BUSINESS LAW AND PRACTICE

BUSINESS LAW AND PRACTICE

Trevor Adams BSc, PhD, Solicitor
Alexis Longshaw MA (Oxon), Solicitor
Christopher Morris BA, Solicitor
Tim Sewell MA (Oxon), Solicitor

JORDANS

2000

Published by
Jordan Publishing Limited
21 St Thomas Street
Bristol BS1 6JS

© The College of Law 2000

All rights reserved. No part of this publication may be
reproduced, stored in a retrieval system, or transmitted in
any way or by any means, including photocopying and recording,
without the written permission of the copyright holder,
application for which should be addressed to the publisher.

British Library Cataloguing-in-Publication Data
A catalogue record for this book is available from the British Library.

ISSN 1352–4488
ISBN 0 85308 655 9

Printed in Great Britain by Hobbs The Printers Ltd of Southampton

PREFACE

In writing this book, we have set out to describe the forms of business organisation most commonly encountered in practice in the context of their 'internal' concerns, their relations with outsiders and their possible tax liabilities. Written for legal practice course students, it is intended to be a comprehensive introduction to the whole field of advising people who run small businesses, whatever the chosen form of organisation.

The style which we have adopted has been chosen in the hope that the contents will be readily understood and appreciated by a student who is totally unacquainted with the subject as well as by one with some prior knowledge. Insofar as this style necessitates a less detailed treatment of topics than some textbooks adopt, we hope that the inclusion of statutory references in the text will encourage the reader to consult the original source materials whenever further research into a topic is required. To this end, we have prepared a companion volume, *Business Law and Practice: Legislation Handbook* (Jordans), which contains the up-to-date text of all the legislation and the principal forms referred to in the book. In addition, we have listed below a few of the many textbooks which the reader may find useful for further study.

Company
Boyle and Birds *Boyle and Birds' Company Law* 4th edn (Jordans, 2000)
Boyle and Sykes *Gore Browne on Companies* (Jordans)
Pennington *Pennington's Company Law* 7th edn (Butterworths, 1995)
Mayson, French and Ryan *Company Law* 16th edn (Blackstone, 1999)
Morse *Palmer's Company Law* (Sweet & Maxwell)

Competition Law
Whish *Whish: Competition Law* 3rd edn (Butterworths, 1993)
Lindrup *Butterworths Competition Law Handbook* 5th edn (Butterworths, 1998)

Drafting Commercial Agreements
Guest *Chitty on Contracts* 27th edn (Sweet & Maxwell, 1994)
Green *Practical Commercial Precedents* (Longman)

Insolvency
Grier and Floyd *Personal Insolvency: A Practical Guide* 3rd edn (Sweet & Maxwell, 1997)

Partnership
Ivamy *Underhill's Law of Partnership* 12th edn (Butterworths, 1986)
Morse *Partnership Law* 4th edn (Blackstone, 1998)
I'Anson Banks *Lindley and Banks on Partnership* 17th edn (Sweet & Maxwell, 1995)

Taxation
Whitehouse *Revenue Law Principles and Practice* 17th edn (Butterworths, 1999)

The law is stated as at 1 May 2000.

In the interests of brevity, we have used the masculine pronoun throughout to include the feminine.

Similarly, in the interests of brevity, we have used the following abbreviations.

BNA 1985	Business Names Act 1985
CAA 1990	Capital Allowances Act 1990
CA 1985	Companies Act 1985
CDDA 1986	Company Directors Disqualification Act 1986
ERA 1996	Employment Rights Act 1996
FA	Finance Act (various years)

IA 1986	Insolvency Act 1986
ICTA 1988	Income and Corporation Taxes Act 1988
IHTA 1984	Inheritance Tax Act 1984
PA 1890	Partnership Act 1890
SGA 1979	Sale of Goods Act 1979
SGSA 1982	Supply of Goods and Services Act 1982
SSGA 1994	Sale and Supply of Goods Act 1994
TCGA 1992	Taxation of Chargeable Gains Act 1992
TMA 1970	Taxes Management Act 1970
UCTA 1977	Unfair Contract Terms Act 1977

PREFACE TO THIS EDITION

Note from Trevor Adams

Chapters 1–27 of this book were originally written by Andrew Harvey and Alison Harvey. Following the retirement of Victor Tonge, I have taken on the task of updating and editing those chapters, save for taxation matters, which are dealt with by Christopher Morris.

Chapters 28–34 are the work of Alexis Longshaw and Tim Sewell, who continue to update and edit them.

My co-authors and I would like to express our thanks to the many colleagues who have made helpful comments and suggestions for this and previous editions.

TREVOR ADAMS
The College of Law
Chester

CONTENTS

PREFACE	v
PREFACE TO THIS EDITION	vii
TABLE OF CASES	xvii
TABLE OF STATUTES	xxi
TABLE OF STATUTORY INSTRUMENTS	xxvii
TABLE OF EUROPEAN LEGISLATION	xxix

PART I		**STARTING A BUSINESS** *Trevor Adams*	1
Chapter 1		INTRODUCTION TO COMMON FORMS OF BUSINESS ORGANISATION	3
	1.1	Introduction	3
	1.2	Sole trader	3
	1.3	Partnership	3
	1.4	Private limited company	4
	1.5	Public limited company	6
Chapter 2		LEGAL AND PRACTICAL CONSIDERATIONS WHEN STARTING UP	9
	2.1	Introduction	9
	2.2	Employees	9
	2.3	Accounting records for tax purposes	17
	2.4	National insurance	18
	2.5	Value Added Tax	18
	2.6	Licences	18
	2.7	Insurance	18
	2.8	Intellectual property	18
PART II		**RUNNING A BUSINESS AS A SOLE TRADER** *Christopher Morris*	21
Chapter 3		TAXATION OF INCOME PROFITS OF SOLE TRADERS	23
	3.1	Introduction	23
	3.2	Income profits	23
	3.3	Basis of assessment and date for payment	28
	3.4	Relief for a trading loss	31
	3.5	Capital profits and loses	34

PART III	**RUNNING A BUSINESS IN PARTNERSHIP** *Trevor Adams*	37
Chapter 4	THE START OF A PARTNERSHIP	39
	4.1 Introduction	39
	4.2 What is a partnership?	39
	4.3 Setting up a partnership	40
	4.4 Formalities required by statute	40
Chapter 5	THE PARTNERSHIP AGREEMENT: DEFINING MUTUAL RIGHTS AND OBLIGATIONS	43
	5.1 Introduction	43
	5.2 Commencement date	43
	5.3 Name	43
	5.4 Financial input	43
	5.5 Shares in income profits/losses	44
	5.6 Drawings	44
	5.7 Shares in increases/decreases in asset values	45
	5.8 Place and nature of business	45
	5.9 Ownership of assets	45
	5.10 Work input	46
	5.11 Roles	46
	5.12 Decision-making	47
	5.13 Duration	47
	5.14 Retirement	48
	5.15 Expulsion	49
	5.16 Payment for outgoing partner's share	49
	5.17 Restraint of trade following departure	49
	5.18 Arbitration	50
Chapter 6	PARTNERS' RESPONSIBILITIES TO ONE ANOTHER	51
	6.1 Introduction	51
	6.2 Utmost good faith	51
	6.3 Further responsibilities implied by the Act	51
	6.4 Contractual responsibilities	52
Chapter 7	LIABILITY FOR FIRM'S DEBTS	53
	7.1 Introduction	53
	7.2 For what will the firm be liable (PA 1890, ss 5–8)?	54
	7.3 Against whom can the firm's liabilities be enforced?	56
	7.4 What if a partner cannot pay?	59
	7.5 Summary	61
Chapter 8	DISSOLUTION	63
	8.1 Introduction	63
	8.2 When does dissolution occur?	63
	8.3 Express terms on dissolution	65
	8.4 The business, its goodwill and other assets following dissolution without continuing partners	65
	8.5 Distribution of proceeds following sale of the business or its assets	66
	8.6 Following dissolution, who winds up the firm's affairs?	67
Chapter 9	TAXATION OF PARTNERSHIPS	69
	9.1 Introduction	69

	9.2	Income tax on partnerships' business profits	69
	9.3	Capital gains tax on disposals by the firm	72
	9.4	Capital gains tax on disposals by partners individually	75
	9.5	Inheritance Tax on disposals by partners individually	75
	9.6	VAT and partnerships	75

PART IV   RUNNING A BUSINESS AS A PRIVATE COMPANY LIMITED BY SHARES   77
Trevor Adams and Christopher Morris

Chapter 10   COMPANY FORMATION   79
- 10.1 Introduction — 79
- 10.2 Documents needed — 79
- 10.3 The certificate of incorporation — 81
- 10.4 How to form a company — 82
- 10.5 Shelf company alternative — 82
- 10.6 Immediate obligations and practicalities — 83
- 10.7 The elective regime — 86
- 10.8 Shareholders' agreements — 87
- 10.9 Holding companies and subsidiary companies — 88
- 10.10 Summaries and checklists — 88

Chapter 11   THE COMPANY'S CONSTITUTION   89
- 11.1 Introduction — 89
- 11.2 The memorandum — 89
- 11.3 The articles of association — 92
- 11.4 Changing the constitution — 94
- 11.5 Summaries and checklists — 96

Chapter 12   MEMBERS AND MEETINGS   97
- 12.1 Introduction — 97
- 12.2 Joining the company — 97
- 12.3 Status of membership — 98
- 12.4 General meetings — 99
- 12.5 Rights of members — 106
- 12.6 Restrictions on members' rights — 111
- 12.7 Rights of minority shareholders — 112
- 12.8 Summaries and checklists — 114

Chapter 13   DIRECTORS   119
- 13.1 Introduction — 119
- 13.2 Appointment — 119
- 13.3 The register of directors — 121
- 13.4 Notification to the registrar — 121
- 13.5 Remuneration (fees) for non-executive directors — 122
- 13.6 Directors' service contracts — 122
- 13.7 Liability of directors — 123
- 13.8 Powers of directors — 125
- 13.9 Board meetings: calling and conduct — 126
- 13.10 General duties ('Fiduciary' duties) — 128
- 13.11 Statutory duties — 130
- 13.12 Statutory restrictions on directors — 132
- 13.13 Disqualification of directors by the court — 133
- 13.14 Disqualification under the articles — 134

	13.15 Removal from office by members	134
	13.16 Summaries and checklists	136
Chapter 14	THE COMPANY SECRETARY	139
	14.1 Introduction	139
	14.2 Appointment	139
	14.3 Terms and remuneration	139
	14.4 Functions	139
	14.5 Removal from office	140
Chapter 15	THE AUDITOR	141
	15.1 Introduction	141
	15.2 Appointment	141
	15.3 Terms and remuneration	142
	15.4 Functions	142
	15.5 Removal from office and resignation	142
Chapter 16	COMPANY ACCOUNTS	145
	16.1 Introduction	145
	16.2 Requirement to file accounts	145
	16.3 Profit and loss account	145
	16.4 Balance sheet	147
	16.5 Management accounts	148
Chapter 17	SHARES	151
	17.1 Introduction	151
	17.2 Issuing shares	151
	17.3 Classes of shares	155
	17.4 Dividends	156
	17.5 Transfer of shares	157
	17.6 Buy-back of shares by the company	158
	17.7 Transmission of shares	159
	17.8 Summaries and checklists	159
Chapter 18	DEBENTURES	161
	18.1 Introduction	161
	18.2 What is a debenture?	161
	18.3 Pre-contract considerations	161
	18.4 Security for the loan	162
	18.5 Typical terms of a debenture	164
	18.6 Procedure for issue of debenture	165
	18.7 Registration	165
	18.8 Remedies of the debenture holder	166
	18.9 Redemption of the loan	167
	18.10 Advantages and disadvantages of debentures: comparison with shares	167
	18.11 Summaries and checklists	169
Chapter 19	SOURCES OF FINANCE	171
	19.1 Introduction	171
	19.2 Share and loan capital – from whom?	171
Chapter 20	LIABILITY	173
	20.1 Introduction	173

	20.2 Liability of the company	173
	20.3 Liability of the officers of the company to the company itself	174
	20.4 Liability of the directors and other officers to outsiders	175
Chapter 21	TAXATION	177
	21.1 Introduction	177
	21.2 Taxation of the company – corporation tax	178
	21.3 Taxation of directors and employees	185
	21.4 Taxation of shareholders	190
	21.5 Taxation of debenture holders	193
PART V	**DISPOSING OF BUSINESS ASSETS OR BUSINESS INTERESTS** *Christopher Morris*	195
Chapter 22	CAPITAL TAXATION ON DISPOSALS	197
	22.1 Introduction	197
	22.2 The subject matter of a charge to tax	197
	22.3 When and how capital taxation applies: principles	198
	22.4 Capital tax reliefs	202
	22.5 Summaries and checklists	215
PART VI	**INSOLVENCY** *Trevor Adams*	217
Chapter 23	INDIVIDUAL INSOLVENCY: BANKRUPTCY	219
	23.1 Introduction	219
	23.2 What is bankruptcy?	219
	23.3 The bankruptcy process	219
	23.4 Effect of bankruptcy on the bankrupt	222
	23.5 Increasing the bankrupt's estate	223
	23.6 Avoiding bankruptcy: individual voluntary arrangements	225
	23.7 Summaries and checklists	226
Chapter 24	CORPORATE INSOLVENCY: LIQUIDATION	229
	24.1 Introduction	229
	24.2 What is liquidation?	229
	24.3 Compulsory liquidation	229
	24.4 Voluntary liquidation	230
	24.5 The company's property	232
	24.6 Distribution of assets	232
	24.7 Dissolution	233
	24.8 Increasing company assets	233
	24.9 Alternatives to liquidation	236
	24.10 Summaries and checklists	239
PART VII	**CHOOSING THE FORM OF BUSINESS ORGANISATION** *Christopher Morris and Trevor Adams*	245
Chapter 25	THE TAX CONSIDERATIONS	247
	25.1 Introduction	247
	25.2 Income profits	247
	25.3 Income loss reliefs	248
	25.4 Pension arrangements	249
	25.5 National insurance contributions	249

	25.6 Relief for interest paid	249
	25.7 Available reliefs for capital gains	250
	25.8 Possibility of double taxation of a company's income and capital profits	251
	25.9 Available reliefs for inheritance tax	252
	25.10 Conclusion	253
Chapter 26	CONSIDERATIONS OTHER THAN TAX	255
	26.1 Introduction	255
	26.2 Liability for debts	255
	26.3 Raising finance	256
	26.4 Management structure	256
	26.5 Status	257
	26.6 Formality in setting up	257
	26.7 Publicity of information	257
	26.8 Statutory obligations and control	257
PART VIII	**CONVERTING THE FORM OF AN EXPANDING BUSINESS** *Trevor Adams*	259
Chapter 27	CONVERSION AND THE IMMEDIATE IMPLICATIONS	261
	27.1 Introduction	261
	27.2 Converting from sole trader to partnership	261
	27.3 Converting from unincorporated business to limited company	262
	27.4 Converting from private to public limited company	266
PART IX	**FORMS OF TRADING** *Alexis Longshaw and Tim Sewell*	267
Chapter 28	DRAFTING COMMERCIAL AGREEMENTS – BASIC PRINCIPLES	269
	28.1 Introduction	269
	28.2 What are the terms of the contract?	269
	28.3 Are the terms clear?	271
	28.4 Statutory control of contract terms under UCTA 1977	274
	28.5 Statutory control of contract terms under the Unfair Terms in Consumer Contracts Regulations 1999	277
	28.6 An exemption clause checklist	277
	28.7 Two examples of exemption clauses	280
Chapter 29	INTRODUCTION TO SALE OF GOODS	283
	29.1 Introduction	283
	29.2 What is a sale of goods contract?	283
	29.3 The statutory framework	283
	29.4 Drafting sale of goods contracts – an outline	284
Chapter 30	SUPPLY OF SERVICES	291
	30.1 Introduction	291
	30.2 Services contracts	291
	30.3 Supply of goods and services	292
Chapter 31	INTRODUCTION TO AGENCY AND DISTRIBUTION AGREEMENTS	295
	31.1 Introduction	295
	31.2 Agency	295

	31.3 Distribution agreement	296
	31.4 Other types of marketing agreement	297
Chapter 32	**THE BASIC PRINCIPLES OF AGENCY**	**301**
	32.1 Introduction	301
	32.2 The normal agency contract	303
	32.3 Agents acting without actual authority	304
	32.4 Undisclosed principals	306
	32.5 Payments to agents	307
	32.6 Termination of agency	307
Chapter 33	**CHOOSING A MARKETING AGREEMENT**	**309**
	33.1 Introduction	309
	33.2 Commercial factors	309
	33.3 Overseas operations	310
	33.4 UK taxation	312
	33.5 Competition law	312
	33.6 Making a choice	313
Chapter 34	**COMPETITION LAW**	**315**
	34.1 Introduction	315
	34.2 Principles and sources of EC competition law	315
	34.3 Other systems of competition law	316
	34.4 EC competition law and commercial agreements	316
	34.5 The relevant Articles of the EC Treaty	318
	34.6 The Commission's powers of investigation and enforcement	322
	34.7 Consequences of infringement	323
	34.8 Avoiding infringement of Article 81	324
	34.9 Applying the Articles to specific commercial agreements	329
APPENDIX 1	**DRAFTING A SALE OF GOODS TRANSFER**	**331**
	Alexis Longshaw and Tim Sewell	
	Part 1 TRANSFER OF OWNERSHIP	335
	A1.1 Introduction	335
	A1.2 Significance of the transfer of ownership	335
	A1.3 Seller with no right to sell	335
	A1.4 When does ownership pass?	337
	A1.5 Retention of title	343
	A1.6 Ownership and risk	345
	Part 2 PRICE AND PAYMENT	349
	A2.1 Introduction	349
	A2.2 Price	349
	A2.3 Payment	350
	A2.4 A seller's rights against the buyer	350
	A2.5 A seller's rights against the goods	351
	A2.6 The above principles applied to the standard example	352
	Part 3 DELIVERY	355
	A3.1 Introduction	355
	A3.2 Time and place of delivery	355
	A3.3 Buyer's rights on incorrect delivery	356
	A3.4 Seller's rights on buyer's non-acceptance of the goods	358

Part 4 DESCRIPTION — 359

A4.1 Introduction — 359
A4.2 The implied term relating to description — 359
A4.3 The buyer's rights if the seller defaults — 360

Part 5 QUALITY — 365

A5.1 Introduction — 365
A5.2 Common features of the two conditions — 365
A5.3 Satisfactory quality — 366
A5.4 Reasonable fitness for the buyer's particular purpose — 369
A5.5 The buyer's rights on the seller's breach — 369

APPENDIX 2 SUMMARY SECTION OF THE CONSULTATION PAPER ON CHANGES ON COMPANY LAW — 371

INDEX — 379

TABLE OF CASES

References are to paragraph numbers. Prefix A refers to paragraph numbers in Appendix 1 materials.

Aluminium Industrie Vaassen BV v Romalpa Aluminium [1976] 2 All ER 552, CA	29.4.2, A1.5.1, A1.5.3
Arcos Ltd v E A Ronaasen & Son [1933] AC 470	A4.2.2
Aswan Engineering Establishment Co v Lupdine Ltd [1987] 1 WLR 1, CA	A5.3.3
Bannerman v White (1861) 10 CBNS 844	28.2.1
Beale v Taylor [1967] 1 WLR 1193, CA	A4.2.1
Bedford Insurance Co Ltd v Instituto de Resseguros do Brazil [1985] QB 966, DC	32.3.3
Bell Houses Ltd v City Wall Properties [1966] 2 QB 656	11.2.3
Bence Graphics International Ltd v Fasson UK Ltd [1997] 3 WLR 205, CA	A5.5.1
Bentley (Dick) Productions v Smith (Harold) (Motors) [1965] 2 All ER 65, CA	28.2.1
Bolam v Friern Hospital Management Committee [1957] 2 All ER 118	30.2.1
Bolton Partners v Lambert (1889) 41 Ch D 295	32.3.3
Bond Worth Ltd, Re [1980] Ch 228, ChD	A1.5.3
Brady v Brady [1989] AC 755, CA	17.2.10
British Sugar plc v NEI Power Projects Ltd (1997) 87 BLR 42, CA	28.3.4
Bushell v Faith [1970] AC 1099, HL	11.3.3, 22.4.3
Butler Machine Tool Co v Ex-cell-o Corpn (England) [1979] 1 All ER 965, CA	28.2.3
Clemens v Clemens Bros [1976] 2 All ER 268	12.6.1, 12.8.1
Clough Mill Ltd v Martin [1985] 1 WLR 111, CA	A1.5.3
Cohen v Roche [1927] 1 KB 169	A3.3.3
Collins v Associated Greyhound Racecourses Ltd [1930] 1 Ch 1	32.4
Compaq Computer Ltd v Abercorn Group Ltd [1991] BCC 484	A1.5.3
Copeman v William J. Flood and Sons Ltd [1941] 1 KB 202	21.2.2
Cornwall v Henson [1900] 2 Ch 298	A4.3.2
Cutsforth and Others v Mansfield Inns Ltd [1986] 1 All ER 577, DC	34.7.2
Drughorn (Fred) Ltd v Rederiaktiebolaget Transatlantic [1919] AC 203	32.4
Dyster v Randall & Sons [1926] Ch 932	32.4
Fleet v Murton (1871) LR 7 QB 126	32.2.2
Foss v Harbottle (1843) 2 Hare 461	12.6.4, 20.3.3
Garden Cottage Foods Ltd v Milk Marketing Board [1984] AC 130, HL	34.7.2
Garner v Murray [1904] Ch 57	8.5
Gillespie Brothers v Roy Bowles Transport [1973] 1 QB 400, CA	28.3.3, 28.7.2
Grant v Australian Knitting Mills [1936] AC 85	A5.3.3
Greer v Downs Supply Co [1927] 2 KB 28	32.6.1
Hadley v Baxendale (1854) 9 Exch 341	28.3.4, A3.3
Harlingdon & Leinster Enterprises Ltd v Christopher Hull Fine Art [1991] 1 QB 564, [1990] 1 All ER 737, CA	A4.2.1

Heil v Hedges [1951] 1 TLR 512 — A5.3.3
Hendy Lennox (Industrial Engines) Ltd v Grahame Puttick Ltd [1984] 1 WLR 485 — A1.5.3
Heron II, The; Koufos v Czarnikow (C) [1969] 1 AC 350, HL — 28.3.4
Hollier v Rambler Motors (AMC) [1972] 2 QB 71, CA — 28.3.3
Humble v Hunter (1848) 12 QB 310 — 32.4

Interfoto Picture Library v Stiletto Visual Programmes [1988] 1 All ER 348, CA — 28.2.3
Irish Sugar [2000] All ER (EC) 198, Court of First Instance — 34.5.6
Italian Flat Glass, Re [1990] 4 CMLR 535 — 34.5.6

L'Estrange v Graucob [1934] 2 KB 394 — 28.2.2
Lambert v Lewis [1982] AC 225, HL — A5.3.4
Lordsvale Finance plc v Bank of Zambia [1996] QB 752, [1996] 3 WLR 688 — A2.4.2

Mallalieu v Drummond [1983] 2 AC 861, [1983] STC 665, HL — 3.2.1
Maple Flock Co Ltd v Universal Furniture Products (Wembley) Ltd [1934] 1 KB 148 — A4.3.2
Martin-Baker Aircraft Co Ltd v Canadian Flight Equipment [1955] 2 QB 556 — 32.6.1
May and Butcher v R [1934] 2 KB 17 — A2.2.2
Millar's Machinery v David Way (1935) Com Cas 204 — 28.3.4
Moore & Co Ltd and Landauer & Co, an arbitration between, Re [1921] 2 KB 519 — A4.2.2

O'Neil and Another v Philips and Others (1999) unreported — 12.5.14
Oscar Chess Ltd v Williams [1957] 1 All ER 325, CA — 28.2.1

Reardon Smith Line Ltd v Yngvar Hansen-Tangen [1976] 3 All ER 570, HL — A4.2.3
Rogers and Another v Parish (Scarborough) Ltd [1987] QB 933, [1987] 2 WLR 353 — A5.3.3
Routledge v McKay [1954] 1 All ER 855, CA — 28.2.1
Rowland v Divall [1923] 2 KB 500 — A1.3.1

Said v Butt [1920] 3 KB 497 — 32.4
St Albans DC v ICL [1996] 4 All ER 481 — A5.2.2
Secretary of State for Trade and Industry v Deverell and Another (1999) unreported — 13.2.6
Sheffield v Pickfords Ltd (1997) 16 Tr LR 337, CA — 28.4.2
Smart v Sandars (1848) CB 895 — 32.6.1
South West Water v ICL (1999) unreported — 28.4.2
Standard Rotary Machine Company Ltd (1906) — 18.7.1

Thornton v Shoe Lane Parking [1971] 2 QB 163, CA — 28.2.3

Victoria Laundry (Windsor) Ltd v Newman Industries Ltd [1949] 2 KB 528, CA — 28.3.4

Wadsworth v Lydell [1981] 1 WLR 598, CA — A2.4.2
Wardar's (Import and Export) Co v W Norwood and Sons Ltd [1968] 2 QB 663, CA — A1.4.2
Watteau v Fenwick [1893] 1 QB 346 — 32.3.2
Williams v Agius [1914] AC 510 — A3.3.1

Wilson v Rickett, Cockerell & Co Ltd [1954] 1 QB 598, CA	A5.2.2
Witter (Thomas) Ltd v TBP Industries Ltd [1996] 2 All ER 573	28.4.2
Wormell v RHM Agriculture (East) Ltd [1986] 1 WLR 336	A5.2.2
Yarmouth v France (1887) 19 QBD 647	3.2.2

TABLE OF STATUTES

References are to paragraph numbers. Prefix A refers to paragraph numbers in Appendix 1 materials.

Administration of Justice Act 1982	
s 15	A2.4.2
Business Names Act 1985	27.2.1
ss 1–5	4.4.1
s 4	27.3.1
Capital Allowances Act 1990	3.2.2
s 3	3.2.2
s 18	3.2.2
s 24	3.2.2
s 77	27.3.2
Companies Act 1985	11.2.3, 12.3.2, 13.10, 15.1, 26.6, 27.4.1, A1.5.3
s 3A	11.2.3
s 4	11.4.2, 12.8.5
s 5	11.4.2
s 9	1.4.2, 11.4.3, 12.8.5
s 17	12.8.5
ss 25–28	15.2
s 28	1.4.2, 11.4.1, 12.3.2, 12.8.5
s 35	12.8.5, 18.3.2, 20.2.1
(2)	12.5.11, 12.7.8
s 35A	13.7.5, 20.2.2
s 35B	13.7.5, 20.2.2
s 43	12.8.5, 27.4.1
ss 43–48	12.8.5
s 51	12.8.5
s 53	12.8.5
s 80	1.4.1, 10.6.7, 11.3.3, 12.8.4, 17.2.2, 17.8.1
s 80A	17.2.2
s 89	10.6.7, 11.3.3, 17.2.3, 17.8.1
s 91	17.2.3
s 95	12.8.5, 17.2.3
s 100	17.2.8
s 120	12.8.5
s 121	17.2.1, 17.8.1
ss 122, 123	17.2.1
s 125	12.4.8, 12.8.5
s 130	17.2.7
s 135	12.8.5
ss 135–137	17.2.9
s 151	17.2.10
s 152(1)	17.2.10
s 153	17.2.10
s 155	12.8.5
ss 155–158	17.2.10
s 159	17.2.9, 17.3
s 159A	17.3
s 160	17.3
s 162	17.2.9, 17.3
s 164–165	12.8.5
s 183	17.5.1
s 185	17.5.1
s 173	12.8.5, 17.6
s 185	12.5.4
s 221	15.1
s 226	15.1, 15.4
(2)	15.1
s 240	12.5.6
s 244	16.2
s 246	16.2
s 246A	16.2
s 249A	15.1
(1)	15.1
s 249B(2), (3)	15.1
s 263	17.4
s 283	14.2
(4)	14.4
s 303	1.4.2, 11.3.3, 12.3.2, 12.6.3, 13.15.2
(2)	13.2, 13.5.2
s 305	13.11.7
s 307	12.8.5
s 308	12.8.5
s 309	13.12.5
s 312	13.12.1
s 317	13.2.6, 13.6.1, 13.9.2, 13.11.1, 13.16.2, 17.18.1, 18.3.1, 19.2.1, 19.11.2
s 318	13.6.3, 13.11.2
s 319	1.4.1, 12.3.2, 13.6.2, 13.12.3
s 320	1.4.1, 13.12.2
s 322B	13.11.8
s 324	17.5.1, 17.8.1
s 346	13.12.2
s 330	13.12.4
s 352	12.5.5
s 359	17.5.2
s 363(1)	13.11.4
s 366	12.5.7
s 368	12.5.9, 12.7.7, 12.8.2
s 369	12.4.6
(3), (4)	12.7.3
s 370	12.4.7, 12.5.2, 13.7.6
s 371	12.5.10, 12.8.2
s 373	12.4.10
s 376	12.5.12, 12.7.1, 12.8.2
s 378(1), (2)	12.4.8
s 379(3)	13.15.2
s 379A	10.7, 12.4.8, 12.7.4
s 381	15.4

Companies Act 1985 *cont*	
s 381A	12.4.15, 12.4.16
s 381B	15.4
s 382	12.4.14
s 382A	12.4.15
s 382B	12.4.16
s 383	12.5.8
s 384	15.1, 15.2
s 386	15.2, 15.5
s 390	15.4, 15.5
s 391	15.5
(3)	15.5
s 392	15.5
s 392A	15.5
s 394	15.5
s 395	18.7, 18.7.1, 24.8.8
(1), (2)	18.7.1
ss 395–397	24.8.8
s 396	18.7
s 403	18.7.3
s 404	18.7.2
s 420	18.7.1
s 458	24.8.3
s 459	12.5.14, 12.7.5, 13.16.6, 20.3.3
s 711	20.2.2
s 716	4.4.1
ss 722, 723	13.7.6
s 730	13.7.6
s 739	13.12.2
s 741(2)	13.2.6
s 744	14.2, 20.4.1
Sch 4	16.2
Sch 15A	17.2.3
(7)	13.6.2
Sch 24	13.7.6, 26.2.1
Companies Act 1989	11.2.3, 18.7.1
Sch 1	16.2
Company Directors Disqualification Act 1986	13.13, 13.16.14
s 2	13.13
s 3	13.13
s 6	13.13
s 10	13.13
s 11	13.14, 23.4.1
s 13	20.4.6
s 15	20.4.6
Competition Act 1998	34.4.1
s 2	33.5
Consumer Credit Act 1974	2.6.1, A1.3.2
Consumer Protection Act 1987	33.2.4
Disability Discrimination Act 1995	2.2.1
Employment Rights Act 1996	
s 1	2.2.2, 27.3.6
Enduring Powers of Attorney Act 1985	32.6.2
Equal Pay Act 1970	2.2.1
Factors Act 1889	
s 2(1)	32.3.2
Fair Trading Act 1973	34.3.2
Finance Act 1991	
s 72	3.4.2
Finance Act 1994	
ss 181, 182	3.3.6
ss 189–194	3.3
Finance Act 1998	21.2.4, 21.2.9
Health and Safety at Work etc Act 1974	2.2.5
Hire Purchase Act 1964	
Pt III	A1.3.2
Income and Corporation Taxes Act 1988	16.1
Pt VI	21.4.1
ss 60–63	3.3
s 74	3.2.1
ss 153–168	21.3.3
s 167	21.3.3
s 198	21.3.5
s 203	21.3.6
ss 219–229	21.4.5
s 284	23.6.3
s 313	21.2.2
s 338	21.2.5
s 348	21.2.5
s 353	9.2.4, 21.2.10, 21.4.2
s 360	21.4.2
s 362	9.2.4, 21.2.10
s 380	3.4.2, 3.4.4, 3.4.5, 3.4.6
s 381	3.4.1, 3.4.2, 3.4.6, 25.3.1
s 385	3.4.2, 3.4.3, 3.4.6
s 386	3.4.5, 3.4.6
s 388	3.4.4, 3.4.5, 3.4.6, 25.3.3
s 393(1)	21.2.2, 21.2.3
s 393A	21.2.3, 25.3.2, 25.3.3
s 414	21.2.10
s 416	21.2.10
s 417	21.2.10
s 419	21.2.10
s 420	21.2.10
s 421	21.4.1
Sch A	3.2, 21.2.8
Sch D	3.2, 3.2.2, 3.3.6, 9.2.1, 9.2.2, 21.2.8, 21.3.5, 21.5.1, 25.2.1, 25.2.2, 27.3.2
Sch D, Case I	3.2, 21.3.6
Sch D, Case II	3.2
Sch E	21.3.2, 21.3.3, 21.3.4, 21.3.5, 21.3.6, 22.3.3, 25.2.1, 25.2.2
Sch F	21.4.1, 22.3.3

Inheritance Tax Act 1984		s 340	23.5.5
s 4(1)	22.3.5	s 341	23.5.4, 23.5.4, 23.5.5
s 10(1)	22.3.4	s 360	23.4.1
s 94	22.3.3	s 423	23.5.6, 24.8.7
ss 103–114	22.4.3	s 435	23.5.4
ss 115–124	22.4.3	Sch 4	12.8.5
ss 227–228	22.4.3	Insolvency Act 1994	23.3
s 270	22.3.4		
Insolvency Act 1986	7.4.2, 23.3, 23.3.5, 24.2		
s 5	24.9.2	Law Reform (Frustrated Contracts) Act 1943	A1.6.3
ss 8, 9	24.9.3		
s 10	24.9.3		
(2)	24.9.3		
s 11	24.9.3	Matrimonial Homes Act 1983	23.3.4
s 14	24.9.3		
s 18	24.9.3		
s 22	24.9.3		
s 45	24.9.4	Partnership Act 1890	5.15, 7.1, 8.1, 8.2, 8.3.1
s 76	17.6	s 1	4.2.1, 5.2, 27.2.1
s 84	12.8.5, 24.4.2	ss 5–8	7.1, 7.2
s 85	24.4.3	s 5	5.11, 7.2.2
s 86	24.4.2	s 9	7.3.1
s 89	24.4.1	s 10	7.2.4
s 90	24.4.1	s 14	7.3.3, 7.3.4, 7.5
s 98	24.4.3	s 17	7.3.1
s 99	24.4.3	s 23	8.2.3
s 109	24.4.3	s 24	5.1
s 110	12.8.5	(1), (2)	6.3
s 122	12.8.5, 24.3.1	s 26	8.2.1
(1)(g)	12.5.15, 12.7.6	s 27	8.2.2
ss 123–125	24.3.1	ss 28–30	6.2
s 129	24.3.2	s 32	8.2.1, 8.2.2
s 130	24.8.2	s 33	5.13.3, 8.2.3, 8.2.4, 23.4.1
s 131	24.3.2	s 34	8.2.5
s 136	24.3.2	s 35	5.13.4, 8.2.6
s 143	24.5	s 36	7.3.4, 7.5
s 146	24.7.1	(1), (2)	7.3.4
s 165	12.8.5	s 38	8.6
s 178	24.8.1	s 39	8.4.1
s 183	24.8.2	s 42	5.16, 8.3.2
s 213	13.7.4, 20.4.4, 24.8.3, 26.2.1	s 44	8.5
s 214	13.7.3, 20.4.3, 24.8.4, 26.2.1	Powers of Attorney Act 1971	32.6.2
s 238	24.8.5	s 5(1)	32.6.2
s 240	24.8.6, 24.9.4		
s 245	24.8.9		
s 247	23.5.2		
s 249	24.8.6	Race Relations Act 1976	2.2.1
s 252	23.6	Resale Prices Act 1976	34.3.1
s 260	23.6	Restrictive Trade Practices Act 1976	34.3.1
s 264	23.3.1		
s 279	23.3.6		
s 281	23.3.6	Sale and Supply of Goods Act 1991	29.4.6, A3.3.1, A4.3, A4.3.1, A5.3, A5.3.1
s 294	23.3.3		
s 306	23.3.4		
s 310	23.3.4	Sale of Goods Act 1979	28.4.3, 29.1, 29.2, 29.4.1, 29.4.2, 29.4.3, A1.1, A1.4, A4.1
s 315	23.5.1		
s 316	23.5.1		
s 339	23.5.4		

Sale of Goods Act 1979 *cont*	
s 2(1)	29.2, A1.2
(4),(5)	29.2
s 7	A1.6.3
s 8	29.4.3
(1)	A2.2.1
(2),(3)	A2.2.2
s 9	29.4.3, A2.2.1
s 10(1)	29.4.3, A2.4.1
s 11(2)	A3.3.2, A4.3
(4)	29.4.5, A4.3.1
ss 12–15	28.6.2
s 12	28.6.2, 29.4.2, A1.3.1
(1)	A1.3.1, A1.3.2
(2)–(5)	A1.3.1
s 13	29.4.5, 29.4.6, A4.3.3, A4.3.4, A5.5, A5.5.2
(1)	A4.2
(2)	A4.2.4
s 14	29.4.6, A5.1, A5.2.1, A5.2.3
(1)	A5.1
(2)	A5.1, A5.2.1, A5.3, A5.4, A5.5, A5.5.2, A5.5.3
(2A)	29.4.6, A5.3.1, A5.3.2
(2B)	29.4.6, A5.3.1, A5.3.3, A5.3.4
(2C)	A5.3
(3)	29.4.6, A5.1, A5.2.1, A5.3.4, A5.4, A5.5, A5.5.2, A5.5.3
(4)	A5.4
(5)	A5.2.3
s 15	29.4.5, A5.1
(1),(2)	A4.2.4
s 15A	29.4.5
(1)–(3)	A4.3
s 16	29.4.2, A1.4.2, A1.4.5
s 17	A1.4.1, A1.4.3, A1.4.5
(2)	A1.4.1, A1.4.2
s 18	29.4.2, A1.4.1, A1.4.2
Rule 1	A1.4.1, A1.4.5, A1.4.6, A1.6.4
Rules 2, 3	A1.4.1, A1.4.5
Rule 4	A1.4.4
Rule 5	A1.4.3, A1.4.5, A1.4.6
Rule 5(1)–(3)	A1.4.2
s 19	29.4.2, A1.5, A1.5.1
s 20	29.4.2, A1.6.2, A1.6.4
(2)	A1.6.2
s 20A	A1.4.2
s 21(1)	A1.3.2
ss 22–25	A1.3.2
s 25	A1.2, A1.5.4
s 27	A2.1, A3.2, A3.4
s 28	A2.3.1, A2.3.2
s 29(1)	A3.2
(2)	29.4.4, A3.2.2
(3)	A3.2
(5)	29.4.4, A3.2
s 30	A3.3.1
(2A)	A3.3.1
(2B)	A3.3.1
s 31(1)	29.4.4, A3.2.2
(2)	A4.3.2
s 32	29.4.4
(1), (2)	A3.2.1
s 33	A1.6.2
s 34	A4.3.1
s 35(1)–(3)	A4.3.1
(5)–(7)	A4.3.1
s 35A	A5.5.3
(1)	A4.3.1
(4)	A4.3.1
s 38(1)	A2.5
s 41	29.4.3
(1)	A2.5.1
ss 44–46	29.4.3, A2.5.2
s 47	A2.5
s 48(3)	A2.5.3
s 49	A1.2
(1), (2)	A2.4.2
s 50(1), (3)	A3.4
s 51	28.3.4
(2)	A3.3
(3)	A3.3.1, A3.4
s 52	A3.3.3, A4.3
s 53	A4.3
(1)	A3.3.1
(2)	A3.3
(3)	A5.5.1
(4)	A3.3.1
s 54	A3.3, A3.4
s 54A(2)	A4.3.2
s 55(1)	29.3.2
s 59	A4.3.1
s 61(1)	29.4.1, 29.4.4, A1.4.1, A1.4.3, A3.2
(5)	A2.4.1
Sale of Goods (Amendment) Act 1995	A1.4.2
Sex Discrimination Act 1975	2.2.1
Sherman Act 1890 (USA)	34.3.2
Supply of Goods and Services Act 1982	28.4.3, 30.2.1
Pt I	30.3
Pt II	30.2, 30.3
s 1(1)	30.3
(3)	30.3
s 12(1)–(3)	30.2, 30.3
s 13	28.6.2, 30.2.1, 30.2.2
s 14(1), (2)	30.2.1
s 15(1), (2)	30.2.1
s 16	30.2.2
(3), (4)	30.2.2
Supply of Goods (Implied Terms) Act 1973	28.4.3

Taxation of Chargeable Gains Act 1992	
s 2A	22.4.1
s 62	22.3.5
s 150C	22.4.1
ss 151A, 151B	22.4.1
ss 152–159	9.3.4, 21.2.4, 22.4.1
s 162	22.4.1, 27.3.3
ss 163–164	22.4.1
s 165	22.4.1
s 281	22.4.1
s 286	22.3.4
s 286(5)	22.3.4
Sch 5	22.4.1
Sch 5B	22.4.1
Sch 6	22.4.1
Sch A1	22.4.1
Taxes Management Act 1970	
ss 59A, 59B	3.3.6
Trade Union and Labour Relations (Consolidation) Act 1992	2.2.1
Unfair Contract Terms Act 1977	28.1, 28.4.1, 28.6, 28.6.2, 29.3.2, 29.4.4
s 1	28.4.3, 28.7.2
s 2(1), (2)	28.4.3, 28.7.2, 30.2.2
s 3	28.4.2, 28.4.3, 29.4.4, A3.3.4, A3.4
(2)(b)	28.4.3, A3.3.4
s 6	28.4.2, 28.4.3, 29.4.2, 29.4.5, 29.4.6
(1)	A1.3.1
(2)	A4.3.3, A5.5.2
(3)	28.7.1, A4.3.3, A5.5.2
s 7	28.4.2, 28.4.3
s 11(1)	28.4.2
(2)	28.4.2
s 12	28.4.2
s 13	28.4.1, A4.3.3
Sch 1	28.6.2
Sch 2	28.4.2, 28.7.1, 28.7.2

TABLE OF STATUTORY INSTRUMENTS

References are to paragraph numbers.

Commercial Agents (Council Directive) Regulations 1993, SI 1993/3053	33.3.3
Companies (Tables A–F) Regulations 1985, SI 1985/805	
Table A	10.2.2, 11.3.2
arts 1–35	11.3.2
art 24	11.3.3
art 30	17.7
art 31	17.7
art 32	12.4.9, 17.2.1
art 35	17.6
arts 36–63	11.3.2
art 38	13.2
art 39	12.4.5
art 40	12.4.7
art 41	12.4.7
art 42	12.4.11
art 46	12.4.10
art 50	12.4.12, 13.2.3
art 53	12.4.15
art 62	12.4.13
arts 64–98	11.3.2
art 64	13.2.1
art 65	13.2.7
art 66	13.2.7
art 70	12.6.3, 18.3.1
art 72	13.2.4, 13.6.1, 13.8.1
art 73	13.2.4, 13.15.1
arts 76–79	13.2
art 78	12.6.3
art 79	13.2
art 81	13.14, 13.16.4, 23.4.1
art 82	13.5, 13.15.2
art 84	13.6.1
art 85	13.10.1
art 88	13.2.3, 13.9.1, 13.9.2
art 89	13.9.3
art 91	13.2.3
art 93	13.9.6, 13.16.2
art 94	11.3.3, 13.9.2, 18.3.1, 18.11.2
(c)	13.9.2, 17.8.1, 18.11.2
art 95	11.3.3, 13.9.3, 13.16.2, 18.3.1
art 96	13.6.1, 13.9.4, 18.6
art 97	13.6.1, 13.9.4
art 98	13.9.4
art 99	14.2, 14.3, 14.5
arts 99–101	11.3.2
art 100	13.9.5
arts 102–110	11.3.2
art 102	12.5.3, 17.4
art 104	12.5.3
arts 111–116	11.3.2
art 111	12.4.5
art 115	12.4.4
Table B	11.2

Company and Business Names Regulations 1981, SI 1981/1685   4.4.1, 11.2.1
Company and Business Names (Amendment) Regulations 1982, SI 1982/1653   4.4.1, 11.2.1
Company and Business Names (Amendment) Regulations 1995, SI 1995/3022   4.4.1, 11.2.1
Competition Act 1998 (Land and Vertical Agreements Exclusion) Order 2000, SI 2000/310   33.5, 34.4.1
    regs 2, 3, 4   34.4.1

Deregulation (Resolutions of Private Companies) Order 1996   12.4.15

Insolvency Rules 1986, SI 1986/1925   24.2
Insolvent Partnerships Order 1994, SI 1994/2421   7.4.2

Rules of the Supreme Court 1965, SI 1965/1776
    Ord 81   7.3.2

Transfer of Undertakings (Protection of Employment) Regulations 1981, SI 1981/1794   27.3.6

Unfair Terms in Consumer Contracts Regulations 1994, SI 1994/3159   28.5
Unfair Terms in Consumer Contracts Regulations 1999, SI 1999/2083   28.5
    reg 5   28.5
    reg 8   28.5
    Sch 2   28.5

Working Time Regulations 1998, SI 1998/1833   2.2.5

TABLE OF EUROPEAN LEGISLATION

References are to paragraph numbers.

Directives

Dir 86/653/EEC on the Co-ordination of the Laws of Member States relating to Self-Employed Commercial Agents OJ 1986 L382/17	33.3.3

Regulations

Reg 17/62 (first company law regulation) OJ Sp Ed 1959-62, 87	34.2.2, 34.6.2, 34.8.11
art 11	34.6.3
art 14	34.6.4
Reg 1983/83 (exclusive distribution agreements block exemption) OJ 1983 L173/1	34.8.7
Reg 1984/83 (exclusive purchasing agreements block exemption)	34.8.7
Reg 4087/88 (franchising agreements block exemption)	34.8.7
Reg 1216/99	34.8.11
Reg 2790/99 (vertical agreements or vertical restraints block exemption)	34.8.7, 34.9.2
art 1	34.8.7
art 2	34.8.7
art 2.1	34.8.7
art 3	34.8.7
art 4	34.8.7
art 4(a), (b)	34.8.7
art 5	34.8.7
arts 6–8	34.8.7
art 12.2	34.8.7
preamble	34.8.7

Treaties and Conventions

Rome Convention relating to contractual obligations 1980	33.3.1
Treaty of Rome 1957 (EC Treaty) as amended by the Treaty of Amsterdam	31.3.4, 34.2.1
Art 2	34.5.1
Art 3	34.5.1
(g)	34.5.1
Arts 28–30	34.5.2
Art 81	33.5, 34.2.1, 34.3.1, 34.5.1, 34.5.3, 34.5.4, 34.5.6, 34.5.7, 34.6.1, 34.7.1, 34.7.2, 34.7.3, 34.8.1, 34.8.2, 34.8.6, 34.8.9, 34.8.10, 34.8.13, 34.8.14, 34.9, 34.9.1, 34.9.2, 34.9.3
(1)	34.4.2, 34.5.3, 34.5.4, 34.8.2, 34.8.3, 34.8.4, 34.8.5, 34.8.6, 34.8.7, 34.8.11, 34.8.12, 34.9.1, 34.9.2
(2)	34.5.3, 34.5.4
(3)	34.5.3, 34.5.4, 34.8.9, 34.8.11
Art 82	34.2.1, 34.3.1, 34.5.1, 34.5.5, 34.5.6, 34.5.7, 34.5.8, 34.6.1, 34.7.1, 34.8.3, 34.8.14, 34.9, 34.9.3
Art 83	34.6.2
Art 234	34.2.3

PART I

STARTING A BUSINESS

Part I aims to introduce the reader to the common forms of business organisation from which the new business person(s) might choose, namely sole trader, partnership and limited company. The subsequent Parts of the book examine each in detail and in Part VII these forms are compared in the context of considering which would be best suited to the possible needs of the business person(s).

Chapter 1

INTRODUCTION TO COMMON FORMS OF BUSINESS ORGANISATION

1.1 INTRODUCTION

There are various forms of business organisation in which a person or persons may choose to operate a business, each of which may offer a number of advantages and disadvantages compared with alternative forms of business organisation. In ascending order of complexity, the most common forms are: sole trader, partnership, private limited company and public limited company. Their respective merits and demerits are considered in Part VII. The essential features of these forms of business organisation are given below.

1.2 SOLE TRADER

A sole trader is a person who alone:

(1) has the right to make all decisions affecting the business;
(2) owns all the assets of the business;
(3) is responsible for paying income tax on all the profits of the business;
(4) is responsible for the debts and obligations of the business without any limit.

1.3 PARTNERSHIP

A partnership consists of two or more persons who, on the basis of a contract between them:

(1) share the right to take part in making decisions which affect the business or the business assets, although they may have agreed that this right shall be limited in relation to one or more of their number. For example, a 'sleeping partner' may have agreed not to be involved in day-to-day matters while reserving the right to be consulted on fundamental matters such as borrowing;
(2) share the ownership of the assets of the business, although they may have agreed that the firm will use an asset which is owned by one of the partners individually;
(3) share the net profits of the business, although the contract need not provide for equal shares;
(4) share responsibility for the debts and obligations of the business without any limit, although if one does not pay then the others must pay his share.

Chapter 1 contents
Introduction
Sole trader
Partnership
Private limited company
Public limited company

1.4 PRIVATE LIMITED COMPANY

A business which is run as a private limited company will be owned and operated by the company itself. The company is recognised in law as having an existence which is separate from the person or persons who formed the company and from the directors and shareholders.

Decisions affecting the business, the company or its assets are made either by directors or by shareholders (ie members). The division of powers between board meetings (by which, generally, decisions of directors are made) and general meetings (by which, generally, decisions of shareholders are made) is a fundamental aspect of company law. It imposes on a company a degree of formality which is absent from the running of a business by a sole trader or a partnership. In many private companies, the same persons hold the positions of directors and shareholders so that it may seem pointless to make any distinction between these roles; nevertheless this distinction must be observed since the validity of many decisions may be in question if the appropriate formality has not been observed.

1.4.1 Decisions of directors

The directors manage the company and its day-to-day affairs. Typically, the directors will be responsible for making the following decisions, although this list is not exhaustive:

(1) entering into contracts (including sales and purchases, borrowing, contracts of employment);
(2) other matters of day-to-day management of the business;
(3) calling general meetings;
(4) taking legal proceedings in the company's name;
(5) approving the registration of the transfer of shares (and thus changes in membership).

Typically, the directors will also have limited authority for the following decisions in the sense that they must first seek approval from the shareholders in a general meeting:

(1) issuing new shares in the company (see CA 1985, s 80);
(2) entering into contracts with individual directors by which the company will buy from or sell to that director something of significant value (see CA 1985, s 320);
(3) awarding to individual directors service contracts of significant duration (see CA 1985, s 319).

Decisions of the directors will normally be made at a board meeting on the basis of one vote per director and a simple majority will suffice.

The board of directors will generally be able to delegate its decision-making to one or more individual directors. The most common example of this is delegation of wide managerial authority to a managing director, but many companies have directors to whom more specific functions have been delegated by the board, for example, sales director, finance director, personnel director.

1.4.2 Decisions of shareholders

The shareholders are the owners of the company. In order to protect their position as owners, the law gives them the right to make some decisions affecting those rights, and to change the directors.

Shareholders will be responsible for making the following decisions, although this list is not exhaustive:

(1) altering any aspect of the company's constitution (eg its name (see CA 1985, s 28), its regulations on calling and conduct of meetings (see CA 1985, s 9));
(2) dismissing a director from the board (see CA 1985, s 303);
(3) appointing directors to the board;
(4) condoning any breach of duty to the company by its directors.

Shareholders will also be responsible for authorising the directors to make the following decisions (as above):

(1) issuing new shares in the company;
(2) entering into contracts with individual directors by which the company will buy from or sell to that director something of significant value;
(3) awarding to individual directors service contracts of significant duration.

Decisions of the shareholders will normally be made by a prescribed majority which depends on the decision in question. Some decisions (eg dismissing or appointing a director) require a simple majority of those voting and are described as 'ordinary resolutions'; some (eg altering the company's name or its regulations on calling or conduct of meetings) require a special majority, being 75 per cent of those voting, and are described as 'special resolutions'; others (eg dispensing with the normal requirement for the company to hold an annual general meeting) require the unanimous vote of all shareholders and are described as 'elective resolutions'.

Regrettably, it is not possible to give any rule for working out which decisions require which type of resolution – this has to be a matter of learning or checking, as necessary. The position in each instance will be governed by provisions in the Companies Act 1985, by common law principles or by provisions in the company's constitution.

Decisions which are to be taken by the shareholders can be made only at a general meeting (or generally by a written resolution which is signed by all the shareholders).

1.4.3 Assets

Assets of the business are usually owned by the company, although it may have been agreed that it will use an asset which is owned by one of the shareholders individually.

1.4.4 Taxation

The company will pay corporation tax on the profits of the business; the directors and shareholders of the company cannot be made liable for payment of corporation tax. Typically, the directors and the shareholders will receive income from the company in the form of salaries and dividends respectively, both of which give rise to a possible charge to income tax dependent on the circumstances of the individual recipient.

1.4.5 Debts

The company alone is responsible for the debts and obligations of the business, so that the directors and shareholders cannot generally be required to pay anything towards the debts of the company even in the event of the company's insolvency. Shareholders enjoy the benefit of limited liability, which means that their liability is limited to paying to the company the price they have agreed to pay for their shares; once shares have been paid for in full, the holder of those shares has no further liability. It is from this principle that the term 'limited liability company' derives. There are only a few exceptional circumstances (such as where the individual has acted dishonestly) where a director or shareholder can be forced to make a contribution to the company's assets in the event of its insolvency.

1.4.6 Publicity

In return for the advantage conferred on its shareholders by limited liability, the limited company has to accept a considerable degree of publicity of information about itself, its directors, its shareholders and its finances (including some or all of its year-end accounts). The prescribed information is required to be filed with the registrar of companies in Cardiff and updated as necessary; all information filed with the registrar of companies is open to inspection by the public.

1.5 PUBLIC LIMITED COMPANY

Whether a company is a public limited company or a private limited company depends essentially on its constitution. To be a public company, the company's constitution must state that it is a public company, must include the words 'public limited company' (or the abbreviation plc) at the end of the company's name and satisfy requirements as to the minimum amount of its share capital. Any company which is not a public company is a private company.

As with a private company, the business will be owned and operated by the company broadly as described in **1.4**, but there are important differences between public companies and private companies, some derived from statute, others derived from practice. Some of these differences are described in **1.5.2**.

1.5.1 Dealings in shares of public companies

A public company may (but need not) apply to have its shares listed on The Stock Exchange or on the Alternative Investment Market; in each case this means that a price will be quoted at which dealings in the company's shares will take place.

The Official List

In general, only a large public company which has traded for at least 3 years can apply for its shares to be listed on The Stock Exchange and the company must comply with the initial and on-going requirements of The Stock Exchange as to publication of information about the company's affairs. These requirements are contained in a volume called The Listing Rules, commonly known as the 'Yellow Book'. Listing on The Stock Exchange means that the company's shares are among the most marketable of all shares; only around 2,500 of the UK's companies are listed on The Stock Exchange, compared with a total of over 1,000,000 companies registered in the UK.

The Alternative Investment Market (AIM)

The Alternative Investment Market, which was set up in June 1995, is less stringently regulated than The Stock Exchange. The AIM deals in the shares of smaller and growing companies and provides a market-place with lower costs and less regulation than The Stock Exchange. There are no minimum capital requirements, no minimum number of shares required to be in public hands and no requirements for a minimum trading record. Currently, around 300 companies are listed on AIM.

1.5.2 Companies Acts requirements

Although, in general, the Companies Acts apply to both public and private companies, there are many differences of detail.

(1) A private company secretary need not be specially qualified or experienced.
(2) A private company can have just one director who may also be the only shareholder; a public company must have at least two directors and at least two shareholders.
(3) A private company can buy back the shares of a member who wishes to leave the company even if the company's accumulated profits are not sufficient so that it is necessary to use capital for the purchase.
(4) A private company is prohibited from offering to issue its shares to the public at large.
(5) There are fewer provisions regulating directors' dealings with their company if the company is a private company.
(6) Private companies up to a certain size may be permitted to file abbreviated accounts with the registrar of companies.
(7) Only a private company may be exempt from the statutory obligation to have its year-end accounts audited.
(8) Only a private company can dispense with the obligation to hold an annual general meeting.
(9) Only a private company can dispense with the formality of holding general meetings by having all its shareholders sign resolutions in writing.

1.5.3 Differences in practice

In a private company, the directors and shareholders are often substantially the same persons. In a public company, there will usually be a significant difference in personnel between the shareholders (who are likely to include institutional investors) and the directors (whose position is more like that of employees who are paid to manage the business).

In a private company, the shareholders cannot easily sell their shares because the articles of association usually contain restrictions on transfer (often in the form of directors' power of veto on the registration of the transfer) and because of difficulties of valuation, given that there is no ready 'market' for the shares. In a public company, there is less likely to be any restriction on transfer and, if the shares are listed on The Stock Exchange or AIM, there can be no restriction.

A private company may, or may not, choose to pay dividends to its shareholders; many private companies pay no dividend at all. In practice, a public company must have a record of paying dividends every year in order to encourage investment in that company by share ownership.

Chapter 2

LEGAL AND PRACTICAL CONSIDERATIONS WHEN STARTING UP

2.1 INTRODUCTION

The new business will require personnel: the owner(s) of the business will need to be aware of his statutory responsibilities and duties when recruiting employees, when acting as their employer and eventually, perhaps, when terminating their employment. Arrangements will have to be put in place for paying income tax (and corporation tax if the business is run by a company), for paying national insurance contributions and for collecting and paying value added tax, if appropriate. Also, the product must be considered: does the business need any licences, should the business carry insurances, is there a need to protect the intellectual property rights of the business? There may be further matters to consider in relation to the business premises, such as planning consents, although these are not considered further in this book.

Chapter 2 contents
Introduction
Employees
Accounting records for tax purposes
National insurance
Value added tax
Licences
Insurance
Intellectual property

2.2 EMPLOYEES

2.2.1 Recruitment

There is a statutory duty, under the Sex Discrimination Act 1975 and the Race Relations Act 1976, not to discriminate directly or indirectly on the grounds of sex, race or married status in advertising or offering employment. Under the Disability Discrimination Act 1995, it is also unlawful to discriminate against a disabled person in the recruitment of employees. (These provisions of the 1995 Act are not applicable to small businesses, ie those which employ less than 15 employees.) In addition, a person should not be refused employment on the ground of his trade union membership (Trade Union and Labour Relations (Consolidation) Act 1992).

There is a further statutory duty under the Equal Pay Act 1970 for an employer to provide equal pay for men and women who are employed by him to do the same or comparable work.

2.2.2 Statement of terms: Employment Rights Act 1996, s 1

Within 2 months of commencement of employment, the employer must, unless the employee's written contract deals with the matters (see **2.2.3**), give the employee a written statement containing details of the following aspects of the relationship:

(1) identity of the employer and employee;
(2) date of commencement of the employment and date of commencement of any previous employment from which this employment has taken over (eg where the business has changed hands);

(3) pay and intervals of payment;
(4) hours of work;
(5) holidays and whether holiday pay is given;
(6) arrangement for sickness and sickness pay;
(7) pensions;
(8) period of notice to be given by employer or employee to terminate the contract;
(9) if the employment is not permanent, the period for which it is expected to continue; if for a fixed term the date of expiry;
(10) job title;
(11) place(s) of work;
(12) particulars of any collective agreement(s) directly affecting the terms and conditions of employment;
(13) if the employee is required to work outside the UK for more than one month, the period of such work, the currency in which he will be paid, benefits provided and terms relating to return to the UK;
(14) disciplinary rules (but only if there are 20 or more employees in total);
(15) grievance procedures;
(16) whether the employer has obtained a contracting out certificate so that he makes no contributions towards the State Earnings Related Pension Scheme (SERPS).

2.2.3 Contract of employment

An employer may be advised to prepare for each employee a formal contract of employment which could itself satisfy the obligation to provide a statement as described in **2.2.2**. The contract should deal with all those matters listed in **2.2.2** and any other terms which might be appropriate. Significant additional terms might include:

(1) A term defining the range of the employee's duties.
(2) A term defining where the employee can be required to work.
(3) A term restraining employees who have left the business from setting up, or working in, a business which competes or might compete with that of the employer. To be enforceable, such a term must be for the protection of a legitimate trade interest and must be limited to what is reasonable in the circumstances regarding the length of time and the geographical area for which the ex-employee is to be restrained. Such a term benefits the employer by preventing his ex-employee from damaging the business by taking advantage of the knowledge and influence that he has gained during the employment in relation to the business and the persons with whom it deals.

2.2.4 Tax and national insurance

An employer is required to operate the PAYE (Pay As You Earn) system, by which he deducts from his employees' pay the appropriate amount of income tax and national insurance and accounts for these deductions to the Inland Revenue. The Inland Revenue provide the employer with the necessary information to operate the system.

2.2.5 Health and safety

An employer has a common law duty to take reasonable care for the health and safety of the employee at work, including the provision of:

(1) safe premises;
(2) safe plant and equipment;
(3) a safe system of work;
(4) competent fellow employees.

An employee who is injured as a result of his employer's failure to discharge this duty will be entitled to damages from the employer.

Much stricter duties are imposed on the employer by Regulations made under the Health and Safety at Work etc Act 1974. An employer who fails to comply with his obligations under the Act and the regulations is liable to criminal prosecution. The Act itself provides no express remedy for the injured employee. Breach of Regulations made under the Act gives rise to criminal liability and also to a civil action for damages for breach of statutory duty. Since most duties are strict, the employer will in many cases be liable to pay damages even though he is not at fault.

The Working Time Regulations 1998, SI 1998/1833 impose a maximum of 48 hours per week, on average.

2.2.6 Insurance

An employer is required to carry insurance against his liability to an employee who is injured or who contracts a disease as a result of his work. The certificate of insurance must be displayed at the place of work.

2.2.7 Understanding future dealings with employees

An employer should understand that he has certain statutory obligations towards his employee during the course of the employment in addition to those matters already described. These include:

(1) allowing employees time off work for:

    (a) ante-natal care;
    (b) trade union duties and activities;
    (c) public duties (eg those of magistrates); and
    (d) maternity and parental leave;

(2) not discriminating on the grounds of sex, race, married status or disability in offering or refusing promotion or training etc to an employee and dismissal; and
(3) allowing an employee to return to work after maternity leave.

An employer should also understand the general rights and remedies of an employee whom he may wish to dismiss.

2.2.8 Dismissal of employees

An employer should understand the possible rights and remedies of an employee whom he wishes to dismiss. Basically, there are three potential remedies: the common law claim for wrongful dismissal and two statutory claims – the complaint of unfair dismissal and the claim for a statutory redundancy payment.

2.2.9 Wrongful dismissal

This is a common law claim which is based on the fact that the contract has been terminated by the employer in a manner which is a breach of the contract of employment. This is likely to be so if the employer terminates a contract for an indefinite term with no notice or with inadequate notice, or if a fixed-term contract is terminated before its expiry date.

Most employment contracts are for an indefinite term and terminable by either side giving the correct contractual notice. If the employer gives the proper period of notice, then no breach will have occurred and there will be no claim for wrongful dismissal whatever the reason for the termination. In a fixed-term contract, the contract is not terminable by notice (unless it contains a 'break clause' allowing it to be ended by notice). In the case of a fixed-term contract without a break clause, termination of the contract prior to its expiry date will be a breach of contract and the employee may claim wrongful dismissal. If there is a break clause then the employer may terminate under it and if he gives the appropriate period of notice, the employee cannot succeed in a wrongful dismissal claim.

The applicable notice period will usually be expressly agreed in the contract, and if the employer gives no notice or short notice he will be in breach. If an expressly agreed notice period is shorter than the statutory minimum period required by s 86 of the Employment Rights Act 1996 (ERA 1996), then the longer statutory period of notice must be given. In the absence of an expressly agreed period of notice, there is an implied term that the employee is entitled to 'reasonable' notice. What will be a reasonable period will depend on the facts of the case. For more senior employees, a longer period will be implied. In any event, any such implied period is again subject to the statutory minimum period stipulated by s 86.

Where a contract of employment can be ended by notice, ERA 1996, s 86 provides for the following statutory minimum periods of notice (which prevail over any shorter contractual period, express or implied). The statutory minimum is:

(a) one week's notice after one month's continuous employment;
(b) 2 weeks' notice after 2 years' continuous employment;

and thereafter one additional week's notice for each year of continuous employment up to a maximum of 12 weeks' notice after 12 years' continuous employment.

It should be appreciated that the claim for wrongful dismissal requires a dismissal in breach of contract. Where an employee simply resigns, he will have no claim, since it is he, the employee, who has then terminated the contract. He, the employee, will be in breach of contract if he does not give the notice that he was required to give under the contract to end it, or, in the case of a fixed-term contract, he terminates it before the expiry date. (In indefinite contracts, the only statutory minimum notice required to be given by an employee is one week's notice after one month's continuous employment.) However, if the employer had committed a repudiatory breach of an express or implied term of the contract, the employee is entitled to treat the contract as discharged. In this case, the employee is entitled to leave, with or without notice and he can bring a claim of wrongful dismissal. Although he has not been actually dismissed by the employer he has been 'constructively dismissed' in breach of contract. However, in such a case, the employee must leave within a reasonable time of the employer's breach, otherwise he will be deemed to have affirmed the contract. Such a repudiatory breach may occur where the employer unilaterally alters the employee's term or breaks the implied duty of good faith owed to employees (eg a change in terms, such as a reduction in pay, or a change of place or hours of work which is not permitted by the contract).

It should be noted that even where there is a prima facie wrongful dismissal, the employer will have a defence if the employee had committed a repudiatory breach of an express or implied term of the contract, such as revealing confidential information or trade secrets, wilfully disobeying the employer's lawful orders or other serious misconduct. The employer can still use this defence even if he did not know of the employee's breach at the time he terminated the contract, but only discovered it afterwards.

Damages for wrongful dismissal are damages for breach of contract and the normal contractual rules apply. The aim is to put the employee in the position he would have been in, so far as money can do this, had the contract not been broken. Thus, in the case of an indefinite contract, the starting point for the calculation is the *net* salary or wages the employee would have earned during the proper notice period. In the case of a fixed-term contract, it is the net salary for the remainder of the fixed term. It should be noted that the income tax and national insurance contributions which would have been paid on that salary or wages, if earned, are notionally deducted in assessing the damages. In addition, the employee may claim damages for loss of other benefits he would have been entitled to for the relevant period (eg lost commission or 'fringe' benefits such as pension rights or use of a company car). Damages can usually be claimed for pecuniary loss only, so they will not generally be awarded for loss of future prospects or for injured feelings.

The employee is under a duty to mitigate his loss. Once his employment has been terminated he will be expected to take reasonable steps to obtain suitable employment and he will not be awarded damages in respect of any loss which has been mitigated or would have been mitigated but for his breach of the duty to mitigate. Note that where an employer has made a payment in lieu of notice, this will be deducted from any damages.

The claim for wrongful dismissal can be brought in either the High Court or the county court or in the employment tribunal. There is no limit to the amount of damages which may be awarded by the court, but there is currently a maximum of £25,000 which may be awarded by an employment tribunal. Where the claim is brought before the tribunal, there is a time-limit of 3 months from the dismissal. In contrast, in cases before the court, the usual limitation of 6 years applies.

2.2.10 Unfair dismissal

Under ERA 1996, s 94, an employee has the right not to be unfairly dismissed. The claim is brought before the employment tribunal. And there is a three-month time-limit from the date of the dimissal. The employee must prove that he is 'qualifying employee'. He must be below the normal retirement age for both men and women in that business, or, if there is no such normal retirement age, below the age of 65. Additionally, he must have one year's continuous employment starting when that employment began and ending with the dismissal. (Prior to June 1999, the requisite period was two years.) Certain classes of employment are excluded from making such a claim (eg members of the armed services, the police force and mariners).

The employee must prove that he has been dismissed. This includes actual dismissal and constructive dismissal. Actual dismissal is dismissal by the employer with or without notice. Constructive dismissal has been discussed above in the context of wrongful dismissal. There is another type of dismissal for the purposes of the statutory claim. This is where the contract was a fixed-term contract which was not renewed on its expiry.

The burden of proof then moves to the employer. He must show the principal reason for the dismissal and that such reason is one of the five permitted reasons. If he can establish that, the employment tribunal must decide whether the employer acted reasonably in treating that reason as a sufficient reason for dismissing the employee. If either the employer cannot show one of the reasons or the tribunal considers that the employer acted unreasonably, then the employee will win. The five potentially fair reasons are:

- the *capability or qualifications* of the employee for doing work of the kind he was employed to do (this could include incompetence, or inability to do the job by reason of illness or injury); or
- the *conduct* of the employee (this must generally relate to conduct within the employment – outside behaviour will only be relevant if it has a direct bearing on the employee's fitness to do the job); or
- the employee was *redundant* (in this case the employee will be entitled to a redundancy payment – see below); or
- the employee could not continue to work in the position held without *contravening some statutory enactment* (eg where a lorry driver loses his driving licence); or
- *some other substantial reason* justifying the dismissal of an employee holding the position which the employee held (it is not possible to give a comprehensive list of such reasons, but this category has been held to include dismissal where the employee refuses to accept a reorganisation affecting his working hours and a dismissal arising out of a personality clash between employees).

If the employer has demonstrated that the dismissal was for a fair reason, under ERA 1996, s 98(4), the tribunal must decide whether 'in the circumstances (including the size and administrative resources of the employer's undertaking) the employer acted reasonably or unreasonably in treating it as a sufficient reason for dismissing the employee [having regard] to equity and the substantial merits of the case.' The tribunal will see whether the employer had a genuine and reasonable belief in the facts based on a reasonable investigation and procedure leading to a reasonable decision. It will look at the size of the business – for instance, an employer with many employees may have found it more easy to cope with an employee who has considerable sickness absence. In particular, the employer may be held to have dismissed unfairly if there are procedural defects.

Thus, in competence cases, the employer should normally have warned the employee about his standard of work and given him the chance to improve, and, perhaps additional training and supervision. Perhaps a reasonable employer would have moved the employee to a job within his competence rather than dismissing him. In dismissal for long-term sickness, the employer should consult with the employee as to the likely duration of the illness and its nature.

In conduct cases, the employer should carry out a thorough investigation and allow the employee to state his case. He should not dismiss unless the misconduct is gross or persistent. Guidance on how to deal with misconduct is given by an ACAS Code of Practice, which in particular recommends a system of warnings for less serious misconduct. The Code does not have the force of law, but will be taken into account by the tribunal to see if the employer acted reasonably.

In cases of redundancy, the employer should warn and consult the affected employees or their representatives and adopt a fair basis of selection for redundancy ('Last in, first out' is often used as a basis for selection.) A fair employer would also consider the possibility of redeployment of affected employees within the business.

The employer should generally give the employee the correct notice due under the contract (or payment in lieu of notice). Failure to do so (other than in cases of gross misconduct) may well lead to a finding of unfair dismissal (as well as exposing the employer to a claim for wrongful dismissal).

If the defence is based on the employee's misconduct, unlike wrongful dismissal, the employer cannot rely on misconduct which he only discovered *after* the dismissal (although, if such misconduct had occurred, the tribunal may reduce any compensation). The remedies for unfair dismissal are as follows.

Reinstatement (getting the old job back) or re-engagement (being given another comparable or suitable job with the same or an associated employer)

It is for the employee to ask for such remedies and few such orders are made.

Compensation

This consists of two awards:

(a) The basic award

This is calculated by reference to a statutory formula which reflects the employee's age, his pay, and length of service. The statutory formula works by multiplying the employee's final week's gross pay (subject to a current maximum of £230) by the following two factors:

(i) his length of service (the maximum period taken into account is 20 years)
(ii) a multiplier of ½ or 1½ depending on the employee's age during those years' service (working backwards from the end of the employment)

   for years worked when 41 or over = 1½
   for years worked when 22 to 40 inclusive = 1
   for years worked when below 22 = ½

Example

Ernie starts work for A Co Ltd on his 30th birthday. His employment ends on his 57th birthday. His final gross week's pay is £295. On the basis of 20 years' service (the maximum), his basic award will be:

	£
16 × 1½ × £230	5,520
4 × 1 × £230	920
	6,440

(b) The compensatory award

In addition to the basic award, the tribunal will award such amount as it considers to be just and equitable having regard to the loss sustained by the employee in consequence of the dismissal insofar as that loss is attributable to the action taken by the employer. The award is subject to a maximum of £50,000 and is calculated under the following heads:

- immediate loss of net wages from the date of the dismissal to the date of the hearing, assuming the employee has not at that date got another job;
- future loss of net wages – based on an estimate as to how long it might take the employee to get another job (assuming he has not yet done so). Here the employee must mitigate his loss and will need to look for another job. Failure to mitigate may result in a reduction of this part of the award. Compensation here is not limited to the employee's contractual notice period;
- loss of fringe benefits;
- loss of statutory protection. In any new job, the employee will have to start building up as against a future employer his statutory rights to a redundancy payment and unfair dismissal protection and a statutory minimum notice. Commonly, a nominal figure is awarded for this. Compensation will also be given for the loss of the employee's minimum statutory notice entitlement.

The tribunal will deduct from the compensatory award any payment in lieu of notice or ex gratia payment received from the employer. In addition, it should be noted that both the basic award and the compensatory award can be reduced due to the employee's conduct.

2.2.11 Redundancy

The person primarily liable to pay a redundancy payment is the employer, and in most cases he pays it without dispute. Where he does not, or the employee disputes the calculation, the employee may refer the matter to an employment tribunal. There is a 6-month time-limit.

To claim a statutory redundancy payment, an employee must be qualified and the factors are very similar to unfair dismissal. The age limits are similar to unfair dismissal, but not exactly the same. He must be below any normal retirement age in that business, *being an age less than 65*. If there is no such normal retirement age, the employee must be below the age of 65. The employee must have 2 years' continuous employment and certain classes of employee are excluded (eg Crown employees, mariners and certain domestic servants). Contracting out is only possible as regards the claim for payments arising on the non-renewal of a fixed-term contract on its expiry.

As in unfair dismissal, the employee must prove that he has been dismissed (actually, constructively or by failure to renew a fixed-term contract on expiry).

Once the above has been proved, a presumption arises that the employee has been dismissed for redundancy. The employer may be able to show a reason other than redundancy, but this may open the door to a claim for unfair dismissal. At this point, it is vital to consider whether or not the reason for the dismissal fits into the statutory definition of redundancy (contained in ERA 1996, s 139). The definition covers three situations:

- *complete closedown* (the fact that the employer has ceased or intends to cease to carry on the business for the purposes of which the employee was employed by him);
- *partial closedown* (the fact that the employer has ceased or intends to cease to carry on that business in the place where the employee was so employed);

- *overmanning* (the fact that the requirements of the business for employees to carry out work of a particular kind, or for employees to carry out work of a particular kind in the place where the employee was employed by the employer, have ceased or diminished, or are expected to cease or diminish). Such a situation could arise where new technology means that some employees are replaced by machines, or where initial overmanning means that fellow employees can take on the work done by the redundant employee.

At this point, the employee may have a prima facie entitlement to a redundancy payment. However, it should be noted that an employee may lose his entitlement if he unreasonably refuses an offer of suitable alternative employment made by his employer or an associated employer to take effect within 4 weeks of the end of the original contract.

The statutory redundancy payment is calculated in general in the same way as the basic award for unfair dismissal. The main difference is that in the case of the redundancy payment, there is a lower age cut-off at age 18 (ie the employee cannot receive half of a week's pay for years worked under that age).

2.2.12 Overlapping claims

The employer should appreciate that a dismissed employee may have more than one potential claim against him. If the dismissal is unfair and without proper notice (or within a fixed term) the employee may claim both wrongful dismissal and unfair dismissal. Should the employee succeed in both claims, the basic principle is that compensation will not be awarded for the same loss twice. Immediate and future loss of wages form a substantial part of the compensatory award for unfair dismissal, and this would substantially reduce any damages awarded for wrongful dismissal.

An employee may have a claim for a redundancy and also for unfair dismissal. This could arise where an employee is unfairly selected for redundancy. The redundancy payment will be set against the unfair dismissal award and usually it simply offsets the basic award (since the two are calculated according to a similar formula). However, if the redundancy payment exceeds the basic award (as it might if the basic award were reduced because of the employee's own conduct) the balance will reduce the compensatory award.

2.2.13 Discriminatory dismissals

If an employer discriminates on the grounds of sex, race or married status or disability in dismissing an employee, the employee will be entitled to claim compensation from the employer. This compensation is not subject to any maximum and can include compensation for injured feelings.

2.3 ACCOUNTING RECORDS FOR TAX PURPOSES

There is no statutory form of accounts which must be maintained, unless the business is run by a company, and only a company is required to have its accounts audited (see **15.4**). Nevertheless, it is necessary to maintain accounts which are sufficient to give a true and fair view of the affairs of a business so that the profits which are liable to tax can be ascertained.

2.4 NATIONAL INSURANCE

A sole trader or partner will pay Class 2 national insurance contributions which are at a flat rate and may also pay Class 4 national insurance contributions which are calculated as a percentage of taxable profits. A limited company will pay the employer's national insurance contributions in relation to each of its employees (including directors) and will collect and pay the employee's own Class 2 national insurance contributions.

2.5 VALUE ADDED TAX

If the annual turnover of the business is expected to exceed £52,000 in the ensuing 30 days, the proprietor must register for VAT. This will mean that VAT must then be charged and accounted for on the output of goods or services by the business. In any case, once the turnover has reached £52,000 within a period not exceeding 12 months, registration for VAT becomes necessary.

2.6 LICENCES

2.6.1 Consumer Credit Act 1974

If the business involves offering credit or hire facilities, the proprietor may require a licence under the Consumer Credit Act 1974 which may be obtained by application to the Office of Fair Trading.

2.6.2 Other licences

Particular types of business require a licence to operate obtained from the appropriate local administration office. Examples include licences for liquor sales (from the local magistrates), for food manufacture (from the Environmental Health Department) and for children's nurseries (from the Social Services Department).

2.7 INSURANCE

A range of possible insurances should be considered, two of which (employer's liability insurance, as described in **2.2.6**, and third party liability motor insurance) are compulsory. Examples of non-compulsory but advisable insurances include fire, theft, product liability, public liability and motor insurance (for more risks than the compulsory third party liability).

2.8 INTELLECTUAL PROPERTY

The business may be using brand names, inventions, designs or products which can be protected from copying by competitors by registration. A patent may be granted for an invention which is capable of industrial application following an application to the Patent Office. A design (ie the outward shape or decorative appearance of a product) may be registered at the Patent Office. A trade mark is a brand name or logo which distinguishes the product in the minds of the public (eg 'Coca-Cola' for soft drinks, or 'Honda' for motorcycles). It may be registered at the Trade Marks Registry, which is part of the Patent Office.

PART II

RUNNING A BUSINESS AS A SOLE TRADER

Whilst any business is subject to certain statutory controls and practical considerations, as described in Part I, the simplest form in which a person can trade is as a sole trader. There are no additional controls or considerations peculiar to this form of trading, although, as with partnerships and companies, if the sole trader chooses to trade under a name different from his own name, he will be subject to the Business Names Act 1985 as described in **4.4.1**.

Given the absence of any such additional controls or considerations, this Part simply considers the tax treatment of the profits of a business run by a sole trader.

Chapter 3

TAXATION OF INCOME PROFITS OF SOLE TRADERS

3.1 INTRODUCTION

A sole trader may make two types of profit: income and capital. Insofar as profits are recurring by nature (eg trading, rent, interest), the sole trader will face a possible charge to income tax. Insofar as the profit derives from the disposal of an asset owned by the sole trader (eg business premises), he will face a possible charge to capital gains tax. This chapter deals largely with income profits (and the possibility of trading losses); the possible charge to capital gains tax on disposal of an asset is considered at **3.5** below and in Chapter 22.

3.2 INCOME PROFITS

The profits of the business will derive mainly from the carrying on of a trade and will therefore be assessed to income tax under Schedule D, Case I, of the Income and Corporation Taxes Act 1988 (ICTA 1988) (and broadly the same rules apply to the profits of a profession or vocation assessed under Schedule D, Case II). These profits will have been worked out, usually by an accountant, by preparing a profit and loss account which compares receipts with expenses to produce a figure for net profit (or net loss). Although the profit and loss account will be used as a starting point for ascertaining the figure which is taxable, some adjustment will usually be required since the profit and loss account will not apply the strict tax rules – some of the expenses likely to be shown in the profit and loss account (such as entertainment of customers) are not allowed as deductions for tax purposes and the calculation must be revised to accord with the tax rules prior to submission to the Inland Revenue. Other sources of income which the business might receive include investment income such as rents (Schedule A) or interest (Schedule D, Case III) but a detailed discussion of these is outside the ambit of this book.

3.2.1 Receipts of the trade less 'income' expenditure

The taxable profits of a trade are the 'chargeable receipts' of the trade less its 'deductible expenditure'.

(1) Chargeable receipts

Receipts of the trade are those which derive from the trading activity rather than from circumstances not directly connected with the trade. Most receipts of the trade, such as those from sales, are easily identified, but some are less so. For example, a sum received on cancellation of a trading contract as compensation would be a receipt of the trade but a gratuitous sum received on termination of a trading relationship as a token of personal appreciation would not be. The former would attract income tax, the latter would not.

Chapter 3 contents
Introduction
Income profits
Basis of assessment and date for payment
Relief for a trading loss
Capital profits and losses

Receipts of the trade are only chargeable to income tax if they are of an income, as opposed to a capital, nature. If something is purchased for the purpose of resale at a profit, such as the stock of an antique dealer, the proceeds of sale will be of an income nature. Conversely, receipts of a capital nature will generally derive from the sale of an asset which was purchased for the benefit or use of the business on a more or less permanent basis rather than for resale. For example, the trader who purchases an antique desk for his office and who eventually (many years later) sells it receives a sum of a capital nature.

Some receipts will arise from types of transaction which are different from the purchase and sale of goods, so that the above principles will have to be applied by analogy. For example, a sum received as compensation for cancellation of a contract for the sale of goods is of an income nature because it represents what would have been an income profit if the goods had been sold.

(2) Deductible expenditure

In calculating taxable profit there must be deducted from chargeable receipts of the trade any expenditure which is of an income nature, which has been incurred 'wholly and exclusively' for the trade and deduction of which is not prohibited by statute (ICTA 1988, s 74).

(a) To describe expenditure as being of an income nature sounds perverse, but the terminology is relevant to the trader's purpose. If expenditure on an item is incurred for the purpose of enabling the trader to sell that item at a profit it is of an income nature. Therefore the expense to the antique dealer of buying his stock is of an income nature and deductible from chargeable receipts in calculating taxable profit. Conversely the expense to the trader of buying his antique desk (buying a permanent asset for his business) is of a capital nature and not deductible (but see **3.2.2** below).

A further relevant (and sometimes more appropriate) test is whether the expenditure has the quality of recurrence, rather than being once and for all expenditure. All expenditure on general overheads like electricity, telephone charges, staff salaries and rent has this quality of recurrence in the sense that the type of expenditure is likely to be incurred repeatedly; it is of an income nature. Also, interest paid on borrowing (eg on overdraft) for business purposes will generally qualify as being expenditure of an income nature. Expenditure on the purchase of fixed assets of the business-like premises, desks and cars will not recur in the foreseeable future in that the asset has been acquired for the on-going benefit of the trade.

(b) To be deductible, the expenditure must also have been incurred wholly and exclusively for the purposes of the trade (ICTA 1988, s 74). Expenditure which has a dual purpose cannot be wholly and exclusively for one purpose. For example, when a taxpayer pays for a meal in a restaurant when working away from home, the greater cost of the meal compared with eating at home was not incurred wholly and exclusively for business purposes; the cost of the meal had a dual purpose which included satisfying a person's basic need to eat. Similarly, when a barrister purchases clothing suitable for wearing in court, the greater cost of that clothing compared with casual clothing was not incurred wholly and exclusively for business purposes; the cost of the clothing had a dual purpose including satisfying a person's basic need to be clothed. In fact, despite this principle which has been clearly established in case-law (see, eg *Mallalieu v*

Drummond [1983] STC 665, HL), the Inland Revenue may allow some expenses to be apportioned so that part is deductible; for example, where a taxpayer works from home, part of the cost of heating and lighting the home will be deductible for tax purposes.

3.2.2 Capital expenditure – 'capital allowances'

As described in **3.2.1** above, capital expenditure cannot, under the basic rules governing income tax, be deducted from chargeable receipts when calculating taxable profits. This can cause severe cash flow problems for a business that needs to invest in expensive capital items to help produce the goods or services in which it deals. Parliament has long recognised this and has passed legislation to allow a specified amount of the cost of certain capital items to be deducted each year in calculating taxable profits. Thus, under the Capital Allowances Act 1990, where expenditure is incurred on certain assets, notably the purchase of machinery and plant and the construction of industrial buildings, an annual percentage of the capital expenditure will be allowed as a deduction in calculating trading profits. These deductions, known as capital allowances, are calculated on separate bases for machinery and plant, and for industrial buildings.

(1) Machinery and plant

(a) Definitions.
'Machinery and plant' is not defined in the Act. In *Yarmouth v France* (1887) 19 QBD 647, it was said that plant includes whatever apparatus is used by the businessman for carrying on his business; this includes all goods and chattels which he keeps for permanent employment in his business but not, for example, stock in trade. Examples of machinery and plant are office equipment, computer software, tools and manufacturing equipment.

(b) The allowance.
For most qualifying assets, the taxpayer is allowed, in each year of ownership of the asset, to deduct a 'writing down allowance' of up to 25 per cent of the reducing balance of the cost of the asset in calculating his trading profit (CAA 1990, s 24). (Note: there are special rules for calculating the capital allowances given for expenditure on cars.)

Example 1
A builder, owning no other machinery or plant, purchases a JCB (digger) for £16,000. Starting in the year of purchase, and assuming no further purchases (and ignoring the enhanced first year allowance, for which see below), his capital allowances are as follows:

Year 1 – 25% of £16,000 = £4,000   writing down allowance, leaving £12,000 as the reduced balance of the cost

Year 2 – 25% of £12,000 = £3,000   writing down allowance, leaving £9,000 as the reduced balance of the cost

Year 3 – 25% of £9,000 = £2,250   writing down allowance, leaving £6,750 as the reduced balance of the cost

etc.
Suppose that his chargeable receipts of the trade less other deductible expenses (see **3.2.1**) are £50,000, £60,000 and £70,000 for Years 1, 2 and 3 respectively. This means (following deduction of the writing down allowance) that his

trading profit from this source for inclusion in his 'statutory income' is as follows:

Year 1: £46,000 (£50,000 less £4,000 writing down allowance)

Year 2: £57,000 (£60,000 less £3,000 writing down allowance)

Year 3: £67,750 (£70,000 less £2,250 writing down allowance)

(c) Long-life assets.
In certain cases, only a writing down allowance of up to 6 per cent of the reduced balance can be claimed each year in respect of machinery and plant with an expected working life, when new, of at least 25 years, when the business spends more than £100,000 per year on such assets.

(d) Sale of assets.
If, in due course, the item of machinery and plant is sold, it will be necessary to compare the reduced balance of the cost at the time of sale with the actual sale price in order to assess whether the sale produces a 'profit' or a 'loss' when comparing these figures. If a 'profit' results, this may (subject to pooling – see below) be the subject of a balancing charge to income tax in the tax year covering the accounting period in which the sale takes place; if a 'loss' results, there may be a balancing allowance for income tax purposes in that year. The purpose of a balancing charge or a balancing allowance is to ensure that the taxpayer has had tax relief for precisely the amount by which the asset diminished in value – no more and no less.

Suppose that the builder in Example 1, at the beginning of Year 4, sells his JCB for £7,000. If so, he has made a 'profit' of £250 compared with its written down value (£6,750) and the £250 will form part of his trading profit in Year 4.

(e) Pooling.
In practice, traders will often own more than one item of machinery and plant. The principles for calculating capital allowances remain the same except that, in general, all expenditure on machinery and plant is pooled and the writing down allowance is granted each year on the balance of expenditure within the whole pool. If an asset is sold, the sale proceeds are deducted from the pool; no balancing allowance or charge should occur therefore until the trade is discontinued and the whole pool sold.

Example 2
Bob, a sole trader, has an existing pool of machinery and plant with a written down value of £80,000. He sells some machinery for £20,000:

	£
Written down value of pool	80,000
Less: disposal value	20,000
	60,000
Less: writing down allowance for the year of 25%	15,000
Value of pool carried forward	45,000

If Bob sells the business in the following year and the value agreed for the assets in the pool is, say, £47,000 a balancing charge of £2,000 will be included in Bob's trading profit for the final accounting period of the business under his ownership.

(f) Enhanced first year allowance.
Since 1997, an enhanced first year allowance has been given for expenditure on machinery and plant incurred by a 'small or medium-sized enterprise'. Instead of the usual writing down allowance of 25 per cent, a larger allowance has been allowed in the first year. The increased allowance is currently 40 per cent for most assets. Thereafter, the usual 25 per cent writing-down allowance applies. To be a 'small or medium-sized enterprise', the business must satisfy at least two of the following conditions:

- its annual turnover must not exceed £11.2 million;
- its assets must not exceed £5.6 million;
- its employees must not exceed 250.

The enhanced first year allowance is not available for expenditure, inter alia, on cars and long-life assets.

Example 3
Tom, a sole trader, owns a manufacturing business which is a 'small enterprise'. In June 2000, he buys new machinery for £50,000. The written-down value of his existing pool of machinery and plant is £80,000. In the current year, he is entitled to the following capital allowances:

First year allowance:

£50,000 × 40%   £20,000   (leaving a reduced balance for the new machinery of £30,000)

Writing down allowance:

£80,000 × 25%   £20,000   (leaving a reduced balance for the existing pool of £60,000)

Total capital allowances for
the year   £40,000

The value of the written-down pool carried forward will be £90,000 (£30,000 + £60,000)

(g) Computer equipment purchased by small businesses.
At present, if a 'small enterprise' purchases certain defined computer equipment (covering most hardware and some software), the enhanced first year allowance is 100 per cent; ie the entire cost of the equipment can be deducted from the business' chargeable receipts in the accounting period of the purchase.

To be a 'small enterprise', the business must satisfy at least two of the following conditions:

- Its annual turnover must not exceed £2.8 million.
- Its assets must not exceed £1.4 million.
- Its employees must not exceed 50.

(2) Industrial buildings

(a) Definitions.
'Industrial building' is defined (CAA 1990, s 18) to include a mill, a factory and a warehouse for the storage of goods or materials connected with a manufacturing trade. It does not include a shop or office premises (although

offices forming less than 25 per cent of the cost of a larger industrial building should not cause the allowance to be lost).

(b) The allowance.
In each year of ownership, a writing down allowance of 4 per cent of the cost of construction of an industrial building is deductible in calculating trading profit (CAA 1990, s 3). The writing down allowances will therefore be spread over a fixed period of 25 years.

Example 1
A machine tool manufacturer builds a new factory at a cost (excluding the land on which it is built) of £100,000. His capital allowances are as follows:

Year 1 – 4% of £100,000 = £4,000 writing down allowance
to
Year 25 – 4% of £100,000 = £4,000 writing down allowance

As with a writing down allowance on machinery and plant, this means that the taxpayer can deduct his writing down allowance (here, £4,000 each year) in calculating his trading profit for inclusion in his 'statutory income'.

(c) Sale of assets.
If an industrial building is sold during the 25-year period covered by the writing down allowance, the position of both the seller and the buyer needs to be considered.

(i) The seller must compare the written down value to the sale price to see whether a balancing charge or allowance will arise.
(ii) The buyer (providing the building continues to be used for an industrial purpose) will be entitled to claim the writing down allowance on that part of the original cost of construction which has not been relieved (taking into account any balancing charge or allowance on the seller) for the remainder of the original period of 25 years (and no longer restricted to the 4 per cent per annum limit).

Example 2
Andrew builds a factory at a cost of £1 million. Ten years later he sells the factory to Jane for £700,000. Jane continues to use the factory for an industrial purpose.

(i) Position for Andrew – Over the 10-year period of his ownership, he has claimed writing down allowances totalling £400,000 (£1 million × 4% × 10) and the written down value of the building is £600,000. On the sale to Jane, he incurs a balancing charge of £100,000.

(ii) Position for Jane – Over the next 15 years she can claim writing down allowances (spread evenly over that period) on the total of the written down value of £600,000 plus the amount of the balancing charge of £100,000; ie on the £700,000 she paid for the factory.

3.3 BASIS OF ASSESSMENT AND DATE FOR PAYMENT

Having calculated the taxable profits of the trade in accordance with the rules described in **3.2**, those profits must be assessed to income tax (for the general rules relating to income tax see the LPC Resource Book *Pervasive and Core Topics* (Jordans)). Income tax on the profits of a trade which commences on or after 6 April 1994 is assessed under the rules described in **3.3.1** to **3.3.4** (ICTA 1988, ss 60–63, inserted by FA 1994, ss 200–205).

3.3.1 The 'normal' rule (relevant to the third and subsequent tax years of a business)

Income tax will be assessed on the profits of the 12-month accounting period which ends in the tax year. For example, if a trader prepares his accounts for calendar years, the trading profits of the accounts prepared up to 31 December 1999 will form part of his statutory income for assessing income tax for the tax year 1999/2000.

3.3.2 The first tax year of a new business

In the first tax year (6 April to the following 5 April) in which the trade is carried on, income tax will be assessed on the profits made during that tax year, ie from the date of commencement to the following 5 April. For example, a trader who commences his trade on 1 January 2000 will have his trading profits from 1 January to 5 April 2000 (inc) assessed as part of his statutory income for the tax year 1999/2000.

3.3.3 The second tax year of a new business

In the second tax year in which the trade is carried on, income tax will generally be assessed on the basis of the 'normal' rule so that the profits to be assessed will be the profits of the 12-month accounting period which ends in the second tax year (ie the first accounting period). If the trader in the example at **3.3.2** prepares his accounts on a calendar year basis, his profits for the period 1 January to 31 December 2000 (including those for 1 January to 5 April already taxed) will be assessed as part of his statutory income for the tax year 2000/01. In some instances (eg an opening accounting period of less than 12 months), the rule is that the taxpayer will be assessed on the basis of the profits of the first 12 months' trading, even though this will not coincide with the taxpayer's own accounting period.

3.3.4 The closing tax year of a business

In the final tax year, income tax will be assessed on the profits made from the end of the latest accounting period to be assessed until the date of cessation, less a deduction for what is described as 'overlap profit'. 'Overlap profit' means a profit which is included in the assessment of two successive tax years as, for example, the first and second tax years of a new business (see the example in **3.3.3**).

3.3.5 Illustration

The above rules for assessment of the opening, second, normal and final tax years of a business may be further illustrated by the following example:

Example

A trader commences his business on 1 January 1996 and decides to prepare accounts for calendar years. Although the trade never suffers a loss, it is not as successful as the trader had hoped and he closes the trade on 31 December 1999. The accounts show the following trading profits:

	£
1996:	20,000
1997:	30,000
1998:	40,000
1999:	10,000

Income tax will be assessed on the following figures:

	£	
1995/96: (1st tax year)	5,000	(¼ of £20,000, representing the 3-month period 1 January 1996 to 5 April 1996).
1996/97: (2nd tax year)	20,000	(profits made in the 1996 accounting period which ends in the tax year).
1997/98: (3rd tax year)	30,000	(profits made in the 1997 accounting period which ends in the tax year).
1998/99: (4th tax year)	40,000	(profits made in the 1998 accounting period which ends in the tax year).
1999/00: (final tax year)	5,000	(profits made from the end of the latest accounting period to be assessed less overlap profit, ie

	£	
	10,000	(for 1999)
less	5,000	(overlap profit)
	5,000)	

The information used in the example may be presented in diagram form as follows:

	'96	'97	'98	'99	
Profit from accounts	£20,000	£30,000	£40,000	£10,000	Total profit = £100,000
	95/6	96/7	97/8	98/9	99/00
	Year 1	Year 2	Year 3	Year 4	Final Year

Total amount assessed to income tax

Tax on: £5,000   £20,000   £30,000   £40,000   £5,000   = £100,000

Note: The purpose and effect of deducting 'overlap profit' in the final tax year in calculating the assessment figure is that the total profit for the lifespan of the business is the same as the total amount assessed to income tax. However, there is still a cash flow disadvantage for the taxpayer in the example who does not receive any credit for the initial double taxation of the 'overlap profit' until the business ceases.

3.3.6 Date for payment (TMA 1970, ss 59A and 59B, inserted by FA 1994, ss 192 and 193)

Income tax assessed under Schedule D, Case I, is payable by two equal instalments, of which the first is due on 31 January in the tax year in question and the second is due on 31 July following the end of that tax year. Since the trader's taxable profit may not be known by the first of those dates (or even the second), generally he will make his two payments based on the previous year's profits. On or before the 31 January following the end of the tax year, the taxpayer will make a tax return on which his actual liability to income tax will be self-assessed and an adjustment (by further payment or by repayment of tax) will be made.

For example, a trader whose accounts are prepared on a calendar year basis will be taxed on profits for 2000 in the tax year 2000/01. The first instalment will be due on 31 January 2001, the second on 31 July 2001 (both payments usually based on the profits for 1999) with a balancing charge or rebate due on 31 January 2002 once the return for 2000/01 has been processed under the self-assessment system.

3.4 RELIEF FOR A TRADING LOSS

Thus far, this chapter has dealt with the calculation and taxation of a trading profit. The calculation of chargeable receipts of the trade less deductible expenditure (including capital allowances) may, however, produce a trading loss. There are various provisions in the ICTA 1988 which allow the taxpayer to deduct a trading loss from other income in order to provide relief from tax on that other income. Where the circumstances are such that relief could be claimed under more than one of the following provisions, the taxpayer may choose under which to claim. It may be that the taxpayer's loss is greater than can be relieved under just one of these provisions; if so, the taxpayer can claim as much relief as is available under one provision and then claim relief for the balance of his loss under any other available provision (although he cannot claim relief for the same loss twice over). Generally, the taxpayer will want to claim relief under whichever provision is best for cash-flow; some allow a repayment of tax previously paid, while others act to reduce the amount of tax which will become due in the future.

3.4.1 Start-up loss relief (ICTA 1988, s 381)

If the taxpayer suffers a loss which is assessed in any of the first 4 tax years of a new business, the loss can be carried back and deducted from all other types of income of the taxpayer in the 3 tax years prior to the tax year of the loss. This provision might be particularly useful to a person who starts a new business having previously had a steady income from a former business or employment. While the new business becomes established, it may make losses but the trader may be cushioned by claiming back from the Inland Revenue some income tax which he has paid in his previous business or employment in the earlier years. This would be especially beneficial if some or all of the income tax which he paid and is now able to claim back was at the higher rate of 40 per cent.

If the taxpayer elects to use this provision, the loss in question must be set against earlier years before later years – the taxpayer cannot pick and choose which year's income is reduced first.

Example

Bruno commences a business on 1 January 2000. In the first few months of trading, he incurs a lot of expense in setting up the business but has few customers. As a result, he makes a trading loss in the first tax year of assessment (for the period 1 January to 5 April 2000 inclusive) of £25,000.

Before starting his own business, Bruno had been an employee of a large company, and had the following income:

Tax year	1996/97	£20,000
	1997/98	£25,000
	1998/99	£35,000
	1999/00 (part)	£35,000

If Bruno claims relief under s 381, his £25,000 trading loss will be relieved as follows:

£20,000 will be set off against his income for 1996/97, reducing the revised income for 1996/97 to nil (so Bruno will get a tax rebate for that tax year).

The remaining £5,000 will be set off against his income for 1997/98, reducing the revised income for 1997/98 to £20,000 (so Bruno will get a partial tax rebate for that tax year).

Note:

(i) The relief is given against 'total' income, ie before deduction of the personal allowance. For 1996/97, Bruno has, therefore, effectively wasted his personal allowance.

(ii) The rule that a loss must be deducted from earlier years before later years means that Bruno has had his income reduced for years when he was a basic rate taxpayer, not when he became a higher rate taxpayer.

3.4.2 Carry-across/1 year back relief for trading losses generally (ICTA 1988, s 380 and FA 1991, s 72)

(1) Set off against income

A trading loss which arises in an accounting period is treated as a loss of the tax year in which the accounting period ends. The loss can be deducted from all other types of income of that tax year or from the preceding tax year. If there is enough of a loss to claim in both tax years, the relief must be given first for the current tax year, and any loss left over can be carried back to the preceding tax year.

As with start-up relief, if the taxpayer claims this relief, the loss must be set against 'total' income which may result in him having no income left against which to set his personal allowance; this would mean that the personal allowance for that year is wasted since there is no provision for personal allowances to be carried forward to another year.

In the example at **3.4.1**, Bruno may have preferred to claim relief for his trading loss under s 380 rather than s 381. This would have enabled him to set his loss of £25,000 against either his income of £35,000 in 1999/2000 or his income of £35,000 in 1998/99 (both years when he was a higher rate taxpayer).

(2) Set off against capital gains

If a claim is made under s 380 and the taxpayer's other income for that year is reduced to nil by the trading loss in question, and some of the loss has still to be used, then if the taxpayer does not opt to relieve the excess loss in some other way (eg by using s 381 or s 385) it can be deducted from the taxpayer's chargeable gains (if any) for the tax year of the loss. If any loss still remains it can be carried back to the preceding tax year and deducted from any capital gains in that year.

This is the only loss relief considered in this chapter which allows relief, in certain circumstances, against a taxpayer's chargeable capital gains as well as against income.

3.4.3 Carry-forward relief for trading losses generally (ICTA 1988, s 385)

If a taxpayer suffers a trading loss in any year of a trade, the loss can be carried forward to be deducted from subsequent profits which the trade produces, taking earlier years first. This has two disadvantages for the taxpayer when compared with relief under s 380 (see **3.4.2**). First, he must wait until future profits of the trade would become taxable before he benefits from his loss relief. Secondly, s 385 is more restrictive than s 380 in that it only provides for the loss to be set against profits which the trade produces – it does not provide for relief against other sources of income or against capital gains.

However, the losses carried forward under s 385 can be carried forward indefinitely until a suitable profit from the trade arises to be relieved.

Example

Carl's business has an accounting period which ends on 31 December each year. In 1999, he makes a trading loss of £40,000. In 2000 he makes a trading profit of £35,000 and in 2001 he makes a trading profit of £20,000. He has no other income. If Carl makes a claim under s 385, his income tax assessments will be based on:

Tax year	Profit/(loss) £
1999/00	(40,000)
2000/01	Nil (£35,000 profit fully covered by carried forward loss)
2001/02	£15,000 (£20,000 profit reduced by remaining £5,000 loss)

3.4.4 Carry-back of terminal trading loss (ICTA 1988, s 388)

If a taxpayer suffers a trading loss in the final 12 months in which he carries on the trade, this loss can (unless otherwise relieved (eg by s 380)) be carried back to be deducted from his trading profit in the 3 tax years prior to his final tax year, taking later years before earlier years. He may thus reclaim from the Inland Revenue tax which he has paid in earlier years. Note that s 388 does not allow relief against non-trading income or against capital gains.

3.4.5 Carry-forward relief on incorporation of business (ICTA 1988, s 386)

If the taxpayer has suffered trading losses which have not been relieved and transfers the business to a company wholly or mainly in return for the issue to himself of shares in the company, the losses can (unless otherwise relieved (eg by s 380 or s 388)) be carried forward and deducted from income which he receives from the company, such as a salary as a director or dividends as a shareholder. In order to be 'wholly or mainly in return for the issue of shares', at least 80 per cent of the consideration for the transfer must consist of shares in the company.

Example

On 30 November 2000, Dee transfers her business to a company wholly in return for shares in the company. Her trading loss from the business at that stage is £10,000. In the remainder of the 2000/01 tax year she receives a small salary from the company of £6,000. In the following tax year, 2001/02, she receives a salary from the company of £15,000 and her shareholding in the company produces dividends of £2,000. She has no other income. If Dee claims relief under s 386:

(i) her income from the salary of £6,000 in 2000/01 is reduced to nil by the losses carried forward; and

(ii) the remaining loss of £4,000 can be set against her income of £17,000 in 2001/02 (reducing the salary by £4,000).

3.4.6 Summary

SECTION OF ICTA 1988	WHEN WILL THE LOSS HAVE OCCURRED?	AGAINST WHAT WILL THE LOSS BE SET?	WHICH TAX YEARS ARE RELEVANT?
s 381 (start-up relief by carry-back)	The first 4 tax years of trading	Any income	The 3 tax years preceding the tax year of the loss
s 380 (carry-across/ carry back 1 year relief)	Any accounting year of trading	Any income and (thereafter) chargeable gains	The tax year in which the accounting year of the loss ends and/or the preceding tax year
s 385 (carry-forward relief)	Any accounting year of trading	Subsequent profits of the same trade	Any subsequent tax year until the loss is absorbed
s 388 (terminal relief by carry-back)	The final 12 months of trading	Previous profits of the same trade	The 3 tax years preceding the final tax year
s 386 (carry-forward relief on incorporation)	Up to incorporation	Subsequent profits	

3.5 CAPITAL PROFITS AND LOSSES

On the sale of a capital asset used in the trade, a capital profit or loss may result. The treatment of capital gains on the disposal of business assets is dealt with in Chapter 22.

Some capital assets may qualify both for capital allowances and be chargeable assets for the purposes of capital gains tax (eg an industrial building). If so, special rules exist to determine whether income tax or capital gains tax will apply to the rise or fall in value of the asset on its disposal. The detail of these rules is beyond the scope of this book, but they are designed to ensure that where capital allowances have been claimed an adjustment is made so that only the 'true' gain or loss on the disposal of an asset is used in the capital gains tax calculation.

PART III

RUNNING A BUSINESS IN PARTNERSHIP

When a business is run by a partnership, the taxation of the business profits becomes more complex than for a sole trader, and various matters other than taxation become relevant.

In addition to taxation of the business profits of a partnership, this Part considers how and on what terms a partnership may be established, the ongoing implications of being in partnership, both as regards fellow partners and as regards debts of the business, and how a partner may retire from or break up the partnership.

Chapter 4

THE START OF A PARTNERSHIP

4.1 INTRODUCTION

Where two or more persons wish to establish a business relationship between themselves without becoming a company, partnership is only one of a number of possibilities. Other possibilities include the relationships of employer and employee, principal and agent, franchisor and franchisee. Some possibilities are described in Chapter 33, but this chapter concentrates on recognising a partnership and the requirements for the start of a partnership.

4.2 WHAT IS A PARTNERSHIP?

4.2.1 Definition

A partnership arises where two or more persons agree that they will run a business together and actually do so. The term 'partnership' therefore describes no more than a business relationship based on an agreement (ie contract). The agreement can be oral or in writing or may even be implied by conduct. A partnership need not necessarily be recognised as such by the parties since the existence of a partnership depends on whether or not the definition contained in s 1 of the Partnership Act 1890 applies. By this section, 'partnership is the relation which subsists between persons carrying on a business in common with a view of profit'.

'Carrying on a business in common' means that two or more persons share responsibility for the business and for decisions which affect the business; effectively, that there are two or more proprietors. In contrast, an employer and his employee may be running a business together, but this will not mean that they are partners: the employee must accept the decisions and instructions of his employer, and he has no right to interfere.

It is important to realise at the outset that the partnership does **not** have a separate legal existence. In contrast, a company does have such a separate legal existence.

In order to be able to identify a particular relationship as being a partnership, it is necessary to appreciate what are the fundamental characteristics of a partnership.

4.2.2 Fundamental characteristics

Typical rights and responsibilities of partners which are fundamental to the relationship include:

(1) the right to be involved in making decisions which affect the business;
(2) the right to share in the profits of the business;
(3) the right to examine the accounts of the business;
(4) the right to insist on openness and honesty from fellow partners;
(5) the right to veto the introduction of a new partner;

Chapter 4 contents
Introduction
What is a partnership?
Setting up a partnership
Formalities required by statute

(6) the responsibility for sharing any losses made by the business.

Theoretically, any or all of these fundamental characteristics can be varied or excluded by the agreement governing the relationship, although at some point variations or exclusions would deny the existence of the partnership.

4.3 SETTING UP A PARTNERSHIP

Since the existence of a partnership is established by applying the definition to the relationship (which may be based on an oral agreement), it follows that there is no necessary formality. However, a written agreement is invaluable as evidence of the relationship and of its terms. It is also useful for the partners to have a written 'constitution' to which they may refer. It may, amongst other things, provide solutions to possible disagreements or disputes and thus perhaps avoid future litigation. Typical terms of a partnership agreement are considered in Chapter 5.

4.4 FORMALITIES REQUIRED BY STATUTE

4.4.1 Business Names Act 1985

Where the Business Names Act 1985 applies (s 1), there are controls over the choice of partnership name (ss 2 and 3) and requirements as to revealing the names and addresses of the partners (s 4). These controls and requirements will not apply, however, if the name consists simply of the names of the partners because the Act itself will not then apply. For example, if Paula Jones and Alan Burns commence business in partnership, the following business names will not be subject to the Act: 'Jones and Burns', 'P Jones and A Burns', 'Paula Jones and Alan Burns'. Conversely, if they choose one of the following business names, they will be subject to the Act: 'P Jones', 'Jones, Burns & Co.', 'JB Services'.

If the Act applies, certain words or expressions forming part of the business name will require the written approval of the Secretary of State for Trade and Industry (and possibly the prior approval of another relevant body). These include words or expressions contained in the Company and Business Names Regulations 1981, as amended by the Company and Business Names (Amendment) Regulations 1982 and 1985. In addition, prescribed information must appear on all stationery and on a notice at any place of business to which customers or suppliers have access. This information consists of the names of the partners and (for each partner) an address in Great Britain for service of documents. Non-compliance with the obligations is an offence punishable by a fine and the partners will be unable to enforce contracts if the other party can show that he was prejudiced by the non-compliance (BNA 1985, s 5).

In some partnerships, it would be unrealistic to comply with the Business Names Act 1985 requirements for stating partners' names on stationery. For example, although, generally, trading partnerships cannot have more than 20 partners (CA 1985, s 716), professional partnerships are not limited in this way. It is provided, therefore, that the partnership can instead include on its stationery a statement that a full list of partners is available at the principal place of business (BNA 1985, s 4).

4.4.2 Other statutory obligations

Other statutory obligations which may arise at the start of a partnership are not peculiar to partnerships and may arise at the start of any business. These include obligations concerning income tax, VAT and national insurance, as noted in Chapter 2; a partnership will have the additional obligation, in this context, of notifying HM Customs and Excise and the Inland Revenue of the identity of the partners.

Chapter 5

THE PARTNERSHIP AGREEMENT: DEFINING MUTUAL RIGHTS AND OBLIGATIONS

5.1 INTRODUCTION

The Partnership Act 1890 (PA 1890), s 24 contains a number of provisions that will be implied into a partnership agreement in the absence of express provision, but the Act is rather limited in scope and inevitably cannot do more than treat all partners equally. The length of a partnership agreement will depend on the imagination and thoroughness of the partners and their advisers. The following range of topics gives some idea of the possible provisions of a comprehensive agreement, although there will always be scope for additional provisions.

5.2 COMMENCEMENT DATE

The existence of a partnership is established when the statutory definition in PA 1890, s 1 is satisfied. The date specified in the agreement will not necessarily be correct therefore, but it is desirable to specify a date from which the parties regard their mutual rights and responsibilities as taking effect.

5.3 NAME

The name of the partnership should be stated since this means that it is fixed and any partner can insist as a matter of contract on there being no change to it. The firm name may be different from the business (or trading) name, in which case both names should be stated in the agreement.

5.4 FINANCIAL INPUT

Each partner is likely to be putting capital into the business, whether this is the result of borrowing or from his own resources. This is one of the ways in which the partnership will finance the purchase of assets needed to run the business. The agreement should state how much capital each partner is contributing and, possibly, deal with the question of future increases in contributions, if such increases are anticipated.

Chapter 5 contents
Introduction
Commencement date
Name
Financial input
Shares in income profits/losses
Drawings
Shares in increases/decreases in asset values
Place and nature of business
Ownership of assets
Work input
Roles
Decision-making
Duration
Retirement
Expulsion
Payment for outgoing partner's share
Restraint of trade following departure
Arbitration

5.5 SHARES IN INCOME PROFITS/LOSSES

Partners may be content to share income profits of the business equally. Indeed, if there is no evidence of contrary agreement, this will be the effect of PA 1890 which will imply such a term. Any losses may also be shared equally; again this will be implied by PA 1890 if there is no evidence of contrary agreement. In practice, the circumstances will often suggest that a different, more detailed, basis for division of profits is appropriate. The partners' agreement may provide for the following possibilities in dividing profits.

5.5.1 Salary

Salaries of differing fixed amounts might be appropriate before any surplus profit is divided between the partners; their purpose is to ensure that certain factors are reflected in the partners' incomes, making them unequal. These factors might include different amounts of time devoted to the business (eg allowing for a part-time or even a sleeping partner) and the different degrees of skill and experience of the partners.

5.5.2 Interest

Interest (at a specified rate) might be allowed on partners' capital contributions, again before any surplus profit is divided between the partners. This is simply to reward partners in proportion to their contribution to the financing of the partnership.

5.5.3 Profit-sharing

A suitable ratio in which the profits remaining after salaries and interest on capital are to be shared should be stated. If salaries and interest on capital have achieved sufficient 'fine tuning', then equal shares may be appropriate. On the other hand, the longer-serving partner or partners may negotiate for a higher share to reflect, for example, seniority in the business.

Any provisions of this kind in the agreement should also state what is to happen in the event of a loss. In particular, are salaries and interest on capital still to be awarded, thus exacerbating a loss?

5.6 DRAWINGS

One source of future ill-feeling and possible dispute between partners is the amount of money that they each withdraw from the business from time to time in respect of their shares of the profits. One partner may be conservative, wishing to maintain a healthy bank balance for the partnership, while another is more cavalier in his attitude. Often a partnership agreement will state a monthly limit on how much each partner can withdraw, perhaps with provision for periodic review. The clause may also stipulate the consequences of exceeding the stated limit.

5.7 SHARES IN INCREASES/DECREASES IN ASSET VALUES

If a fixed asset of the partnership (such as premises) is sold, realising an increase or a decrease in its value, how is this to be shared between the partners? If the assets are revalued without disposal to show their current value in the accounts (eg in anticipation of a new person joining the partnership), how is this increase/decrease to be reflected in the value of each existing partner's share in the business, as shown in the accounts? Partners may be content to share these increases/decreases equally and, as with income, this will be the effect of PA 1890 which will imply such a term if there is no agreement to the contrary. However, as with income, there may be circumstances where the partners would agree a different basis for division. In particular, if there is disparity in capital contributions, the partner who contributes the greater share of the capital may feel that he should receive the greater share of any gain. The basis for division of increases (or decreases) in asset values is sometimes known as the 'asset-surplus sharing ratio'. As with all aspects of any agreement, this provision will be a matter for negotiation and the other partners may feel that, if interest on capital is to be allowed (as in **5.5**), this provides sufficient recognition of the disparity in contributions.

5.8 PLACE AND NATURE OF BUSINESS

The agreement may contain clauses which describe the premises at which the business will be carried on, the geographical area of its operations and the nature of the business which will be carried on. Once agreed, any change would need the unanimous consent of the partners.

5.9 OWNERSHIP OF ASSETS

A partnership asset is an asset where beneficial ownership rests with all the partners, although not necessarily in equal shares. Many disputes have arisen over the factual question of what is a partnership asset and what belongs to a partner individually. This may arise as a result of the partnership being formed where certain assets which are to be used by the business (eg freehold premises or a lease of premises) already belong to one of the persons who is becoming a partner and there is no clear agreement as to what was intended as to ownership. That partner could have continued to own the asset personally (allowing the firm the use of the asset) or the asset could have become partnership property, either by its value representing a capital contribution from that partner or by that partner receiving payment from the others. Equally, a dispute may arise over an asset which has been acquired during the partnership where there was no clear agreement (either express or implied) as to the partners' intentions as to ownership.

In many instances no dispute will arise because there will be evidence of what was intended. Title deeds may indicate who was the owner, but these need not be conclusive since one partner may have legal title in his sole name whilst holding as trustee for all the partners beneficially so that the asset is in fact a partnership asset. The accounts of the partnership should reveal what capital contributions have been made and should correspondingly record what are the assets of the partnership, but these may not be conclusive evidence. To avoid the possibility of there being a dispute over the available evidence or no clear evidence, the agreement should stipulate what are the assets of the partnership (eg by referring to a list contained in a schedule to the agreement).

If there is a dispute, what circumstances are likely to trigger it? The dispute may arise on dissolution when it becomes necessary to establish how much each partner is entitled to receive; the value of an asset owned by just one partner will not be shared. It may be that a profit is made out of a particular asset; a profit on an asset owned by just one partner will not be shared. Any or all of the partners may incur liability to capital gains tax or inheritance tax by reference to a particular asset and wish to claim certain reliefs; liability to tax and the availability or amount of certain reliefs will depend on whether the asset is or is not a partnership asset.

5.10 WORK INPUT

The Partnership Act 1890 will imply a term into a partnership agreement, in the absence of contrary agreement, that all partners are entitled to take part in the management of the business, albeit without any obligation to do so. There is no implication that a partner must devote his full time and attention to the business. Wilful neglect of the business (as opposed to a degree of laziness) may mean that the other partners are entitled to be compensated for the extra work undertaken by them.

The agreement should set out the degree of commitment expected of each partner. The term might require the partner to work in the business full-time or part-time or even not work at all (being a dormant or sleeping partner). To express these degrees of work with precision in terms of fixed hours of work may well be inappropriate, particularly for full-time working partners. Often the agreement will be expressed in more general terms so that, for example, a full-time working partner 'must devote his whole time and attention to the business'. In order to reinforce this rather widely-expressed obligation, often there is further provision to the effect that such partners must not be involved in any other business whatsoever during the partnership. This absolute bar is enforceable and does not fall foul of the public policy issues which may make such covenants in restraint of trade void after termination of the relationship of the partners (see **5.17**).

Inevitably, there must be qualifications to the main statement as to the amount of work required of a partner. There must be provisions dealing with holiday entitlement, with sickness and with any other reasons for being absent from work, such as maternity. The Partnership Act 1890 offers no guidance as to what would be implied here in the absence of express provision.

5.11 ROLES

Partners may have differing functions within the partnership so that not only must the agreement describe the amount of work input but also each partner's function. For example, a sleeping partner's role might be defined as being limited to attending meetings of the partners and the agreement would state that he has no authority to enter into contracts on behalf of the partnership. The agreement might state that a particular partner (with limited experience) only has authority to make contracts within specified limits, thereby partly defining his role.

Whatever is agreed along these lines is binding between the partners and any partner who ignored any such restriction would be acting in breach of contract. The question of whether any contract made by him in breach of the partnership agreement would be enforceable against the firm by the third party depends on the application of s 5 of PA 1890 which is considered in Chapter 7.

5.12 DECISION-MAKING

Unless the agreement provides to the contrary, all partnership decisions will be made on the basis of a simple majority (where each partner has one vote), except that decisions on changing the nature of the business or on introduction of a new partner require unanimity. In certain circumstances, it may be that the agreement should be more detailed, perhaps describing certain decisions which may be made by any partner on his own (such as ordinary sales and purchases of stock), certain decisions that will require a simple majority (such as hiring staff) and certain decisions that will require unanimity (such as borrowing money). In this context, it is important to appreciate that anything contained in the agreement (eg type of business) is a term of the contract between the partners and therefore cannot be altered without the consent of all parties to the contract (ie all partners would have to consent). That consent might be built into the contract itself in that the agreement might contain provision for altering its terms (eg that a change in the type of business is to be effective if agreed by a majority of the partners).

5.13 DURATION

5.13.1 Dissolution by notice

How long is the partnership to last before it may be dissolved either by just one partner who wishes to leave or by all the partners wishing to go their separate ways? If there is no provision in the agreement, the partnership can be dissolved at any time by any partner giving notice to the others; this is described as a partnership at will. The notice of dissolution can have immediate effect and need not even be in writing unless the agreement itself was by deed. Although having the advantage of allowing each partner freedom to dissolve the whole partnership at any time and for any reason, a partnership at will has the corresponding disadvantages for the firm as a whole of insecurity and instability. Frequently, therefore, a partnership agreement will restrict the right of partners to dissolve the partnership.

5.13.2 Other solutions

One possible provision is that any notice of dissolution must allow a minimum period (of, say, 6 months) before taking effect. This at least gives time to settle what should happen on the dissolution (eg, some partners might negotiate the purchase of the interest of another in order to continue the business).

Another possibility is to agree a duration of a fixed term of a number of years (or months). This provides certainty but is inflexible in committing each partner to the partnership for a certain duration. A fixed term can also be criticised if it fails to provide for what should happen if partners wish to continue after the expiry of their fixed term. However, this can be dealt with by providing that the partnership will continue automatically on the same terms after the fixed term except that thenceforth it will be terminable by, say, 3 months' notice.

Yet another possible provision is that the partnership is to continue for as long as there are at least two remaining partners despite the departure of any partner by reason of retirement (see **5.14**), expulsion (see **5.15**), death or bankruptcy. This provision has the merit of providing some degree of security and stability whilst allowing individuals the flexibility of being able to leave. In case the departure of a partner might present financial problems for the others in purchasing his share from him, ancillary provisions can be included delaying payment to the outgoing partner so that he is, in effect, forced to lend money to the partnership.

5.13.3 Death and bankruptcy

Under PA 1890, s 33, unless there is contrary agreement, the death or bankruptcy of a partner will automatically cause dissolution of the entire partnership. Therefore, when providing for the duration of the partnership, it is appropriate to add a further provision that, on the death or bankruptcy of a partner, the remaining partners will automatically continue in partnership with one another on paying for the deceased or bankrupt partner's share in the business.

5.13.4 Court order

Situations may arise where a partner is 'locked into' a partnership by an agreement which contains no provision allowing him to dissolve the partnership or even to retire. To deal with this, PA 1890, s 35 provides that, on certain grounds, the court can make an order for dissolution. This effectively enables the partner to break his agreement with his partners without being liable for breach of contract. If none of the grounds in the Act are satisfied, the partner has no escape without being liable for breach of contract (see Chapter 8).

5.14 RETIREMENT

It is easy to assume that a partner must have the right to retire from the partnership when he pleases and yet the agreement may contain provisions on duration which will have the effect of preventing retirement other than by the partner acting in breach of contract (such as a fixed term with no further provisions). Even if there is no provision on duration, strictly a partner's exit route is by dissolving the entire partnership by giving notice. It would then be for the others to re-form in partnership if they could reach agreement with the outgoing partner for the purchase of his share.

It is usually desirable therefore to have express provision governing the question of when a partner can retire (without dissolving the partnership so far as the others are concerned) and of payment for his share by the others (see **5.16**).

In the context of partnership law, the word 'retirement' does not mean being eligible to collect the old age pension. It means leaving the partnership, perhaps to follow other business opportunities.

5.15 EXPULSION

Expulsion of a partner is analogous to retirement save that expulsion happens at the instigation of the other partners while retirement is a voluntary act of the outgoing partner. It amounts to terminating the contract (the partnership agreement) with the outgoing partner without his consent and is an important sanction for breach of the agreement or for other stipulated forms of misconduct. As with retirement, PA 1890 does not provide for the possibility of a partner being expelled by the others without his consent. There should therefore be provision in a partnership agreement for the possibility of expulsion. The agreement should state on what grounds the right to expel is to be exercisable and how it will be exercised (eg by an unanimous decision of the other partners with immediate effect). As with a retirement clause, the expulsion clause should also deal with the question of payment for the outgoing partner's share.

5.16 PAYMENT FOR OUTGOING PARTNER'S SHARE

Where a person ceases to be a partner by reason of retirement, expulsion, death or bankruptcy and others continue in partnership together, the remaining partners will need to pay for the outgoing partner's share in the business. To avoid any need to negotiate the terms of the purchase at the time, the agreement should contain the appropriate terms. If the agreement is silent on this and a settlement cannot be agreed at the time, s 42 of PA 1890 becomes relevant. Under this section, if a person ceases to be a partner and others continue in partnership but there is delay in final payment of the former partner's share, then the former partner or his estate is entitled to receive either interest at 5 per cent on the amount of his share or such share of the profits as is attributable to the use of his share.

The terms that may be appropriate for inclusion in the partnership agreement will depend on the circumstances but they should deal with the following.

(1) Whether there is to be a binding obligation on the partners to purchase the outgoing partner's share, or whether they are merely to have an option to purchase. Apart from the question of certainty as to what will happen, these alternatives have differing tax implications; in order to obtain business property relief for inheritance tax, an option to purchase is preferable (see **22.4.3**).
(2) The basis on which the outgoing partner's share will be valued.
(3) Provision for a professional valuation if the partners cannot reach agreement between themselves.
(4) The date on which payment will be due (or dates, if payment by instalments is agreed).
(5) An indemnity for liabilities of the firm if these were taken into account in the valuation.

5.17 RESTRAINT OF TRADE FOLLOWING DEPARTURE

5.17.1 Competition

There will be no implied term preventing an outgoing partner from setting up in competition with the partnership or joining a rival business or even poaching the employees of the partnership to work in a rival business. To protect the business connections of the continuing firm (broadly to preserve its customers and its employees) and to protect its confidential information, there should always be a provision limiting an outgoing partner's freedom to compete with the firm. The drafting of such clauses is critically important because a restraint of trade clause which is held to be unreasonable will be void as a matter of public policy.

5.17.2 Drafting a non-competition clause

One type of clause commonly used to restrain an ex-partner's activities is a clause which seeks to prevent the person from being involved in any way in a competing business. The key issues to address in drafting such a clause (a non-competition clause) are:

(1) What is the clause aiming to protect? There must be a legitimate interest; this will usually be the firm's business connections, its employees and/or its confidential information.
(2) Is the clause reasonable, as drafted, for the protection of that interest? It must be limited as to its geographical area and as to its duration, and both the area and the duration must not be greater than is reasonable for the protection of the legitimate interest in question.

Suppose, for example, that the partnership of X, Y and Z carries on business as double glazing installers throughout Cheshire and North Wales, where all three partners are fully involved throughout the area. Their agreement contains a clause stipulating that, on leaving the partnership, a partner will not work in any way in the building trade for 10 years in England or Wales. This clause will be void because it is unreasonably wide on all three aspects. If the clause had stipulated that, on leaving the partnership, a partner would not work in the business of double glazing installation for 12 months throughout Cheshire and North Wales, this might be valid and enforceable.

5.17.3 Other forms of restraint of trade

Other forms of restraint of trade clause may also be considered. A 'non-dealing clause' seeks to prevent the former partner from entering into contracts with customers or former customers or employees of the partnership which he has left. A 'non-solicitation clause' merely seeks to prevent him from soliciting contracts from such customers or employees. Both types of clause are less restrictive of the former partner's freedom to ply his trade and therefore more likely to be held enforceable, provided that the effect of the clause is limited to what is reasonable for the protection of the firm's legitimate interest.

5.18 ARBITRATION

To avoid the expense, delay and adverse publicity arising out of litigation between partners, the agreement may provide that certain disputes should be referred to arbitration. Usually the disputes in question will be described as those arising out of the interpretation or application of the agreement itself rather than disputes over the running of the business.

Chapter 6

PARTNERS' RESPONSIBILITIES TO ONE ANOTHER

6.1 INTRODUCTION

Although a partner has no definable role other than under the terms of the partnership agreement (which may be express or implied), he does have certain responsibilities towards his fellow partners and correspondingly certain rights against his fellow partners which arise as a result of the existence of the partnership relationship.

6.2 UTMOST GOOD FAITH

By common law, partnership is a relationship onto which is imposed a duty of the utmost fairness and good faith from one partner to another. Particular applications of this principle, contained in the PA 1890, ss 28–30, are that:

(1) partners must divulge to one another all relevant information connected with the business and their relationship;
(2) they must be prepared to share with their fellow partners any profit or benefit they receive that is connected with or derived from the partnership, the business or its property without the consent of the other partners; and
(3) they must be prepared to share with their fellow partners any profits they make from carrying on a competing business without the consent of the other partners.

Examples

In negotiating to sell to the partnership business premises owned by him, a partner must not suppress information which will affect the valuation. The doctrine of caveat emptor does not apply to partners' dealings with one another.

If a customer of the firm asks a partner to do some work for cash in his spare time, the cash belongs to the partnership unless the other partners choose to allow him to keep it.

If a partner sets up a competing business in his spare time, the profits of that business belong to the partnership unless otherwise agreed.

If the partnership owns a lease of its business premises which contains an option to purchase the freehold, a partner who exercises the option in his own name must allow his fellow partners to share in the profit that he makes.

6.3 FURTHER RESPONSIBILITIES IMPLIED BY THE ACT

Further responsibilities that can be enforced by the partners against one another are:

Chapter 6 contents
Introduction
Utmost good faith
Further responsibilities implied by the Act
Contractual responsibilities

(1) the responsibility for bearing a share of any loss made by the business (the particular share depending upon the terms of their agreement) (PA 1890, s 24(1));
(2) the obligation as a firm to indemnify fellow partners against bearing more than their share (as above) of any liability or expense connected with the business (PA 1890, s 24(2)).

6.4 CONTRACTUAL RESPONSIBILITIES

Most of the responsibilities of a partner to his fellow partners derive from the terms of their partnership agreement and may be express or implied.

Chapter 7

LIABILITY FOR FIRM'S DEBTS

7.1 INTRODUCTION

Transactions which may affect a partnership generally involve contracts. Contracts may be made by all of the partners acting collectively (eg they all sign a lease of business premises) or by just one of the partners. Some or all of the partners may seek to deny that they are liable on the contract (or for breach of it). In such cases, it is necessary first to identify whether the firm itself is liable and then, if the firm is liable, to identify which individuals are liable. These matters are governed by the following sections of the Partnership Act 1890; they are based on agency principles and are explained in the text which follows.

> '**5 Power of partner to bind the firm**
>
> Every partner is an agent of the firm and his other partners for the purpose of the business of the partnership; and the acts of every partner who does any act for carrying on in the usual way business of the kind carried on by the firm of which he is a member bind the firm and his partners, unless the partner so acting has in fact no authority to act for the firm in the particular matter, and the person with whom he is dealing either knows that he has no authority, or does not know or believe him to be a partner.
>
> **6 Partners bound by acts on behalf of firm**
>
> An act or instrument relating to the business of the firm and done or executed in the firm-name, or in any other manner showing an intention to bind the firm, by any person thereto authorised whether a partner or not, is binding on the firm and all the partners.
>
> Provided that this section shall not affect any general rule of law relating to the execution of deeds or negotiable instruments.
>
> **7 Partner using credit of firm for private purposes**
>
> Where one partner pledges the credit of the firm for a purpose apparently not connected with the firm's ordinary course of business, the firm is not bound, unless he is in fact specially authorised by the other partners; but this section does not affect any personal liability incurred by an individual partner.
>
> **8 Effect of notice that firm will not be bound by acts of partner**
>
> If it has been agreed between the partners that any restriction shall be placed on the power of any one or more of them to bind the firm, no act done in contravention of the agreement is binding on the firm with respect to persons having notice of the agreement.'

Remember that a partnership has no legal existence separate from that of the partners (unlike a company). So, when the PA 1890 refers to the 'firm', it means the partners.

Chapter 7 contents
Introduction
For what will the firm be liable? (PA 1890, ss 5–8)
Against whom can the firm's liabilities be enforced?
What if a partner cannot pay?
Summary

7.2 FOR WHAT WILL THE FIRM BE LIABLE? (PA 1890, ss 5–8)

7.2.1 Actions which are actually authorised

The firm will always be liable for actions which were actually authorised. An action may be actually authorised in various ways.

(1) The partners may have acted jointly in making the contract; clearly they are not then at liberty to change their minds.
(2) The partners may have expressly instructed one of the partners to represent the firm in a particular transaction or type of transaction. For example, one of the partners may have the function, under their agreement, of purchasing stock for the business. That partner is then acting with actual authority and the firm is bound by any contract that he makes within the scope of that authority.
(3) The partners may have impliedly accepted that one or more partners have the authority to represent the firm in a particular type of transaction. If all the partners are actively involved in running the business without any limitations being agreed between them, it will be implied that each partner has authority, for example, to sell the firm's products in the ordinary course of business. Alternatively, authority may be implied by a regular course of dealing by one of the partners in which the others have acquiesced.

7.2.2 Ostensible authority

The firm may be liable for actions which were not actually authorised but which may have appeared to an outsider to be authorised. This liability derives from application of the principles of agency law, based on the fact that each partner is an agent of the firm and of his fellow partners for the purposes of the partnership business. Thus, even though as between the partners there is some express or implied limitation on the partner's authority, the firm will be liable by application of s 5 where:

(1) the transaction is one which relates to the type of business in which the firm is apparently engaged (ie 'business of the kind carried on by the firm' per s 5); and
(2) the transaction is one for which a partner in such a firm would usually be expected to have the authority to act (ie 'in the usual way' per s 5); and
(3) the other party to the transaction did not know (or have reason to suspect) that the partner did not actually have authority to act; and
(4) a person deals with a person whom he knows or believes to be a partner.

It can be seen that points (3) and (4) relate to the knowledge or belief of the third party who has dealt with the partner. It will be a subjective test as to whether these conditions are satisfied. On the other hand, points (1) and (2) call for an objective test of what would appear to an outsider to be the nature of the firm's business and what authority one would expect a partner in such a firm to have.

Example 1

At a partner's meeting of the firm of A B & Co, it is decided that the firm should enter into a contract for the purchase of new premises at 21 High Street and a contract for the sale of their present business premises at 13 Side Street. Both written contracts are duly signed by all of the partners. The firm is bound by these contracts because they were actually authorised by means of the partners acting together. Note that the result would be the same if one partner had been instructed to sign the contract on behalf of the firm.

Example 2

Without consulting his fellow partners, C, the senior partner of C, D & Co seizes an unexpected opportunity to purchase new business premises at 12 High Street and to sell the firm's present business premises at 31 Side Street by signing a written contract for each on behalf of the firm. Although undoubtedly connected with the firm's business, the firm is not bound by the contract because C was not actually authorised and, because a third party would not normally expect that one partner would have authority to make such a major contract on his own, there is no apparent authority. However, C is personally liable to the third party under the contract.

Example 3

E, a partner in E F Plumbers, has placed several unconnected orders on credit in the name of the firm without consulting his partner F. In each case, the supplier has assumed that E was authorised to make the contract on behalf of his firm. The orders were:

(1) a quantity of copper piping;
(2) a jacuzzi and luxury bathroom suite;
(3) a brand-new van with 'E F Plumbers' printed on the side;
(4) a quantity of roofing felt and heavy timber.

In the first three instances, each contract is apparently connected with the business and so it would only be necessary to resolve whether a single partner would usually be expected to have the authority to make the contract. The order for the van may be too major for there to be apparent authority, but the other two contracts would seem to be binding on the firm. The contract for the roofing felt and timber has no apparent connection with the firm's business and therefore it is likely that the firm would not be bound unless there were special facts (eg some representation by the firm and not just by E) which led the supplier to believe that E had the authority to make this contract.

Example 4

J K Hairstylists are visited by Morris, a salesman for a manufacturer of a new range of shampoos for salon use. After an inspection of his products, Morris hears J and K discussing their merits and J being adamant that the firm should stick with its present supplier and order nothing from Morris. Ignoring this deadlock with his partner, K orders a supply from Morris.

Although K would have had apparent authority to make such a contract if Morris had not been aware of their discussion, in fact Morris has reason to believe that K had no authority to make the contract and so the firm is not liable.

7.2.3 Personal liability

In any of the above instances the partner who has acted will be personally liable to the other party under the contract irrespective of whether or not the firm is liable. There is privity of contract between him and the other party. Also, if the partner who has acted has done so without actual authority but has made the firm liable by virtue of his apparent authority, then he is liable to indemnify his fellow partners or to compensate them for any liability or loss which they incur. This is on the basis that he has broken his agreement with his fellow partners by acting without actual authority.

7.2.4 Tortious liability

Only liability in contract has been considered so far. Occasionally the firm (as well as the partner in question) is liable for some act of a partner which is tortious by nature, for example, negligence. The position here is governed by s 10 which makes the firm liable for any wrongful act or omission of a partner who acts in the ordinary course of the firm's business or with the authority of his partners.

7.3 AGAINST WHOM CAN THE FIRM'S LIABILITIES BE ENFORCED?

7.3.1 Potential defendants

The person who is seeking to enforce a liability of the firm under the principles considered in **7.2**, or who is seeking to claim damages for breach of such a contract, will want to know who can be sued. The range of potential defendants may be quite extensive.

(1) The partner with whom the person made the contract can be sued individually because there will be privity of contract between them on which the potential plaintiff can rely.
(2) The firm can be sued as a group of persons. All those who were partners at the time when the debt or obligation was incurred are jointly liable to satisfy the judgment (PA 1890, ss 9 and 17).
(3) Any person who was a partner at the time when the debt or obligation was incurred can be sued individually. It is unlikely that a creditor would sue only one partner in this way, but any partner who is so sued is entitled to claim an indemnity from the firm as a whole so that the liability is shared between the partners.
(4) Although generally someone who left the firm before the debt or obligation was incurred or who has joined the firm since that time is not liable (PA 1890, s 17), such a person may be sued or made liable for a judgment against the firm as a result of:

   (a) 'holding out' (see **7.3.3**); or
   (b) failure to give appropriate notice of retirement (see **7.3.4**); or
   (c) a novation agreement (see **7.3.5**).

7.3.2 Suing in the firm's name

In practice, the most appropriate way of proceeding if court action is necessary is to sue the partners as a group of persons in the firm's name (Rules of the Supreme Court 1965, Ord 81). This has the merit that if judgment is obtained against the partners in the firm's name, this can be enforced against the partnership assets and also potentially against assets owned personally by any of the persons who were partners at the time that the debt or obligation was incurred (or who were liable as if they were partners (see **7.3.1**)).

Example

'Hot Pots' are distributors of potatoes for the catering industry. Originally, the firm consisted of A, B and C as partners. In December, 2 weeks after A had retired from the firm, Hot Pots agree to purchase the entire crop of Farmer Giles's potatoes in the coming year at a price which is fixed. As a result of ideal growing conditions, there is a glut of potatoes and the contract price turns out to be much higher than the market price at the time of delivery. Hot Pots cancel the order and Farmer Giles sues for breach of contract. Before judgment is obtained against the firm, B retires and D joins the firm. Once judgment is obtained against Hot Pots it can be enforced against the assets of the partnership and/or the assets of B personally and/or the assets of C personally. It could not be enforced against the assets of A (unless there was a 'holding out' (see **7.3.3**) or a failure to give appropriate notice of retirement (see **7.3.4**)), or against the assets of D (unless there was a novation agreement (see **7.3.5**)).

7.3.3 Persons liable by 'holding out' (PA 1890, s 14)

Where a creditor of a partnership has relied, when giving credit to the firm, on a representation (or 'holding out') that a particular person was a partner in that firm, he may be able to hold that person liable for the firm's debt even though it transpires that the person has never been a partner or, perhaps, has been a partner but had retired before the contract was made. The representation in question may be oral (eg where the person is described as a partner in conversation), in writing (eg on headed notepaper) or even by conduct (eg in a previous course of dealing). The representation may be made by the person himself or, providing it is made with the person's knowledge, by another person.

Example 1

A has retired from the firm of 'Hot Pots', leaving B and C to carry on the business. After A's retirement B and C wrote to Farmer Giles on some of the firm's old headed notepaper offering to purchase his entire crop of potatoes at a fixed price. On the notepaper, A's name still appears as a partner and Farmer Giles has observed this and relied upon it. If A knows that the firm is using up the old stock of notepaper without removing his name, this may operate as a representation with his knowledge that he is a partner. Conversely, if he stipulated that the old notepaper should be destroyed on his retirement, but B and C have failed to do this, then any such representation is not made with his knowledge and he is not liable.

Example 2

Varying the facts of Example 1, the contract between 'Hot Pots' and Farmer Giles for the purchase and sale of potatoes was made orally when B and C met Farmer Giles on his farm and the contract was subsequently confirmed on the old notepaper; since the contract was already made before Farmer Giles saw the notepaper, he cannot have relied on the notepaper as containing any representation and therefore cannot hold A liable.

Example 3

Again varying the facts of Example 1, Farmer Giles in fact knew that A had retired when goods were ordered on the old notepaper; because of his knowledge of the retirement, he cannot have relied on the notepaper as containing any representation and therefore cannot hold A liable.

7.3.4 Persons liable by failure to notify leaving (PA 1890, s 36)

The firm's debts can be enforced against all those who were partners at the time when the debt or obligation was incurred (see **7.3.1**). Although a person may retire from a partnership, he remains liable on those contracts already made; the terms for the purchase of his share in the business should include a provision whereby the purchasing partner(s) indemnify him against liability for any such debts which were taken into account in valuing his share (see **5.16**).

A separate point arises under s 36. Where a partner leaves the partnership (eg on retirement or expulsion), he must give notice of his leaving since otherwise he may become liable under s 36 for the acts of his former partner or partners done after he leaves the firm, if the creditor is unaware of the fact that he has left. The notices which he should give are prescribed by s 36 and consist of:

(1) actual notice (eg by sending out standard letters announcing his leaving) to all those who have dealt with the firm prior to his leaving (s 36(1)); and
(2) an advertisement in the *London Gazette* (or, for Scotland, the *Edinburgh Gazette*) as notice to any other person who knew who were the partners in the firm, that knowledge being judged at the date when the partner leaves (s 36(2)).

A creditor who was unaware of the partner's leaving and who can establish that the type of notice appropriate to him (as above) was not given will be able to sue the former partner for the firm's debt, in spite of the fact that he has ceased to be a partner. The principle on which s 36 is based, unlike that on which s 14 is based, does not depend on the creditor having relied on some representation at the time of the transaction. Rather the creditor is given the right to assume that the membership of the firm continues unchanged until notice of the prescribed type (as above) is given. It follows that, if the creditor was never aware that the person had been a partner, no notice of any sort will be required since that creditor cannot be assuming the continuance of that person in the partnership.

If the reason for ceasing to be a partner is death or bankruptcy (rather than retirement or expulsion), no notice of the event is required; the estate of the deceased or bankrupt partner is not liable for events occurring after the death or bankruptcy.

Example 1

If, in the 'Hot Pots' examples (see **7.3.2** and **7.3.3**) Farmer Giles had dealt with 'Hot Pots' previously, he is entitled to assume that A remains a partner until he receives actual notice of his retirement. If Farmer Giles has not heard that A has retired, he will be able to sue A, as well as the others, on the contract for the potatoes.

Example 2

If Farmer Giles has never dealt with 'Hot Pots' previously, but was aware that A was a member of the firm, he will be able to assume that A remains a partner unless the fact of A's leaving is advertised in the *London Gazette*. Therefore, if A's retirement has not been so advertised and Farmer Giles has not heard that A has retired, he will be able to sue A, as well as the others, on the contract for the potatoes. Where the retirement has been so advertised there is no requirement that Farmer Giles was aware of the advertisement or even that he had heard of the *London Gazette*! The advertisement operates as deemed notice to Farmer Giles.

Example 3

If Farmer Giles has never dealt with 'Hot Pots' previously and was not aware that A was a member of the firm, he cannot hold A liable to him on the basis of s 36 even if A fails to give any notice of his retirement.

7.3.5 Liability under a novation agreement

A novation agreement in this context is a tripartite contract involving the creditor of the firm, the partners at the time the contract with the creditor was made and the newly constituted partnership. The partnership may change because one partner leaves and/or a new partner joins. Under this contract of novation, it may be agreed that the creditor will release the original partners from their liability under the contract and instead the firm as newly constituted will take over this liability.

It may be that a retiring partner will be released from an existing debt whilst substituting an incoming partner. This is clearly advantageous to the retiring partner whilst disadvantageous to the incoming partner, and the latter will usually agree to this only as part of the broader package of terms on which he is taken into partnership. It may be that a partner retires and no new partner joins. In this case, in order to ensure that the novation is contractually binding, either there must be consideration for the creditor's promise to release the retiring partner from the liability or the contract must be executed as a deed.

A novation agreement, which, as described, is a tripartite agreement releasing a retiring partner from an existing debt, should not be confused with an indemnity in relation to existing debts. Such an indemnity is a bipartite agreement between the retiring partner and the other partners. Since the firm's creditors will not be party to this agreement they are not bound by it and can still sue the retired partner. It would then be for the indemnifying partners to meet the liability and thus protect the retired partner from it.

Example

In the example in **7.3.2**, the incoming partner D was not liable to Farmer Giles. If Farmer Giles, the partners in 'Hot Pots' and D had entered into a novation agreement as described above, then in fact D would be liable to Farmer Giles.

7.4 WHAT IF A PARTNER CANNOT PAY?

7.4.1 Non-payment generally

A creditor can sue the firm as a group of persons or can sue individually any of the persons who are liable as partners. If the creditor has obtained judgment against a partner individually and that partner cannot pay, the creditor is then at liberty to commence fresh proceedings in order to obtain judgment against the firm. Even if the firm cannot pay out of its assets, either because it cannot raise the cash to do so or because its assets in total are insufficient to meet its liabilities in total, judgment against the firm can be enforced against the private assets of any person liable as a partner. If the claim of the creditor cannot be satisfied in any of these ways, it follows that the firm is insolvent and all of the individuals liable as partners are also insolvent, so that insolvency proceedings are likely to follow.

7.4.2 Insolvency

Insolvency is considered in Chapters 23 and 24. The law on insolvency of a partnership and of its partners individually is governed by the Insolvent Partnerships Order 1994 and the Insolvency Act 1986. The provisions are complex, but the main point is that, although a partnership is not a person in its own right, nevertheless an insolvent partnership may be wound up as an unregistered company or may avail itself of the rescue procedures available to companies, such as a 'voluntary arrangement' with creditors or an 'administration order' of the court (see **24.9.2** and **24.9.3**). A partnership is not governed by the laws on bankruptcy which relate to individuals. Thus, the partnership may be subject to a winding up order and the individual partners may be subject to bankruptcy orders.

7.5 SUMMARY

(S.5 PA 1890)

The question is:

Where a contract has been made by a partner (X), is the firm (and therefore all the partners and possibly other persons) liable in relation to that contract?

The path to the answer is:

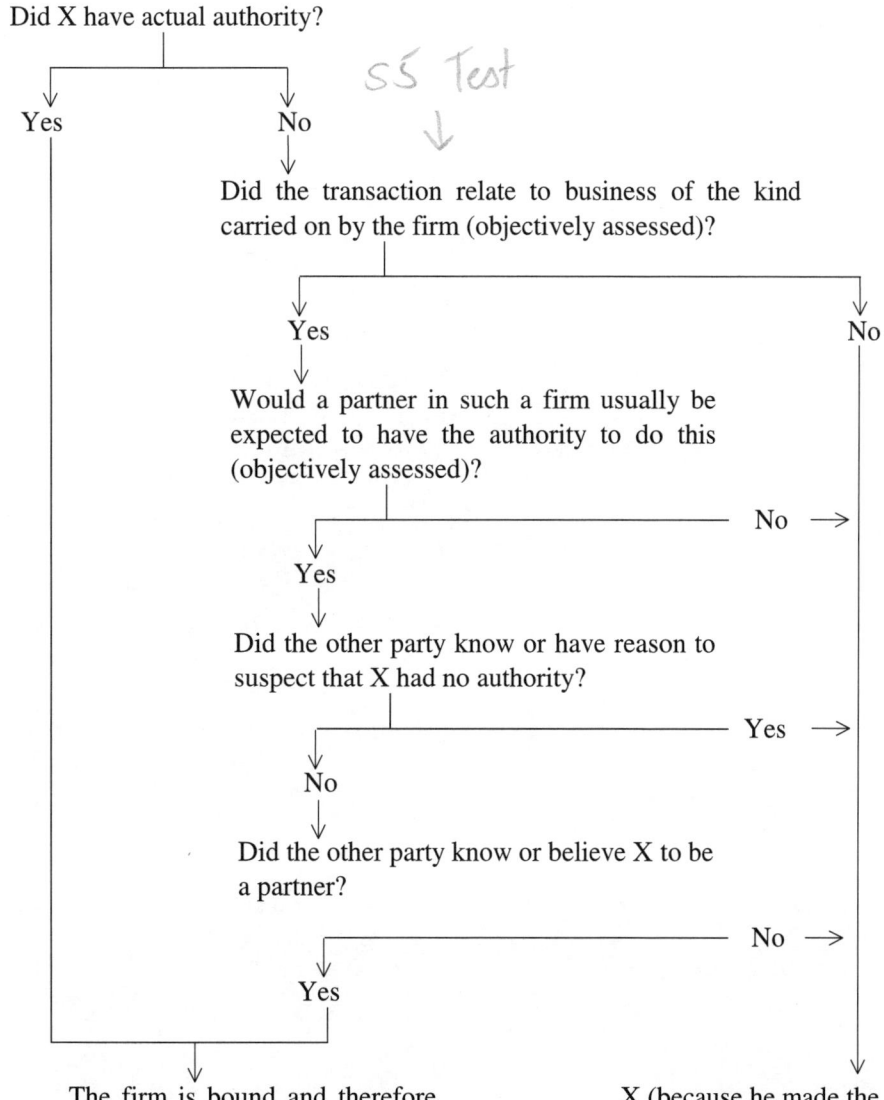

Did X have actual authority?
- Yes →
- No → *s5 Test*
  - Did the transaction relate to business of the kind carried on by the firm (objectively assessed)?
    - Yes →
      - Would a partner in such a firm usually be expected to have the authority to do this (objectively assessed)?
        - Yes →
          - Did the other party know or have reason to suspect that X had no authority?
            - No →
              - Did the other party know or believe X to be a partner?
                - Yes →
                - No → X liable alone
            - Yes → X liable alone
        - No → X liable alone
    - No → X liable alone

The firm is bound and therefore also all those who were partners at the time and possibly others under s 14 and s 36

'holding-out' as partner

partner must give notice of leaving p'ship otherwise will remain liable

Novation agreement

X (because he made the contract) is liable but no one else

Chapter 8

DISSOLUTION

8.1 INTRODUCTION

Dissolution is when a partnership ends; it may be by agreement between the partners, it may be where one partner is in a position to insist (contrary to the wishes of the other(s)) or it may be by circumstances which had not been anticipated. One of the main implications of dissolution is the question of what happens to the business and its assets: should one or more of the partners take over the business by paying off the other(s)? The circumstances for, and the consequences of, dissolution should be dealt with in a partnership agreement but, failing that, the Partnership Act 1890 (PA 1890) provides the details.

8.2 WHEN DOES DISSOLUTION OCCUR?

Dissolution of a partnership means that the contractual relationship joining all of the current partners comes to an end. It may be that some of the partners in fact succeed to the business and continue in a new partnership with one another. For example, if one of the partners retires and the others continue in partnership, strictly one partnership is dissolved and a new one formed.

Under PA 1890, a partnership is expressed to be dissolved on the occurrence of any one of several events, although most of these provisions can be excluded by agreement (see **8.3**).

8.2.1 Notice

A notice of dissolution can be given by any partner to the other or others (PA 1890, ss 26 and 32). This notice need not state any reason for the dissolution and can have immediate effect. It need not even be in writing unless the partnership agreement was by deed. A partnership which is terminable under s 26 is known as a partnership at will.

8.2.2 Expiry of fixed term

A partnership dissolves on the expiry of a fixed term for which the partners have agreed to continue in partnership unless their agreement provides for continuance after the fixed term has expired (PA 1890, s 32). This must be taken to give effect to what the partners intended in agreeing a fixed duration. If the partners in fact continue their relationship after the fixed term has expired (and hence after the original partnership has dissolved), they will be presumed to be partners on the same terms as before except that their new partnership is a partnership at will and its terms must be consistent with that type of partnership (s 27).

Chapter 8 contents
Introduction
When does dissolution occur?
Express terms on dissolution
The business, its goodwill and other assets following dissolution without continuing partners
Distribution of proceeds following sale of the business or its assets
Following dissolution, who winds up the firm's affairs?

8.2.3 Charging order over partner's assets

A notice of dissolution may be given by the other partners to a partner whose share in the partnership assets has been charged under s 23 by order of the court as security for the payment of that partner's private debt (PA 1890, s 33).

A judgment creditor of a partner in his private capacity may use s 23 as a means of enforcing the judgment. He is not permitted to make any direct claim on the partnership assets even though the partner will be joint owner of those assets. The effect of a charging order under s 23 is that the creditor of that partner has an indirect claim by becoming the chargee of the partner's share in those assets. The creditor's charge may also entitle him to receive the partner's share of the profits of the partnership. At this stage, the other partners have the right to pay off the creditor and then look to their partner for recompense. If this does not happen, then, in order to enforce the charge (and hence the indirect claim on the partnership assets), the creditor may obtain an order of the court for the sale of the partner's share in the assets. If such a sale is ordered the most likely buyers are the other partners, but if they do not wish to purchase the share an outsider may do so. This will not make the outsider a partner in the firm since he is merely the owner of a share in the assets. Since this situation is likely to be unsatisfactory from the other partners' point of view, they have the right just mentioned to give notice of dissolution of the partnership.

8.2.4 Death or bankruptcy

Death or bankruptcy will automatically terminate the partnership (PA 1890, s 33) so that the personal representatives of the deceased or the trustee in bankruptcy of the bankrupt can collect for his estate the amount to which the former partner was entitled for his share.

8.2.5 Illegality

Where it is illegal to carry on the business of the partnership, the partnership will dissolve (PA 1890, s 34). This situation might arise where the partnership business consists of the sale of alcohol and the partnership loses its licence to sell alcohol or where the partnership business is that of a solicitors' practice and one of the partners is struck off the Roll of Solicitors.

8.2.6 Court order for dissolution

The court has power (PA 1890, s 35) to order dissolution on various grounds, one of which (the 'just and equitable' ground) provides the court with such a wide discretion that it effectively makes the other, more specific, grounds unnecessary. Broadly, the other grounds are designed to cover circumstances where one partner ought to leave (eg on account of his conduct) but he is unwilling to do so and the others cannot expel him because their agreement failed to provide for this. Cases under s 35 are unusual because most partnerships, whether governed by an express or an implied agreement, can be dissolved without court intervention. This may be because there is nothing in their agreement to prevent a partner from giving notice to dissolve the partnership. Even if this is prevented by their agreement, the partners may be able to negotiate dissolution, for example where one partner will leave and be paid for his share, allowing the others to re-form in partnership.

On occasions, however, there will be a partnership agreement which would prevent dissolution unless all of the partners agreed. For example, the agreement may state that the partnership will continue for a long fixed term, or even for the joint lives of the partners. In such cases, unless the agreement provides for an unhappy partner to retire or for a troublesome partner to be expelled, it may be necessary to apply to the court for an order for dissolution. The order effectively breaks the partnership agreement without any partner being liable to the others for breach of contract.

8.3 EXPRESS TERMS ON DISSOLUTION

8.3.1 Restrictions on dissolution

Generally, it will be inappropriate to leave the question of duration and dissolution to be governed by the PA 1890. The partners will not want the insecurity of a partnership at will, nor will they want the death or bankruptcy of one partner to cause a dissolution of the partnership between the survivors. Usually, therefore, it will be appropriate for the partnership agreement to exclude at least these possibilities and to make express provision as to the duration of the partnership (see **5.13**).

8.3.2 Purchase of outgoing partner's share

If dissolution occurs where one partner leaves (by retirement, expulsion, death or bankruptcy) and the others are to continue as partners, the agreement should contain provisions allowing for the remaining partners to purchase the share of the former partner and fixing the terms of the purchase. If the agreement does not contain such provisions, it may be possible for the parties involved to negotiate terms for the outgoing partner's share to be purchased by the continuing partners. Inevitably, it may be some time after the partner has left that a price is settled and the others agree to purchase. If the agreement does not deal with the question of payment for the use of the former partner's share in the assets since he left, he will be entitled to receive, at his option, either interest at 5 per cent per annum on the value of his share, or such sum as the court may order as representing the share of profits made which is attributable to the use of his share (PA 1890, s 42). The purchase agreement can exclude this entitlement (see **5.16**).

8.4 THE BUSINESS, ITS GOODWILL AND OTHER ASSETS FOLLOWING DISSOLUTION WITHOUT CONTINUING PARTNERS

8.4.1 Disposal of the business

Sometimes dissolution occurs where the partners cannot reach agreement as to some of the partners carrying on with the business and purchasing an outgoing partner's share. Then it will be necessary for there to be a disposal of the business and for the proceeds of sale to be used to pay off creditors and then to pay to the partners the amount to which they are entitled. This disposal of a business may be by sale as a going concern or, if a buyer cannot be found, by breaking up the business and selling its assets separately. This position is reinforced by s 39 of PA 1890 which gives every partner the right to insist on a disposal and payment as above, if necessary by application to court for the business and affairs of the firm to be wound up.

8.4.2 Goodwill

There is a serious financial disadvantage to the partners if the business is not purchased as a going concern but is broken up with the assets being sold separately. A valuable asset of any successful business is its goodwill. Goodwill can be described as the benefit of the business's reputation and connections and the benefit of having its own momentum so that profits will continue to be earned because the business is established.

A common basis for valuing goodwill is to take a number (perhaps two) of years' profit. For example, if the business generated £25,000 and £30,000 profit in the previous 2 years, the goodwill of the business might be valued at £55,000. Another approach to understanding the meaning of goodwill is to consider a person who is contemplating either purchasing an established business as a going concern or setting up a new business. In either instance, the cost would include the purchase of the necessary tangible assets like premises, equipment, stock, etc, but if purchasing an established business the buyer will have to pay for the benefit of its being established and already making a profit. This payment (of whatever amount is negotiated) is for goodwill. It can be seen therefore that, in the context of dissolution of partnership, the question of someone (whether it be continuing partners or an outsider) taking over the business as a going concern (and therefore paying for goodwill) is of considerable financial significance to a partner who is leaving.

Financial considerations apart, one other aspect of selling goodwill is worth considering at this point. The buyer of goodwill is likely to insist on the seller(s) entering into a covenant in restraint of trade for the protection of the goodwill which he is purchasing. If the seller was free to become involved immediately in a competing business, the benefit of having purchased (effectively) an established set of customers might be seriously undermined. Therefore, in return for the financial benefit of selling his share in the goodwill, an outgoing partner will have to accept the limitations imposed on his future activities by a covenant in restraint of trade. It should be remembered that a covenant in restraint of trade will be valid only if it is reasonable in the circumstances (see **5.17**).

8.5 DISTRIBUTION OF PROCEEDS FOLLOWING SALE OF THE BUSINESS OR ITS ASSETS

Unless there is agreement to the contrary, the proceeds of sale of the business or its assets will be used in the following sequence (PA 1890, s 44). First, creditors of the firm (ie anyone with a claim against the firm except for the partners themselves) must be paid in full. If there is a shortfall so that the firm is insolvent, the partners must pay the balance from their private assets, sharing the loss in accordance with their partnership agreement. Secondly, partners who have lent money to the firm must be repaid, together with any interest to which they are entitled. Thirdly, partners must be paid their capital entitlement. Finally, if there is a surplus, this will be shared between the partners in accordance with their partnership agreement.

Example

A, B and C are partners sharing profits equally. The firm has borrowed £7,000 from A and £9,000 from B, in addition to their capital contributions of £16,000 and £8,000 respectively. C has put no money into the firm. The firm is now dissolved; it owes £18,000 to creditors and has assets which will realise £49,000.

The £49,000 will be applied as follows:

(1) £18,000 will be paid to the creditors, leaving £31,000 to be used to pay to A, B and C what they are entitled to receive;
(2) £16,000 will be used to repay the loans of £7,000 and £9,000 from A and B respectively (all interest due had already been paid).

This leaves £15,000 to repay the total capital of £24,000 owing to A and B. It follows that the firm has made a loss of £9,000 (£24,000 capital owing less £15,000 net assets available). Under their agreement A, B and C share profits equally and therefore by implication the loss of £9,000 will be shared equally, each partner losing £3,000.

A will receive only £13,000 of the £16,000 capital owing to him. B will receive only £5,000 of the £8,000 capital owing to him. C must pay £3,000 to the firm since he has no capital entitlement to lose. Thus, in addition to recovering the loans, A and B together receive £18,000, made up of the net assets available (£15,000) plus C's contribution of £3,000. In the event that C is insolvent and cannot contribute the £3,000 which he owes, the capital entitlement of A and of B is reduced proportionately; since A's capital (£16,000) was twice that of B (£8,000), A loses a further £2,000, reducing his entitlement to £11,000, while B loses a further £1,000, reducing his entitlement to £4,000. This basis for allocating C's share of the original loss between the other partners was established in *Garner v Murray* [1904] Ch 57.

8.6 FOLLOWING DISSOLUTION, WHO WINDS UP THE FIRM'S AFFAIRS?

Each partner (except a bankrupt partner) has continuing authority to act for the purposes of winding up the firm's affairs (PA 1890, s 38). It may be that there is no need for any person outside the partnership to become involved in the dissolution. On the other hand, if there is a dispute between the partners, or if the assets are in jeopardy, any partner (or the trustee in bankruptcy of a bankrupt partner or the personal representatives of a deceased partner) may apply to the court for the appointment of a person (even one of the partners) as receiver to deal with the assets or as receiver and manager to conduct the business in addition to the above, perhaps with a view to selling the business as a going concern. The receiver or receiver and manager is an officer of the court and will be entitled to receive remuneration for his services from the partnership assets, although not from the partners' personal money.

Chapter 9

TAXATION OF PARTNERSHIPS

9.1 INTRODUCTION

Chapter 3 considered taxation of the two types of profit (income and capital) which a sole trader might make. This chapter looks again at these two types of profit but in the context of a partnership. It will be seen that, although the principles are the same, there is a further consideration in the context of a partnership: how are the profits allocated between the partners in ascertaining their tax liability?

9.2 INCOME TAX ON PARTNERSHIPS' BUSINESS PROFITS

9.2.1 General principles

The principles described in Chapter 3 for the income tax treatment of a sole trader also apply for the taxation of a partnership. These principles are:

(1) calculation of trading profit under Schedule D, Case I;
(2) the basis of assessing the taxable profit of a given tax year for each partner;
(3) income tax relief for trading losses.

9.2.2 Application of general principles to partnerships

(1) A partnership is not treated as an entity distinct from the partners themselves and so there is no assessment to income tax on the firm as a whole.
(2) The assessment of income tax in the context of a partnership will therefore entail the following steps.

   (a) The trading profit of the business will be calculated in the same way as if the business were run by a sole trader, applying the rules of Schedule D, Case I. This will include the deduction of allowable expenditure on machinery and plant and industrial buildings by means of capital allowances (note that the enhanced allowances referred to in **3.2.2** are available to partnerships whose businesses qualify as 'small or medium sized').
   (b) The trading profit will be allocated between the partners according to the way in which income profits were shared under their agreement for that accounting period (eg salaries, interest on capital and then profit shares).
   (c) Each partner's income will then be included in his tax return and will be assessed in the ordinary way, taking account of whatever reliefs and allowances he is entitled to receive. Each partner is only liable to the Inland Revenue for income tax on his share of the profits – he cannot be required to pay income tax on the profits which are allocated to his partners.

Chapter 9 contents
Introduction
Income tax on partnerships' business profits
Capital gains tax on disposals by the firm
Capital gains tax on disposals by partners individually
Inheritance tax on disposals by partners individually
VAT and partnerships

Example

A, B, C and D started a business on 1 January 1998. They share income profits as follows.

- A, B and C each receive 'salaries' of £10,000 per annum to reflect the fact that they work full-time whereas D only works part-time.
- All partners receive interest on capital at 10% per annum; their contributions were as follows:

    A: £20,000
    B: £20,000
    C: £10,000
    D: £50,000

- Profits remaining after 'salaries' and interest on capital are shared equally between the partners.

The firm's accounts are prepared for calendar years and, in the calendar year 1999, the firm makes a profit before allocation between the partners of £100,000. The partners' entitlement is:

	A	B	C	D	Totals
'Salary'	10,000	10,000	10,000	–	30,000
Interest	2,000	2,000	1,000	5,000	10,000
Profit	15,000	15,000	15,000	15,000	60,000
	£27,000	£27,000	£26,000	£20,000	£100,000

The figure produced at the foot of each partner's column (eg £27,000 for A) is the figure for inclusion in that individual's statutory income for the tax year 1999/2000 (see **3.3** as to the 'basis of assessment').

(3) In the event of the business making a trading loss, that loss will be allocated between the partners for income tax purposes in accordance with the agreement for that accounting period and the partners then choose individually how they will claim the benefit of income tax relief for their share of the loss. See **3.4** for the possible alternatives for claiming relief for a trading loss.

9.2.3 Change in firm's membership

(1) Where a new person joins an existing partnership, he will be assessed to income tax for his first 2 tax years on the basis described in **3.3.2** and **3.3.3**, because as far as he is concerned this is a new business. The existing partners will continue to be assessed on the basis described in **3.3.1**.

(2) Where a person leaves a continuing partnership (eg on retirement or on expulsion), he will be assessed to income tax for his final tax year on the basis described in **3.3.4**, because as far as he is concerned the business is coming to an end. The remaining partners will continue to be assessed on the basis described in **3.3.1**.

(3) These rules may be illustrated by the following example:

Example

A, B and C start a business in partnership on 1 January 1997; they will prepare accounts for calendar years. On 1 January 1999, D joins the partnership. On 30 June 2000, A retires. Profits for these 4 years are:

	£
1997	20,000
1998	27,000
1999	40,000
2000	60,000

(1) D's assessments to income tax:

    (a) D's first tax year (1998/99)

    D will be assessed to income tax on his share of the £10,000 profits for the (roughly) 3-month period 1 January 1999 to 5 April 1999 (this figure being one-quarter of the profit for the full year 1999).

    Note: For 1998/99, A, B and C will be assessed individually to income tax on their shares of the £27,000 profits made in 1998 (this being the profit for the accounting period which ends in the tax year).

    (b) D's second tax year (1999/2000)

    D will be assessed to income tax on his share of the £40,000 profits for his first 12 months in the business (this being the profit for 1999).

    Note: For 1999/2000, A, B and C will also be assessed by reference to this period because it is the accounting period which ends in the tax year.

(2) A's assessment to income tax for his final tax year (2000/2001).

    A will be assessed to income tax on his share of the profits made from the end of the latest accounting period to be assessed (ie 1999) until the date of his retirement LESS a deduction for his 'overlap profit'. This means that he will be assessed on his share of the £30,000 profits for the 6-month period from 1 January 2000 to 30 June 2000 (this figure being one-half of the profit for the full year) LESS a deduction for his share of the £5,000 profits made in the period 1 January to 5 April 1997 which were assessed in both his first and second tax years (1996/97 and 1997/98).

    Note: For 2000/2001, B, C and D will be assessed individually on their shares of the £60,000 profits made in 2000 (this being the profit for the accounting period which ends in the tax year).

9.2.4 Income tax relief on a partner's borrowings (ICTA 1988, ss 353 and 362)

A person who borrows money (eg from a bank) in order to buy a share in a partnership or to lend money to a partnership can deduct the interest he pays each year (on the money he has borrowed) from his statutory income (ie income from all sources). The relief is designed to encourage investment in business and a similar provision exists for investment in certain companies (see **21.4.2** and **25.6**).

9.3 CAPITAL GAINS TAX ON DISPOSALS BY THE FIRM

9.3.1 General principles

Normal capital gains tax principles apply to partnerships (in accordance with an Inland Revenue Statement of Practice (SPD/12 dated 17 January 1975)). Thus capital gains tax may arise where there is a disposal of a chargeable asset resulting in a chargeable gain.

A partnership as a whole is unlikely to make gifts of the partnership assets and so the likely 'disposal' which is relevant is their sale. Bearing in mind that certain assets are not chargeable assets for capital gains tax, the partnership assets which are most likely to be subject to capital gains tax are premises, fixed plant and machinery, goodwill and certain investments. Apart from investments, such assets will be eligible for the higher rate of taper applicable to business assets.

Disposal by an individual partner of his interest in an asset, or his interest in the partnership, is considered in Chapter 22.

9.3.2 Disposal by the firm

Where the firm disposes of a chargeable asset, this is treated for capital gains tax purposes as being separate disposals by the partners of their individual interests in that asset. These interests are established by applying the terms of the partnership agreement relating to the sharing of capital profits (gains); often this is in the same proportion as income profits (and this is the fall-back position), although the partners may have expressly agreed on different proportions (eg to share the capital profits in the same relation as their capital contributions) (see **5.7**).

Example

If a firm consists of three partners who have equal shares in all profits, then each partner is treated as owning one-third of each asset.

If the firm consists of three partners (A, B and C) who share all profits in the ratio of A:2, B:1 and C:1, then A owns half of each asset, B one-quarter and C one-quarter.

9.3.3 Calculation of gain

When calculating the gain made by each partner by the firm's disposal of an asset, it will be necessary to apportion the sale price and the acquisition cost among the partners according to the fraction appropriate to their fractional interest in the asset.

Example

D, E, F and G have been partners for many years and share all profits equally. In 1995 they purchased shop premises, paying £60,000 as the purchase price. In July 2000, they sell the shop premises for £120,000. Each of the partners is taken to have disposed of one-quarter of the chargeable asset (the shop) at one-quarter of the sale price (ie £30,000). To each of them, there will be allocated one-quarter of the acquisition cost and of any relevant expenditure. In order to show the calculation of D's gain (by way of illustration), the following assumptions will be made:

- there was no relevant expenditure other than the purchase price;
- an indexation factor of 0.1 will apply for the period of ownership up to 5 April 1998;
- D made no other disposals in the 2000/01 tax year (so the annual exemption is available in full);
- no other relief is available;
- D is a 40% income tax payer;
- D qualifies for 2 years' enhanced business taper relief (on a business asset held for 2 whole years since 6 April 1998).

	£	£
Disposal price		30,000 (b4 indexation)
LESS		
Acquisition cost	15,000	
Indexation allowance	1,500	
		16,500
Indexed gain		13,500 (after indexation)
Tapered gain (£13,500 × 75%)		10,125
LESS		
Annual exemption		7,200
		2,925
CGT @ 40%		1,170

9.3.4 Business relief – roll-over relief on replacement of qualifying assets (TCGA 1992, ss 152–159)

On a disposal of a chargeable partnership asset, each partner may use taper relief and his annual exemption (if available) to reduce any chargeable gain on his share of the asset (as described in **9.3.3**). Alternatively, it may be possible for each partner to postpone paying tax on his share of the gain by using roll-over relief on the replacement of a qualifying asset. The relief is designed to encourage businesses to expand and thrive by allowing the capital gains tax due on the disposal of a qualifying asset used in the business to be effectively postponed when another qualifying asset is purchased by way of replacement. The following points should be noted in connection with the relief.

(1) The principal qualifying assets for the purposes of the relief are goodwill, land, buildings, and fixed plant and machinery. Assets held by the partnership as investments are not qualifying assets.

(2) If a qualifying asset is sold and, within certain time-limits (see below), the proceeds of sale are used for the purchase of another qualifying asset to be used in a business, then any liability to capital gains tax from the sale can be postponed (at least until the disposal of the 'new' asset) by 'rolling over' the gain on the sale (after allowing for any indexation) into the acquisition cost of the 'new' asset. This means that the indexed gain realised on the sale of the 'old' asset is deducted from the acquisition cost of the 'new' asset to give a lower base cost for use in subsequent capital gains tax calculations. Thus a later disposal of the 'new' asset may produce a gain which comprises both the rolled-over gain and any gain on the new asset itself so that at this stage capital gains

tax becomes payable on the entire gain. However, the entire gain could be postponed again if the proceeds are again used for the purchase of a qualifying asset.

(3) Provided both the asset disposed of and the asset acquired are qualifying assets (as defined above), it is immaterial whether or not they are of the same type. For example, it is permissible to sell qualifying fixed plant and machinery and roll the gain into the purchase of qualifying buildings.

(4) The time-limits mentioned above are that the 'new' asset must be purchased within one year before or 3 years after the disposal of the 'old' asset.

(5) If the gain (after any indexation) is rolled over into the purchase of another qualifying asset, the gain cannot be tapered prior to the roll-over. Only the period of ownership of the asset ultimately disposed of (with no replacement qualifying purchase) will qualify for taper relief.

(6) If the (indexed) gain is rolled over, the annual exemption cannot be used prior to rolling over the gain.

Example

If the partnership in the example in **9.3.3** buys replacement shop premises for £200,000, D would be treated as paying one quarter of this, ie £50,000. Instead of paying CGT of £1,170 as in the example, he could (provided that the purchase was within the relevant time-limits) roll-over his indexed gain into the acquisition cost of the qualifying replacement asset. Thus his share of the replacement premises would be taken to have cost him £36,500 (ie £50,000 less his indexed gain of £13,500). The effects of this are as follows.

- D pays no CGT on the disposal of the original premises.
- When the replacement premises are sold, D's gain will be calculated on the reduced acquisition cost (£36,500) with the effect that his 'gain' is the original £13,500 *plus* any increase in the value of the replacement premises. Assuming no further replacement asset is acquired, D will be entitled to reduce the gain by taper relief for the period of ownership of the new asset and by his annual exemption for the tax year of this final disposal (if not already used), but his annual exemption for the year of the original disposal (2000/01) is not available.

It would be possible for one partner to roll-over his share of the indexed gain on the disposal of the 'old' asset whilst another chose to taper his share of the indexed gain, use his annual exemption and pay any tax arising. In the example, D might therefore choose to pay the tax of £1,170 whilst E, F and G each elected to roll-over his share of the indexed gain into the 'new' qualifying asset.

Further reliefs which may be available if the partners together dispose of the partnership business and assets on discontinuance are considered in Chapter 22.

9.3.5 Payment of tax

Once each partner's chargeable gain and resultant tax liability have been calculated, the tax is payable by that partner individually; as with income tax on the firm's income profits, capital gains tax can only be assessed on each partner for his own share of the firm's gain.

9.4 CAPITAL GAINS TAX ON DISPOSALS BY PARTNERS INDIVIDUALLY

A partner may dispose of his fractional share in each of the partnership assets when his fellow partners are making no disposal. For example, on retirement a partner may sell to his fellow partners (ie they are 'buying him out') or he may sell to a third party. In these instances, the principles described in **9.3.2** and **9.3.3** will govern the identification of his fractional share, and the calculation of his (indexed) gain. The relief described in **9.3.4** and those described in Chapter 22 may be available and any tax due as a result of the disposal will be payable in accordance with **9.3.5**.

9.5 INHERITANCE TAX ON DISPOSALS BY PARTNERS INDIVIDUALLY

As noted in **9.3.1**, it is unlikely that the partnership as a whole will make gifts of assets. If an individual partner disposes of his share of the partnership asset(s) at less than full value, inheritance tax should be considered and the general inheritance tax rules apply to any transfer of value that a partner makes (eg on a gift of his share to a relative). Exemptions and reliefs which may be available are described in Chapter 22.

9.6 VAT AND PARTNERSHIPS

A detailed discussion of VAT is beyond the scope of this book but it should be noted that, unlike the position for the assessment and payment of income tax, capital gains tax and inheritance tax, a partnership is treated as a separate entity for VAT purposes.

PART IV

RUNNING A BUSINESS AS A PRIVATE COMPANY LIMITED BY SHARES

When a business is run by a company, it is owned by a person (the company) which is quite separate from the individuals involved, even though they are the directors and shareholders of the company. The company's separate legal personality leads to a number of complications in running the business. Decisions affecting the business must be made either by the directors or by the shareholders. Broadly, it depends on the Companies Acts or on the company's constitution (in particular its 'articles of association') whether a particular decision rests with the directors or with the shareholders. Taxation of the business profits may involve two taxes, corporation tax and income tax, imposed on three different persons, namely the company (corporation tax on its profits) the directors (income tax on their salaries) and the shareholders (income tax on their dividends).

In addition to taxation, this Part describes how to form a company, how to manage the company and its affairs in compliance with the Companies Acts and its constitution (the memorandum and articles of association), how to join and leave a company, and what liability may be incurred by the company and its directors in running the business.

Chapter 10

COMPANY FORMATION

10.1 INTRODUCTION

If a client wishes to run his business as a company, either a company must be created or an existing 'shelf' company will have to be bought. Once the client owns 'the company', it may then be necessary to adapt it to suit that client's needs and to consider what action to take in order for the business to begin trading as a company.

10.2 DOCUMENTS NEEDED

In order to form a company, four documents must be sent to the registrar of companies at Companies House in Cardiff (the Companies Registry), together with a fee, currently £20. Those documents are the memorandum, the articles of association, Form 10 and Form 12.

10.2.1 The memorandum

The intended name of the company must be inserted in the memorandum. A client may already have in mind the name by which he wishes the company to be known, but he does not have complete freedom of choice. A company cannot be registered with a name which is the same as that of an existing company. Therefore it is important to search the index of names at Companies House at an early stage to ensure that the desired name is not already in use. It would also be wise to search the Trade Mark Index to make sure that the proposed name is not already registered as a trademark. The registrar will not accept a company name if it is offensive, or suggests criminal activity, and the use of certain words requires written approval of the Secretary of State (see **11.2.1**). If the chosen name is not already in use by another company, there is no procedure for reserving that name. Consequently, there is no means of preventing the formation of a new company which bears the name the client has chosen between the date of the search and the date on which the application for incorporation is received by the registrar.

The memorandum also gives details of the country of the registered office of the company, whether or not the liability of the members is limited and the amount of the nominal capital. Additionally, it will set out the objects of the company, ie the purpose for which the company is in business, either in general terms (a 'general commercial company') or more specifically.

The memorandum must be printed and then signed by at least one subscriber. Any subscriber automatically becomes a member of the company as soon as the company is registered. The following must be written in the memorandum:

(1) the name, address and occupation of each subscriber; and
(2) the number of shares he intends to take in the company when it is formed.

Chapter 10 contents
Introduction
Documents needed
The certificate of incorporation
How to form a company
Shelf company alternative
Immediate obligations and practicalities
The elective regime
Shareholders' agreements
Holding companies and subsidiary companies
Summaries and checklists

Usually there are two subscribers. It is common for them to agree to take one share each at this stage, the true number of shares they require being allotted to them after incorporation. Alternatively, the subscribers may agree to take the full number of shares they ultimately require. The main purpose of signing as subscriber at this stage is to ensure that there will be at least one member of the company when it comes into existence. The subscribers' signatures to the memorandum should be witnessed and the document dated. One person can witness both the subscribers' signatures where there are two subscribers.

10.2.2 The articles of association

The Companies Act 1985 provides a precedent for a set of articles of association for a private company limited by shares, namely Table A. The articles of a company can comprise Table A in its entirety without amendment. Alternatively, Table A could be totally rejected in favour of a different set of articles specifically drafted for a particular company. Neither of these options is usually chosen. The most common way of providing articles for a company is to utilise most of Table A, but to make specific amendments to it in order to make it more appropriate to the particular company.

The articles must be printed and signed by the subscribers to the memorandum. The date must be included and the signatures must be witnessed in the same way as for the memorandum.

10.2.3 Form 10

Form 10 is a standard form which has to be completed. Unlike the articles and the memorandum (where a lengthy objects clause is required), no drafting is necessary here.

The postal address of the registered office must be given on this form. Provided the company's address remains within the country stated in the memorandum, the address of the registered office is freely alterable; all that is needed to alter it is a resolution of the board (and notification to the registrar of companies on Form 287).

The company is obliged to keep most of its 'statutory books' (see **10.6.1**) at the registered office, for example internal registers and minutes of meetings. However, the registered office does not have to be, and frequently will not be, a place where the company carries on business. As the company has no physical existence, it has a registered office so that those who need to do so can 'find' it, for example to serve official notices or legal documents. It is not unusual for the registered office of a company to be its auditor's office or its solicitor's office. The registered office can be a place where the company carries on its business, provided that the statutory books are properly kept there.

Details of the people who are to be the first directors and the first secretary of the company must be inserted in Form 10. Those named will take office automatically on the incorporation of the company without further formality. The details required here for directors are the same details as are necessary for the register of directors (ie name, address, business occupation, nationality, details of any other directorships, date of birth), and each person named must sign to indicate that they consent to act as director (or secretary).

Form 10 must also be signed either by the subscribers to the memorandum or, on their behalf, by the solicitor engaged in the formation of the company.

10.2.4 Form 12

Form 12 is a statutory declaration that all the requirements of the Companies Act in relation to formation of a company have been complied with. It can be made by any of the people named as director or secretary on Form 10, or by the solicitor involved in forming the company, but, like any statutory declaration, it must be sworn before a solicitor or commissioner for oaths.

10.3 THE CERTIFICATE OF INCORPORATION

If all the documents required are correctly prepared and sent to the registrar, together with the fee, the registrar will issue a certificate of incorporation, and it is this which brings the company into existence. Once the certificate is issued, it is conclusive evidence that the company has been properly formed and came into being on the date stated. When a company is formed, it will be allocated a company number by the registrar, and from then on every document sent to the registry must bear that number, as that is the way in which the company is identified at Companies House.

10.3.1 Separate legal identity of the company

Once the certificate of incorporation has been issued, the company then exists as a legal person, which means that the company can, for example, own property or owe money quite independently of the people who are involved in the running of that company, ie the directors and shareholders. So, for example, employees are employed by the company, and the company will be named as the employer in any contract of employment. Even though it will be the directors who allocate employment duties and arrange for wages to be paid, they do so on behalf of the company and not in a personal capacity. Therefore, any employment claims, such as claims for breach of contract or redundancy, should be made by employees against the company and not against the directors (or shareholders), and only the company's money is available to pay any such claims.

10.3.2 Pre-incorporation contracts

Prior to incorporation the company does not exist, and there is no guarantee that it will ever exist. Any attempt to act on behalf of the company prior to the date stated on the certificate of incorporation is ineffective. The company, when it is incorporated, has no obligation under any contract purportedly made on its behalf before its registration. Any person who tries to act on behalf of the company before incorporation does so at his own risk, as he is personally liable on any contract made. If, when the company is formed, the directors wish the company to be party to the pre-incorporation contract, they cannot adopt the existing contract but must enter into a contract of novation (an entirely new contract) with the other party, replacing the earlier contract.

10.4 HOW TO FORM A COMPANY

When considering the best methods by which to form a company for a client, perhaps the most obvious way is to prepare all the documents personally after discussion with the client. (A company formed in this way is often called a 'tailor-made' company.) This would involve preparing the memorandum, including the objects clause (using precedents), having searched, or instructed agents to search, the index of names; drafting the articles, using Table A and other precedents (many firms will have their own in-house precedents for the more complex documents); having both of these printed; completing the two forms; and sending all these to the registrar of companies with the necessary fee.

It is also possible to take all the required documents to the Companies Registry, where the new company can be incorporated on the same day provided that all the necessary documentation is in order, the name does not require approval (see **11.2.1**) and the documents are submitted before 3 o'clock in the afternoon. The main Companies Registry is at Companies House in Cardiff, but there are branches of the Registry located in London, Birmingham, Manchester, Leeds and Edinburgh which also provide this speedier service, for which the fee is currently £20.

Alternatively, a company could be formed with the assistance of law stationers (ie a company whose business includes the provision of services in connection with company formation and administration). (This is sometimes known as a semi-tailored company.) The law stationers would arrange a search in the index of names, and would normally supply a standard memorandum, Table A articles with standard amendments (and possibly some optional amendments as well) and the two forms (Forms 10 and 12). The solicitor would complete the forms, discuss the other documents with his client, obtain the client's signature where necessary, and return all documentation to the law stationers who would then lodge the papers and the fee with the registrar for registration.

The third possibility is a shelf company – see **10.5**.

10.5 SHELF COMPANY ALTERNATIVE

Where a client wants to run a business through the medium of a company, it is possible to buy a company which has been incorporated already and therefore already exists, ie a shelf company. The shelf company will not have been trading, but will have been formed in anticipation of somebody wanting to buy it and use it as a method of running a business. As the company is already in existence, this can be a much quicker way of getting a client in business in the form of a company than creating a company from scratch, which may be time-consuming because of the need to apply for registration. This method of obtaining a company is therefore used frequently.

Shelf companies are generally formed with standard articles and an objects clause stating that the company is a general commercial company, making it suitable for most purposes (see further **11.2.3**). If a shelf company is purchased, the supplier will send the buyer the certificate of incorporation, the memorandum and articles (and possibly other documentation, eg internal registers).

Nominees (usually employees of the supplier of the shelf company) will have been named as directors on Form 10, will have signed as subscribers to the memorandum and thus will have become the first two members and directors of the company on incorporation. Before sending 'the company' to the buyers they will have to hold a board meeting at which they appoint the buyers as directors (having received their signed consents to act as such). The buyers may become directors of the company from that time. The original two directors will send with the other documentation their resignations, which may take effect immediately or from the next board meeting (which will be held by the buyers) and in this way the original directors are replaced by those who have bought the shelf company.

The subscribers' shares must also be transferred into the names of the buyers. The correct way to do this is to ensure that the original subscribers' names are entered on the register of members and they then transfer their shares in the usual way by stock transfer form (see **17.5.1**). A common practice has grown up whereby the original subscribers are not entered on the register of members but simply renounce their right to take up their shares in favour of the buyers without completing a stock transfer form, and, although not strictly correct, this method does not seem to cause any problems in practice.

Any changes to the memorandum and articles which might be necessary can be made in due course, but the advantage of this method is that the client can be trading throughout. The registered office will have to be changed, and it may be appropriate to change the name of the company as the existing name is unlikely to be one which the client would have chosen. Alternatively, the original company name may be retained, with the business operating under a separate business name. A new company secretary will also have to be appointed. The articles may need amending, as those supplied will probably be Table A with or without certain standard amendments.

10.6 IMMEDIATE OBLIGATIONS AND PRACTICALITIES

Once a company has been formed or a shelf company acquired, certain matters will have to be dealt with as a matter of priority.

10.6.1 Statutory books

The statutory books comprise the register of members, register of directors, register of company secretaries, register of directors' interests (in shares and debentures of the company), register of charges, minutes of board meetings and of general meetings, accounting records, and copies of directors' service contracts. These must be written up on incorporation, and amended from time to time to reflect any changes so that they are always up to date. If this requirement is not satisfied, any director or other officer of the company in default may be liable to a fine.

10.6.2 Registration for VAT

Most businesses, except those with a very small turnover (see **2.5**), must register for VAT with HM Customs and Excise. The company will be allocated a VAT number and must make returns every 3 months.

10.6.3 Stationery

All stationery used by the company must bear the company name, its place of registration, its registered number, the address of the registered office, and either the names of all the directors or the names of none of them. If the company trades under a business name, the company name must appear on all stationery, as must an address within Great Britain where documents can be served on the company (usually the address of the registered office).

10.6.4 Employees: PAYE and national insurance

If the company is to have employees working for it (in many cases the directors themselves will be employees) then the directors should contact the local tax inspector (Inland Revenue) to arrange for the deduction of income tax from wages under the PAYE scheme and should arrange with the DSS for the payment of national insurance contributions by them and on their behalf.

10.6.5 Insurance

Insurance should be taken out in the company's name, for example for any motor vehicles, for injury to employees or for occupier's liability.

10.6.6 Bank account

Although not legally necessary, it is essential from a practical point of view that the company has a bank account. The bank will require the directors to sign a mandate form, giving specimen signatures and specifying who can sign cheques on the company's behalf and whether there is any limit. For example the directors might decide that one director's signature is sufficient for cheques up to, say, £500, but that for any amount in excess of that sum two directors must sign the cheque. Thus the directors can tell the bank when it is authorised to pay out company money. They will probably make this decision at the first board meeting of the company.

10.6.7 The first board meeting

The directors will need to hold the first board meeting soon after incorporation because they will need to make decisions on a variety of matters.

At the start of the meeting a chairman may be elected from among the directors and the person so elected will then take charge of the meeting.

A list of some of the things which might be done at the first board meeting of a company is given below. It is not necessary for the directors to deal with all the items listed. Many other matters may be dealt with and almost certainly trading matters will be discussed. There is no particular format for board meetings, and exactly what happens in individual cases will depend on the circumstances pertaining and the people involved.

Opening a bank account
See **10.6.6**.

Appointing an auditor

The first auditor of the company is appointed by the directors. Theoretically, there is no urgency about this appointment, because the only requirement is that an auditor is appointed before the first AGM, but it is common for the directors to appoint an auditor much earlier than this, often at the first board meeting.

Awarding directors' service contracts

Directors often deal with the terms of their own service contracts (including terms as to remuneration, working hours, holidays and duration) at this meeting. If they attempt to award themselves fixed-term service contracts for more than 5 years, the fixed-term element can be valid only if approved in advance by the members in general meeting by ordinary resolution. (See further **13.6**.)

Adopting a company seal

The company seal is one way in which the company can sign documents, although the counter-signatures of either two directors or one director and the secretary are necessary in addition. A company does not have to have a company seal: it can rely instead on the signatures of directors or the secretary, but most companies do have one, and it does make company documents look more official. If the company is to have a seal then it must be formally adopted by the board of directors and needs a resolution of the board to authorise its use each time it is required.

Fixing an accounting reference date

The accounting reference date is the date to which the company must make up its accounts each year, ie it is the final day of the company's accounting year. When a company is formed, the registrar will allocate a date, which will be the last day of the month in which the company was incorporated. For example, if the date given on the certificate of incorporation is any date in June, the company will be given 30 June as an accounting reference date. At the first board meeting, the directors may wish to consider choosing a different date. If they select a different date, they must file Form 225 with the registrar of companies. The accounting reference date can be changed at any time during the companys's existence by a resolution of the board and the filing of Form 225.

Using a business name

For practical reasons, if a business name different from the company's name is to be used it should be used immediately in order to build up the goodwill of the business. This decision lies with the directors, so if they want to trade under a business name they should decide to do so at the first board meeting. (See further **11.2.1**.)

Allotting shares

The directors are likely to issue some or all of the nominal capital at the first board meeting as this will raise money for the company and give it some working capital. (The details of issuing shares are given in Chapter 17.) The directors must ensure that they have authority to allot shares (it must either be included in the articles or given by ordinary resolution of the members at a general meeting: CA 1985, s 80) and that they are not bound by the statutory pre-emption rights in s 89 of the Companies Act 1985, which can be removed either by the articles or by special resolution of the members. If the directors do issue shares, they must also resolve to stamp the company seal (if the company has one) on the share certificates issued to members.

Approving the cost of formation

As the company does not exist before its incorporation, the cost of forming the company cannot be incurred on behalf of the company, and those instructing the solicitor to act are personally liable for any costs. However, once the company is in existence, it is common for the directors to resolve that the expense of incorporating the company should properly come out of company funds.

10.7 THE ELECTIVE REGIME

When a company is first incorporated, or during the currency of its existence, the members may wish to consider whether they want to adopt, in full or in part, the elective regime (CA 1985, s 379A). This possibility is only available to private companies, and is only a practical consideration for a small private company, where a small number of people are involved in running the company. It is most likely that the elective regime will be adopted where the directors and the members of the company are largely the same people, and there is therefore no need for members to have safeguards and checks against the directors. The aim of the elective regime is to deregulate the company; to lessen the formal requirements where they are not necessary. At present, if the necessary elective resolutions are passed with the unanimous consent of members, five requirements can be relaxed. The Companies Act 1989 contemplates the possibility that, if this experiment proves successful, legislation might be introduced in the future allowing companies to de-regulate in a greater number of ways. Under the elective regime at present the members can agree:

(1) to give directors the power to allot shares for a period greater than the usual 5-year maximum. The members can specify that the directors' authority is to last for a fixed period of time greater than 5 years, or it could be indefinite (see **17.2.2**);

(2) to remove the need to lay accounts before the members at a general meeting. Accounts must still be prepared and sent out to members every year, but will not necessarily be put before the members at the AGM each year (see **12.5.6**);

(3) to remove the requirement to hold an AGM each year. Any member would still have the right to ask for an AGM if he wanted one, but one would not be held as a matter of course (see **12.5.7**);

(4) to remove the requirement that the auditor is appointed for only one year at a time. Usually members will simply re-appoint the same auditor year after year. The passing of this elective resolution recognises that fact and allows the appointment to be indefinite (see **15.2**);

(5) to reduce the percentage shareholding required to consent to short notice for an EGM (Extraordinary General Meeting). Usually an EGM can only be held on short notice if a majority in number of the members holding at least 95 per cent of the shares agree to do so. By elective resolution the members can agree to reduce the figure of 95 per cent, but they cannot reduce it below 90 per cent (see **12.4.6**).

Members can adopt all or any combination of the elements of the elective regime. Although an elective resolution (see **12.4.8**) is necessary for the introduction of any of these relaxations, any or all elements so adopted can be removed by an ordinary resolution of the members. Thus, it is easier for the members to cancel the elective regime than to introduce it. If it is passed, an ordinary resolution reversing an elective resolution is one of the few ordinary resolutions of which a copy is required by the registrar of companies.

10.8 SHAREHOLDERS' AGREEMENTS

A shareholders' agreement is essentially a contract. It can be made by all members of a company, or just some of them, and even people who are not shareholders can be party to the agreement if this is appropriate.

A shareholders' agreement can be made at any time during the lifetime of a company, but is most commonly made when a new company is set up, thereby establishing areas of agreement between those involved.

10.8.1 Why use a shareholders' agreement?

Members are already bound by one contract: the articles. However, the articles only form a binding contract in respect of membership rights, and are ineffective so far as non-membership rights are concerned. Therefore, if members wish to agree between themselves some matter which is unrelated to their membership rights, for example, that one of them should act as the company solicitor, they may enter into a shareholders' agreement to this effect.

The articles are a public document, open to public inspection at the Companies Registry. Any agreement which members wish to keep secret can be dealt with in a shareholders' agreement, which is a private contract between the parties which the general public have no right to see.

Additionally, the articles can be altered at any time by special resolution of the members, ie 75 per cent of the votes of those present at a general meeting. A shareholders' agreement, like any other contract, cannot be amended except with the unanimous consent of the parties to that contract. Therefore any attempted variation of a shareholders' agreement will provide a remedy for breach of contract where a variation of the articles would not.

10.8.2 Common provisions in a shareholders' agreement

A shareholders' agreement usually contains a series of mutual promises by the parties to the agreement, which provide the consideration for the contract. For example, one shareholder might require the others to promise that his child should be appointed as a director when the child reaches 25 years of age, another might require the others to agree to his appointment as auditor of the company for the next 10 years, and another might require that the others buy his shares from him at market value when he wants to retire.

10.9 HOLDING COMPANIES AND SUBSIDIARY COMPANIES

A business may be so structured that it is run by a 'group' of companies, consisting of a holding company (sometimes called the parent company) and one or more subsidiary companies. A company is a holding company if it owns a majority of shares in the subsidiary company, or if it has power to control the composition of the board of directors. In some ways, a group of companies can be seen as one big organisation (eg annual accounts must be produced for the group as a whole and not just for each individual company). However, the principle that each company is a separate legal entity still applies, so that, save in exceptional circumstances, the debts of the subsidiary company cannot be claimed from the funds of the holding company and vice versa.

Owners of a business may decide to set up a group of companies rather than just one company for a variety of reasons, for example there may be tax advantages, or each subsidiary company may be concerned with a different aspect of the group's business.

10.10 SUMMARIES AND CHECKLISTS

10.10.1 Documents, etc needed for company formation

- memorandum
- articles
- Form 10
- Form 12
- fee (£20)

Alternatively, buy a shelf company.

10.10.2 Matters to consider

- practicalities, eg registration for VAT, ordering stationery
- first board meeting

and if appropriate

- elective regime
- shareholders' agreement
- group structure

Chapter 11

THE COMPANY'S CONSTITUTION

11.1 INTRODUCTION

Every company is obliged to have a memorandum and a set of articles, which comprise the company's constitution. The memorandum is concerned with the company's relationship with and dealings with outsiders, whereas the articles govern the internal workings of the company.

Chapter 11 contents
Introduction
The memorandum
The articles of association
Changing the constitution
Summaries and checklists

11.2 THE MEMORANDUM

Every company must have a memorandum. Five clauses must appear in the memorandum: name, objects, registered office, liability and capital. A specimen memorandum for a private company limited by shares has been produced in the form of a statutory instrument (SI 1985/805) and is called Table B.

11.2.1 The name clause

Every company must have a company name, and this must be stated in the memorandum. Obviously a name has to be chosen when a company is first formed, but it is possible to change the name of a company if the members agree to this by special resolution. Those involved in forming a company may have definite views on the name they would choose for their business, but there are various restrictions on their choice of company name. The final word of the company name must be 'Limited', or the abbreviation 'Ltd'. This warns outsiders dealing with the company that liability of the shareholders is limited and that they can look only to company funds for payment of company debts.

A name cannot be used if there is already a company with that name on the index of names at the Companies Registry, and therefore it is important to check the index at an early stage to ensure that the desired name is not already in use. It is also wise to check the Trade Mark Index to ensure that the proposed name is not already registered as a trademark. The registrar may refuse the use of a proposed name if it is offensive or suggests a criminal offence (eg Hookers Ltd would almost certainly be refused). The written approval of the Secretary of State is required if the proposed name contains any of the words specified in the Company and Business Names Regulations 1981, as amended by the Company and Business Names (Amendment) Regulations 1982 and 1995. For example, any word which suggests a connection with the royal family, or with the government can only be used with the approval of the Secretary of State. The use of certain other words also requires approval, and the Regulations specify from which relevant body such consent must be obtained.

Once a company is registered with a particular name, that does not guarantee that there will be no problems in the future. If, for example, the name is misleading as an indication of the company's business activities, then the registrar can order the company to change its name. The company may also face a passing-off action in tort if it has adopted a name which is so similar to that of any existing business (whether it is a company or an unincorporated business) that the general public is likely to believe that there is some connection between the two and thus the company is appropriating some of the other business's goodwill. There is no foolproof way of preventing this from happening, as there is no requirement for partnerships or sole traders to register the name under which they trade but telephone and trade directories should be checked for the same or similar names in the same area of business. If a passing-off action is successful the company will be restrained by injunction from trading under its current name.

Although the company must always have a 'company name', it may decide to trade under, and thus be known to the general public by, a business name. The directors of a company have the power to decide on the use of a business name, so all that is needed to implement this is a resolution of the board. A business name need not contain the word 'Limited' but, if a business name is used, the company name must also appear on all company stationery so that the warning to the general public about the limited liability of the members is still apparent. However, the directors may still have to obtain written consent for the use of those words listed in the Company and Business Names Regulations 1981, and must still ensure that they do not use a name which is already in use.

11.2.2 The registered office clause

In the memorandum, all that need appear is the country in which the registered office is situated. The full postal address of the registered office appears on Form 10 and is freely alterable within the chosen country, but the country of the registered office must remain constant. This is the only clause of the memorandum which cannot be altered.

11.2.3 The objects clause

The objects clause of the memorandum should set out the purpose for which the company is in business and what it is empowered to do. This is now of little importance to third parties who deal with the company, but it is still relevant to members, as they have the right to apply to the court in advance of any action being taken or legal obligation incurred to restrain a proposed ultra vires act, ie one not authorised by the objects clause (see **20.2.1**).

For many years, Parliament has intended that the objects clauses of companies should be stated succinctly, but this has not happened because the courts, when attempting to protect the investor from misuse of his investment, have tried to limit the scope of what a company can do by a strict interpretation of the objects clause. The result of this is that objects clauses tend to be lengthy and cumbersome because the draftsman attempts to cover every activity in which the company might become involved.

There is usually a main objects clause, followed by a number of sub-clauses. The Companies Act 1989 introduced the possibility of having a main objects clause stating simply that the company is a 'general commercial company'. If this wording is used as the main objects clause, then the company can carry on any business it wishes, thereby enabling it to diversify its business without encountering problems with limitation from the objects clause. This wording also enables the company to do anything incidental or conducive to its business. However, many companies now trading were formed before this possibility was introduced in 1989, and their main objects clause would have had to set out comprehensively the business which the company was to carry on. These 'old' main objects clauses are frequently fairly lengthy, in order to give the company as much freedom as possible for future business activities.

The sub-clauses which follow the 'old' main objects clause attempt to list everything the company might possibly want to do during its existence, sometimes extending to several pages of print. The most important of these sub-clauses are:

(1) a *Bell Houses* clause (so called after *Bell Houses Ltd v City Wall Properties* [1966] 2 QB 656) whereby the company is authorised to 'carry on any other trade or business whatsoever which can, in the opinion of the board of directors, be advantageously carried on by the company in connection with, or ancillary to, any of the above businesses or the general business of the company';

(2) an independent main objects clause, which allows the company to have more than one object, each of the objects existing independently of the others, rather than being subject to the interpretation that there is only one main object for the company, anything other than that being merely subsidiary to that one.

Most shelf companies are now formed with an objects clause which is a combination of the old and new styles. It will have as a main objects clause the new wording 'general commercial company', but additionally will contain many of the old sub-clauses. This combination is being used because there is some doubt as to whether, without the additional sub-clauses, the company would be entitled to do anything it may want. For example, it is not clear whether a company would be acting intra vires if it sold off the whole of its business, or made gifts to charities. Although the Companies Act 1989 allows the company to do anything 'incidental or conducive to its business' as a general commercial company (CA 1985, s 3A), it is not certain whether the examples given above would be covered by this, and therefore most of the old-style sub-clauses from a pre-1989 standard objects clause are still being used.

11.2.4 The liability clause

Where the liability clause merely states that the liability of the members is limited, this means that the company is a private company limited by shares (see **12.3.1**). If liability is 'limited' in any other way (eg by guarantee), then the clause must say so explicitly.

11.2.5 The capital clause

The figure stated in the memorandum is the amount of nominal (or authorised) capital of the company. This figure is the maximum nominal value of the shares which the company can issue; it effectively provides a ceiling for the issue of shares. The figure chosen (eg £100,000) will be divided into shares of a certain nominal (or 'par') value. For example £100,000 might be divided into 100,000 shares of £1 each, 200,000 shares of 50 pence each or 100 shares of £1,000 each. A company does not have to issue all its nominal capital; the nominal capital figure represents simply the maximum number of shares that it can issue. Its issued share capital will be the nominal value of the shares actually allotted to members. Once all the nominal capital has been issued, no more shares can be allotted to members until the nominal capital figure in the memorandum has been increased. This is done by ordinary resolution of the members in general meeting.

11.3 THE ARTICLES OF ASSOCIATION

Every company must have a set of articles of association which give detailed instructions as to how the company is to work. This is where the internal management structure is set out, so the articles will often provide the answer to the question as to whether the members or the directors are permitted to do some proposed act.

11.3.1 Contractual status

The articles form a contract between the company and all its members, but it is a contract which is valid only insofar as it deals with membership rights (see **12.5**). These include such entitlements as the right to vote, the right to attend general meetings and the right to a dividend if one is declared. Anything in the articles which purports to bind the company and its members but which deals with rights other than those of a member in his capacity as member (such as the right to be a director or the right to be appointed the company's solicitor) will be unenforceable if included in the articles of the company; it should be dealt with in a separate contract, such as a shareholders' agreement (see **10.8**).

11.3.2 Table A

A specimen set of articles for a private company limited by shares has been produced in the form of a Statutory Instrument and this is called Table A. Table A is a comprehensive document, dealing with virtually every aspect of the internal workings of a company, and it will apply to a company unless it is specifically excluded or modified. As discussed at **10.2.2**, a company can adopt Table A in full, without modification, as its articles, but it is more common to make some amendments. The main areas of operation dealt with in Table A are as follows:

Articles 1–35:	shares
Articles 36–63:	members and general meetings
Articles 64–98:	directors and board meetings
Articles 99–101:	administration
Articles 102–110:	profits
Articles 111–116:	notices

11.3.3 Special articles

A company could, if it wished, exclude Table A altogether and devise a set of special articles specifically designed for its requirements. It is rare for a company to do this as many of the provisions of Table A are suitable for the majority of companies. It is also not particularly common for a company to adopt Table A in full without any amendment, as most company shareholders will require some provision which differs from the standard. It is usual to find that although a company has used most of Table A as the basis for its articles, it has made certain amendments by way of special articles.

Special articles can be inserted either when the company is first formed, or during the currency of its existence. Examples of special articles which are commonly required are as follows.

To give the directors the power to allot shares

Directors must specifically be given the power to allot shares by the members (CA 1985, s 80; see **17.2.2**). When a company is first formed, it is useful if this power is already in the articles because the directors can then issue shares and raise capital needed for the company to start up in business without having to call a general meeting in order to obtain the members' authority to do so.

To give the directors freedom to allot shares to whomsoever they wish

This is a special article which gives the directors the freedom to allot the shares to whomsoever they wish by removing the statutory pre-emption rights of existing members (CA 1985, s 89; see **17.2.3**). This enables the directors to get on with the business of issuing the shares and raising the necessary capital for the company without having to call a general meeting of the members to ask them to release these pre-emption rights. Alternatively, there may be a special article giving existing members a right of first refusal of new shares.

To enable the directors to vote on issues in which they have a personal interest

A special article may be included which allows directors to vote on any issue at board meetings, even where they have a personal interest in the matter in question. Table A forbids this except in very limited circumstances (art 94), but where the company has very few directors this restriction can prove extremely inconvenient as it is common for directors to have such a personal interest (eg when discussing the forms of a proposed contract with a separate company in which one of the directors is a shareholder, or when deciding the amount of their own salaries), and if an insufficient number of directors is entitled to vote (and count in the quorum: art 95) then no business can be conducted on this matter at the board meeting. (See further **13.9.2**.)

To restrict members' rights to transfer shares

An article which restricts members' rights to transfer (give away or sell) their shares is likely to be required in a small company where those involved in the business want to retain control over membership. Under Table A (art 24), the directors only have a limited discretion to refuse to register the transfer, so members can generally transfer their shares to whomsoever they like, which means that if one of the members disposes of his shares the others may be forced into running the business with someone they would not choose. A restriction is therefore usually imposed in a small company, either directing to whom members should offer their shares if they wish to dispose of them (eg members of the family or other members of the company) or simply giving the directors an absolute discretion to refuse to register a proposed new member, which gives the directors control over the composition of the membership as registration is crucial (see **12.2.2**).

To prevent removal of directors

An article can be included which gives directors who are also members extra votes on a resolution to remove them as director at a general meeting (a *Bushell v Faith* clause). In many small companies, most of the people involved in the company will be both directors and shareholders. In this situation, the position of director is very important because most decisions which govern the running of the company will be taken at board meetings. It is an intrinsic part of company law that members have the right to remove a director by ordinary resolution (CA 1985, s 303) (see **13.15.2**). One way in which a director can effectively be given job security is by the inclusion in the articles of a *Bushell v Faith* clause which will multiply by a given figure the number of votes to which the director-shareholder is entitled on a poll vote (see **12.4.10**). Provided this gives that director-shareholder at least 50 per cent of the total votes exercisable at a general meeting, he cannot be removed from office. In order to give total job security, the special article must give the director-shareholder weighted voting rights not only on a resolution to remove him but also on a resolution to change the articles to take away or change his weighted voting rights. Provided this gives him sufficient votes on a poll vote to block the necessary special resolution (more than 25 per cent), the director-shareholder cannot be removed from office without his own consent or failure to vote.

11.4 CHANGING THE CONSTITUTION

As a company evolves, the directors and shareholders may find that elements of the constitution which were, or were thought to be, suitable are no longer so. Circumstances change and sometimes the company's constitution must be amended to reflect this. If a shelf company has been used to start up a new business then changes may be necessary immediately in order to structure the company in the way the buyers wish.

11.4.1 Change of name

The name of a company is changed by the members passing a special resolution to that effect (CA 1985, s 28). There are restrictions on the choice of name (see **11.2.1**) and therefore it is essential to search the index of names at the Companies Registry, and the Trademarks Index, prior to calling the necessary EGM. There is a fee of £10 which must be sent to the registrar of companies, together with the reprinted memorandum and copy of the special resolution. The registrar will send back a new certificate of incorporation and the company will have to have new stationery.

A company which has been in business for a while is unlikely to change its name because of the possible loss of goodwill which this might cause. Where a shelf company is purchased, it is highly likely that the buyers will not want the existing name given to the shelf company and will wish to change it. (Shelf companies tend to have purely functional names, eg 'CoL 12345' or 'Jordans 56789'.) Alternatively, they could retain the company name as it is and trade under a business name (see **11.2.1**).

11.4.2 Change of objects

The objects clause may also be changed by a special resolution of the members (CA 1985, s 4). Changing the objects clause was never very common, but is even less so today because a company can be incorporated as a 'general commercial company'. Any change in the objects of a company would necessitate amending the memorandum. The reprinted memorandum and copy of the special resolution must be sent to the registrar of companies. Minority shareholders who object to the change have the right of appeal to the court within 21 days on limited grounds (CA 1985, s 5).

11.4.3 Change of articles

A special resolution of the members in a general meeting is required to change the articles of a company (CA 1985, s 9) and the articles would have to be reprinted to reflect whatever change was made. Both must be sent to the registrar of companies. Members are restricted in the changes they can make to the articles; they must be bona fide in the best interests of the company as a whole (see **12.6.2**).

It is common for the articles of a company to be amended during its existence, for a variety of reasons, including the need to deal with new situations. When a shelf company is purchased, it is extremely likely that the articles supplied will not be exactly what the buyers would wish and so changes will frequently have to be made.

11.4.4 Increase in nominal capital

The nominal capital will have to be increased if all the capital specified in the memorandum has been issued and the company wishes to issue more shares. An increase in nominal capital is achieved by an ordinary resolution of the members. This is one of the exceptional ordinary resolutions which must be sent to the registrar of companies if it is passed at a general meeting of the company. Any change in the nominal capital figure will also involve amending the memorandum, which must also be filed, together with Form 123 (see **17.2.1**).

11.4.5 Procedure

In outline, the procedure for making all the above changes is as follows.

(1) One or more directors will call a board meeting on reasonable notice.
(2) At the board meeting the directors will resolve to call an EGM (Extraordinary General Meeting).
(3) Notice of the EGM will be sent out to the members. If the only change proposed is an increase in the nominal capital (requiring an ordinary resolution), then 14 clear days' notice must be given. For any of the other changes which require a special resolution, 21 clear days' notice is needed.
(4) The EGM is held and the resolution(s) passed.
(5) Copies of the resolution(s) which have been passed are sent to the registrar of companies, together with the amended memorandum and/or articles as appropriate. If there has been a special resolution to approve a change of name, a fee must also be sent to the registrar. If the authorised share capital has been increased, Form 123 should also be filed at Companies House.

The calling and conduct of meetings is dealt with in greater detail at **12.4**.

11.5 SUMMARIES AND CHECKLISTS

11.5.1 The company's constitution

```
                    Company's constitution
                   /                      \
         memorandum                        articles
         • name, and                       • Table A, or
         • registered                      • specially drafted, or
           office, and                     • Table A, with
         • objects, and                      amendments
         • liability, and
         • capital
```

11.5.2 Resolutions to change the constitution

name	–	special resolution
objects	–	special resolution
capital	–	ordinary resolution
articles	–	special resolution

Chapter 12

MEMBERS AND MEETINGS

12.1 INTRODUCTION

The terms 'members' and 'shareholders' are synonymous. The members of a company are its financial backers. The members finance the company by purchasing shares in it. This gives them certain rights as members but very few liabilities as they are protected by the company being 'limited'. Members may or may not also be directors of the company.

12.2 JOINING THE COMPANY

12.2.1 The subscribers to the memorandum

Those people who, prior to incorporation, signed the memorandum as 'subscribers' automatically become the first members of the company when the registrar of companies issues the certificate of incorporation. Their names should be entered on the register of members but their status as members is not dependent upon this being done.

12.2.2 Others

If anyone other than one of the subscribers wishes to join the company by becoming a shareholder, he must ensure that his name is entered on the register of members, as only then does he become a member of the company. This applies irrespective of the method by which he acquires his shares, whether by sale or gift, allotment by the company or transfer by an existing member.

The directors cannot refuse to enter the name of a person who has received shares by transfer on the register of members unless the articles of the company allow them this discretion and, if the directors wrongly refuse to do so, the prospective new member can apply to the court for an order for rectification of the register.

Directors must ensure that the new name is entered within a reasonable time (which should not be longer than the 2-month period within which a new share certificate must be issued). The prospective new member's status between the date on which he acquires the shares and the date on which his name is entered on the register of members is that he is beneficially entitled to the shares but he is not the registered legal owner of them. This means that, although the original member will receive notice of general meetings and be entitled to attend, he must vote in accordance with the instructions of the prospective member, and although the original member will receive any dividends which are declared in connection with the shares, he must account to the prospective member for such amounts.

Chapter 12 contents
Introduction
Joining the company
Status of membership
General meetings
Rights of members
Restrictions on members' rights
Rights of minority shareholders
Summaries and checklists

12.2.3 The register of members

Every company must keep a register of the names of those who own shares in it. The register will show the names and addresses of every member, together with the number of shares held by each of them. This register must be updated whenever necessary to reflect any changes in the membership of the company.

If the company becomes a company with only one member because the membership has fallen to one, the register of members must contain not only the name and address of the sole member, but also a statement that the company has only one member and the date upon which the company became a company with only one member.

If a company's membership increases from one to more than one, then the register of members must contain the name and address of the person who was previously the sole member and a statement that the company has ceased to have just one member, together with the date on which the number of members was increased.

If these special requirements for one-person companies are not complied with, then the company and every officer in default is liable to a fine. In addition, there is a daily default fine if the error is not rectified immediately.

12.3 STATUS OF MEMBERSHIP

The members of a company own the shares in that company and thereby own the company in proportion to their shareholdings. (In common parlance, 'member' is the same as 'shareholder'.) The directors (usually) will decide how many shares to issue and, initially, will sell the shares to those persons who wish to become members. This process is known as allotment or issue of shares and occurs when a company commences its business. Later in the company's life the directors may decide that the company should have more shares, which will entail them allotting or issuing these additional shares either to the current members or to new shareholders. Members may dispose of their shares to other people by sale or gift (transferring the shares to the buyer or donee), subject to any restriction imposed by the company's articles.

Members thus provide the financial backing for the company. The money produced by the sale of the shares from the company to its members enables the company to commence and continue in business (although companies frequently also require assistance in the form of loans). In exchange for leaving his money with the company (ie having bought the shares), a member may receive an income payment from the company (called a 'dividend') and may benefit from the capital appreciation of the value of his shares. Equally, a member's shares may decrease in value if the company is not successful.

12.3.1 Limited liability

Any liability of a member of a limited company is generally 'limited' to the agreed price of his shares. Other than in exceptional circumstances, members have no personal liability for the company's debts, however great those debts may be. For example, if a member buys 100 £1 shares in a company and that company becomes insolvent, owing millions of pounds to its creditors, the worst that can happen to the member is that he loses the £100 he invested. This is because the company is a legal person in its own right (see **10.3.1**) and any debts owed by the company are the responsibility of that company and not of any individuals involved in it, save in particular circumstances (see **20.3** and **20.4**). This is why limited companies must have as part of their name the word 'Limited' or 'Ltd'; it warns members of the public that the only money available to pay the company's debts is that which belongs to the company and that generally creditors cannot look to members (or directors) for payment of the company's debts.

12.3.2 Functions of a member

The degree of involvement by members in their chosen company will vary enormously depending, for example, on the size of shareholding, the size of company and the wishes of the member. A member may also be a director of the company (or of any other company) but is not required to be so. There is not necessarily any link between the two roles within the one company. The directors generally make the day-to-day decisions. However, more major decisions which may have an effect on members' rights are usually required by the Companies Act 1985 to be approved by the members in a general meeting. Thus, the Companies Act 1985 states that only certain acts can be done by the members, for example removing a director from office (CA 1985, s 303), changing the name of the company (CA 1985, s 28) or authorising a service contract for a director which gives him job security for more than 5 years (CA 1985, s 319). It can be seen that the members only have very limited powers over the directors, apart from dismissal.

12.4 GENERAL MEETINGS

Although general meetings are meetings of members, it is normally the directors who have the power to call these meetings, and the board may resolve to call a meeting of the shareholders at any time, for any reason. All members are entitled to attend a general meeting and to speak at the meeting. Directors are also permitted to attend and speak, but cannot vote unless they are also shareholders. A general meeting will be an Extraordinary General Meeting (EGM) except for once a year when the company has its Annual General Meeting (AGM).

12.4.1 The AGM

The directors are obliged to call an AGM once in each calendar year. Although, commonly, the date of the AGM will be fixed from year to year (eg it might always be the first Monday in March, or the last Thursday in October), this does not have to be the case, and the only rule is that there must not be a gap of more than 15 months between AGMs. There is a special rule which applies when the company is first incorporated: no AGM need be held in the year of incorporation, or in the following year, provided the first AGM is held within the first 18 months of the company's existence.

Notice of 21 clear days is required for an AGM, although it is open to members to agree that a shorter period of notice is acceptable. Their decision, however, must be unanimous.

In larger companies, where it is much less likely that all the members will be directors, the AGM provides those shareholders who are not on the board with a yearly opportunity to confront the directors, particularly on the question of the company's finances as this is also their opportunity to see the annual accounts. Members are not limited to challenging the directors on financial matters and may, for example, be able to remove a director from office.

In many smaller companies, however, the members may all be directors, in which case the AGM is of less significance. In recognition of this, it is possible for the members to pass an elective resolution, which requires the unanimous agreement of members, that there will not be an AGM as a matter of course. Even if this is done, any member will still have the right to insist on an AGM being held, but no AGM will take place unless someone asks for one (see **12.5.7**).

12.4.2 EGMs

Although EGM stands for extraordinary general meeting, this is the name given to every meeting of members other than the AGM. The period of notice required for an EGM depends on the type of resolution(s) to be proposed at the meeting. If only ordinary or extraordinary resolutions are on the agenda and they do not concern the appointment of a director, then 14 clear days' notice is required for an EGM. In all other cases, 21 clear days' notice is required (see **12.8.2** and **12.8.3**).

12.4.3 The power to call general meetings

The directors are primarily entitled to call general meetings. When they do so, they can also prepare a statement setting out their views on the issues to be raised at the meeting and urging members to vote in support of their policy. They are entitled to use company funds to pay for any expense incurred in doing this. In this way, directors who are not shareholders, or who are minority shareholders, can exert considerable influence over general meetings.

Alternatively, the directors may try to retain power within the company by not calling general meetings, thus excluding the shareholders from involvement in the running of the company and keeping them in ignorance about company matters.

To redress the balance, members too have a right to call a general meeting and to circulate their views, but only in certain circumstances (see **12.5.9** and **12.5.13**).

12.4.4 Notice of general meetings

Notice of general meetings must be given in writing. It must be sent to all members, to the personal representative of a deceased member, to the trustee in bankruptcy of a bankrupt member, to all directors and to the auditor. Notice can be served personally on all of these people or sent by post to the address which appears on the register of members. If notice is sent by post, it is deemed to be served 48 hours after posting (Table A, art 115).

Members (and those others entitled) must be given either 21 or 14 'clear' days' notice of a meeting, depending on the type of meeting and the type of resolutions to be proposed at that meeting. 'Clear' days means that, when allowing for the amount of notice required, the day on which the notice is served and the day on which the meeting is held cannot be counted. For example, if notice of an AGM is served on all those entitled to it on 4 July, 5 July then becomes the first of the 21 clear days' notice required for the meeting. By looking at a calendar, it is clear that the twenty-first of the 21 clear days is 25 July and thus the AGM can validly be held on 26 July.

The written notice can be in any form but must fulfil certain requirements. It must state the name of the company and the date, time and place of the meeting. It must say whether the meeting is an AGM or an EGM and must give details of the resolutions which are to be proposed at the meeting. The exact wording of special, extraordinary and elective resolutions must be set out, and this requirement means that at the general meeting itself no amendment can be made to the wording of any such resolution. In the case of ordinary resolutions, the requirement is that sufficient detail must be given to enable members to decide whether or not it is an issue on which they have a view and would wish to attend. The exact wording of such resolutions need not be given (although it may be given) and thus it is possible for there to be an amendment to an ordinary resolution at the general meeting provided the change is not so radical that it would make the notice of the meeting ineffective. Notice of a general meeting must also contain a 'proxy notice', which is a statement telling the recipient member that if he is unable to attend or does not wish to attend the meeting he can send someone else in his place, and that the person he sends need not be a member of the company (see **12.4.13**).

12.4.5 Invalid notice

It is essential that written notice be given in the proper form to all those entitled to it, because if this is not done then any resolutions purportedly passed at the meeting are invalid (Table A, art 111). This rule is strictly applied. However, to allow some leniency on this, the articles of a company will usually contain a provision which states that, provided the error is accidental, the resolutions passed at the meeting are still valid (Table A, art 39). The important word here is 'accidental'; this provision will not assist the company where there is any suggestion that the 'mistake' was deliberate, for example, if a dissenting member has not been given notice in a deliberate attempt to exclude him from the meeting.

12.4.6 Short notice

If there is agreement between the members, general meetings can be held on short notice, ie less than the 21 or 14 clear days required. If the meeting is an AGM, all members must agree to this; if the meeting is an EGM then the meeting can be validly held on short notice provided a majority in number of the members agree and those members hold at least 95 per cent of the shares in the company (CA 1985, s 369).

For example, if, in a company, there are ten shareholders who each own 10 per cent of the shares, then although any six of them would be a majority in number of the members, they would not together hold 95 per cent of the shares. Even nine of them would not do this and so, in this example, short notice could only be achieved by unanimous consent.

However, if a different company had six shareholders, one who owned 95 per cent of the shares and five others who each owned 1 per cent then, although the majority shareholder has the required percentage of the shares, he does not constitute a majority in number of the members. As there are six members of this company, short notice can only be effective if the majority shareholder and three of the others (four in total) agree.

Members can reduce the 95 per cent shareholding requirement for an EGM if they pass an elective resolution to that effect, but they cannot reduce it below 90 per cent (see **10.7**).

12.4.7 Quorum

Resolutions are only validly passed at a general meeting if that meeting is quorate, ie a certain number of people must be present at the meeting. The Companies Act 1985, s 370 and Table A, art 40 fix the quorum for general meetings at two, unless either the company in question is a company with only one member (in which case the quorum is one) or the company agrees otherwise. If the company is not a one member company, the quorum cannot be reduced to one (save in exceptional circumstances by the court, see **12.5.10**) because generally one person cannot constitute a 'meeting'. It can, however, be increased to any figure thought appropriate for that company by the members amending the articles by special resolution. In a small company, the statutory quorum of two may be suitable. In a two-person company, it is essential to prevent one person having complete dominance. In a larger company, the members may feel that it is inappropriate to validate a meeting when only two shareholders are present and a larger number may be specified in the articles as the quorum.

If a member sends a proxy to the meeting in his place, the proxy can count as part of the quorum. However, generally, there must be at least two people physically present in the room for there to be a 'meeting', so one person who attends as a member himself and is also a proxy for another member cannot, on his own, fulfil the requirement of a quorum of two.

A general meeting must be quorate when it starts and must remain quorate throughout (Table A, art 41). If insufficient people are present at the start of the meeting, or if someone has to leave and the meeting ceases to be quorate, the chairman will adjourn the meeting, usually to the same time and place in the following week, when a further attempt will be made to hold a quorate meeting.

12.4.8 Types of resolution

Members of a company act by passing resolutions at general meetings. As to voting methods and the meaning of majority, see also **12.4.10**. There are four types of resolution.

Special resolution (CA 1985, s 378(2))

A special resolution requires a 75 per cent majority for it to be passed. This means that on a vote on a show of hands at least three-quarters of the number of members present and voting must vote in its favour. On a poll, 75 per cent of the votes of those members or their proxies present and voting must be in favour of the resolution.

Example

If a company has issued 100 shares, 10 shares to each of ten members, then if all ten members are present at a general meeting, or send a proxy, any eight of them can pass a special resolution because between them they would have 80 per cent of the votes. However, if only eight shareholders turned up to the meeting and the other two did not send proxies in their place, any six of those members present would between them hold 75 per cent of the votes, and thus could pass a special resolution.

If a special resolution is to be proposed, 21 clear days' notice of the meeting is required, whether the meeting is an AGM or an EGM. A special resolution is needed to change the company's name, for example, or to change the articles of the company.

Extraordinary resolution (CA 1985, s 378(1))

Like a special resolution, an extraordinary resolution requires a 75 per cent majority for the resolution to be passed. The amount of notice required for an extraordinary resolution, however, depends on the type of meeting: 21 clear days if the resolution is to be proposed at an AGM, 14 clear days if at an EGM. There are very few occasions on which the members are required to use an extraordinary resolution, the main examples being where the members wish to pass a resolution to put the company into voluntary liquidation (see **24.4.1**) and to vary the rights attaching to certain classes of shares in certain circumstances (CA 1985, s 125).

Ordinary resolution

An ordinary resolution is passed if a simple majority of the members present and voting at the meeting are in favour of it. Thus, the resolution will be passed if, on a show of hands, a majority in number of the members present vote for the resolution or if, on a poll, more than 50 per cent of the votes cast are in favour. The period of notice required for an ordinary resolution depends on the type of meeting at which it is proposed: 21 clear days for an AGM, 14 for an EGM.

Elective resolution (CA 1985, s 379A)

An elective resolution is carried only if it obtains the unanimous consent of all members of the company. Unlike the other types of resolution, which require the approval of a certain percentage of those members (or their proxies) present and voting, all members of the company must be present, or have sent a proxy, and all must vote in favour of the elective resolution for it to have effect. An elective resolution always requires 21 clear days' notice. This type of resolution is used only to introduce one or more elements of the elective regime into the company (see **10.7**).

12.4.9 Which resolution to use?

The most commonly used types of resolution, and therefore the most important, are special and ordinary resolutions. Members can act by ordinary resolution (straight majority) unless they are required to use some other sort of resolution either by statute or by the company's articles. The Companies Act 1985 insists that for certain decisions only a certain type of resolution is adequate; for example, a special resolution is needed to change the company's name or articles. Therefore, for these amendments to be validly made, a special resolution must be used. Where, however, the Act or the articles specify that an ordinary resolution may be used, or do not specify any particular type of resolution to be used, then although members can use an ordinary resolution it is open to them to change the articles to require that either a special or extraordinary resolution shall be used, as both of these require a higher percentage of the votes to be cast in favour for the resolution to be passed. Therefore, for example, the articles of a company could specify that in order to increase the nominal capital of that company, the members must pass a special resolution (75 per cent) whereas most companies operate under art 32 of Table A which prescribes an ordinary resolution (see **11.4.4**).

The two exceptions to this are removal of a director and removal of an auditor. The right to remove a director or auditor by a simple majority of the members under the Companies Act 1985 is a right which cannot be taken away.

12.4.10 Voting

Members can vote at general meetings in one of two ways: on a show of hands or on a poll. If a vote is taken on a show of hands every member has one vote but if any person is there as a proxy for an absent member, that person cannot vote on a show of hands in that capacity. If a poll vote is taken, each member has one vote for every share he owns, and in this case a proxy can vote, exercising the same number of votes as the member he represents.

Example

A company has issued 100 shares; six members each hold 10 shares, eight members each hold 5 shares. If all members are present at a general meeting then on a vote on a show of hands the eight 5 per cent shareholders would outvote the six 10 per cent shareholders, but on a poll vote the 10 per cent shareholders would between them have 60 per cent of the votes and would therefore be able to pass an ordinary resolution.

Initially, all votes will be taken on a show of hands, but this method is clearly disadvantageous to a majority shareholder and to a proxy. If, therefore, the result of the show of hands is not unanimous, or not the desired result of a proxy in attendance, then a poll vote may be demanded.

The articles will specify who can ask for a poll vote, and a proxy has the same right as the member he represents to ask for a poll vote. The only restriction on this is that the articles cannot be amended so that more than five members or holders of more than 10 per cent of the company's shares must request a poll in order for one to be held (CA 1985, s 373). Subject to this, the members have complete freedom to decide who can demand a poll.

Under Table A (art 46), a poll vote must be taken if requested by the chairman, any two members or any member(s) holding at least 10 per cent of the shares. Therefore, under Table A, the only member or proxy who has no right to a poll vote is a single member who owns less than 10 per cent of the company's shares. If the members wanted to amend this to allow any single member to insist on a poll being held, they could do so by passing a special resolution to change the articles. Clearly, there would be little point in a shareholder with a very small percentage of the shares asking for a poll vote if he was the only member who wished to overturn the result of the vote on a show of hands. Such a member's right to demand a poll may be important, however, where he holds the few votes that could affect the outcome of the vote.

12.4.11 The chairman

The chairman at general meetings of members will usually be the same person as is appointed to be the chairman for board meetings (Table A, art 42). His task is to preside at meetings and to keep order. For example, he will take items in turn from the agenda, and will decide whether proposed amendments to ordinary resolutions can be allowed, bearing in mind the detail which was given on the notice of the meeting. He will declare whether a particular resolution has been passed or defeated, and his statement on this is conclusive unless the vote was on a show of hands and a poll is subsequently demanded, or unless his declaration is clearly bad on the face of it. For example, if there are ten members present at the meeting, each of whom holds 10 shares in the company, and, on a show of hands, nine of them vote for the resolution and one votes against, but the chairman declares that the resolution is defeated, that is a ruling which is clearly bad on the face of it.

12.4.12 The chairman's casting vote

The chairman will have a casting vote in addition to any other vote he may have (Table A, art 50) unless a special article has been included to remove this. The casting vote only operates if, without it, the number of votes for and against the resolution is equal. In a two-member company, it is usually thought inappropriate for the chairman to retain a casting vote as this effectively gives him complete control. In other cases, the casting vote is often considered to be a useful way of reaching a decision where there is deadlock. Without the chairman's casting vote the rule is that where the number of votes for and against a particular resolution is equal then the negative view prevails and the resolution is defeated.

12.4.13 Proxies

A proxy is a person who attends a general meeting in place of a member of the company. If a member wants to send a proxy to a meeting rather than attending personally, he must formally appoint a person as his proxy by depositing notice in writing at the registered office (Table A, art 62). The company cannot insist on more than 48 hours' notice prior to a general meeting of the appointment of a proxy.

A proxy may be appointed for one meeting or for several meetings, and the appointee may be told whether to vote for or against particular resolutions by the member who appoints him, or he may be required to attend the meeting, hear the arguments put forward and vote in whatever manner he feels appropriate.

A member could ask another member of the company to attend the meeting as his proxy, or he could ask a complete outsider to stand in for him.

A proxy cannot vote on a show of hands but he can vote if there is a poll, and he has the same right as his appointor to request that a poll be taken. A proxy can, however, speak at a general meeting, and therefore a member may wish to appoint a proxy not only where the member is unable to attend general meetings but also where he feels that a proxy may be more articulate or persuasive when speaking on a particular issue.

12.4.14 What must be done after the meeting?

Copies of every special resolution, extraordinary resolution, elective resolution or written resolution which takes the place of a special, extraordinary or elective resolution must be sent to the registrar of companies within 15 days of the resolution being passed. Usually, copies of ordinary resolutions are not sent to the registrar, but there are some exceptions, notably an ordinary resolution to increase the nominal capital of the company (see **11.4.4**), an ordinary resolution to give the directors the authority to allot shares (see **17.2.2**), and an ordinary resolution to revoke an elective resolution (see **10.7**).

Minutes must be kept of every meeting which has been held (CA 1985, s 382). These are usually written up by the secretary and then signed by the chairman as being an authentic record of the meeting.

12.4.15 Is it necessary to have a general meeting?

Where there is a possibility that a resolution will receive the unanimous support of the shareholders, the directors may attempt to ask the members to pass a resolution by means of a written resolution rather than calling a general meeting.

The Deregulation (Resolutions of Private Companies) Order 1996, which came into force on 1 June 1996, has modified the procedure for members passing a written resolution in place of calling a general meeting.

The procedure involves sending a copy of the resolution to the auditor and all the members (CA 1985, s 381A). Provided that all the members sign the resolution, then it will be validly passed as if passed at a general meeting. Failure of a company officer to send a copy of the resolution to the auditor is now a criminal offence, punishable with a fine, although the resolution would be validly passed.

Table A, art 53 provides an alternative way of passing a written resolution in which a copy is not sent to the auditor. However, there is some doubt as to whether certain resolutions which the Companies Act 1985 states should be passed at a general meeting can be validly passed in this way.

If a written resolution is passed by the members, it must be recorded in minutes in the same way as if it was passed at a general meeting (CA 1985, s 382A). The date of the resolution will be the date on which the last member signed. A written resolution cannot be used to remove a director or auditor from office.

12.4.16 Decisions taken by a sole member

The sole member must either pass the resolution by means of a written resolution (CA 1985, s 381A) or must provide the company with a written record of his decision (CA 1985, s 382B). Failure to do so renders the sole member liable to a fine, but does not affect the validity of the decision.

12.5 RIGHTS OF MEMBERS

Generally, the rights of members in any particular company will be governed by the articles of that company. Additional rights may be given by special articles, but a shareholder in any company can expect to have the following rights.

12.5.1 The right to vote (CA 1985, s 370)

The right to vote is an extremely important right for members as this is the way in which they exercise their powers. They can attend general meetings and vote in person, or they have the right to send a proxy to attend, speak, and vote in their place. All except (usually) members with a very small percentage of the company's shares have the right to demand a poll vote, as only then is the size of their shareholding taken into account. By exercising their votes, members have the right to appoint additional directors to the board, and can remove directors from office; thus they can control the composition of the board.

12.5.2 The right to receive notice of general meetings (CA 1985, s 370)

All members must be given proper notice of a general meeting, and if this is not done any business transacted at the general meeting is invalid. Members must be given sufficient information in the notice of the general meeting to enable them to know what is to be proposed: the exact wording of special, extraordinary and elective resolutions must be set out and enough information on any ordinary resolutions for members to decide whether they feel strongly enough about the issue to make it crucial that they attend.

12.5.3 The right to a dividend, if one is declared (Table A, art 104)

Initially, the directors decide whether it is appropriate to pay a dividend to members. If they decide that the company has sufficient funds, they will recommend the amount of the dividend and then the members in a general meeting will actually declare the dividend. The members cannot vote to pay themselves more than the directors have recommended, although they could decide that a smaller amount was more appropriate (Table A, art 102).

12.5.4 The right to a share certificate (CA 1985, s 185)

Every shareholder must receive from the company a share certificate, which must bear the company's seal (if it uses one). A member is entitled to receive the share certificate within 2 months of either allotment (if new shares are being issued) or lodging the transfer with the company (if existing shares are being transferred). The certificate will say how many shares the member owns, and acts as prima facie evidence of title.

12.5.5 The member's right to have his name entered on the register of members (CA 1985, s 352)

This right of a member to have his name entered on the register of members is subject to the articles of the company. In a private company, the directors are often given, by special article, the right to refuse to register a 'new member'. In the absence of a special article to this effect, the board must enter the name of any new shareholder within a reasonable time, which will not be longer than the 2 months within which they are required to issue the new share certificate.

12.5.6 The right to a copy of the annual accounts (CA 1985, s 240)

Even if an elective resolution has been passed dispensing with the need for the accounts to be laid before members at the AGM, accounts must still be sent to all members each year, and every member then has the right to ask for a general meeting to be held to discuss the accounts if he feels that this is necessary.

12.5.7 The right to an AGM (CA 1985, s 366)

The right to an AGM is more important where there are some members who are not also directors than where the composition of the board and the shareholders is identical. It gives members a chance at least once a year to confront the directors and to express their opinions. It is at the AGM that the annual accounts will usually be considered and discussed and, on this occasion, members may also take the opportunity to refuse to re-elect a director whose turn it is to retire by rotation (see **13.15.1**).

If an elective resolution is in force dispensing with the requirement to hold an AGM each year, any member has the right to insist that an AGM is held. If the member requesting an AGM wants it to be held in the current calendar year, he must make his demand known to the company before 1 October of that year. If any request is made within the final 3 months of the calendar year (ie between 1 October and 31 December), the company is permitted to postpone the holding of the AGM until the following calendar year.

12.5.8 The right to inspect minutes of general meetings (CA 1985, s 383)

Minutes of all general meetings must be kept at the registered office of the company and members must be permitted to read those minutes if they so wish.

12.5.9 The right to call an EGM (CA 1985, s 368)

Many of the rights of members mentioned above are subject to the provisions of the company's articles, but the right to call an EGM cannot be excluded by any contrary provision in the articles. Members holding at least 10 per cent of the company's shares have the right to requisition a meeting by depositing a written request at the company's registered office. The requisition must say why a meeting is requested, and must be signed by those making the request. The directors are then obliged to take action to convene a meeting within 21 days, and the meeting must actually be held within 28 days of notice of the meeting being sent out, which means that the maximum permitted delay between receipt of the requisition and the day of the meeting is 7 weeks. If the directors do not take the required action then the requisitionists themselves can call a meeting, and their meeting must take place within 3 months of the date of the original request. They can recover any cost incurred in doing this from the company, and the company can deduct this amount from the fees of the directors. If members call an EGM in this way, they, rather than the directors, fix the agenda for the meeting.

12.5.10 The right to ask the court to call an EGM (CA 1985, s 371)

Any member can apply to the court for an order that an EGM be held if for some reason it is impracticable for one to be held otherwise (eg where other members are refusing to attend general meetings and it has proved impossible to hold one which is quorate). The court has the power to make such ancillary directions as it might think appropriate; in the situation in the example above, it might order that the quorum for one general meeting should be reduced to one.

12.5.11 The right to restrain an ultra vires act (CA 1985, s 35(2))

This right to restrain an ultra vires act only exists before the ultra vires act is done. Once the company has incurred some legal obligation in relation to an ultra vires transaction, it is too late for members to take any action. Prior to the ultra vires act, however, any member can apply to the court asking for an injunction to restrain the company from pursuing the course of action in question (see **20.2.1**).

12.5.12 The right to have an item placed on the agenda for an AGM (CA 1985, s 376)

Any shareholder or shareholders owning 5 per cent or more of the company's shares have the right to have an item placed on the agenda for an AGM. The request must be given to the company in writing 6 weeks prior to the AGM. He (or they) must sign the requisition and leave it at the registered office of the company, together with a sum of money to cover the company's expenses (although the general meeting may later vote that this is returned). Where the date of the AGM is fixed from year to year (eg it is always held on the first Wednesday in November), then it is easy for any member wishing to avail himself of this right to determine the date by which he must give notice to the company. If, however, the date of the AGM has not been fixed, the member concerned should simply give notice to the company whenever he chooses and the item must then be placed on the agenda at the next AGM to be called. If the directors attempt to frustrate the member by calling the AGM within 6 weeks, they will not succeed in this, because if that happens the member is deemed to have given the required amount of notice. This right is extremely useful as it is the only way in which members can have matters which they want discussed and voted on included in the agenda for a general meeting other than when members requisition a meeting under s 368.

12.5.13 The right to circulate a written statement (CA 1985, s 376)

The right to circulate a written statement is also given to holders of 5 per cent or more of the shares in the company. Any request from members that the directors should send out such a statement in writing must be made, by written requisition deposited at the registered office, at least one week before the relevant general meeting. This right is given to members in relation to both AGMs and EGMs. It is an important right because it is the counter-balance to the directors' power to circulate their views in advance of the meeting (see **12.4.3**).

12.5.14 The right not to be unfairly prejudiced (CA 1985, s 459)

If any member feels that what is happening within the company is 'unfairly prejudicial' to him, he has a right to petition the court. The complaint may be based on past, present or even anticipated future events, and may be unfairly prejudicial to all of the members or only some or one of them. Whether what has happened, is happening or will happen amounts to 'unfair prejudice' is judged on an objective basis, from the perspective of an impartial outsider. For the petition to be successful, the member must prove that he has been affected in his capacity as member, although this has been given a very wide interpretation. For example, if it was one of the terms of a takeover that the previous owner of the business would receive shares in the acquiring company and become a director of that company, it may follow that the loss of the directorship constitutes 'unfair prejudice' to the member as the two positions are inextricably linked. In order to establish unfair prejudice, it is not necessary to prove that the value of the member's shares has been adversely affected, although frequently this will have happened. Examples of potential unfair prejudice are:

(1) non-payment of dividends;
(2) directors awarding themselves excessive remuneration;
(3) directors exercising their powers for an improper purpose (ie to 'freeze out' a minority shareholder);
(4) exclusion from management in a quasi-partnership type of company (ie a small company formed on the understanding that all those involved will share the running of the business and the profits).

If the court finds that a member has suffered unfair prejudice, it can make any order it thinks appropriate. However, the most common remedy given is an order that the other shareholders or the company itself should purchase the shares of the petitioner at a fair value. The House of Lords in *O'Neil and Another v Philips and Others* (1999) unreported, held that the court's powers were wide under s 459 but did not give an automatic right to withdrawal from a company where trust and confidence had broken down.

12.5.15 The right to have the company wound up (IA 1986, s 122(1)(g))

Any member can make an application to have the company wound up on the ground that it is just and equitable to do so, provided he can prove that he has a 'tangible interest', ie that the company is solvent and he will therefore get back some or all of the money originally invested. The court has granted such applications in a wide variety of situations, for example where the management is in deadlock, where the members have no confidence in the management, where the company can no longer carry on the business for which it was formed and, in the quasi-partnership situation, where one of those involved is being excluded from management. A petition for winding up is a remedy of last resort, because if it is successful the company will cease to exist, which means that the members will no longer have an investment and the directors will no longer have a job.

12.6 RESTRICTIONS ON MEMBERS' RIGHTS

Any restrictions on what members can do are found in the articles of association of the company.

12.6.1 Voting

Generally, there are no restrictions on the way in which members exercise their voting rights. When voting at general meetings they need only have regard to their own self-interest and need not consider whether they are acting in the best interests of the company as a whole. Even if a member is also a director, when exercising his votes as a member he can ignore the duty to the company which he is obliged to take into account when exercising his vote as a director.

However, where a director is also the majority shareholder (he owns more than 50 per cent of the shares), there is a restraint. Arguably, such a person should not use his majority of the shares at a general meeting to sanction an abuse of power by him in his capacity as a director. The same applies where a number of directors together constitute a majority shareholding at general meetings. They cannot use this to sanction their own misdemeanours.

Although there is generally no restraint on majority shareholders voting in accordance with their own self-interests, if the effect of their doing so amounts to 'unfair prejudice' to other members then those other members may obtain a remedy by petitioning the court (see **12.5.14**). There was one case (*Clemens v Clemens Bros* [1976] 2 All ER 268) which stated that the voting of majority shareholders was subject to 'equitable considerations' which might make it unfair for them to vote in a particular way. The court's decision was that a particular resolution passed by the majority shareholder should be overturned, but it is uncertain to what extent this reasoning would be appropriate in any other given situation.

12.6.2 Changing the articles

Although members can change the articles by special resolution there are restrictions on what changes they can make. Generally, they can only make a change if it is bona fide in the best interests of the company as a whole. The test for this is that of the hypothetical individual shareholder: if, from an objective perspective, the proposed change is for the benefit of the 'typical' shareholder, then it is also in the best interests of the company as a whole. This is so, even though it may not be beneficial to all shareholders. However, a change to the articles will not be in the best interests of the company if it amounts to a fraud on the minority, ie something which benefits majority shareholders at the expense of those with a minority holding. The proposed inclusion in the articles of a provision stating that any member who holds less than 10 per cent of the shares cannot vote at general meetings would be a fraud on the minority, as would a proposed amendment providing that any member holding less than a certain percentage of the shares must offer them for sale to the other members.

12.6.3 Powers of the directors

Members are not empowered to do those things which have been delegated to the board of directors. The question of who has power to do what within a company will be governed by the articles, but usually the directors take all management decisions (unless otherwise directed by special resolution (Table A, art 70)) and only those matters required by statute to be decided by the members are left in the hands of the shareholders. The effect of this is that if the members do not like the way in which the board is running the company, they cannot simply overturn the decisions of the board. They have the right to remove directors from office (CA 1985, s 303) and the right to appoint new directors to office (Table A, art 78), both by ordinary resolution. Thus, members could remove all the existing directors and replace them, or they could appoint a sufficient number of new directors to outnumber those currently on the board. The disadvantage with either of these methods is that, although the members may effect a change in the running of the company in the future, these steps do not have retrospective effect.

12.6.4 Restrictions on minority shareholders

Minority shareholders are restricted in what they can do. Generally within a company there is majority rule. Even where some wrong is done to the company, or there is some irregularity in internal management, it is for the directors or, if they cannot or will not take action, for the majority shareholders to decide whether to take action in the company name (the rule in *Foss v Harbottle* (1843) 2 Hare 461). Clearly, there is little point in allowing minority shareholders the right to commence legal action in the company name when the wrong can easily be ratified by an ordinary resolution passed by the majority. Thus, in many cases, the rule preventing minority shareholders from taking legal action is justifiable as it means that the court's time is not wasted.

However, there are exceptional situations where a minority shareholder is permitted to bring a 'derivative action' in the company's name. A derivative action will comprise two stages: first, a preliminary hearing to decide whether the applicant is entitled to bring a derivative action, then the hearing itself.

Minority shareholders can bring a derivative action in two main types of situation: where the majority cannot ratify what has been done (eg where the company acts illegally, where an ordinary resolution has been used when a special or extraordinary resolution was required or where the company acts on a resolution which was not validly passed because notice was not properly given); and where it would be unfair not to allow a derivative action (eg where there is fraud on the minority or where there is 'unfair prejudice'). The rule in *Foss v Harbottle* is relevant only when members wish to bring an action on the company's behalf. If they wish to take action in respect of their personal rights against the company then they do so in their personal capacity and a derivative action is unnecessary.

12.7 RIGHTS OF MINORITY SHAREHOLDERS

Those members holding 50 per cent or less of the company's shares have little power within the company as they cannot, without the backing of other shareholders, be certain of passing any resolutions at a general meeting. Thus minority shareholders may appear to be powerless in the hands of the directors and of the other members. To redress the balance, some rights of members are especially useful to protect the position of a minority shareholder within the company.

12.7.1 The right to have an item placed on the agenda for an AGM (CA 1985, s 376)

This right is available to holders of at least 5 per cent of the company's shares (see **12.5.12**).

12.7.2 The right to circulate a written statement (CA 1985, s 376)

This right too can be exercised by a member or members holding at least 5 per cent of the company's shares (see **12.5.13**).

12.7.3 The right to refuse to consent to short notice

An AGM can only be held on less than 21 clear days' notice if all the members consent (CA 1985, s 369(3)), so any member can prevent this happening. An EGM can be held on short notice if a majority in number holding at least 95 per cent of the shares consents (CA 1985, s 369(4)), and therefore any member who has more than 5 per cent of the shares in the company can frustrate those who want the meeting held within the normal 14-day period. Even if an elective resolution is passed reducing the requirement of 95 per cent to a lower figure (but not less than 90 per cent), a sole minority shareholder may be in a position to prevent a meeting from being held on short notice; anyone with more than 10 per cent of the shares certainly would. In any case, such an elective resolution could only be introduced with the consent of all members.

12.7.4 The right to prevent the introduction of the elective regime (CA 1985, s 379A)

An elective resolution requires unanimous consent and therefore any member, however small his shareholding, can prevent the introduction of any or all of the elements of the elective regime (see **10.7**).

12.7.5 The right not to be unfairly prejudiced (CA 1985, s 459)

Any member can petition (see **12.5.14**).

12.7.6 The right to have the company wound up (IA 1986, s 122(1)(g))

Any member can petition (see **12.5.15**).

12.7.7 The right to call an EGM (CA 1985, s 368)

Holders of at least 10 per cent of the company's shares can exercise this right (see **12.5.9**).

12.7.8 The right to restrain an ultra vires act (CA 1985, s 35(2))

Any member can take action (see **12.5.11**).

12.7.9 The right to block a special resolution

This can be done provided that the member holds more than 25 per cent of the company's shares.

12.8 SUMMARIES AND CHECKLISTS

12.8.1 Power of membership

SHAREHOLDING	WHAT THEY CAN DO	RESTRICTIONS
100%	anything	– legality
75%	pass special resolution	– fraud on minority – *Clemens v Clemens* – weighted voting rights – unfair prejudice
50%+	pass ordinary resolution	– fraud on minority – *Clemens v Clemens* – weighted voting rights – unfair prejudice
25%+	block special resolution	
10%	– call EGM – demand poll vote	
5%	– have item on agenda for AGM – circulate a written statement	
any shareholder	– vote – notice of GMs – dividend – share certificates – name on register – copy of accounts – AGM – inspect minutes – ask court for EGM – restrain ultra vires act – unfair prejudice – winding up – block written and elective resolutions	– see above – if declared – subject to articles – before legal obligation incurred – if company solvent

12.8.2 General meetings

(a) Examples of reasons for calling:

- to change constitution (articles, name, objects, capital)
- to give directors authority to issue shares, buy-back shares, etc

- to approve directors service contracts over 5 years, substantial property transactions involving directors, etc

- to suspend restriction on directors voting

- to suspend pre-emption rights on issue of new shares

- to declare dividends (if recommended)

(b) Who calls?

- AGM – the board of directors (unless excluded by elective resolution)

- EGM – the board of directors, whenever it thinks fit
  – members holding 10 per cent shares can requisition a meeting (s 368)

- Any member can apply to the court (s 371) for either type of meeting

Note: Written resolution can be signed by all members instead of holding a general meeting (unless proposed resolution to dismiss a director or the auditor)

(c) Notice

- Agenda – normally decided by the directors

    – AGM – holders of 5 per cent shares can have item included on the agenda (s 376)

    – EGM – members decide the agenda if they requisition a meeting (s 368)

    – if meeting ordered by the court on member's application, member's proposed resolutions included

- Contents – date, time, place, type of meeting (AGM or EGM)

    – proxy notice

    – exact wording of special, extraordinary and elective resolutions

    – general notice of ordinary resolutions

- Length of notice

TYPE OF MEETING	NOTICE	SHORT NOTICE?	MEMBERS' RIGHTS
AGM	21 clear days	unanimous consent	– item on agenda – circulate statement
EGM	21/14 clear days	majority in number holding 95% (90%) shares	– circulate statement – call meeting

12.8.3 Resolutions

TYPE	NOTICE	VOTES NEEDED TO PASS
special	21 clear days	75% (of those present and voting)
extraordinary	AGM – 21 clear days EGM – 14 clear days	75% (of those present and voting)
ordinary	AGM – 21 clear days EGM – 14 clear days NB – 21 clear days if resolution is to appoint a director	50%+ (simple majority of those present and voting)
elective	21 clear days	100% (unanimous consent of all members entitled to vote)

12.8.4 After meeting

- File with registrar

    – all special, extraordinary and elective resolutions

    – altered memorandum/articles

    – appropriate forms

    – some ordinary resolutions, eg
    - increased capital
    - authorise share issue (or revoke s 80 authority)
    - cancel elective resolution

- Update statutory books, eg
    - register of members
    - register of directors
    - register of directors' interests
    - minute book

12.8.5 Special and Extraordinary Resolutions

Special resolutions are required in the following cases.

Under the Companies Act 1985:

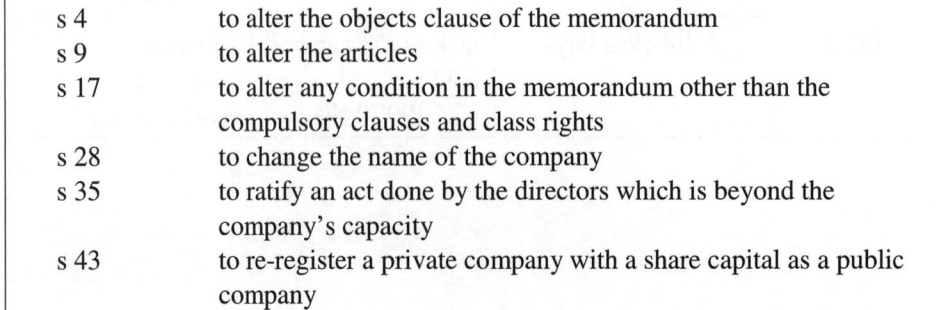

s 4	to alter the objects clause of the memorandum
s 9	to alter the articles
s 17	to alter any condition in the memorandum other than the compulsory clauses and class rights
s 28	to change the name of the company
s 35	to ratify an act done by the directors which is beyond the company's capacity
s 43	to re-register a private company with a share capital as a public company
ss 43–48	to re-register an unlimited private company as a public company

s 51	to re-register an unlimited (private) company as limited
s 53	to re-register a public company as a private company
s 95	to withdraw or modify the statutory pre-emption rights
s 120	to create reserve capital
s 135	to reduce capital with the consent of the court
s 155	to approve the giving of financial assistance by a private company for the acquisition of shares in itself
ss 164–165	authority to purchase own shares 'off market'
s 173	to approve a payment out of capital by a private company for the redemption or purchase of its own shares
s 307	to make the liability of the directors unlimited
s 308	to approve the assignment of office by a director

Under the Insolvency Act 1986:

s 84	to wind up voluntarily
s 110	to sanction the sale of the company's property, by the liquidator in a members' voluntary winding up, for shares in another company
s 122	to effect a winding up by the court

Extraordinary resolutions are required in the following cases.

Companies Act 1985, s 125: at a class meeting to sanction a variation of class rights in certain circumstances.

Insolvency Act 1986, s 84: to wind up the company voluntarily because it cannot continue its business because of its liabilities.

Insolvency Act 1986, s 165 and Sch 4: in a members' voluntary winding up, to sanction the exercise by the liquidator of the following powers:

(i) to pay any class of creditors in full;
(ii) to make a compromise or arrangement with creditors;
(iii) to compromise all calls, debts and claims between the company and a contributory or other debtor.

Editor's note: some of the above sections are not on the LPC course but are included in this table for completeness and to aid you when you are in practice. No claims are made that these are absolutely all the possible instances when special or extraordinary resolutions are required!

Chapter 13

DIRECTORS

13.1 INTRODUCTION

The directors of a company are the people who manage the company. They take business decisions and make trading contracts on the company's behalf. The company exists as a legal person but needs agents to act on its behalf. The directors are the company's agents and they have a considerable amount of power within the company structure. As a result, various safeguards are usually built into the company structure, both by statute and by the articles, in order to protect members. These subject the directors to a large number of restrictions and controls. Generally, the directors, like the members, are protected from personal liability by the fact of the company being 'limited', but there are a number of exceptions to this.

13.2 APPOINTMENT

The first directors of any company will be those persons named as directors on Form 10. They will automatically become directors on incorporation of the company.

Subsequently, directors can be appointed either by an ordinary resolution of the members in general meeting or by a resolution of the board. Whichever method is adopted, the procedural requirements will be laid down by the articles of the company. If the appointment is at a general meeting to replace a director who is removed at the same general meeting, then a 'special notice' of the resolution must be given by the proposing shareholder(s) to the company as required by CA 1985, s 303(2) (see **13.15.2**).

Where appointment is to be made by the members, a detailed procedure is set out in Table A (arts 76–79) which requires specific information to be given to the company and to the members (the same information as is required on Form 10 and also appears on the register of directors) within various time-limits. Table A also requires 21 clear days' notice of the meeting to be given to the members where a resolution must be given by the proposing shareholders to the company as to be proposed concerning the appointment of a director, even though the resolution is only an ordinary resolution (Table A, art 38).

It is much simpler for a new director to be appointed by the existing board. However, under Table A (art 79), such an appointee holds office only until the next AGM, at which point his continued position is subject to re-appointment by the members.

Any person seeking appointment as a director must be prepared to sign a form (Form 288a) indicating his consent to act as a director. Thus a person cannot be appointed to office against his will or without his knowledge.

Chapter 13 contents
Introduction
Appointment
The register of directors
Notification to the registrar
Remuneration (fees) for non-executive directors
Directors' service contracts
Liability of directors
Powers of directors
Board meetings: calling and conduct
General duties ('fiduciary' duties)
Statutory duties
Statutory restrictions on directors
Disqualification of directors by the court
Disqualification under the articles
Removal from office by members
Summaries and checklists

13.2.1 Number of directors

Normally a company can have as many directors as are required, but it must have at least two (Table A, art 64). If a different minimum number is required (eg if there is to be only one director or it is felt that there should always be four directors), then either a special article to this effect should be included on formation of the company or the existing articles should be changed by special resolution of the members.

13.2.2 Qualification shares

Although not required by statute or by Table A, it is sometimes thought to be appropriate to require directors to hold qualification shares, ie they are required to own at least a certain number of the company's shares in order to qualify for the office of director in that company. Any such requirement will appear as a special article of the company. This is of more significance in a large company than in a small one, as in many small companies the tendency is for most, if not all, directors to be shareholders as well.

13.2.3 Chairman of the board

The directors usually have the power in the articles to elect one of themselves to be the chairman (Table A, art 91). Nominally the chairman is the head of the company, although he has no special powers other than his casting vote in the event of an equal vote for and against a resolution if the articles so permit. Table A, arts 88 and 50 give the chairman the casting vote at board and general meetings, respectively. Even this one privilege may not be preserved by the articles if it is thought to be inappropriate. The main task for the chairman is to take charge at board and general meetings and to preserve order. The chairman is appointed and can be removed from his position by the board at any time.

13.2.4 Managing director

The directors also usually have the power to appoint a managing director, to whom they usually give authority to run the company on a day-to-day basis (Table A, art 72: see **13.8.1**). The board will fix the terms of the managing director's service contract, including the level of remuneration he is to receive. The managing director must be a director of the company, so if he is removed from the position of director he automatically also loses the managing directorship. The power to remove the managing director from office also lies with the board of directors. Any director holding the office of managing director (or other executive office – see **13.2.5**) is excluded from the requirement in Table A, art 73 that directors must retire by rotation (see **13.15.1**).

13.2.5 Executive and non-executive directors

Broadly speaking, an executive director is involved in the day-to-day management of the company, whereas a non-executive director merely attends board meetings.

In the past, non-executive directors were often well known personalities in the business world or members of the nobility whose reputation, or fancy title, gave some additional status to the reputation of the company. Today, non-executive directors are expected to be more involved, for example by monitoring the management of the company's affairs by its executive directors. They will often be encountered in public companies but much less frequently in private (Limited) companies.

13.2.6 Shadow directors

A person is a shadow director if he gives directions or instructions to the directors of a company and those directors are accustomed to act in accordance with his directions or instructions (CA 1985, s 741(2)). A person advising in a professional capacity does not become liable as a shadow director under this provision. In the case of *Secretary of State for Trade and Industry v Deverell and Another* (1999) unreported, the Court of Appeal held that a shadow director was anyone, other than a professional adviser, who exercised real influence in the corporate affairs of a company. Many of the provisions of the Companies Act 1985 which apply to directors also apply to shadow directors, eg CA 1985, s 317 on disclosure by directors of interests in contracts.

13.2.7 Alternate directors

An alternate director is someone who attends board meetings in place of the real director, ie a stand-in director. The ability to send a substitute to board meetings is governed by the articles of the company. Under Table A, directors are permitted to appoint alternate directors, but there are restrictions on their choice (Table A, art 65). They can appoint another director of the company as their alternate, in which case that other director would have his own vote plus the absentee director's vote (ie he would have two votes as opposed to the usual one for each director). If a director wishes to appoint an outsider as his substitute, this is permissible only under Table A if the appointee is someone of whom the other directors approve, so board approval must be sought before the appointment can be effective.

An alternate director should be given notice of all meetings, and can attend and vote in the same way as the real director (Table A, art 66).

13.3 THE REGISTER OF DIRECTORS

Whenever and however directors are appointed, their names must be entered in the register of directors, together with certain information, for example details of other directorships, nationality and occupation. This register must be altered whenever there is a change in the composition of the board.

13.4 NOTIFICATION TO THE REGISTRAR

Except for the first directors of the company named on Form 10, whenever a director is appointed to or removed from office the registrar of companies must be informed by sending either Form 288a (appointment) or Form 288b (resignation) to Companies House. Where a new director is being appointed, his signed consent to act must appear on Form 288a. Any change in the particulars of a director or secretary (eg change of address) should be notified on Form 288c.

13.5 REMUNERATION (FEES) FOR NON-EXECUTIVE DIRECTORS

Being a director of a company is not necessarily a full-time job (see **13.2.5** and **13.10.3**). If a director merely attends board meetings (a non-executive director), then he would not expect a service contract giving him a salary. This would be more appropriate where the director was also working for the company in some other capacity as an employee, for example as head of sales or as marketing director. However, where a person is appointed to be a director of a company and does give up his own time to attend board meetings (albeit without devoting any other time to the company's business), he will expect some financial recompense. This is given in the form of directors' fees, the amount of which is decided by the members in general meeting (Table A, art 82).

13.6 DIRECTORS' SERVICE CONTRACTS

Where directors are to work for the company not just as directors but in some other, often full-time, capacity, they are likely to want written service contracts (contracts of employment). Such directors are known as executive directors.

13.6.1 Contracts awarded by the board

Directors are empowered to award service contracts to themselves (Table A, art 84). The board will decide the terms of each service contract, including the amount of salary to be paid to each such director and any authority the director is to have to act on behalf of the board (Table A, art 72 – see **13.8.1**).

When service contracts are being discussed and voted upon at a board meeting, the directors who are to be awarded the service contracts must declare formally to the board that they have a personal interest in this matter (CA 1985, s 317). There are restrictions on these directors concerning voting and counting in the quorum for that meeting. Under Table A, art 97, each service contract can be taken as a separate issue, and a director can vote and count in the quorum on every other director's service contract, but not on his own. This will create a problem where there are only two directors and the quorum for board meetings is, as in Table A, two. The problem can be overcome either by changing the articles (by special resolution of the members) to allow directors to vote whenever interested in the matter (including in relation to their own service contracts), which would perhaps be seen as undesirable in the interests of fairness. The alternative is to relax temporarily the rules on voting and counting in the quorum on this particular resolution by ordinary resolution of the members (Table A, art 96).

13.6.2 Fixed-term contracts

Sometimes directors will think it appropriate to award themselves fixed-term contracts, under which they are contractually guaranteed to be employed for a certain period of time. For example, one of the directors may, by his service contract, be appointed for a period of 10 years. The advantage of this type of contract is that if the company breaches the contract by removing him from this job within the 10-year period, the now ex-director can claim damages, the amount of which would be based on the salary he would have received over the whole 10-year period had he not been dismissed.

Where directors are proposing to award themselves service contracts for a fixed term greater than 5 years, they are required to obtain the prior consent of the members in a general meeting by ordinary resolution (CA 1985, s 319). Where they call a general meeting for this purpose, all the proposed terms of the service contracts in question must be available for inspection by members at the meeting and for 15 days prior to the meeting at the registered office. If a written resolution of the members is to be used instead of calling a meeting, the terms of the proposed service contracts must be sent out to members with the written resolution itself (CA 1985, Sch 15A(7)).

If the approval of the members is not sought and obtained, the service contract will still be effective, save for the clause stating that the director is to be employed for a fixed term. Instead of that director's job being guaranteed for a specified period of time, the contract will be capable of termination on reasonable notice. All the rest of the terms of the contract decided upon by the directors will be valid and enforceable against the company, but the fixed-term element will not. Therefore, if the director concerned were to be dismissed in breach of contract, his damages would be based not on the fixed period of time stated, but on the period of time deemed by the court to be 'reasonable notice'.

13.6.3 Inspection of service contracts

Copies of all directors' service contracts must be kept at the registered office where they are open to inspection by members (CA 1985, s 318). The exceptions are those for a fixed term with less than 12 months of the term still remaining and those for an indefinite term where the notice period required is less than 12 months. Members may wish to check the service contract of any director they are proposing to dismiss to ascertain the likely cost of removing him in breach of contract.

13.7 LIABILITY OF DIRECTORS

Generally, in the absence of misconduct, directors have no liability whatsoever for any debts they incur on the company's behalf. If a director is also a shareholder in a company which goes into insolvent liquidation, then the worst that can happen to that director is that he loses his job as director, together with the salary that goes with it. He also loses whatever money he invested in the company when he bought his shares.

Although this is the general rule, there are situations where a director can incur personal liability.

13.7.1 Personal guarantees

It is common for banks to require that directors personally guarantee any loan to a company, particularly where the company is a small company or a new company. In this case, the risk of the bank's loan being in excess of the company's assets is greater. This effectively destroys the advantage of limited liability enjoyed by those trading as a company, because it means that if the company is unable to repay the loan for any reason, that debt is enforceable against the director and all his personal assets. If this happens the effect may be that the director is forced into bankruptcy. Directors often have little choice but to accept this however, because without the personal guarantees the bank is unlikely to approve the loan to the company.

13.7.2 Acting while disqualified

If a person who has been disqualified as a director by the court (see **13.13**) acts in breach of that order, he thereby incurs personal liability for any debts incurred by the company during the period in which he illegally acted as a director.

13.7.3 Wrongful trading

A director is trading wrongfully when, broadly, he knows or ought to know that the company is likely to go into insolvent liquidation and he fails to take action to minimise the loss to the company's creditors (see **24.8.4**). Although a director who is found by the court to have been trading wrongfully does not actually become directly liable for the company's debts, he can be required to contribute to the assets of the company where the company is in the process of liquidation (IA 1986, s 214).

13.7.4 Fraudulent trading

Actions for fraudulent trading are possible only when the company is in the process of being wound up voluntarily or due to insolvency. A director is liable under this provision if he is knowingly a party to fraudulent trading, ie if he is carrying on the business and continuing to incur debts on the company's behalf at a time when he knew there was little or no prospect of those debts being paid on time or within a reasonable period (see **24.8.3**). Any director found to have been trading fraudulently can be required by the court to contribute to the company's assets, although, as with wrongful trading, he does not become directly liable for debts incurred by the company (IA 1986, s 213).

13.7.5 Breach of warranty of authority

Where a director purports to act on behalf of the company, but is acting outside the scope of his actual and apparent authority, he may not bind the company by his actions. This liability is based on the assumption that the director has impliedly warranted to an outsider that he has the authority to enter into the contract. If he has exceeded the powers of himself, or of the board of directors, or of the company, then he has broken that warranty and he is liable accordingly.

Section 35B of the Companies Act 1985 provides that an outsider dealing with a company is not bound to check on the powers of the directors or of the company. Section 35A provides that, as regards an outsider, the power of the directors to bind the company shall not be limited by the company's constitution, ie the outsider is not affected by any such restraints inside the company.

In addition, the company could also be liable (as well as the director) under the common law principle of 'holding out' where the director is allowed to deal with third parties in a way which would normally imply authority to enter into such contracts.

13.7.6 Failure to maintain company records

All directors and officers of the company are required to maintain proper up-to-date records both at Companies House and internally (the statutory books). Under CA 1985, ss 722 and 723, the relevant information to be kept in 'books' or other registers may in fact instead be kept as computer records, and printed out whenever required. Failure to keep proper records renders those in default liable to a fine (CA 1985, s 730 and Sch 24).

13.8 POWERS OF DIRECTORS

Generally, directors are given most of the powers of management required to run the company, and they exercise these powers by passing resolutions at board meetings. Their powers will be given to them by the articles. The usual provision is that they can do anything not required to be done by the members in general meeting either by statute or by the articles themselves (Table A, art 70).

Once directors have been given a certain power, that power then belongs to the board and cannot generally be exercised by the members. This means that the members cannot overrule the board or retrospectively alter a decision of the board. All that members can do if they dislike the way in which the directors are running the company is to alter the composition of the board, or change the articles by special resolution to take certain powers from the board. Both of these affect the position only in the future and have no retrospective effect. However, if directors become unable to exercise their powers, for example if the board is deadlocked, then powers may revert to the members.

13.8.1 Delegation of powers

Generally, directors are required to exercise their powers by acting as a board. However, it is usual to find in the articles of a company certain provisions which enable directors to delegate some, if not all, of their functions (Table A, art 72).

If the board decides to appoint a managing director (see **13.2.4**), the board will, at the same time, decide which powers are to be delegated to him. It is common to give the managing director the ability to make day-to-day decisions on behalf of the company, more radical and important issues being reserved to the board as a whole. The managing director can be given all or any of the powers of the board, but these can be varied or withdrawn at any time by the board.

Directors can also delegate their functions to employees of the company, and will not be personally liable for failure by those employees to carry out their tasks satisfactorily, unless circumstances existed whereby the director concerned should have been on warning that the relevant employee might prove incompetent.

If a director is unable to attend one or more board meetings, he could appoint an alternate director to be there in his place, so delegating his powers to the alternate director (see **13.2.6**).

13.8.2 Authority of directors

People who are appointed as directors of a company have certain authority to bind the company. They will have actual authority in the articles, and they will have apparent (ostensible) authority because they hold the position of director. For example, the managing director will have apparent authority to make day-to-day business decisions on behalf of the company because that is what is expected from the holder of that office.

Directors will bind the company if they act with either actual or apparent authority. If they exceed this they will not bind the company, and they will be personally liable for breach of warranty of authority to any third party with whom they were dealing.

13.8.3 The chairman of the board

Table A, art 91 provides that the directors may appoint one of their number as chairman of the board of directors. They may remove him from office at any time. He chairs every meeting at which he is present and is willing so to do. If he is not willing, or is not present 5 minutes after the start of the meeting, the directors present may appoint one of their number to be the chairman of the meeting.

13.9 BOARD MEETINGS: CALLING AND CONDUCT

13.9.1 Notice

Any director can call a board meeting at any time on reasonable notice (Table A, art 88). There is no need for notice of a board meeting to be in writing, but it must be given to every director who is not out of the country. What amounts to reasonable notice will depend upon how serious or controversial are the issues to be discussed, and upon the composition of the board. For example, if all directors work full time for the company and there is a mundane decision to be made, any one director could call a board meeting on, say, 5 minutes' notice. However, more notice would be needed if some of the directors were not present, or if a major or sensitive issue was to be the subject of discussion.

13.9.2 Voting

At a board meeting, each director has one vote and all resolutions can be passed by majority vote. If there is an equal number of votes for and against a resolution there is a deadlock and the negative view prevails, which means that the resolution is defeated. The chairman may be able to ensure that the resolution is passed by using his casting vote, depending on whether he has been given this power in the articles (Table A, art 88 gives the chairman a casting vote). If the chairman's casting vote has been removed by a special article, then, where the voting is deadlocked, the rule is that the negative view prevails and therefore the resolution is defeated.

Directors must be aware of any restrictions in the articles on their capacity to participate in voting on matters where they have a personal interest (direct or indirect) in the outcome of the vote. For example, if a director is a shareholder in another company with which the company of which he is a director is proposing to make a contract, then clearly he has a personal interest in that contract. Another example of a personal interest is where a director wants to acquire more shares in the company and the directors meet to decide whether or not to allot to him the number of shares he has requested at the price he has offered to pay. Whenever a director has a personal interest, he must declare that interest to his co-directors at the first board meeting at which the matter is discussed (CA 1985, s 317). Even where the director concerned may think it obvious to his fellow directors that he has such a personal interest, it is still necessary for him to make the formal declaration. If he fails to do so, he commits a criminal offence and any resulting contract is voidable at the instance of the company.

Having made the necessary declaration, the director concerned may then be unable to vote on this particular issue, depending on the articles. Table A, art 94 prevents a director with a personal interest from voting on most relevant matters but provides a limited number of narrow exceptions. The main one is that a director can participate in the voting where he is buying shares in the company or lending money to the company (art 94(c)).

13.9.3 Quorum

The quorum for a board meeting is two (Table A, art 89) unless the directors themselves decide otherwise or there is a special article varying the number required. Any director unable to vote on a matter because he has a personal interest (see **13.9.2**) is also prevented from counting in the quorum (Table A, art 95). This may cause problems for any company where the directors are personally guaranteeing a loan to the company and therefore they all have a personal interest because it is not clear whether an exception in art 94 applies to this situation. It can be particularly frustrating in a small company where the result of this rule may be that it is impossible to obtain a quorum on a number of issues.

13.9.4 Resolving the problems

If there is any dispute over the ability of a particular director to vote and count in the quorum on any issue, it is the chairman who must decide this and his decision is final (Table A, art 98).

The restrictions on directors voting and counting in the quorum can be overcome in various ways. When the company is formed, a special article can be included allowing directors to vote and count in the quorum even where they have a personal interest in the matter under discussion. Alternatively, at a later stage, the articles can be changed by special resolution of the members to remove the restrictions imposed by Table A and allow more freedom. Another possibility is that the rules can be relaxed or suspended by the members passing an ordinary resolution to this effect (Table A, art 96). Even where one of these possible courses of action is adopted by the company and directors are allowed to participate at board meetings irrespective of their personal involvement, they must still remember to declare any personal interest to the other directors, as this requirement cannot be dispensed with. There is a special provision when the subject under discussion is that of directors' service contracts (Table A, art 97) which enables each director to vote and count in the quorum on all other service contracts except his own.

13.9.5 Minutes

Minutes must be written up for every board meeting (Table A, art 100) and kept at the registered office. They are open to inspection there by the directors, but not by the members. The minutes for each meeting will usually be signed by the chairman as being an authentic record of the business transacted at that meeting.

13.9.6 Use of written resolutions

If there is a possibility that all directors will agree to a proposed resolution, that resolution could be passed as a written resolution without the need to hold a board meeting. A copy of the proposed resolution should be sent to every director and if each director then signs his copy of the resolution and returns it to the company the resolution is validly passed: unanimous consent is necessary (Table A, art 93).

13.10 GENERAL DUTIES ('FIDUCIARY' DUTIES)

Directors are in a position of trust within the company and as such they owe certain duties to the company. Their duty, however, is to the company and not to the shareholders. They might owe a duty to shareholders where, for example, they agreed to act as agents for the members, or they assumed responsibility for giving advice to members, but generally it is the best interests of the company that directors must have in mind.

The duties of directors have evolved through decisions of the courts. Although the Companies Act 1985 regulates certain activities of directors, it does not impose any general duty of good faith or competence. The duties of directors are an amalgamation of several elements.

(1) *Agent*, in that the director acts not on his own behalf but that of the company.
(2) *Trustee*, in that he controls the assets and exercises powers for the company's benefit, not his own. As such, he owes fiduciary duties to the company.
(3) *Employee*, in that an executive director is an employee with the same rights and duties to those of any other employee.
(4) *Professional adviser*, in that he renders services for reward (even as a non-executive fee earner) and must accept the burden of skill and care which falls upon independent contractors of that type.

The duties imposed on directors break down into two broad categories – 'good faith' and 'skill and care'.

13.10.1 Not to make a secret profit

In relation to company property, the directors' position can be said to be similar to that of trustees. Company property includes money, tangible assets and also confidential information such as trade secrets and details of business opportunities. If any company property is misapplied, the directors are answerable as trustees. Therefore, directors should not allow their personal interests and their duty to the company to conflict. For example, if a director is in possession of information about business opportunities such as contracts soon to be available, and he has gained this information solely because he holds the office of director in the company, then he should not use that information to his own advantage, ie he should not enter into the contract in his personal name and take the profit from it. If he does so, he will be obliged to account to the company for any profit made unless he fully discloses all relevant facts to the members of the company and obtains their approval by ordinary resolution at a general meeting. Members can only ratify directors' actions in this way if doing so would not constitute a fraud on the minority, ie if the directors concerned are not themselves the majority shareholders (see **12.6.1**).

The articles of most companies, however (Table A, art 85), now contain a relieving provision permitting a director to have personal interests separate from those of the company and to keep any profit resulting from those personal interests, provided he discloses to the board the full nature and extent of any such interests, and he is not cheating the company. For example, if a director is awarded a service contract at a realistic salary by the board, he can keep his 'profit' (his salary) by virtue of this provision of Table A. However, if a director sells an asset to the company for a price substantially in excess of what the asset is worth, he does not gain the protection of art 85.

13.10.2 Not to exceed or abuse their powers

As they are in a fiduciary position, directors owe a general duty of good faith to the company and should therefore exercise only the powers they have been given by the articles of the company and should not exceed those powers. In addition, the directors should use the powers they have been given for the purpose for which they were given, and not for some unauthorised reason (eg to enable them to keep control of the company). The directors could ask the members to sanction the use of their powers for an unusual reason by ordinary resolution at a general meeting, but only where this would not constitute a fraud on the minority.

13.10.3 Duty of skill and care

The standard of skill required of directors is judged on a subjective basis. They are required to exercise the degree of competence which could reasonably be expected from someone with their degree of knowledge and experience. It therefore follows that, for example, a higher standard is imposed on a director who is professionally qualified or who has had years of experience than on a complete newcomer to the business world. The standard of care required of directors is judged on an objective basis. They are required to exercise the degree of care which a reasonable person would exercise on his own behalf.

All that directors are obliged to do is to attend board meetings and to vote on the proposed resolutions when they are reasonably able to do so. A person may be a non-executive director (broadly a director who does not hold a full-time position in the company), but it is common for directors also to hold an executive position with the company, eg sales director, and thus be full-time employees of the company. A full-time director may owe duties of skill and care under a service contract.

13.10.4 Breach of duty

If a director does act in breach of any of his fiduciary duties owed to the company, the company (ie either the other directors, if they constitute a majority of the board, or the members), can take action against him for breach of duty, requiring him to compensate the company for any loss it has suffered and/or to account to the company for any profit made.

13.11 STATUTORY DUTIES

Various duties are also imposed upon directors of a company by statute. One of the ways in which the Companies Act 1985 exercises control over directors is that it requires that certain information cannot be kept secret.

13.11.1 Declaration of personal interests

If a director has a personal interest (direct or indirect) in any matter to be discussed at a board meeting, he must formally declare to his co-directors that he has such an interest (CA 1985, s 317). He may be prevented from voting on that matter and counting in the quorum (depending on the terms of the company's articles).

13.11.2 Service contracts

Even where approval of the members is not required because the service contract is not for a fixed term exceeding 5 years, members still have the right to inspect the terms of directors' service contracts at the registered office (CA 1985, s 318). Contracts capable of lawful termination within 12 months do not have to be lodged at the registered office for inspection.

13.11.3 Annual accounts

It is the directors' responsibility to ensure that full accounts are produced each year and that they are sent to all members within 10 months of the accounting reference date (the final day of the company's accounting year to which the accounts are made up).

The accounts consist of:

(1) a profit and loss account, which shows whether the company has made a profit or a loss over the last year;
(2) a balance sheet, which sets out the company's financial position on a specified day, the accounting reference date;
(3) the auditor's report, which should say whether these final accounts present a true and fair view of the company's finances; and
(4) details of any loans to directors in the last year (loans to directors are generally forbidden but there are exceptions (see **13.2.4**)), details of directors' salaries and directors' pensions and any situations in the last year when directors have had personal interests in proposed contracts;
(5) the directors' report, which deals with what has happened to the company over the last year.

The accounts must also be sent to the registrar of companies each year, whereupon they become a public document open to public inspection. The time-limit within which they must be sent to Companies House is also 10 months from the accounting reference date. 'Small' and 'medium-sized' companies are permitted to deliver abbreviated accounts to the registrar giving less detailed information than companies which do not qualify for this concession, but they must still supply full accounts to their members. The auditor will certify that for this purpose a company can be categorised as 'small' or 'medium-sized'.

Auditing of accounts is not required in the case of very small private companies – those with a turnover of less than £350,000 and a balance sheet total of less than £1.4 million.

13.11.4 The annual return

It is the directors' responsibility to submit an annual return (Form 363) to the registrar within 28 days after its 'return date' (the date to which the annual return is made up) (CA 1985, s 363(1)). A company's first return date is the anniversary of its incorporation. Otherwise, it is the anniversary of the previous return date.

The annual return is designed to ensure that the information at Companies House is kept up to date. In practice, the registrar of companies will send Form 363 to the company partially completed, using the information already stored at Companies House. It is then for the company to check the accuracy of the information, to complete the form as necessary and then to return it to the registrar. The information required on the annual return is the address of the registered office, details of the company's main business activities, details of the directors and the company secretary, details of issued share capital, the names of past and present members and whether elective resolutions are in force dispensing with AGMs or with the need to lay the annual accounts before the members. All this information is kept at Companies House and is available to anyone who chooses to make a company search.

The fee for filing an annual return is £15.

13.11.5 The register of directors

Details about each director (name, address, business occupation, date of birth, nationality and details of other directorships) must appear on the register.

13.11.6 The register of directors' interests

The register of directors' interests records the number of shares and debentures in the company held by each director. It also records the number of shares or debentures held by the spouse of any director and by his children under the age of 18. It is the responsibility of each director to notify the company formally of such holdings of shares or debentures within 5 days of him either becoming a director or acquiring the shares or debentures, and the company secretary will then enter that information on the register of directors' interests.

13.11.7 Notepaper

To prevent the public being misled, either the names of all directors must appear on the company notepaper or the names of none of them (CA 1985, s 305).

13.11.8 Contracts with a director who is also the sole member

Where a contract is to be made between the company and the only member of that company, and that sole member is also a director of the company, then either the contract itself must be in writing or the terms of the contract must be set out in a written memorandum or must be recorded in the minutes of the first board meeting following the making of the contract (CA 1985, s 322B). If this is not done, the company and every officer in default is liable to a fine. This provision is also relevant to the situation where a contract is proposed between the company and a sole member who is also a shadow director.

13.12 STATUTORY RESTRICTIONS ON DIRECTORS

The board is limited by statute in various ways. Certain actions are forbidden and some things can only be done with the consent of the members.

13.12.1 Gratuitous compensation to directors

If a director is removed from office, he may be entitled to compensation for breach of contract or for unfair dismissal or a redundancy payment. These are payments to which the director is legally entitled, and such payments can be made by the directors without needing to consult the members. However, if the board wishes to pay a director who is leaving a 'golden handshake', ie a genuinely gratuitous payment (eg as an expression of appreciation for years of loyal service), they are required to obtain the prior approval of members by ordinary resolution (CA 1985, s 312).

13.12.2 Substantial property transactions

If a director, in his personal capacity, is buying something from or selling something to the company, then the prior consent of the members by ordinary resolution is necessary if the asset being bought or sold is of 'requisite value', ie a substantial property transaction (CA 1985, s 320). If the asset in question is worth less than £2,000, it is not of requisite value and the transaction will not be a substantial property transaction. If the asset is worth more than £100,000, it will always be a substantial property transaction. If the asset being bought or sold is worth between £2,000 and £100,000 then it will qualify as being of requisite value if it is worth more than 10 per cent of the company's net relevant assets (the net assets figure shown on the latest set of accounts or, if no accounts have been prepared, the amount of the company's called-up share capital). This provision also covers other dealings with non-cash assets, for example charging or leasing an asset of requisite value (see CA 1985, s 739(2)).

If a substantial property transaction takes place without the members' authority being obtained in advance, the contract is voidable by the company and the director who was party to the transaction and any other director who authorised the transaction become liable to indemnify the company for any loss it has suffered and to account to the company for any gain they have made.

This provision applies to all directors of a company, including any shadow directors.

On incorporation of a business, it is very likely that s 320 will be relevant as the former partners or sole trader will become directors of the new company (which has a net asset value of virtually nil) and will sell their business to the company. The business will inevitably be worth more than 10 per cent of the company's net relevant assets.

NB Section 320 is also relevant to transactions between the company and persons 'connected' with a director (eg family members – spouses and children under 18, companies with which the Director is 'associated' (broadly, where the director owns 20 per cent of the shares) and partners acting in their capacity as partners) (CA 1985, s 346).

13.12.3 Service contracts

If directors wish to award themselves service contracts for a fixed term in excess of 5 years, the prior approval of the members in general meeting by ordinary resolution is necessary (CA 1985, s 319).

If such approval is not obtained in advance, although the rest of the terms contained in the service contract are valid, the fixed term is ineffective and the contract is terminable on reasonable notice (see **13.6.2**).

13.12.4 Loans to directors

Generally, loans to directors (including shadow directors) are unlawful (CA 1985, s 330), but there are limited exceptions where to make loans is permissible, for example small amounts of money can be lent. In fact, in a private company, breach of s 330 is not a criminal offence and the section therefore has no sanction to enforce it other than simply giving the company the right to recover the loan at any time.

Nevertheless, if money is lent to a director in breach of the statutory restriction then the director who borrowed the money and any other director who authorised the loan may be required to account to the company for any profit made and to indemnify the company against any loss it has suffered.

13.12.5 Interests of employees

There is a statutory obligation imposed on directors (and shadow directors) to have regard to the interests of the employees of the company (CA 1985, s 309). It may sometimes be necessary therefore to balance the interest of members against those of employees where the two do not coincide. However, employees have no right to enforce this obligation.

13.13 DISQUALIFICATION OF DIRECTORS BY THE COURT

The court has power to disqualify individuals from holding the office of director under the Company Directors Disqualification Act 1986 (CDDA 1986). The period of disqualification can range from 2 to 15 years. The director's previous behaviour and the seriousness of the current offence will be relevant in determining the length of disqualification.

A director can be disqualified by the court if he is guilty of general misconduct in relation to the running of a company, for example if he has been found guilty of a criminal offence in conjunction with running a company (CDDA 1986, s 2) or has been in persistent default in complying with the filing requirements (CDDA 1986, s 3); if he is thought to be unfit to hold the office of director (CDDA 1986, s 6), which the court may consider to be the case if the director has been disqualified previously; or if he has been found liable for wrongful trading (CDDA 1986, s 10), ie if he knew or ought to have known that the company was likely to go into insolvent liquidation and at that point failed to take every step to minimise the loss to creditors.

13.14 DISQUALIFICATION UNDER THE ARTICLES

It is usual for the articles of a company to provide that in certain circumstances a person is disqualified from acting as a director. Article 81 of Table A provides that a director shall automatically cease to hold office in a variety of situations, for example if he is absent from board meetings for more than 6 months without permission and the board resolves that he should cease to be a director, if he becomes bankrupt or if he is mentally ill.

It is an offence for an undischarged bankrupt to act as a director except with leave of the court (CDDA 1986, s 11).

13.15 REMOVAL FROM OFFICE BY MEMBERS

13.15.1 Retirement by rotation

Table A requires directors to retire by rotation (art 73). At the first AGM of the company, all the directors are required to retire from office but will automatically be re-appointed unless a resolution to the contrary is passed by the members. At each subsequent AGM, one-third of the total number of directors must retire from office and be subject to re-election (or a number as near to one-third as can be achieved). Executive directors, including the managing director, are exempt from the requirement to retire by rotation (Table A, art 84). The other directors must take it in turns to be one of those within the one-third. It is thus open to the members to remove a director from the board when his position as director is subject to confirmation in this way.

The requirement that non-executive directors retire by rotation is an important safeguard to members as it enables them periodically to consider removal of a director from office without the need to ensure that the matter is put on the agenda for a general meeting. However, in a company where the composition of the members and the directors is largely the same, this device is unnecessary, in which case the articles can be amended by a special article excluding the relevant provisions of Table A.

13.15.2 Removal by ordinary resolution

Members always have the right to remove a director from office at any time, and this right cannot be taken from them by anything contained in the director's service contract or in the articles (CA 1985, s 303).

Any member wanting to propose a resolution to remove a director must give the company 'special notice' (CA 1985, ss 303(2) and 379). He must leave a formal notice at the registered office at least 28 days before a general meeting setting out his request. (If a director is to be appointed at the same meeting, special notice must be given of this appointment as well.)

If a general meeting has already been called for a fixed date, a member will know whether he has time before the meeting to give the required notice. However, if no date has been fixed for a general meeting, the member should give the notice to the company and then, if the directors attempt to call a general meeting within the next 28 days, the member will be deemed to have given proper notice (CA 1985, s 379(3)). This provision prevents the directors from being able to defeat the members by calling a meeting within the 28-day period.

Alternatively, the directors may try to frustrate the member's intentions by not calling a general meeting at all. There may not even be an AGM if an elective resolution dispensing with this requirement has been passed. Faced with this situation, a member could either request an AGM and, providing he owns at least 5 per cent of the shares in the company, use his right to have an item included on the agenda for an AGM to ensure that the resolution was put to the meeting (see **12.5.2**) or, if he owns at least 10 per cent of the shares in the company, requisition an EGM and thus fix the agenda for that meeting (see **12.5.9**).

Whenever the company receives 'special notice' of a resolution to remove a director, the board must ensure that the director concerned is informed immediately. That director then has the right to make written representations to the members and can circulate a statement in writing to them. He can also speak at the meeting, whether or not he is also a member.

An ordinary resolution is required to remove a director from office in this way, so if an EGM is called purely for this purpose, only 14 clear days' notice of the meeting is required from the company to the members (although on the wording of CA 1985, s 379(2) it is arguable that 21 days' notice is required) and only a majority of the votes cast at the meeting is needed to pass the resolution.

Before giving special notice to the company for the removal of a director, a member should check the articles to see whether or not they contain a *Bushell v Faith* clause, giving directors who are also members weighted voting rights on a resolution for their removal. Provided the director is also a member of the company, this could prevent the members from being able to remove the director from his position as director as long as his shareholding is sufficient to defeat an ordinary resolution when multiplied by the figure stated in the special article. A member wishing to remove a director should check whether it would be possible to remove the special article by passing a special resolution at a general meeting or whether directors have also been given weighted voting rights in this respect.

Even if there is no such special article, or if the multiplier is not sufficient to protect the director concerned, the member proposing the ordinary resolution should also check the director's service contract (open to inspection at the registered office) to check the amount of compensation which might be payable for breach of contract (wrongful dismissal) as it could be extremely expensive for the company to get rid of him, particularly where the director concerned has been given a long fixed-term contract.

If a director is removed from the board, then he automatically loses any executive position he might hold within the company (eg marketing director), because the two are inter-dependent. This may entitle the ex-director to make a claim against the company for wrongful dismissal, unfair dismissal, or even possibly redundancy.

If a director is removed from the board, the officers of the company are under an obligation to notify the registrar of companies by filing with him Form 288b, and must delete that person's name from the register of directors and (if also a shareholder) the register of directors' interests.

13.16 SUMMARIES AND CHECKLISTS

13.16.1 Appointment

First directors	– Form 10
Subsequently	– by board (until next AGM), or
	– by members – ordinary resolution
	– 21 clear days' notice (or consent to short notice)
	– Form 288a to registrar
	– register of directors (and register of directors' interests)
Alternate directors	– notify company (restrictions on choice)

13.16.2 Board meetings

- Called on reasonable notice by any director
- Check whether any director has a personal interest – must declare it (s 317) and may be prevented from voting and counting in the quorum (see Table A, arts 94 and 95)
- Resolutions passed by simple majority
- Can use written resolutions instead (Table A, art 93)

13.16.3 Service contracts

- Board decision – but term over 5 years' duration needs prior consent of members by ordinary resolution
- Contract kept at registered office if more than 12 months left to run

13.16.4 Disqualification

- Under Company Directors Disqualification Act 1986
- Under the articles (Table A, art 81)

13.16.5 Dismissal – procedure

- Special notice to the company 28 days prior to general meeting (if already called)
- Board informs director forthwith
- Director entitled to circulate written representations to members
- (If not already called, board calls general meeting to pass ordinary resolution. Special notice not invalidated if called within 28 days)
- Director entitled to speak at general meeting
- File Form 288b and complete register of directors (and register of directors' interests)
- *Note:* Written resolution cannot be used

13.16.6 Possible claims available to dismissed director

- Statutory employment claims – unfair dismissal, redundancy payment
- Wrongful dismissal (for breach of contract)
- Unfairly prejudicial conduct if also a member (s 459)

Chapter 14

THE COMPANY SECRETARY

14.1 INTRODUCTION

Although every company must have a company secretary, it is for the directors of that company to decide exactly what the secretary of their company should be required to do. The functions of a company secretary are not prescribed and can vary enormously, but will generally centre around the administration of the company.

14.2 APPOINTMENT

A company must have a company secretary (CA 1985, s 283). He is an officer of the company (CA 1985, s 744). The first secretary of any company will be named on Form 10 with the first directors (see **10.2.3**) but need not be a director as well. Like them, he automatically takes office when the certificate of incorporation is issued. Subsequently, if any change occurs, the company secretary is appointed by the board of directors (Table A, art 99).

14.3 TERMS AND REMUNERATION

The directors decide the contractual terms on which the company secretary is to hold office and they fix the amount of his remuneration (Table A, art 99).

14.4 FUNCTIONS

The company secretary is in charge of the administrative side of running the company. His exact duties will depend upon the requirements of the directors which are likely to be influenced by the size of the company and whether or not he works for the company full time. The full-time company secretary of a large company may be the head of an administration department; that of a small company may well hold this post as an 'extra' on top of other full-time duties, such as a director (although a sole director cannot also be the secretary: CA 1985, s 283(4)). Alternatively, a professionally qualified person, such as a solicitor or accountant, may be the company secretary, in which case the requirement that the company pays him for whatever he does in this capacity will usually restrict the activities he is asked to undertake.

The duties commonly assigned to a company secretary are to write up the minutes of board meetings and general meetings, to keep up to date the company's internal registers and to send the necessary returns to the registrar of companies.

The company secretary also has apparent authority on behalf of the company to make contracts connected with the administrative side of the company's business, for

Chapter 14 contents
Introduction
Appointment
Terms and remuneration
Functions
Removal from office

example to order hire cars. He will usually also have actual authority to enter into contracts of this type and so bind the company. He has no apparent authority to enter into trading contracts on the company's behalf, for example to borrow money in the company's name.

14.5 REMOVAL FROM OFFICE

The directors have power to remove the company secretary from office at any time (Table A, art 99). The consequences of such removal (eg whether any compensation is due for breach of contract) will depend upon the terms of the contract fixed by the directors at the time of his appointment.

Chapter 15

THE AUDITOR

15.1 INTRODUCTION

A company has a duty to keep records of its accounts, under CA 1985, s 221. These accounts must give a 'true and fair view of the state of affairs of the company as at the end of the financial year' (CA 1985, s 226(2)). There is a general duty to appoint auditors to review those accounts independently every year (CA 1985, s 384). These duties are to ensure that those who have put up the money for the business (the shareholders) are not defrauded or mislead by those in charge of the company's finances, that is the directors.

The audit requirement is, however, relaxed for small private companies with a balance sheet of not more than £1.4 million and a turnover of not more than £350,000. Such a company is exempt from the statutory audit requirements (CA 1985, s 249A(1)).

To comply with the exemption the directors have to declare on the balance sheet, under s 249B(4), that:

- the company falls within this exemption;
- the directors acknowledge their responsibility:
    (a) to keep accounting records that comply with s 221; and
    (b) to prepare accounts that give a true and fair view in accord with s 226.

However, shareholders holding not less than 10 per cent of the issues share capital can require the company to have its accounts audited by lodging a written notice at the registered office during the financial year in question, but not more than one month before the end of the financial year (CA 1985, s 249B(2), (3)).

Note that there are some types of company that cannot use the s 249A relaxation but the detail of these is not necessary for the present course.

Chapter 15 contents
Introduction
Appointment
Terms and remuneration
Functions
Removal from office and resignation

15.2 APPOINTMENT

If a company must have an auditor, it must appoint someone who is qualified (a certified or chartered accountant) and independent (not connected with anyone involved in the company) (CA 1989, ss 25–28). Usually a firm of accountants is appointed to be the company's auditor, which means that any qualified member of that firm at the date of the appointment can undertake the audit (see **15.4**).

The directors will appoint the first auditor. This must be done before the first AGM of the company, but often will be done at the first board meeting. The directors' appointee will then hold office until the end of the first AGM. At each AGM the members will decide who the auditor is to be for the period until the next AGM (CA 1985, s 384).

As the same auditor is usually appointed year after year, the members may have passed an elective resolution dispensing with the need to reappoint the auditor annually (CA 1985, s 386) in which case the auditor is simply deemed to be reappointed (see **10.7**).

15.3 TERMS AND REMUNERATION

The terms on which the auditor holds office and his fee for doing so will be a matter for negotiation between him and the company. The directors approve the contract with the first auditor; in subsequent years the approval of members is necessary.

15.4 FUNCTIONS

The main duty of the auditor is to report to the members on the annual company accounts. The auditor must check that proper accounting records have been kept and that the final accounts (profit and loss account and the balance sheet) accord with those records. The auditor is required to certify that the accounts give a true and fair view of the company's financial position (CA 1985, s 226). If the auditor qualifies his report in any way, he is warning the members that there may have been some unethical business dealings or even fraud.

On any matter where a written resolution is being proposed rather than a general meeting being held, the auditor must be sent a copy of the proposed resolution (CA 1985, s 381B). Failure to send him a copy is a criminal offence for the officer(s) concerned (see **12.4.15**).

Notice of all general meetings must be sent to the auditor, and he then has a right to attend and speak at any such meeting, although he does not have a right to vote (CA 1985, s 390).

15.5 REMOVAL FROM OFFICE AND RESIGNATION

The auditor can be removed from office at any time by the members (CA 1985, s 391). The procedure is exactly the same as that required for the removal of a director, ie an ordinary resolution of which special notice has been given by the proposing shareholder to the company is required (see **13.15.2**). Members must hold a general meeting; a written resolution cannot be used to achieve this. The consequences of removal (eg whether compensation is payable) are dependent upon the terms of the contract between the company and the auditor (CA 1985, s 391(3)).

An auditor may resign from office by notice in writing sent to the registered office (CA 1985, s 392).

In the event of any cessation of office by an auditor, the auditor must give a written statement. This must either state that all is well, or explain the circumstances connected with the cessation of office which he feels need to be brought to the attention of the shareholders or the creditors (CA 1985, s 394). In the case of a resignation, he may also demand an extraordinary general meeting be called to consider these matters (CA 1985, s 392A).

These provisions prevent an auditor from just walking away from fraud, for example, without warning the shareholders or the creditors.

Chapter 16

COMPANY ACCOUNTS

16.1 INTRODUCTION

At the end of its accounting year, a company will prepare a profit and loss account and a balance sheet. The profit and loss account shows the calculation of its net profit for the year (described in the example below as 'Profit before taxation') by subtracting the company's various expenses from its income. This figure (after adjustment by the Inland Revenue to comply with ICTA 1988) will be used for calculating the company's corporation tax liability. The profit and loss account then goes on to show how the net profit is to be used by the company. Typically, part will be required for payment of corporation tax, part will be paid out to shareholders as dividend and the balance will be retained by the company as additional finance for the business. The balance sheet then describes everything which the company owns (described in the example at **16.4** as 'Fixed Assets' and as 'Current Assets') and everything which the company owes to its creditors (as opposed to its shareholders). The difference between what the company owns and what it owes represents the amount which the shareholders may expect to receive if the company were wound up, consisting of repayment of their investment plus distribution of any accumulated profit. This is described in the example at **16.4** as 'Capital and Reserves'.

16.2 REQUIREMENT TO FILE ACCOUNTS

A company must file with the registrar of companies its year-end accounts or, in the case of 'small' or 'medium-sized' companies, an abbreviated version of its year-end accounts (CA 1985, ss 246, 246A). The time-limit for filing accounts is 10 months from the end of the accounting reference period for a private company, and 7 months therefrom for a public company (CA 1985, s 244). The form and content of company accounts is prescribed by Sch 4 to the Companies Act 1985, as amended by Sch 1 to the Companies Act 1989, and will also be governed by standards set by the accountancy profession and contained in Financial Reporting Standards (FRSs) and Statements of Standard Accounting Practice (SSAPs).

16.3 PROFIT AND LOSS ACCOUNT

Broadly, for a single company (not part of a group of companies) whose only income derives from trading, the profit and loss account must show the information indicated by the following example, although the actual format may vary.

Chapter 16 contents
Introduction
Requirement to file accounts
Profit and loss account
Balance sheet
Management accounts

Example

Profit and loss account for the year ended 31 December 1999

		£	£	£
	Turnover	500,000		
Less	Cost of sales	300,000		
	Gross profit		200,000	
Less	Distribution costs	90,000		
	Administration expenses	50,000		
			140,000	
				60,000
Less	Interest payable			10,000
	Profit before taxation			50,000
Less	Taxation on profit			10,000
	Profit after taxation			40,000
Less	Dividends paid			25,000
	Profit retained			15,000
Add	Profit brought forward from			
	previous years			65,000
				80,000

There must also be a set of notes to the accounts (usually consisting of a considerable number of pages) which provide supplementary or explanatory information on a number of the items shown in the profit and loss account.

'Turnover' describes the total value of sales made during the year.

'Cost of sales' describes the cost of goods sold. The bulk of this will be the cost of stock acquired during the year. Adjustments will have been made to allow for stock held at the start of the year (opening stock) and stock left over at the end of the year (closing stock).

'Gross profit' is the resulting subtotal which describes the profit made by the business before taking into account the general overheads of the business.

'Distribution costs and administration expenses' describe the general overheads (or expenses) incurred in running the business. Examples include wages, electricity, postage, telephone, advertising and any allowance for the depreciation in value (eg through wear and tear) of items like machinery.

'Interest payable' (eg on a loan) is another example of an expense incurred by the company and will be shown separately from other expenses.

From the profit thus described, corporation tax must be deducted in order to show the figure for 'profit after taxation'. In fact, this need be paid only within 9 months after the end of the accounting period, but it is necessary to identify the liability to pay.

The company may choose to pay a dividend out of its profit and this will further reduce the company's profit figure.

Any remaining profit is being retained by the company and can then be added to the profit retained in previous years. The total represents the amount by which the company's assets have increased in value as a result of the company's successful trading activities. Broadly, it follows that the shares of the shareholders have increased in total value by this amount. This becomes evident when examining the company's balance sheet.

16.4 BALANCE SHEET

Broadly, the balance sheet describes everything owned by the company, all the liabilities of the company and the amount to which the shareholders would be entitled in the event of the company's affairs being wound up. It will inevitably 'balance' because whatever is left after comparing the company's assets with its liabilities is shown as representing the shareholders' funds. As with the profit and loss account, the following example illustrates the accounts of a single company (not part of a group of companies).

Example

Balance sheet as at 31 December 1999

	£	£	£
FIXED ASSETS			
Tangible assets			350,000
CURRENT ASSETS			
Stocks	125,000		
Debtors	75,000		
Cash at bank and in hand	50,000		
		250,000	
LESS CREDITORS: amounts falling due within one year			
Trade creditors	65,000		
Taxation and social security	20,000		
Accruals	15,000		
		100,000	
NET CURRENT ASSETS			150,000
TOTAL ASSETS LESS CURRENT LIABILITIES			500,000
LESS CREDITORS: amounts falling due after more than one year			
Debenture loans			60,000
			440,000
CAPITAL AND RESERVES			
Share capital			300,000
Share premium account			60,000
Profit and loss account			80,000
			440,000

As with a profit and loss account, there must also be a set of notes which will provide supplementary or explanatory information on a number of the items shown in the balance sheet.

The heading refers to a specific date at which the balance sheet is accurate. Unlike a profit and loss account, whose purpose is to show profit or loss over a period of time (usually 12 months), a balance sheet serves as a 'snapshot' of the company's financial position on a single day. It is inevitable that the assets and liabilities will not remain static.

'Fixed assets' are those of the company's assets which are owned on a more or less permanent basis, like its premises, machinery, fixtures, fittings, tools and equipment. These are all examples of tangible fixed assets. A company may own other fixed assets which should be shown separately. These might include investments and intangible assets like patents and the goodwill of the business.

'Current assets' are those of a less permanent character in the sense that there will be a turn-round of these items from one year to the next.

'Creditors' are split between those where the amount falls due within one year and those where the amount falls due after one year. In the illustration, the company has an obligation to pay outstanding creditors £100,000 within the current year, including £15,000 for 'accruals' representing anticipated liabilities (such as wages and electricity which have not yet been invoiced); its long-term debts total a further £60,000. This split by reference to the length of time before payment is due is of considerable significance when analysing the ability of a company to pay its way. A common reason for failure of businesses is that they are unable to satisfy their immediate creditors who are unwilling to wait for payment. For this reason, the figure for 'net current assets' is an important indicator of the ability of the company to continue to operate. A company will reckon to pay its current liabilities out of its current assets and, although existing cash may not be sufficient, the other current assets may be expected to realise cash in the short term. A company may have net current liabilities whereas the company in this illustration has net current assets. Such a company expects to pay more to its short-term creditors than it currently has in cash or other assets which will realise cash. While not necessarily signalling disaster, a balance sheet which shows net current liabilities should at least raise questions about the company's ability to continue in business.

'Capital and reserves' describes the funds attributable to the shareholders. If the company's assets were all sold, realising the figures given in the balance sheet, and then all creditors (whether short-term or longer-term) were paid off, the amount left over would be the amount available to the shareholders. Assuming the company has not made overall losses through its lifetime, the amount left over will represent a return of the money originally invested in the company (both the nominal value of the shares and any premium paid to the company over and above the nominal value) and a surplus representing the company's accumulated profits. In the example, these three elements are represented by 'share capital' (the nominal value of the shares), the 'share premium account' (any premium over and above nominal value) and the profit and loss account (representing the company's accumulated profits).

16.5 MANAGEMENT ACCOUNTS

Although the Companies Act 1985 imposes certain minimum obligations in relation to preparation of a profit and loss account and balance sheet, in practice the directors, and possibly other persons such as a substantial investor, will require 'management accounts' which contain more detailed information than is required by statute. Apart from including a more detailed profit and loss account and balance sheet, management accounts may include a manufacturing account, detailing the direct costs of production, and cash flow forecasts. Broadly, management accounts enable the person reading them to analyse the company's performance and/or prospects in greater depth than is possible with the accounts required by statute.

Chapter 17

SHARES

17.1 INTRODUCTION

Members of a company own shares in that company and will be given a share certificate as evidence of title. The value of shares is not constant. Depending on the company's performance, the capital value of shares may appreciate or depreciate and they may or may not produce income in the form of a dividend.

Chapter 17 contents
Introduction
Issuing shares
Classes of shares
Dividends
Transfer of shares
Buy-back of shares by the company
Transmission of shares
Summaries and checklists

17.2 ISSUING SHARES

Shares can be issued by the directors provided the company has sufficient unissued nominal capital and the directors have authority to do so.

17.2.1 Nominal capital

The company is only permitted to issue shares up to the amount of the nominal capital (also known as the authorised capital) as stated in the memorandum. For many private companies, the initial nominal capital is £100. Once all the nominal capital has been issued, the company can only raise additional finance by issuing more shares if the nominal capital figure is increased by an ordinary resolution of the members in general meeting (CA 1985, s 121), and this can only be done if the articles allow it. Table A does permit an increase in the nominal capital (Table A, art 32).

Where the directors call a general meeting asking the members to pass a resolution to increase the nominal capital, the notice convening the meeting must specify the amount of increase which is proposed. If the necessary resolution is passed, a copy of that ordinary resolution must be sent to the registrar of companies (one of the unusual ordinary resolutions which is publicised in this way) together with Form 123 and the amended memorandum (CA 1985, ss 122, 123).

17.2.2 Directors' power to issue shares

The board will usually want to allot shares in the company at the first board meeting of a new company, and may subsequently wish to issue more shares to raise additional finance. The directors can issue shares only in the company if they have authority to do so, and this authority must be specifically given either in the articles (by a special article) or by ordinary resolution of the members in a general meeting (CA 1985, s 80). Where a new company is formed, it is useful if the authority is contained in a special article so that the matter does not have to be considered at a general meeting. If an ordinary resolution is required, this is one of the exceptional ordinary resolutions which must be filed with the registrar.

However the necessary authority is given, it must state the number of shares which the directors are authorised to allot. Authority can be given for the directors to allot just one batch of shares, or it can be given generally, allowing them to issue any number of shares up to the amount of the nominal capital. It must also give the period of time for which the authority is to last, which cannot normally be longer than 5 years, although it can be renewed at any time for a period not greater than 5 years. In order to ensure that the authority does not expire by oversight, a company should have renewal of the authority as a standing item on the agenda for the AGM. The directors' power to allot shares can be revoked by the members at any time by the passing of an ordinary resolution.

Unusually, an ordinary resolution is sufficient to remove this authority even if the authority was originally given by the articles (which normally require a special resolution for any amendment). Any such ordinary resolution is one of the exceptional ordinary resolutions which must be filed with the registrar.

If the members pass an elective resolution they can remove the 5-year maximum duration of the directors' authority (CA 1985, s 80A). The authority to allot shares can then last for a fixed period exceeding 5 years, for example for 10 years, or indefinitely (see **10.6**).

17.2.3 Statutory pre-emption rights

Even where directors have the authority to issue shares, they cannot necessarily allot them to whomsoever they may choose. The Companies Act 1985, s 89 provides that where shares are being issued in exchange for cash, those shares must first be offered to the existing members of the company, the number that each current member is offered being dependent upon the percentage of the shares he currently holds. The offer to the existing members must remain open for at least 21 days and only if the present members decline to take up the shares can they be offered elsewhere. Where shares are issued wholly or partly for non-cash consideration, s 89 has no application. It is relevant only where the shares are to be paid for in cash.

The statutory pre-emption rights can be removed either by a special article (CA 1985, s 91) or by a special resolution of the members (CA 1985, s 95). With notice of the general meeting called to pass such a special resolution, directors must send to all members a written statement setting out their reasons for proposing the special resolution, the consideration which the company is to receive and their justification of this amount. As is the case with the s 80 authority, the pre-emption rights can be dispensed with either for just one particular issue of shares or generally. The maximum period for which removal can last is the same as for the s 80 authority (ie usually for 5 years), but can be longer if an elective resolution has been passed. If a written resolution is used to remove the statutory pre-emption rights, a written statement by the directors (as above) must be circulated to members at the same time as the written resolution is sent out (CA 1985, Sch 15A).

If the directors do not wish to allot new shares to the existing members in accordance with their current shareholdings, they should first check the articles to see whether the statutory pre-emption rights have been removed. If not removed by the articles, a special resolution is necessary to dispense formally with the need to offer the shares to the present members. However, it is possible for all the members to decline to take up the shares they are offered if this is thought to be quicker and simpler than holding a general meeting. The danger in relying on this procedure is that there is no guarantee that all members will refuse the offer. The directors may feel that a more formal removal of the right to be offered the shares is preferable.

17.2.4 Procedure

The procedure which must be followed in order to allot shares in the company is as follows.

(1) A board meeting must be called by any director on reasonable notice.
(2) Directors must check:

    (a) whether there is sufficient unissued nominal capital;
    (b) whether they have authority to allot the shares;
    (c) whether they are obliged to offer the shares to current members first.

If there is any problem with any of these three issues the directors will need to call a general meeting. If they propose to remove the statutory pre-emption rights, 21 clear days' notice will be required for the meeting (because a special resolution is necessary). Otherwise only ordinary resolutions are needed, and therefore 14 clear days' notice is sufficient. Notice in writing must be sent to all members. The general meeting will then be held and the resolutions passed. Copies of all resolutions will be sent to the registrar of companies and, if the nominal capital has been increased, Form 123 and the amended memorandum must also be sent.

(3) If there is no problem with any of the above matters, or if any problem has been resolved by a general meeting, then the directors can issue the shares at a board meeting. They will resolve to issue the shares to those persons who have made written application for them. Private companies are not permitted to offer their shares to members of the public. Therefore, it is necessary that the offer to buy comes from the prospective member and that that offer is accepted by the company.

(4) If the company has a seal, the directors will resolve to seal the share certificate, which will be sent to the new member, and will instruct the secretary to enter the name of the new member on the register of members. They will also instruct him to notify the registrar on Form 88(2) that new shares have been issued.

17.2.5 Payment for shares

A prospective member must normally pay for his shares in cash. He can only provide non-cash consideration if the company, ie the board, agrees. If consideration in kind is acceptable to the directors, they must send Form 88(2) to the registrar, and must also send the written contract. If the contract is not in writing, Form 88(3), setting out the main details of the contract, should be sent to the registrar in place of the contract itself.

17.2.6 Partly paid shares

When the directors of a company decide to issue shares they will expect the prospective new shareholder to pay for those shares. For example, if a prospective new member offers to buy 100 £1 shares at £1 each the directors will expect him to pay the company £100 (or they may agree to accept assets worth £100 in payment for the shares). Throughout this book, it has been assumed that company shares are fully paid shares. However, the directors may agree to issue shares partly paid, which means that although the full price of the shares must be paid eventually, it does not have to be paid immediately. For example, the directors could issue 100 £1 shares on the basis that 50p per share was payable on issue and the remaining 50p per share was payable 6 months later.

17.2.7 Issue at a premium

The nominal value of each share, as stated in the memorandum of the company, is also known as the par value. Depending on their market value, the shares may be issued for a price greater than their nominal value, but if this happens the excess amount of consideration paid above the nominal value of the shares must be recorded in a separate share premium account (CA 1985, s 130) where it is treated as share capital, and thus subject to the requirement that this fund must be maintained (see **17.2.9**).

17.2.8 Issue at a discount

Shares may not be issued for less than their nominal value. If this happens the shareholder is obliged to pay the amount of discount to the company with interest (CA 1985, s 100).

17.2.9 Maintenance of share capital

After members have paid for their shares, the money produced constitutes the company's capital. Creditors will expect this fund to be available to meet the company's debts and, because the liability of the members of the company is limited, this capital sum should not be diminished. The impact of this on the members of the company is that, having bought their shares in the company, they cannot normally hand back their share certificate to the company in exchange for the consideration they originally provided. If they want to realise their investment, they must sell their shares. The company cannot reduce its share capital by exchanging members' shares for valuable consideration.

However, there are exceptional situations where a company is permitted to reduce its share capital. By virtue of the Companies Act 1985, ss 135–137, it can do so with the approval of the members by special resolution and with the consent of the court. It is rare for a company to do this but it could:

(1) cancel further liability on partly paid shares;
(2) actually pay back to members capital which is not needed; or
(3) reduce the value of the company's shares to reflect capital losses.

The first two methods reduce the amount of capital available to pay creditors. The third simply recognises a capital loss which has already been made and therefore does not prejudice creditors.

Under the Companies Act 1985, a company may additionally be permitted to issue redeemable shares (s 159) or to buy back ordinary shares which have been issued (s 162). This may have the effect of reducing share capital but does not need the consent of the court (see **17.3** and **17.6**).

17.2.10 Financial assistance for the purchase of shares

If someone wants to buy shares in the company but cannot afford to do so without a loan, that person may ask the company itself to lend him the necessary money, or may ask a financial institution such as a bank to do so and the bank may then ask the company to guarantee the loan. The general rule is that a company cannot give a prospective or actual member any financial assistance to enable him to purchase shares in the company (CA 1985, s 151).

Financial assistance means a gift, loan, indemnity, guarantee, assignment or other transaction by which the acquirer is directly or indirectly put in funds (CA 1985, s 152(1)). Any other transaction may amount to assistance if it materially reduces the company's assets, for example the payment by the target company of the legal fees of a bidder company on a takeover.

Section 153 of the Companies Act 1985 exempts from s 151 two categories of transaction, that is those where the principal purpose was not the giving of financial assistance, or where it was incidental to some larger purpose. However, these provisions are vague and difficult to rely on, for example *Brady v Brady* [1989] AC 755. There are also specific common sense exceptions to s 151 in s 153, such as the payment of a dividend to shareholders.

Section 151 is a problem in company law which rears its head in the most unexpected situations. It can be the bane of a company lawyer's life.

However, in certain circumstances, the giving of financial help to a prospective purchaser of shares in a private company is permitted, subject to various procedural safeguards. (This is the so-called 'whitewash procedure'.) The main requirements are that the members must give their consent by special resolution and the directors must make a statutory declaration of solvency stating that the company is currently solvent and will remain so for the next 12 months. The directors' declaration must be supported by confirmation from the auditor. If a director makes a statutory declaration without having reasonable grounds, then he faces criminal sanctions (CA 1985, ss 155–158).

The provision of financial assistance by the company can be useful where a new member wishes to join the company and the current members and directors are keen that he should do so. It is also useful where one member wishes to leave the company and the other members want to buy him out rather than have someone new involved in the business. However, if the person seeking financial help from the company is also a director of the company, an additional restriction applies as loans to directors are generally prohibited (see **13.12.4**).

17.3 CLASSES OF SHARES

A company may decide to create different classes of shares. Usually some shares will be described as ordinary shares, but there may be more then one class of ordinary shares within the company. For example, two different classes of ordinary shares may carry different voting rights.

The directors may also decide to issue preference shares, which will entitle their holders to some kind of preferential right, such as first claim to any dividend, or to return of capital, or both. Exactly what preferential treatment is given to the holders of preference shares will depend upon the terms of their issue. For example, the preferential right to a dividend may be cumulative or may just relate to the profits for each year and preferential shareholders may have no voting rights.

It is also possible for a company to issue redeemable shares (CA 1985, s 159). Such shares can only be redeemed by the company if they have been paid for in full (partly paid shares cannot be redeemed) and, prior to the redemption, the company has issued other shares which are not redeemable. A company cannot be financed solely by the issue of redeemable shares. Table A permits a company to issue redeemable shares (art 3) but gives no further details. Therefore, if the directors decided to issue redeemable shares they would need to ensure that a special article was included in the company's articles setting out details of the terms and conditions of issue (CA 1985, s 159A). For example, shares may be redeemable at the option of the member, or the company, or either. If shares are redeemed, they are effectively cancelled. This reduces the issued share capital of the company, although the nominal capital ceiling is unaffected, and those shares which have been redeemed can be re-issued. If the company redeems shares, it can repay the member concerned using money which has come from profits, from the proceeds of a fresh issue of shares or, if neither of those is possible, from capital, subject to certain safeguards being observed (which are the same requirements as those which are necessary when the company buys back its own shares (CA 1985, ss 160, 162) (see **17.6**)).

The remainder of this book assumes only one class of shares within a company.

17.4 DIVIDENDS

Initially, it is the directors who must decide whether or not to pay a dividend to members. They are only permitted to recommend the payment of a dividend (an income payment on shares) if there are 'profits available' (CA 1985, s 263). To ascertain whether there are profits available, the directors must deduct from all the realised profits of the company to date all the realised losses to date. If there is any profit left after doing this, that money is available to pay a dividend. The directors can find this information by looking at the latest set of audited accounts. This means that even if the company has not made a profit this year, it may still be able to pay a dividend if the profits from previous years are sufficient.

If a dividend is paid when there are insufficient profits available for the purpose, the directors who authorised the payment are jointly and severally liable to the company for the full amount. Any member who has received the dividend must refund it to the company if he knows or has reasonable grounds for believing that the payment is unauthorised.

If funds are available and the directors decide that a dividend should be paid, they suggest the amount of dividend which they think appropriate and propose this to the members in a general meeting. It is the members who actually declare the dividend. They can vote to pay themselves the same amount as the directors have recommended or less, but they cannot decide to declare a larger dividend than the directors have suggested (Table A, art 102). The form of the dividend is usually that shareholders receive, for example, 5p in the £, which means that for every £1 share they hold they receive 5p.

17.5 TRANSFER OF SHARES

Shares are transferred if the member who owns them sells them or gives them to another person.

17.5.1 Procedure for transfer

The seller or donor of the shares ('the transferor') should complete and sign a stock transfer form, which he should then give to the buyer or recipient ('the transferee') (CA 1985, s 183). There is no need for the transferee to sign the stock transfer form (unless the shares are partly paid) and there is no need for the signature of the transferor to be witnessed. The transferor should also hand the share certificate to the transferee.

If the shares are being sold, the buyer must pay stamp duty (currently charged at 50p per £100) on the stock transfer form. If the shares are a gift, no stamp duty is payable. The minimum stamp duty is £5.

The transferee should then send the share certificate and stock transfer form to the company.

The company should send the new member a new share certificate in his name within 2 months, and should also ensure that his name is entered on the register of members (CA 1985, s 185).

If the new member is also a director, he must formally notify the company in writing within 5 days of the fact that he has acquired the shares and that information must be recorded on the register of directors' interests (CA 1985, s 324).

The change in the composition of the membership of the company is notified to the registrar of companies on the annual return (Form 363), which is submitted each year.

17.5.2 Restrictions on transfer

The ability of the members of a company to transfer their shares to whomsoever they choose will be governed by the articles of the company. Under Table A, there is no restriction on the transferability of fully paid shares, but it is common to find a special article placing some restraint on members wishing to transfer their shares. For example, directors may be given an absolute discretion in this matter by empowering them to refuse to place a name on the register of members. Alternatively, members may be permitted to transfer their shares without restriction only to other members of the company or to members of their own family. A further alternative is that members may be allowed to consider transferring their shares to people who are not already members of the company only if they first offer those shares to the other shareholders at a fair value and those shareholders reject this offer and that directors should have an absolute discretion to refuse registration of such a transfer even so.

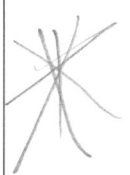

Unless they are given power by a special article, the directors cannot refuse to place a new member's name on the register of members. If they wrongly refuse to do so, their decision can be challenged by an application to the court for an order for rectification of the register (CA 1985, s 359). If directors are given some discretion in this matter, they must make a decision within a reasonable time, which will be not more than the 2-month period within which they are obliged to deliver the new share certificate. If directors exercise their discretion and refuse to register a new member, the court generally will not interfere with that decision unless the transferee can show that the directors did not act in good faith. If the directors properly exercise their power to refuse to register the name of the transferee, the transferee has no claim for damages or for rescission of the contract. The transferor remains the legal owner of the shares, his name continues to appear on the register of members, and he holds the shares on trust for the transferee (see **12.2.2**).

17.6 BUY-BACK OF SHARES BY THE COMPANY

Generally, a company is forbidden to take back its shares because the share capital, once raised, must be maintained in the interests of fairness to creditors. However, a company can buy back its own shares from its members (CA 1985, s 162) provided various conditions are satisfied. The main requirements are that the articles of the company must permit this, and Table A does (Table A, art 35). The members must authorise the purchase by special resolution (the member whose shares are to be bought cannot vote) and the contract must be available for inspection at the registered office for 15 days before the meeting and at the meeting itself. It must then be kept at the registered office for 10 years afterwards.

In addition, the company can only buy its own shares if it has the funds available to do so. It can use money produced by profits, in which case, reserves of profit are allocated to a capital redemption reserve to replace shares bought back; or the company can use the proceeds of a fresh issue of shares, the fresh issue being used to replace the shares bought back. As a last resort, a private company can use some of its capital (CA 1985, s 171), but various additional conditions must be satisfied in order for the company to be able to use its capital in this way (CA 1985, s 173). The main requirements are that the articles of the company must permit the use of capital (Table A does: art 35). Various people, including creditors of the company, must be officially notified that this is happening. The directors must make a statutory declaration of solvency, stating that the company is solvent and will remain so for the next 12 months. The directors should not make such a declaration without careful thought, because if the company is wound up within one year of their declaration and proves to be insolvent, then both the seller of the shares and the directors of the company may be required to contribute to the financial deficiency of the company (IA 1986, s 76). In addition, directors face criminal sanctions for making such a declaration without having reasonable grounds (CA 1985, s 173(6)). If shares are to be bought back from capital, a second special resolution must be passed, specifically authorising the use of capital in this way, in addition to the one simply authorising the buy-back of shares.

If shares are bought back by the company, a duly stamped return must be sent to the registrar of companies (Form 169) stating the number of shares involved and their nominal value, and the register of members must be altered to reflect the change. The register of directors' interests may need updating if the member concerned was also a director. The effect of the company purchasing its own shares in this way is that those shares are simply treated as cancelled.

The ability of the company to buy back its own shares can be useful in a variety of situations, for example when the majority of shareholders want to buy out a dissenting member, when a member wants to leave and when a shareholder dies and the other members do not want to increase their own shareholdings or to take in a new member.

17.7 TRANSMISSION OF SHARES

Transmission is the automatic process whereby, when a shareholder dies, his shares immediately pass to his personal representatives (PRs) or, if a member is declared bankrupt, his shares automatically vest in his trustee in bankruptcy.

When this happens, the PRs or trustee are entitled to any dividend declared on the shares but they cannot exercise the votes which attach to the shares as they are not members of the company (Table A, art 31).

The PRs of a deceased shareholder must produce to the company the grant of representation to establish their right to deal with the shares as PRs of the estate, but they then have a choice (Table A, art 30).

(1) They can elect to be registered as members themselves. In such a case, the entry on the register of members does not show that they hold the shares in a representative capacity. This choice is subject to the articles of the company which may give the directors a discretion to refuse to place any name on the register of members. The directors cannot prevent the PRs from acquiring the shares by transmission in their capacity as PRs, but they can prevent their being registered as members if the articles give them the power to refuse registration. If the PRs are registered as members of the company, they can then transfer the shares in the usual way (see **17.5.1**), either passing them to the beneficiary under the deceased member's will or selling them to a third party for the benefit of the deceased member's estate.

(2) They can transfer the shares directly to the ultimate beneficiary or to a third party in their representative capacity. There is no need for them to be registered as shareholders in order to do this. This choice is also subject to the articles of the company.

A trustee in bankruptcy has the same choice, ie he can elect to be registered as a member and then sell the shares or he can sell them directly in his representative capacity. He must produce the court order concerning his appointment in order to establish his right to deal with the shares.

17.8 SUMMARIES AND CHECKLISTS

17.8.1 Procedure on allotment of shares

- Is a general meeting necessary?
  For example:
    - to increase nominal capital – ordinary resolution (s 121)
    - to give directors authority to allot – ordinary resolution (s 80)
    - to remove or suspend pre-emption rights – special resolution (s 89)

  If so, board meeting held to call general meeting to pass resolution(s) as above, then further board meeting as follows.

- Board meeting
  - receive application(s) for shares
  - if directors buying shares, they must declare personal interest (s 317) but can vote and count in quorum (Table A, art 94(c))

    resolve to
    - allot shares
    - seal share certificate (if company has seal)
    - instruct secretary to file all relevant returns and write up the relevant statutory books

  - if director has purchased shares, he must officially notify the company of this (s 324)

- File all relevant returns
  For example:
  - Form 123, ordinary resolution and amended memorandum
  - ordinary resolution under s 80
  - special resolution under s 89
  - Form 88(2) – return of allotments (with stamped contract if non-cash consideration)

- Write up minutes of board (and general) meetings(s) and update register of members (and register of directors' interests if director has bought shares).

17.8.2 Procedure for transfer of shares

- Give share certificate and transfer form to transferee

- Buyer pays stamp duty (no stamp duty on a gift)

- Apply to company for registration

- Board considers whether to refuse registration (if the articles give them this power)
  Note: Generally, Table A does not allow the directors to refuse to register a transfer of fully paid shares – check the articles

- Board resolves to seal new share certificate (if company has seal)

- Update
  - register of members
  - register of directors' interests (if relevant)

17.8.3 Procedure on death/bankruptcy of shareholder

- Shares pass automatically by transmission to PR/Trustee

- PR/Trustee in bankruptcy can either:
  - have himself entered on the register; or
  - transfer shares to some other person

  Note: Both of these are subject to any restrictions on transfer which may be contained in the articles

Chapter 18

DEBENTURES

18.1 INTRODUCTION

Debentures can be an alternative form of investment in a company. They are a more secure investment than shares in that interest payments must be made by the company and they can include the provision of security to guarantee the investment in the event of default. Debenture holders are not members of the company, hence they do not acquire membership rights.

18.2 WHAT IS A DEBENTURE?

Companies frequently borrow money, either from individuals who are willing to lend to them or from institutional lenders, such as banks. If a company borrows money, it will give the lender a form of IOU, a document which is evidence of the existence and terms of the loan. This document is called a debenture. Like any loan, the capital sum borrowed is repayable at a future date and during the currency of the loan the company must pay interest to the lender. A debenture holder is therefore a creditor of the company, ie someone to whom the company owes money. In order to improve his chances of recovering the debt from the company in the event of its financial collapse, a lender may take a charge over some or all of the company's property, thereby becoming a secured creditor. This increases his chances of being repaid, even on insolvency of the company, as secured creditors must be repaid in full before any ordinary unsecured creditors receive anything. Therefore, although there is no requirement that a debenture must be secured by a charge over some or all of the company's property, most debentures will include some form of security for practical, commercial reasons.

18.3 PRE-CONTRACT CONSIDERATIONS

18.3.1 For the directors of the company

The board should check that the company has the power to borrow money. If it does not have such power then borrowing would be an ultra vires act, ie one outside the capacity of the company. A trading company has implied power to borrow, but institutional lenders sometimes insist on there being an express power to borrow explicitly stated in the objects clause of the memorandum before they will sanction the loan. This is a factor to consider when drafting the objects clause for a new company (see **11.2.3**).

The directors should ensure that they have been given the power to borrow on behalf of the company by the articles and thus will not be acting outside their authority and in breach of duty. They are usually given power to do so (Table A, art 70).

Chapter 18 contents
Introduction
What is a debenture?
Pre-contract considerations
Security for the loan
Typical terms of a debenture
Procedure for issue of debenture
Registration
Remedies of the debenture holder
Redemption of the loan
Advantages and disadvantages of debentures: comparison with shares
Summaries and checklists

The lender may require the directors of the company personally to guarantee a loan to the company, particularly, but not exclusively, where the company is a small company or where it is a new company. If the directors are guaranteeing the loan in this way, they have a personal interest in the matter and must declare that interest formally at the first board meeting at which the question of the loan is discussed (CA 1985, s 317). The articles will then determine whether they can vote and count in the quorum (Table A, arts 94 and 95) (see **13.9.2** and **13.9.3**).

18.3.2 For the lender

The lender should check that the proposed loan is not an ultra vires act for the company. Although the lender is protected by s 35 of the Companies Act 1985 even if the loan is ultra vires (see **20.2.1**), any member can apply to the court for an injunction to restrain a proposed act which is outside the capacity of the company. It is therefore a wise precaution for the lender to ensure that the loan is authorised by the objects clause before he incurs any expenditure in connection with the matter, or uses any valuable time negotiating the terms.

He should also make sure that the directors have the authority to act on behalf of the company in the transaction and that the people he is dealing with have actually been properly appointed as directors of the company. He can do this by inspecting the articles of the company and searching at Companies House for Forms 10, 288a, 288b and 288c.

If, as is usually the case, the loan is to be secured by a charge contained in the debenture, it would also be sensible to search at Companies House for details of any charges currently registered against the company's property to ensure that there is sufficient equity in that property to provide adequate security for the proposed loan. Even if the loan is to be unsecured, the lender should search at Companies House to determine the extent of the company's current secured borrowing. From the charges register, the lender can discover:

(1) the date of creation of any existing charge;
(2) the amount secured;
(3) which property is the subject of the charge;
(4) who holds that charge.

If the charges register reveals any floating charges already in existence, the lender should obtain from the chargeholder a letter of non-crystallisation (a letter in which the chargeholder confirms that his floating charge has not yet crystallised) as it will not be apparent from the company search whether the floating charge has crystallised or not (see **18.4.2**).

If the lender is proposing to take a charge over land held by the company, he should also search at HM Land Registry or Land Charges Department as appropriate.

18.4 SECURITY FOR THE LOAN

18.4.1 Fixed charge

A fixed charge is like a mortgage. It can be taken over specific property (land, buildings, fixed plant and machinery) and the company cannot sell any property it owns which is the subject of a fixed charge or do anything which might devalue the asset, such as subletting the premises, without the consent of the chargeholder. This means, for example, that if the company's office premises are the subject of a fixed charge to the bank, the company cannot sell its office premises and move to another location without the consent of the bank, which may entail repaying the current loan and applying for a new one. This may be forthcoming, or it may be refused, or it may be granted but the new loan may be on less favourable terms.

18.4.2 Floating charge

A floating charge, unlike a fixed charge, does not attach to any particular asset. It floats over a class of assets, during which time the component parts of that class of assets may be constantly changing, as the company has the power to deal with any of the assets within that class without needing to consult the holder of the floating charge. For example, a floating charge may be taken over the company's stock or future assets of the company. This does not prevent the company from selling its current stock, but any new stock it buys in to replace that which is sold immediately becomes the subject of the floating charge as it falls into the class of assets which are covered by the charge. Therefore the floating charge is secured on any property within the specified class (eg any stock) which happens to be owned by the company on a particular day. It is common for institutional lenders to take a floating charge over the whole undertaking of the company (having already taken a fixed charge over any of the company's assets which it is possible to make the subject of a fixed charge). Inevitably the value of the security will vary from day to day as the company carries on business, but if the floating charge crystallises the value of the security is then fixed.

A floating charge will 'crystallise' when the company ceases to carry on business, or goes into liquidation, or when the debenture holder appoints a receiver to enforce his security, which is what he will do if the company defaults on the agreement in any way. When a floating charge crystallises, it no longer hovers over the class of assets which are the subject of the charge, but lands upon those assets and attaches itself to them in the same way as a fixed charge. At this point the company is no longer able to deal with those assets. The floating charge, once crystallised, operates in the same way as a fixed charge and prevents the company from dealing with any item within the class of assets without the consent of the chargeholder.

18.4.3 Prohibition on creation of later fixed charges taking priority

Where a lender is taking a floating charge over, say, the whole undertaking of the company, there may be sufficient equity in the fixed assets of the company to enable the directors, who are able to deal with all the company's assets until such time as the floating charge crystallises, to grant a fixed charge at a later date over some or all of those fixed assets. This presents a potential problem for the floating chargee, as, in the event of the winding up of the company, debts secured by fixed charges must be paid off before those secured by floating charges. This means that the security represented by the floating charge could be far less valuable than was expected when the floating charge was first taken.

In order to prevent this, a debenture containing a floating charge as security for a loan should also contain a clause which imposes a prohibition on the company granting later fixed charges over the property which is the subject of the floating charge, as these would take priority for repayment over the floating charge. This is referred to as a 'negative pledge'.

18.4.4 Personal guarantees

Directors are sometimes required personally to guarantee a loan to their company. Usually only company money can be used to pay company debts because of the principle of limited liability, but if the directors give personal guarantees for a loan they will have to pay the lender whatever amount is outstanding if, for some reason, the lender is unable to recover the loan in full from the company, for example because the company is insolvent. Directors who do give personal guarantees in this way risk the loss of their personal assets if the company fails, possibly even loss of their home. A director who cannot pay the sum he guaranteed from his own resources may even face bankruptcy.

18.5 TYPICAL TERMS OF A DEBENTURE

18.5.1 Repayment date

The amount the company borrows under the debenture will have to be repaid at some future date. Sometimes a loan will be for a fixed period of time (eg 12 months) and there will be a specified date when repayment is due. Sometimes, for example in the case of a bank overdraft, the loan will be repayable on demand.

18.5.2 Interest

The debenture must specify when interest is payable and how much is agreed. There may be a fixed rate of interest, or the interest rate may be linked to bank rates and may therefore fluctuate.

18.5.3 Security

Although there is no need for a loan to be secured, the lender's position is improved if he does take a charge over the company's property and therefore secured loans are very common. The security could be in the form of a fixed charge or a floating charge, or could be a combination of the two, for example a fixed charge on anything owned by the company over which it is possible to take a fixed charge and a floating charge over the whole of the company's undertaking.

18.5.4 Power to appoint a receiver

If the company defaults under the terms of the debenture, because it does not pay either the interest or the capital when due, the debenture holder's right to recover the money owed to him is achieved by the appointment of a receiver, and therefore power to make such an appointment should be contained in the debenture. A receiver appointed by a debenture holder whose security included a floating charge over the whole, or substantially the whole, undertaking of the company is known as an administrative receiver.

18.5.5 Power of sale

The receiver appointed by the debenture holder will need power to sell the assets which are the subject of the charge in order to recover the sum due to his appointor, and therefore a power of sale should be included in the debenture.

18.5.6 Other powers of the receiver

It is advisable to provide for the receiver to have all the powers he will need to achieve his objective, for example power to take legal proceedings in the company name. An administrative receiver will also need the power to manage the business of the company.

18.6 PROCEDURE FOR ISSUE OF DEBENTURE

It is the directors' decision whether to borrow money in the company name and it is they who will negotiate with the lender the terms on which the loan is to be made. A resolution of the board of directors is sufficient to authorise borrowing by the company.

However, there may be problems over the ability of the directors to vote and count in the quorum on the resolution to borrow, particularly where the directors have been asked personally to guarantee the loan, as the articles may prevent any director who has a personal interest (possibly all directors) from being involved in the decision to borrow (see **13.9.2** and **13.9.3**). It may therefore be necessary to call an EGM either to suspend the prohibition in the articles by ordinary resolution (Table A, art 96) or to change the articles by special resolution.

Once the directors have resolved to enter into the loan, the debenture will be signed by either two directors or a director and the secretary, and the directors will also resolve to affix the company seal (if the company has one) to the debenture.

18.7 REGISTRATION

Section 396 of CA 1985 lists those types of charge which are registrable.

Once the company has formally entered into the loan, it is the company's responsibility to register prescribed particulars of any charge contained in the debenture at Companies House on Form 395, together with the original charging document, within 21 days of creation of that charge (CA 1985, s 395) (fee – £10). If the debenture contains a floating charge and a prohibition on the creation of later fixed charges taking priority, the prohibition should be noted on Form 395. Although it is primarily the responsibility of the company to register prescribed particulars of any charge, it is the chargee who suffers if the charge is not registered or is registered late (see **18.7.1**). Possibly, the debenture holder should undertake the registration of the charge himself. The registrar of companies will return the original charging document with a stamp signifying registration, as well as a certificate which is conclusive evidence that the charge is properly registered.

If a fixed charge is taken over land (for practical reasons, floating charges are generally not used where land is concerned) then this must also be registered at HM Land Registry or Land Charges Department.

If such a charge is not registered at HM Land Registry (or Land Charges Department), then a buyer of the land in question can take free of the fixed charge, even if he actually knew of its existence. The position of a buyer is governed solely by what is apparent from the Land Registry/Land Charges Department documents, even if the fixed charge over land has been registered at Companies House.

Details of any charge created by the company should also be kept in the company's own register of charges at its registered office, but failure to do this does not affect the validity of the charge in any way.

18.7.1 Failure to register at Companies House

Registration of a registrable charge at Companies House gives constructive notice of that charge to those persons who could reasonably be expected to search the register (*Re Standard Rotary Machine Company Co Ltd* (1906)), including, of course, subsequent chargees. It seems unlikely that it would constitute notice to purchasers of the company's property.

Failure to register renders the charge void against the company's liquidator or administrator, and also against the company's other secured creditors (CA 1985, s 395(1)). It is not void as such against purchasers of the company's property but they may take free of it under the rule on a bona fide purchaser without notice for value. The security remains valid against the company itself although the money secured by the charge becomes payable immediately (CA 1985, s 395(2)).

Editor's note: New ss 395–420 were to have been inserted in to CA 1985 by CA 1989 but these changes were never implemented. It now seems unlikely that they ever will be. Readers should beware that some textbooks on company law assume that the new regime was implemented and such books are therefore in error.

18.7.2 Late or inaccurate registration

If the 21-day registration period is missed or the details supplied on Form 395 are inaccurate, then the court has the power under the Companies Act 1985, s 404 to order an extension of time or allow rectification of the register, as appropriate, but the remedy is far from automatic. The court may order that, although the charge can be registered late, it will be subject to any charges registered in the meantime.

18.7.3 Memorandum of satisfaction

When a debt, or other obligation, secured by a registered charge is repaid then the fact may be made public by filing a memorandum of satisfaction with Companies House in the prescribed form (CA 1985, s 403).

18.8 REMEDIES OF THE DEBENTURE HOLDER

If the company defaults under the terms of the debenture, the chargee can appoint a receiver to enforce his security. The receiver should formally notify the company, the registrar of companies and the creditors of his appointment. The receiver's job is to take possession of the property which is subject to the charge and, after making provision for the payment of any prior creditors of the company, to sell enough of the property charged to pay what is due to the debenture holder, together with interest and costs. When he has achieved this, the receiver retires from office and the company is permitted to carry on its business again. Frequently, however, the appointment of a receiver and the sale of some of its assets will, in practice, prevent the company from continuing in business and the company is forced into liquidation.

If the charge in question is a floating charge over the whole or substantially the whole of the company's undertaking then the receiver will be an administrative receiver and will have powers of management of the company, the powers of the directors being suspended during the currency of the administrative receiver's appointment and only being resumed when he retires from office (see **24.9.4**).

18.9 REDEMPTION OF THE LOAN

When the loan is repaid to the lender, a director or the company secretary will make a statutory declaration that the debt has been paid on Form 403a and will send this to the registrar of companies. The lender will endorse his receipt of the money on the debenture.

If any entries were made against land at HM Land Registry or Land Charges Department, these should now be removed.

18.10 ADVANTAGES AND DISADVANTAGES OF DEBENTURES: COMPARISON WITH SHARES

18.10.1 For the investor

Involvement in the company
A shareholder is a member of the company, which gives him certain rights within the company (see **12.5**), including the right to attend general meetings and to vote. A debenture holder is merely a creditor of the company and has no say whatever in the way the company is run.

Income
A shareholder has no guaranteed income from the investment in shares. A dividend will only be paid if the directors decide to recommend one, and they can do so only if the company is sufficiently profitable. A debenture holder must be paid the agreed rate of interest at the times specified in the debenture itself. The payment of such interest is a debt owed by the company and is not dependent upon the company making a profit.

Repayment of capital
Generally, a shareholder's capital is not repaid by the company. A lender will agree with the company a date for repayment of the capital sum loaned, and this date will be stated in the debenture. On that date the company must repay the loan.

Restrictions on sale

If a member wishes to sell his shares in order to realise his capital investment in the company, the transfer of his shares is governed by the articles, which may restrict his choice. If a debenture holder wishes to realise his capital earlier than the repayment date agreed, he can sell his debenture to whomsoever he chooses. No restriction in the articles will affect his right to sell.

Capital value of the investment

The value of a company's shares may increase or decrease. Many shareholders make such an investment hoping for capital appreciation rather than income.

The capital value of a debenture generally remains constant, being the value of the loan. There is usually no possibility of capital appreciation or depreciation with this type of investment; the purpose of an investment in this form is the receipt of income.

18.10.2 For the company

Payment of income

The company can pay a dividend to its members only if there are profits available (see **13.9.2**). Even if the company is sufficiently profitable, the directors have a complete discretion as to whether a dividend should be paid.

Debenture interest must be paid in accordance with the terms of the debenture whether or not the company has profits available. If there are no profits which can be used, the company must use capital to make the interest payment. If the company fails to make a payment of interest, the debenture holder is entitled to enforce the terms of the debenture by the appointment of a receiver.

Tax treatment of income payments

The payment of a dividend is not a deductible expense for the company. It is simply a distribution of profit, after it has suffered corporation tax.

Payment of debenture interest, as it is incurred for the purposes of the trade, is a normal trading expense and so deductible in computing trading profit, before corporation tax is assessed.

Involvement of investor

If a person buys shares in the company and has his name entered on the register of members, he is then a member of the company and has certain rights as a member. He could thus have a degree of influence over the way in which the company is run. Even a minority shareholder may be a nuisance (at the very least) to those persons running the company, if that member's views are not in accordance with those of the directors and other members.

A debenture holder generally cannot interfere in the way the company is run. If the company complies with the terms of the debenture, the debenture holder can take no action to influence company policy.

Repayment of capital

The company generally does not have to repay to members the capital which they have invested until the company ceases in business and is wound up. Therefore, this is not a matter which the directors need to consider.

Debenture capital must be repaid at some date in the future (possibly on demand), therefore the directors must make provision for this and ensure that funds are available to repay the loan whenever it falls due.

18.11 SUMMARIES AND CHECKLISTS

18.11.1 Preliminary considerations for the lender

- Is the company financially sound? — check published accounts and, if possible, more recent accounts

- Is satisfactory security offered? — take fixed and/or floating charge(s)
  - check for existing charges
  - get personal guarantees from directors
  - take charge(s) over directors' assets (eg their homes)

18.11.2 Procedure on borrowing

- Check — that the company has the power to borrow
  - that the directors have the authority to borrow

- Prepare debenture — what property is charged?
  - rate of interest and repayment date
  - fixed and/or floating charge?
  - define default
  - methods of enforcement
  - prohibition on later charges taking priority
  - etc

- Board meeting to enter into contract and execute debenture

- If directors are lending money to the company, they must declare their personal interest (s 317) but can vote and count in the quorum (Table A, art 94(c))

    Note: Giving personal guarantees may prevent them from voting – see Table A, art 94

- Registration — at Companies Registry within 21 days
  - at HM Land Registry/Land Charges Department

- Write up statutory books — register of charges (if relevant)
  - register of directors' interests (if director has

taken debenture)
- Charge may be invalid/ineffective security if:
  - not registered
  - insolvent liquidation in near future (see **24.8**)
  - assets are supplied under *Romalpa* clause (see **A1.5.1**)

Chapter 19

SOURCES OF FINANCE

19.1 INTRODUCTION

The essential choice for a company in obtaining the bulk of its finance is between share capital (raised by issuing shares) and loan capital (raised by issuing debentures). Persons who invest by purchasing shares become members of the company with the attendant rights and powers under the Companies Acts, under the company's constitution and under the terms of issue, while those who invest by lending to the company become creditors whose rights generally are contractual and derive from the terms of the debenture (see **18.10**).

The need for these two types of finance can be limited by looking at alternative ways in which the company can acquire or use the assets which the business requires. For example, the company might enter into leasing contracts for the cars used by its directors and the company might acquire premises on a lease rather than acquiring the freehold. Also, certain assets like machinery might be acquired under hire-purchase contracts rather than by immediate purchase.

19.2 SHARE AND LOAN CAPITAL – FROM WHOM?

19.2.1 Directors and shareholders

Initially, a significant amount of the company's capital will have to be provided by the individuals who will run the company (the directors and shareholders). In terms of value, their own investment may be expected to match any 'outside' investment in the company although, depending on circumstances, outside investors may be willing to provide three or four times as much capital as the 'inside' investors. It may also be possible for the persons setting up or running the company to encourage family or friends to provide some finance.

19.2.2 Loan finance

In addition to the finance in the form of share and, perhaps, loan capital provided by those running the company (and possibly their family and friends), many companies will obtain loan finance by bank borrowing in the form of an overdraft. This offers the advantages of relative informality in setting up the overdraft facility and flexibility in the amount actually borrowed. It has the disadvantages that the bank will probably require personal guarantees from the directors and that usually the overdraft is repayable on demand by the bank; the latter disadvantage is particularly significant in the sense that the bank has the power to 'pull the plug' on the company.

Chapter 19 contents
Introduction
Share and loan capital – from whom?

19.2.3 Fixed-term loan

Another way in which loan finance may be obtained from a bank, or other lender, is in the form of a fixed-term loan of a specific amount. This may be especially appropriate for the purchase of a particular asset, like premises, on which the lender will be able to take a fixed charge by way of security. It has the advantage from the company's point of view that, unlike an overdraft, it is not repayable on demand.

19.2.4 Venture capital

Where major 'outside' finance is required (say £500,000 or more), this may be sought from a venture capital organisation. These are generally organisations looking for investment in businesses which have the potential for fairly rapid growth so that after a few years the company may apply to The Stock Exchange for its shares to be listed on the Alternative Investment Market. In this way, the venture capitalist will have the opportunity of selling its investment and realising a substantial gain. Typical features of venture capital include the following.

(1) The investment will be in ordinary shares in the company. The shareholding taken will be a substantial stake in the company but not normally a majority stake since such a surrender of control would usually be unacceptable to the individuals already running the company.
(2) Part of the investment may be in the form of loan finance.
(3) The venture capitalist may require that there are management changes in the company, including a seat on the board for its own representatives.
(4) Before investing, the venture capitalist will carry out a thorough investigation into the company's finances and future prospects by an examination of management accounts.

Chapter 20

LIABILITY

20.1 INTRODUCTION

The effect of a company being 'limited' is that, generally, liability for all debts and obligations rests with the company itself and does not pass to individuals involved in the company, However, there are circumstances in which the officers of the company do become personally liable either to the company itself or directly to third parties.

20.2 LIABILITY OF THE COMPANY

Although a company is a separate legal entity, it does not have a physical existence and therefore it needs real people to act on its behalf (agents). When an agent acts for the company, he may be restricted in what he can do by the objects clause of the company and by his own authority. An act may be unauthorised because it is ultra vires the company or because it is outside the scope of the authority of the agent acting for the company.

20.2.1 Ultra vires acts

A particular course of action is ultra vires the company if it is not within the scope of the company's permitted activities as stated in the objects clause in the company's memorandum. Once an act is undertaken (ie some legal obligation has been incurred) that action cannot be challenged, even if it is outside the scope of the objects clause. Both the company and the other party to the transaction are bound by it, and the validity and enforceability of the contract is not affected by the fact that the action was outside that which is permitted by the company's memorandum (CA 1985, s 35). However, any member can challenge a proposed ultra vires act on the basis that the company does not have the capacity to enter into the transaction concerned, and may ask the court to grant an injunction restraining the proposed action. This can only be done before any legal obligation is incurred by the company on the contract. After that, an aggrieved member's only remedy is to claim against the directors for breach of duty.

The outsider dealing with the company is not obliged to check the constitution of the company to see whether a particular transaction is authorised by the objects clause. The only relevance of the ultra vires rule to a third party dealing with the company is that an act which is not permitted by the memorandum may be restrained by injunction prior to it being undertaken, by which time both sides may have spent a great deal of time and effort conducting protracted negotiations.

20.2.2 Liability for acts of agents

The agents acting for the company are, principally, the directors and the secretary. This relationship is governed by the normal rules of agency. The officers of the

Chapter 20 contents
Introduction
Liability of the company
Liability of the officers of the company to the company itself
Liability of the directors and other officers to outsiders

company may have actual authority to act, thereby binding the company by their actions, or they may bind the company by acts within their apparent (ostensible) authority. Apparent authority may derive from holding a particular position within the company, or from representations from those having actual authority that a particular agent holds a position which would enable him to act on behalf of the company.

For example, the company secretary has apparent (and also, normally, actual) authority to make contracts on behalf of the company relating to the administrative side of the company's business. If a person had never formally been appointed to the post of company secretary but had been held out by the directors as holding that position, the person in question would have the same apparent authority as if he was the company secretary. The third party has no duty to make enquiries unless there is some reason for him to doubt the authority of the agent with whom he is dealing.

In addition, s 35A of CA 1985 provides that where the directors act as a board, their actions will bind the company irrespective of any restrictions there may be in the memorandum or articles. This power to authorise others to bind the company is also deemed to be without limitation.

An outsider dealing with the company is entitled to assume that the power of the directors to act on behalf of the company is unfettered. The third party is not required to consult the memorandum or articles (CA 1985, s 35B), and a company cannot escape liability on a contract by denying the authority of the board to act on its behalf, provided the outsider is acting in good faith. He will be acting in good faith even if he knows that the directors are acting outside the scope of their actual authority. For these purposes, bad faith involves some element of fraud or deception, for example conspiracy with the directors to cheat the company, and thereby the members.

If a member hears in advance that the directors are proposing to act beyond their authority, that member can apply to the court for an injunction to restrain the proposed misconduct. Once the unauthorised act has taken place, the aggrieved member's only remedy is to require the directors who are in breach of duty to indemnify the company for any loss it has suffered and account to the company for any profit they have made.

20.3 LIABILITY OF THE OFFICERS OF THE COMPANY TO THE COMPANY ITSELF

Where the company has entered into an ultra vires transaction, or an agent has made a contract which was outside his actual authority but within his apparent authority, thereby binding the company, the company cannot escape liability to the third party involved in these matters. However, since the action which has taken place was unauthorised, this is relevant to the question of the directors' (and other agents') liability to the company.

20.3.1 Liability for ultra vires acts

If the directors make the company party to an ultra vires transaction, they are acting in breach of duty and are therefore liable to indemnify the company for any loss it has suffered because of the ultra vires act and to account to the company for any profit they have made as a result.

The directors can be absolved from such liability if the members of the company are willing to pass two special resolutions; one ratifying the ultra vires act which has taken place and a second indemnifying the directors against any liability.

20.3.2 Liability for exceeding actual authority

Where a director or other agent of the company (eg the company secretary) binds the company by acting within his apparent authority, but exceeds his actual authority, that director or agent is acting in breach of duty. The person concerned is therefore liable to indemnify the company for any loss it has suffered and to account to the company for any profit he has made.

Any action by an officer of the company which is in breach of his duty to the company can be sanctioned by the company if the members agree to ratify the breach of duty by passing an ordinary resolution to that effect. This absolves the director or agent only if such approval of the members does not amount to a fraud on the minority. The ratification may be ineffective if those holding the majority of the shares in the company and thereby passing the ordinary resolution are the same people as those who have acted in breach of duty.

20.3.3 Enforcement

If a wrong is done to the company (eg if the directors have acted in breach of duty in some way), then the proper plaintiff in any legal action for breach of duty is the company itself. This means that generally it is for the directors or (if they are the ones in breach of duty and therefore unable to take action) the members to institute legal proceedings in the name of the company. The rule in *Foss v Harbottle* ((1843) 2 Hare 461) generally prevents minority shareholders from taking legal action on the company's behalf, although there are certain limited exceptions (see **12.7**). However, an action under CA 1985, s 459 may be more realistic.

20.4 LIABILITY OF THE DIRECTORS AND OTHER OFFICERS TO OUTSIDERS

20.4.1 Criminal penalties

Criminal sanctions usually apply not just to the directors of the company, but also to any 'officer' of the company. The term 'officer' applies to the directors, any manager and the company secretary (CA 1985, s 744). For example, the company secretary is liable, along with the directors, for failure to file the necessary returns with the registrar of companies.

20.4.2 Breach of warranty of authority

Where a director or other agent purports to act on behalf of the company but is acting outside the scope of his actual and apparent authority, he will not bind the company by his actions. The third party will, however, have a remedy against the director or other agent for breach of warranty of authority. He can claim against the director or other agent for any loss he has suffered as a result of that person's lack of authority.

20.4.3 Wrongful trading

If a director fails to take every step to minimise loss to creditors of the company at a time when he knew or ought to have known that there was no reasonable prospect of the company avoiding insolvent liquidation, then he will be liable for wrongful trading if the company goes into liquidation (IA 1986, s 214). The effect of this is that he can be required to contribute to the assets of the company, thereby increasing the amount available to pay creditors. A director will incur liability for wrongful trading if he fails to meet an objective standard of skill and care. He will be found liable, even though he was ignorant of any risk, if the court decides that he ought to have realised that the company was in serious financial difficulties.

20.4.4 Fraudulent trading

If anyone involved in running the company is knowingly a party to fraudulent trading, he too can be required to contribute to the assets of the company. Actions for fraudulent trading can be brought only when the company is in the process of being wound up, and liability is imposed only on those who actively and knowingly participated. Fraudulent trading involves continuing to incur debts and to trade while knowing that there is little chance of those debts being paid on the due date or within a reasonable time (IA 1986, s 213).

20.4.5 Personal guarantees

If directors have personally guaranteed a loan to the company and the company defaults under the terms of that loan, the lender (the debenture holder) may choose to enforce the guarantees against the personal assets of the directors. In extreme cases, directors could be required to sell their homes to repay the company's debt, or even be declared bankrupt.

20.4.6 Acting as director while disqualified

Any director who is guilty of acting while disqualified causes himself to be personally liable for the company's debts incurred during the period when he did so act (CDDA 1986, s 15). He is also liable to a fine on imprisonment (CDDA 1986, s 13).

Chapter 21

TAXATION

21.1 INTRODUCTION

Chapter 21 contents
Introduction
Taxation of the company – corporation tax
Taxation of directors and employees
Taxation of shareholders
Taxation of debenture holders

21.1.1 Taxation in the context of companies

A company is not charged to income tax or capital gains tax; it is charged to corporation tax. This difference between companies on the one hand and sole traders and partners on the other is not as fundamental as it might appear because, in calculating the company's profits chargeable to corporation tax, income profits are broadly calculated on the principles applicable to income tax and capital gains are broadly calculated on the principles applicable to capital gains tax.

The profits of the company may also be partly or wholly paid out to those involved with the company (such as directors and employees and/or shareholders) and so their tax position must also be considered. Finally, those who lend money to a company will usually receive interest on such loans, and the tax on that source of income is also considered in this chapter.

21.1.2 A company's income profits

The following aspects of taxation of business profits of an income nature were considered in Chapters 3 and 9 by reference to the position of a sole trader and that of a partnership:

(1) calculation of trading profit under Schedule D, Case I;
(2) the basis of assessing taxable profit for a given tax year;
(3) tax relief for expenditure on machinery and plant and industrial buildings by means of capital allowances;
(4) tax relief for trading losses.

In the context of a company, two of the above aspects are similarly applicable, one is significantly different and one needs to be adapted to the fact that the company is a legal person separate from its directors and shareholders:

(1) calculation of trading profit under Schedule D, Case I applies to companies as well as to sole traders and partnerships;
(2) the basis of assessing taxable profit of a company is significantly different to that for a sole trader or for partners (see **21.2.6**);
(3) tax relief for expenditure on machinery and plant and industrial buildings by means of capital allowances is available to companies;
(4) tax relief on trading losses is available to companies, albeit with some differences compared with sole traders and partnerships (see **21.2.3**).

21.1.3 A company's capital profits

The basic rules of capital gains tax apply to the disposal by a company of a chargeable asset belonging to it but with some important variations (see **21.2.4**).

21.2 TAXATION OF THE COMPANY – CORPORATION TAX

21.2.1 Introduction

A company is liable to pay corporation tax on its income profits and capital gains and the method of calculation of this is dealt with in detail at **21.2.2–21.2.8** below. In short, it involves the following steps:

Step 1 – Calculate income profits (see **21.2.2** and **21.2.3**)
Step 2 – Add chargeable gains (see **21.2.4**)
Step 3 – Deduct any charges on income (see **21.2.5**)
Step 4 – Calculate the tax (see **21.2.6** and **21.2.7**)

21.2.2 Income profits

A company's income profits chargeable to corporation tax will be calculated under the rules of the appropriate Schedule, most notably Schedule D, Case I, being applicable to profits from the carrying on of a trade. Calculation is likely therefore to involve the following steps.

(1) Trading profit – It will be necessary to calculate the chargeable receipts of the trade less expenditure of an income nature incurred wholly and exclusively for the purposes of the trade, as considered in Chapter 3.

　(a) Examples of a company's chargeable receipts of the trade will be similar to those previously considered for sole traders and partnerships.

　(b) Particular examples of payments which a company will be able to deduct for corporation tax purposes are:

　　(i) Directors' salaries or fees and benefits in kind. Occasionally there may be a problem over deductibility if a director is paid a salary that is excessive as remuneration for his services. If the salary is paid for personal reasons and not wholly and exclusively for the purposes of the trade, then it will not be deductible. It has been held (in *Copeman v William J. Flood and Sons Ltd* [1941] 1 KB 202) that a substantial salary paid to a director who performed minimal duties should be apportioned into two parts; that part which was reasonable for the duties performed would be deductible in calculating the company's taxable profits and the other excessive part would not. It is unlikely that this problem would arise over a salary paid to a director who works full-time for the company where the salary would be fully deductible for corporation tax purposes.

　　(ii) Contributions to a pension scheme for employees. These are fully deductible.

　　(iii) Payment to a director on termination of employment. Where a payment is made to a director by way of compensation for loss of office or employment, this will qualify as a deductible expense under the normal rules. Where a payment is made in return for a director's undertaking not to compete with the company's business following termination of his employment, such a payment is deductible under specific provisions (ICTA 1988, s 313, as amended, and see **21.3.4**).

　　(iv) Interest payments. These will generally be deductible under the normal rules.

(v) In calculating its trading profit, a company may also deduct capital allowances claimed on expenditure on machinery and plant and on industrial buildings. These are available by way of writing down allowance in the same way as described for sole traders (see **3.2.2**) and balancing charges or allowances also work similarly. The increased first year allowance available to small and medium businesses for expenditure on machinery and plant, and the 100 per cent allowance available for expenditure by small businesses on certain computer equipment are available to companies which satisfy the criteria for a 'small' or 'medium' enterprise respectively (there are special provisions to deal with groups of companies).

(2) The company may be able to reduce its trading profit by claiming relief for a loss previously suffered in the trade and 'carried forward' under s 393(1) of ICTA 1988 (see **21.2.3**).

(3) Finally, income from other sources may have to be added in (eg rental income calculated under Schedule A or interest on investments under Schedule D, Case III).

21.2.3 The scope for loss relief

The above calculations under Schedule D, Case I may produce a trading loss for which relief may be available. On the other hand, a trading loss from another accounting period may be allowed as a deduction from a trading profit just calculated. For companies, as for sole traders and partnerships, relief for trading losses is available in a variety of ways depending on the circumstances. The provisions available for companies work in a way which is broadly similar to that for sole traders and partnerships (see **3.4** and **9.2.2**); however, there is no provision for a company's start-up losses to be carried back and deducted from previous income of the proprietors (contrast the start-up losses of an unincorporated business). For a comparison of loss reliefs available to companies with those available to individuals, see **25.3**. The reliefs available to companies are as follows.

(1) Carry-across or carry-back relief for trading losses (ICTA 1988, s 393A)

A company's trading loss for an accounting period can be carried across to be deducted from profits (income or capital) from any source for the same accounting period. If these are insufficient to absorb (or fully to absorb) the loss, the loss (or remaining loss) can then be carried back to be deducted from profits (income or capital) from the previous accounting period (provided that the company was then carrying on the same trade); in this way, the company may recover corporation tax previously paid.

(2) Terminal carry-back relief for trading losses (ICTA, s 393A)

When a company ceases trading, a trading loss sustained in the final 12 months of trading can be carried back and set against the company's profits of any description from any accounting period (or part thereof) falling in the 3 years previous to the start of that final 12 months, taking later periods first. For example, a company with an accounting period that ends on 31 December and which makes a trading loss in 1999 and ceases trading on 31 December 1999, could deduct the 1999 loss from any profits made in 1998, then 1997, and finally 1996 until all the losses have been relieved.

(3) Carry-forward relief for trading losses (ICTA 1988, s 393(1))

A company's trading loss for an accounting period can be carried forward indefinitely to be deducted from subsequent profits which the trade produces. Section 393(1) does not allow relief against non-trading income or against capital gains.

21.2.4 Capital gains

A company's capital gains chargeable to corporation tax will be calculated under the general rules of capital gains tax with important modifications.

(1) A charge to corporation tax may arise where the company has made a disposal of a capital asset which results in a chargeable gain. This is calculated by deducting from the disposal value (on a sale, the sale price) the acquisition value (the purchase price) plus relevant expenditure and the indexation allowance. Note that the restrictions introduced on indexation as from 6 April 1998, by the Finance Act 1998, apply only to gains made by individuals and not to those made by companies. Note also that taper relief, also introduced by that Act, similarly applies only to chargeable gains made by individuals. For a company, therefore, the indexation allowance will be calculated on the acquisition value for the period from the month of acquisition to the month of disposal.

(2) The company may be entitled to set a relief against its gain. In the context of a company which is continuing its business, the main relief is the roll-over relief on replacement of qualifying assets (TCGA 1992, ss 152–159). This relief is the same as for partnerships and sole traders. For explanation and illustration of the working of the relief, see **9.3.4**. As a reminder:

   (a) the principal qualifying assets are goodwill, land, buildings, fixed plant and machinery (assets held as investments are not qualifying assets);

   (b) if one qualifying asset is sold and, within certain time-limits, the proceeds are used for the purchase of another qualifying asset, any liability to corporation tax on the sale of the 'old' asset can be postponed, at least until disposal of the 'new' asset, by rolling the indexed gain on sale into the acquisition value of the 'new' asset. The time-limits are that the 'new' asset must be purchased within one year before or within 3 years after the disposal of the 'old' asset.

(3) It is worth noting that, unlike a sole trader or partner, a company does not qualify for any annual exemption.

21.2.5 Deduction of charges on income (ICTA 1988, ss 338 and 348)

A company's income profits and capital gains for an accounting period will be added together to produce the company's total profit for that period. From these total profits may be deducted charges on income (eg patent royalties).

21.2.6 Calculating the tax

The series of steps described so far will establish the company's taxable profit for the accounting period and the corporation tax will be calculated on that figure by applying the appropriate rate. Where the company's accounting period is a period different from the corporation tax financial year (1 April to 31 March (see **21.2.7**)) and the rates of tax have changed from one tax year to the next, it will be necessary to apply the different rates to the appropriate portions of the accounting period. If, for example, a company has accounting periods of 1 January to 31 December, one-quarter of the full year's profit (representing the first 3 months) will be taxed at the appropriate rate for the finiancial year ending 31 March of that year and the remaining three-quarters of the profit will be taxed at the appropriate rate for the subsequent financial year. In this context, it is worth noting that, whereas income tax is assessed by reference to income tax years (on the profits of the accounting period which ends in the tax year), corporation tax is assessed (as just described) by reference to the company's own accounting period. The corporation tax thus calculated is payable within 9 months from the end of the accounting period. The company must make a payment to the Inland Revenue within this time-limit in relation to its anticipated corporation tax liability for that period, even though the final assessment may not have been agreed with the Inland Revenue (the deadline for the company's self-assessment return is 12 months after the end of the company's accounting period).

For large companies, a new system for the payment of corporation tax came into effect as regards accounting periods ending on or after 1 July 1999. Under the new system, such a company has to pay its corporation tax by four instalments. The system is being introduced through a transitional period of 4 years before it is fully effective. A 'large' company for this purpose is one with annual profits of £1,500,000 or over.

21.2.7 Rates of corporation tax

Corporation tax rates are fixed by reference to financial years, being the period from 1 April in one year to 31 March in the following year; this is marginally different from the income tax year which runs from 6 April to 5 April in the following year. Financial years are described by reference to the period in which they commence, so that the correct description for the corporation tax year running from 1 April 2000 to 31 March 2001 is 'Financial Year 2000'; this also is marginally different from the description of the income tax year which is described by reference to the years in which it begins and ends.

The full rate of corporation tax for the Financial Year 2000 is 30 per cent; this only operates where a company's profits reach £1,500,000, and the rate is applied to all of the company's taxable profits rather than just the excess over £1,500,000.

For companies whose annual profits do not exceed £10,000, there is a 'starting rate' of 10 per cent applied to all the taxable profits. For companies whose profits fall between £50,000 and £300,000, there is a 'small companies' rate of 20 per cent which again is applied to all the company's taxable profits. Special provisions exist for companies whose profits fall between £10,000 and £50,000, or those with profits between £300,000 and £1,500,000.

If a company's profits exceed £10,000, but do not reach £50,000, the first £10,000 is charged at 10 per cent and the excess over £10,000 is charged at a marginal rate of, effectively, 22.5 per cent. Once the company's profits exceed £50,000 the whole amount is taxed at 20 per cent until profits reach £300,000.

For a company whose profits exceed £300,000 but do not reach £1,500,000, the first £300,000 is charged at 20 per cent and the excess over £300,000 is charged at a marginal rate of, effectively, 32.5 per cent. As mentioned above, once a company's profits exceed £1,500,000 corporation tax is charged on the entire profit at 30 per cent.

The reason for these rather complex provisions is to 'smooth' the transition from one tax band to the next. As a company's profits approach a relevant threshold (£50,000 for the 20 per cent small companies' rate and £1,500,000 for the 30 per cent full rate) the marginal rate has the effect of bringing the total tax bill up towards the same figure as if the small companies' rate or the full rate (as the case may be) had been charged on the entire profit.

This can be represented in diagrammatic form:

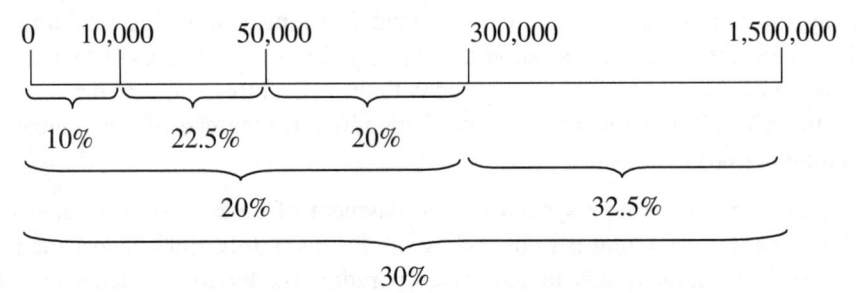

```
0     10,000      50,000           300,000              1,500,000
|_____|_____|_____|_____|
   10%      22.5%        20%
   _____/  _____/
            20%                          32.5%
   _____/
                            30%
```

In establishing the **rate** at which the company's profits are liable for corporation tax, it is not only the company's taxable profit that is relevant. The relevant profit figure is the taxable profit plus the company's 'franked investment income'. Franked investment income consists broadly of dividends received by the company (from companies which are not in the same group as it) plus the 10 per cent tax credit. However, in calculating **how much** tax is payable, franked investment income is not actually charged to corporation tax. The effect of the franked investment income is to reduce the amount of the starting rate band or small company rate band (as the case may be) available to a company that also receives dividends from other companies.

Example

Company A has trade profits of £1,400,000 and franked investment income of £100,000. Company A is not taxed on the £100,000 franked investment income but, because the total of its trade profits plus the franked investment income reaches £1,500,000, it will be taxed at 30 per cent on the whole of its trade profits.

21.2.8 Illustration of corporation tax calculation

The accountant of A Co Ltd produces the following figures relevant to calculation of the company's income profits for the year:

- chargeable receipts are £95,000
- £18,000 is deductible in respect of salaries
- £10,000 is deductible in respect of capital allowances
- income from rents (after deductible expenditure) is £48,000.

In addition, the company has sold some land which was surplus to requirements and has made a chargeable gain of £50,000; it has no plans to buy replacement assets.

The company has paid in total £8,000 in dividends to its shareholders (these are not deductible – see **21.2.9**).

The calculation of the company's corporation tax liability may be summarised as follows:

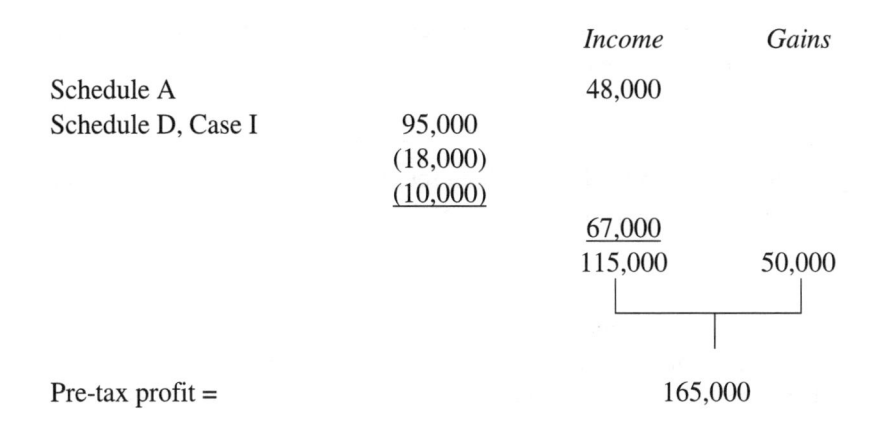

		Income	*Gains*
Schedule A		48,000	
Schedule D, Case I	95,000		
	(18,000)		
	(10,000)		
		67,000	
		115,000	50,000

Pre-tax profit = 165,000

Corporation tax on £165,000 at 20% = £33,000

21.2.9 Dividends

Dividends paid by a company are not deductible in calculating the company's taxable profit, but are treated as distributions of profit. Similarly, when a company buys back its own shares from shareholders (see **17.6**), the payment is not deductible in calculating the company's taxable profit and that part of the price which is over and above the allotment price may be treated in the same way as a dividend. Neither of these payments reduces the company's profits chargeable to corporation tax.

21.2.10 'Close companies'

(1) Introduction

In addition to the general rules governing the taxation of companies, special provisions exist that apply to companies controlled by a small number of people. These companies are known as 'close companies' and the rules exist to try and stop trading via a company being significantly more or less attractive (from a tax perspective) than trading as a sole trader or via a partnership.

(2) Definitions (ICTA 1988, ss 414, 416 and 417)

(a) A 'close company' is one which is controlled by five or fewer participators or by participators (however many) who are directors (or shadow directors) (ICTA 1988, s 414).
(b) A 'participator' is essentially a person owning, or having the right to acquire, shares in the company.
(c) Broadly, 'control' exists in the hands of those having, or having the right to acquire, more than half of the shares or more than half of the voting power. The test for 'control' does not depend on whether particular shareholders whose combined shareholdings represent a majority actually act together, but rather on whether, if they were to act together, the company would be under their control. In establishing who has control, any rights of a participator's 'associate' (defined so as to apply principally to a close relative or a business partner) are treated as rights of that participator.

Example 1

AB Company Ltd has nine shareholders. This must be a close company because, whatever the distribution of shareholdings, there must be at most five who, between them, own a majority – even if all nine shareholders have equal shareholdings, five of them must hold a majority compared with the other four.

Example 2

CD Company Ltd has 100 shareholders of whom four own between them 51 per cent of the shares. This is a close company.

Example 3

EF Company Ltd has 18 shareholders, consisting of nine married couples. This is a close company because a married couple can be identified as a participator and an associate and therefore only counts as one person in assessing control. Effectively, therefore, there are nine participators for gauging control and five of them must hold a majority of the shares (as in Example 1).

Example 4

GH Company Ltd has 25 equal shareholders, none of whom are 'associates' of one another. They are all directors. This is a close company under the second part of the s 414 definition because, although control is in the hands of 13 participators (being the bare majority), those participators are all directors.

(3) *The special provisions applying to close companies*

(A) THE CHARGE TO TAX IMPOSED WHEN A CLOSE COMPANY MAKES A LOAN TO A PARTICIPATOR (ICTA 1988, s 419)

(i) The company's position

Subject to exceptions (see below), when a close company makes a loan to a participator or to his associate, the company must pay to the Inland Revenue a sum equivalent to one-quarter of the loan. Thus it will cost a close company £100,000 to lend £80,000 to a participator or to his associate, since on top of the loan it must pay an additional £20,000 to the Inland Revenue.

The sum paid to the Inland Revenue is in the nature of a deposit since it will be refunded to the company if, and when, the recipient of the loan (the participator or his associate) repays the loan to the company or if the loan is written off.

(ii) The borrower's position

From the borrower's point of view, the loan has the advantage that it is a receipt of money which is not taxable in his hands so long as it remains a loan; however, if the debt is written off by the company, it is charged under the Schedule F regime as if the borrower received a payment net of 10 per cent tax (see **21.4.1**).

Example

In June 1999 A Ltd, a close company, lends £80,000 to B, a participator (shareholder) in the company. In June 2000 the debt is written off by the company so B does not have to repay it.

(1) At the time of the loan A Ltd must pay £20,000 (one quarter of £80,000) to the Inland Revenue. There are no tax consequences for B at this stage.
(2) When the debt is written off, the Inland Revenue will repay the £20,000 to A Ltd. B is treated as receiving a net payment of £80,000 with a 10 per cent tax

credit. The gross sum of £88,888 will form part of B's statutory income for 2000/01.

(iii) The exceptions (ICTA 1988, s 420)

The charge to tax described does not apply:

(1) if the loan is made in the ordinary course of a money-lending business (eg a bank loan to someone who happens to hold shares in the company);
(2) if the loan (together with any outstanding loan to the same person) does not exceed £15,000 and the borrower works full-time for the company and owns less than 5 per cent of the company's shares.

(iv) The reason for the charge

These provisions may seem particularly complex for what they achieve, but their significance can best be appreciated by considering the provisions as being directed at tax avoidance. Without such provisions, a major tax saving could be achieved by the use of close companies, particularly for a participator who is a higher rate income tax payer. Whereas any withdrawal of the company's profits in the form of salary (as employee director) or dividend (as shareholder) will attract a charge to income tax in the hands of the recipient, money which is borrowed from the company is not income at all and therefore cannot in principle attract income tax.

A clear disadvantage to the borrower is that a loan must normally be repaid, perhaps with interest, but if the company is closely controlled the company may not enforce the obligation to repay for many years, if at all. Therefore, subject to that possible disadvantage, there would be a clear incentive to use the borrowing device to avoid the payment of income tax.

Section 419 of the ICTA 1988 helps to close that loophole, although the use of loans may still help defer the payment of tax for the individual borrower which may have a cash flow advantage. A higher rate taxpayer may also benefit by postponing the time when the payment is treated as chargeable in his hands to some future date when he may no longer be a higher rate taxpayer (eg following retirement).

When loans are made to directors, consideration should also be given to the provisions of CA 1985, s 330 (see **13.12.4**).

(B) INCOME TAX RELIEF ON A SHAREHOLDER'S BORROWINGS (ICTA 1988, ss 353 and 362)

Not all provisions relating to close companies are aimed at preventing tax avoidance. A shareholder who takes out a loan in order to purchase shares in a close company or to lend money to it may be able to claim tax relief on the interest he pays on his borrowings. This relief is described at **21.4.2**.

21.3 TAXATION OF DIRECTORS AND EMPLOYEES

21.3.1 Introduction

A substantial proportion (sometimes the whole) of the company's trading receipts may be absorbed by paying salaries or fees and other benefits to the company's directors and other employees. Since these are deductible in calculating profits chargeable to corporation tax, it follows that a substantial proportion of the company's trading receipts may ultimately attract income tax as the income of the directors/employees rather than corporation tax as the company's taxable profit. The charge to income tax on directors and employees is under Schedule E.

21.3.2 The income chargeable generally under Schedule E

Income tax is charged under Schedule E on the emoluments of an office or employment. 'Emoluments' include all benefits received by the director or employee which derive from his office or employment as a reward for his services, whether they are paid by the employer or by a third party. Thus, salaries, bonuses and tips are taxable emoluments; a gift on the other hand for purely personal reasons would not be a taxable emolument since it is not a reward for services. In relation to non-cash benefits such as company cars, there are particular provisions which require separate consideration.

21.3.3 Non-cash benefits

(1) The general rules

(a) Common examples of non-cash benefits provided or paid for by the employer are:

   (i) the use of a company car for private as well as business use;
   (ii) the provision of private medical insurance;
   (iii) an interest-free or low-interest loan;
   (iv) rent-free or low-rent living accommodation;
   (v) an expenses allowance;
   (vi) vouchers exchangeable for goods or services (eg a season ticket for a football club).

(b) The provisions make a fundamental distinction in the taxation of non-cash benefits between:

   (i) employees whose emoluments are at least £8,500 pa (described hereafter as 'higher-paid employees') and company directors generally; and
   (ii) other non-director employees (described hereafter as 'lower-paid employees').

   Often, a director will be an employee of the company in a defined role (eg as sales manager) but this is not always the case. A non-executive director may simply attend board meetings and receive fees for doing so; this is why company directors generally are brought within the legislation along with higher-paid employees. The phrase 'higher-paid employee' may seem a misdescription when the threshold level of emoluments is set at £8,500 – this is because the threshold has not been raised since 1979!

(c) Higher-paid employees and company directors generally (ICTA 1988, ss 153–168).

   In assessing whether or not a person is 'a higher-paid employee', the value (assessed as explained below) of all taxable emoluments must be taken into account. Thus an employee with a salary of £7,500 pa plus the unrestricted use of a company car and with private medical insurance paid for by the employer is bound to have emoluments of at least £8,500 pa, because the cost to the employer of providing the company car and insurance will, taken with the salary, reach and exceed the £8,500 limit. A company director (unless, broadly, he has no more than 5 per cent of the shares in the company and works full-time for the company (ICTA 1988, s 167)) is treated in the same way as a higher-paid employee irrespective of the level of his emoluments.

Higher-paid employees and company directors generally are liable to income tax under Schedule E on all benefits which derive from the office or employment.

Generally, the taxable value of the benefit is taken as the amount of the cost incurred by the employer in providing that benefit. Thus where the employer pays premiums for private medical insurance provided for the employee, pays rent for a house provided for the employee and pays for the employee's season ticket for his local football club, the employee will be assessed to income tax on the benefits valued on the amount of the premiums paid, the rent paid and the cost of the season ticket. Naturally, if the employee reimburses the employer to any extent (eg paying half of the rent), this reduces the cost incurred by the employer and hence reduces the taxable value of the benefit.

In some instances the taxable value of the benefit is calculated on a different basis; for example if the employer actually owns the asset, there may be no ongoing cost to the employer in providing that asset. In this case, Parliament sets prescribed methods for calculating the value of the benefit to the employee in each year. Particular examples are as follows.

(i) Private use of a company car: the taxable value of the benefit is generally 35 per cent of the list price of the car (and accessories). This is reduced to 25 per cent if the employee puts in at least 2,500 business miles during the year and to 15 per cent for 18,000 business miles or more.

(ii) Private use of other company assets such as a house or a yacht: the taxable value of the benefit is its annual value; for a house this will usually be its rateable value, whilst for other assets this will be 20 per cent of the market value of the asset at the time it was first provided as a benefit.

(iii) Loan by the employer: the taxable value of the benefit is the interest 'saved' by the director/employee as compared with the official interest rate as set each tax year. For 2000/01, the official rate is 6.25 per cent. Thus if a director/employee pays no interest on a loan from his employer in 2000/01, the amount he has saved by not paying interest at 6.25 per cent will be treated as part of his income under Schedule E. (However, see the exception below.)

(d) Lower-paid non-director employees.
The lower-paid, non-director category of employee is treated more favourably in relation to non-cash benefits.

Lower-paid non-director employees are generally taxed on a non-cash benefit only if the benefit can be converted into money by the employee. This means that these employees would suffer no charge to tax on the use of a company car, private medical insurance or an interest free loan (provided the total level of all taxable emoluments in the tax year does not reach the £8,500 threshold). By way of exception, however, lower-paid, non-director employees are liable to tax in the same way as higher-paid employees on the benefits of rent-free or low-rent accommodation and of vouchers.

An expenses allowance is not liable to tax unless the Inland Revenue can establish that it is an emolument of the employment rather than a genuine expenses allowance. (The position is reversed for higher-paid employees who will suffer tax on the expenses allowance unless they can establish that the expenditure to which the allowance relates is deductible under Schedule E (see **21.3.5**).)

The taxable value of a non-cash benefit on which a lower-paid, non-director employee suffers a charge to tax is the amount of money into which it could be converted. Thus if such an employee receives a gift of a suit of clothing from his employer, he will be liable to tax on the second-hand value of the suit; the higher-paid employee would have been assessed on the cost to the employer of providing the benefit.

(2) Exceptions

There are exceptions in the following cases, where the charge to tax described above will not apply to either lower- or higher-paid employees:

(a) Certain accommodation

In certain instances, employees are not charged to tax (but generally directors are) on the benefit of rent-free or low-rent accommodation. Common examples are caretakers (exemption because occupation is necessary for the performance of the employee's duties) and police and fire officers (exemption because occupation is customary and for the better performance of the employee's duties).

(b) Interest-free or low-interest loans

There is no charge to tax where the total outstanding on all beneficial loans from the employer does not exceed £5,000 at any time in the tax year.

(c) Employer's pension contributions

The director/employee is not charged to tax on the benefit of those contributions.

(3) Share schemes

The employer company may provide the employee or director with non-cash benefits which relate to shares in the company. These can take a variety of forms including a gift of the shares, a sale of the shares at a favourable price, a sale of the shares on terms where payment for them is postponed, an option to purchase shares in the future and various schemes involving the use of trusts. The tax treatment of such benefits requires more detailed explanation than is appropriate here, but it is worth noting that there are possible tax and other advantages to both the company employer and the employee or director in using these schemes.

21.3.4 Other income chargeable

A number of other receipts are fully chargeable under Schedule E:

(1) maternity pay;
(2) a lump sum received at the beginning of the employment and referrable to future services (a 'golden hello');
(3) a lump sum received at the end of the employment when the employee was entitled to the payment under his contract of employment;
(4) a lump sum received in return for the employee entering into a covenant not to compete with the employer's trade on cessation of employment (ICTA 1988, s 313, as amended);

(5) pensions;
(6) other payments.

A sum received on termination of office which is not otherwise chargeable to income tax is brought into charge by ICTA 1988, s 148, even though it does not derive from the office or employment as a reward for services. Examples include a redundancy payment, compensation for unfair dismissal, damages for wrongful dismissal or even a gratuitous payment (a gift) on termination of the employment. However, the first £30,000 of any such sum is exempt so that (in view of the maximum available) there will be no actual charge on, for example, a statutory redundancy payment.

Any payment on termination which exceeds £30,000 will attract income tax on the excess. Because of the exemption for the first £30,000, it is clear that it is advantageous to the employee from a tax viewpoint if any termination payment is caught by s 148 rather than the ordinary rules of Schedule E. The ordinary rules of Schedule E take priority to s 148. It may therefore be undesirable, for example, for the employee's contract to provide for a lump sum payment on termination or for payment in lieu of notice, since this would be taxable under the ordinary rules and there would be no £30,000 exemption. On the other hand, if the lack of contractual obligation means the employer chooses to make no terminal payment, the employee may lose the entire payment, not just the tax element of it.

21.3.5 Deductible expenditure

(1) The general test (ICTA 1988, s 198)

In calculating what is taxable under Schedule E, an employee or director is generally entitled only to deduct expenditure which is incurred 'wholly, exclusively **and necessarily** in the performance of his duties'. Travelling expenses and certain other items of expenditure are considered separately below. The 'wholly and exclusively' part of the test is the same as that considered in **3.2.1** in relation to Schedule D, Case I, where duality of purpose is generally fatal to a claim for deduction.

The Schedule E test is more severe in two respects:

(a) it contains the additional requirement of necessity, so that it must be shown that the employee's duties could not be performed without the expenditure in question;

(b) it contains the additional requirement that the expenditure was incurred in the performance of the duties so that, for example, expenditure incurred when preparing for the duties (eg in finding the job through an agency) is not deductible.

(2) Concessions

The Schedule E test is so severe that there are few examples of expenditure that will satisfy the test. In a few instances the position is alleviated by extra-statutory concessions:

(A) TRAVELLING EXPENSES

Deductibility of travelling expenses depends on a slightly different test in that the expenditure must be necessarily incurred in the performance of the duties; it need not be wholly and exclusively incurred. It is clear that the employee/director who incurs expenditure when travelling from one place of work to another can treat that expenditure as deductible. However, this must be distinguished from travelling from home to the place of work; this travel cannot be in the performance of the duties, because the performance will only commence when the employee gets to work.

(B) PENSION CONTRIBUTIONS

An employee, or director, is entitled to deduct his contributions to an occupational pension scheme or to a personal pension scheme, although if such contributions exceed certain limits the excess will not be deductible. On the other hand, national insurance contributions of the employee or director are not deductible.

21.3.6 Collection of Schedule E tax (ICTA 1988, s 203)

Tax on the emoluments of an office or employment is deducted at source by the employer under the PAYE (Pay As You Earn) system and paid to the Inland Revenue on the basis of earnings received in the tax year. This applies to most emoluments of the employment, whether cash or non-cash (only the tax on non-cash benefits which are not readily convertible into cash is not collected via PAYE). Tax is collected at all appropriate rates (starting, basic and higher). The system works by the Inland Revenue allocating to each taxpayer who is a director or an employee a code number based on information relating to his earnings and allowances. This code number is communicated to the employer who is provided with Tables which enable him to calculate how much tax should be deducted before the director or employee's earnings are paid to him. The tax is then paid by the employer to the Inland Revenue. Employees/directors are, therefore, taxed on their income sooner under Schedule E than a sole trader or partner who is assessed under Schedule D Case I (see **25.2.1**).

21.4 TAXATION OF SHAREHOLDERS

21.4.1 Income tax under Schedule F on dividends and certain other receipts (ICTA 1988, Pt VI)

(1) Dividends

Schedule F charges income tax on dividends received in the current tax year.

(A) DEDUCTIBLE EXPENDITURE

There are no provisions in Schedule F for expenditure of any description to be deducted in calculating the amount of income which is taxable. For example, a shareholder cannot obtain relief for pension contributions against taxation of his dividend income. However, if the shareholder has borrowed money to purchase his shares, the interest payments may be deductible from his income generally (ie from his 'statutory income') (see **21.4.2**).

(B) TAX CREDIT

The dividend payment which the shareholder receives is treated as being paid net of tax at 10 per cent, and so with the dividend payment the shareholder receives a tax credit, fixed by reference to the 'tax credit fraction'. This fraction is one ninth of the dividend received, and it results in a tax credit of 10 per cent of the aggregate of the dividend received *plus* the tax credit. Thus, if a company pays a dividend of £900 on 1 July 2000, the credit (of one ninth of the dividend received) will be £100, being 10 per cent of the dividend *plus* the credit (ie 10 per cent of £1,000).

(C) RATES OF TAX

Dividend payments are treated as the 'top slice' of a person's income. If, taking a person's other income into account for the tax year in question, the taxpayer is liable to income tax at either starting rate or basic rate, the dividend will be taxed at the 'Schedule F Ordinary Rate' of 10 per cent. This rate is the same as the tax credit and so no further income tax will be due from the taxpayer. If the taxpayer is liable to tax at the higher rate, it will be chargeable at the 'Schedule F Upper Rate' of 32.5 per cent. The taxpayer is then liable for the difference between the tax credit of 10 per cent and tax at 32.5 per cent. Note that the tax credit is non-repayable to a non-taxpayer.

(2) Written-off loan to a participator in a close company (ICTA 1988, s 421)

If the company in question is a close company (see **21.2.10**) and makes a loan to a shareholder, there may ultimately be income tax consequences for the shareholder. The company suffered the immediate consequence of having to pay to the Inland Revenue corporation tax equivalent to one-quarter of the loan (see **21.2.10**). The income tax consequences for the shareholder only arise if and when the company writes off the loan, so that the shareholder no longer has any obligation to repay. At this point the loan is treated as Schedule F income but with the benefit of the 10 per cent tax credit (see the example at **21.2.10**).

(3) 'Profit' on sale of shares back to the company

A charge to income tax under Schedule F may be made when a shareholder sells his shares back to the company itself. The profit represented by the excess of the sale price over and above the issue price of the shares may be treated in the same way as a dividend (as described above). Note that it is not possible for the seller to recover the tax credit if he is not liable to income tax. The treatment does not always apply and the profit may attract capital gains tax instead where certain conditions are satisfied; this possibility is considered further in **21.4.5**.

21.4.2 Income tax relief on a shareholder's borrowing

(1) The relief

Where a taxpayer pays interest on a loan taken for a 'qualifying purpose', that interest qualifies for tax relief (ICTA 1988, ss 353 and 360). As with a charge on income it is deductible from the taxpayer's statutory income (ie income from all sources under the different Schedules) in calculating the taxpayer's total income (from which will be deducted personal reliefs in calculating taxable income for the year).

(2) Conditions

(a) The 'qualifying purpose' of a loan which is relevant in this context is the purchase of ordinary shares in a close company which carries on a trade or for the borrower then to lend the money to such a company.
(b) It is a further condition that the borrower must either:

   (i) control (by personal ownership or through another person) more than 5 per cent of the company's ordinary shares; or
   (ii) be a shareholder (however few shares he owns) and work for the greater part of his time in the management or conduct of the company.

Any shares acquired as a result of the borrowing are counted in applying either limb of this condition.

21.4.3 Income tax relief under the Enterprise Investment Scheme (EIS) or under a Venture Capital Trust (VCT)

(1) EIS

(a) The Enterprise Investment Scheme (EIS) is the latest in a line of initiatives by successive governments to encourage investment in risky 'enterprise' companies.

(b) The relief is complex but, in general terms, if an individual has issued to him (in return for cash) ordinary shares in a qualifying EIS company, he can obtain income tax relief on the investment (up to a maximum investment of £150,000 in any one tax year). The relief is given by deducting a sum equal to 20 per cent of the cost of the investment from the shareholder's tax liability for the tax year of the investment (the maximum deduction is, therefore, £30,000).

(c) Only certain companies qualify for the purposes of the relief. The company must be unquoted and carry on a trade which is not excluded (excluded activities include property development, farming, banking and share dealing). There are also limits on the value of the company's assets and on the type of shares which can be issued (essentially only ordinary shares qualify).

(d) During the 2 years before and the 3 years after the issue of the shares to him, the shareholder must not be 'connected' to the company. In general, a person will be connected to the company if he or his associate is an employee or paid director of the company (subject to exceptions) or if he owns (alone or with an associate) more than 30 per cent of the capital or voting power of the company. 'Associate' is defined as for a close company (see **21.2.10**) but does not include brothers and sisters. For further details of the conditions attaching to EIS investments, see the LPC Resource Book *Pervasive and Core Topics* (Jordans). The relief may also be lost if the individual disposes of his qualifying shares within 3 years of their issue to him.

(2) VCT

A Venture Capital Trust (VCT) is a quoted company which acts as a 'wrapper' to hold shares in unquoted companies which match the EIS criteria. An investor can then acquire shares in the VCT, thus spreading the risk of his investment across several businesses. The income tax relief for acquiring new shares in a VCT is roughly similar to that for EIS relief, but to qualify the shares must be held for 3 years and the maximum investment each tax year is £100,000 (so the maximum tax deduction in any one tax year is £20,000). An additional income tax relief for VCT shares is that any dividends from the VCT are tax free.

21.4.4 Capital taxation on disposal of shares generally

Where shares are sold for their full value, there may be a charge to capital gains tax (or possibly income tax if sold back to the company). Where shares are given away or sold for less than their full value, there may be charges to capital gains tax and inheritance tax. These topics are considered in Chapter 22.

21.4.5 Taxation on sale of shares back to the company (ICTA 1988, ss 219–229)

As mentioned at **21.4.1**, the 'profit' on a sale of shares by a shareholder back to the company which issued the shares is usually charged to income tax.

If certain conditions are satisfied, however, the shareholder's 'profit' on sale of his shares back to the company must be taxed on a CGT basis and therefore not on the income tax basis described in **21.4.1**.

Broadly, the conditions are as follows.

(1) The company must be a trading company and its shares must not be quoted on The Stock Exchange itself (although the shares may be dealt in on the AIM).
(2) The purpose of the buy-back must not be to avoid tax; it must either be to raise cash to pay IHT arising from a death or be for the benefit of the company's trade. For example, the latter purpose might arise where the selling shareholder is at odds with the other shareholders so that the proper functioning of the company can best be achieved by the departure of the seller.
(3) The seller must have owned the shares being sold back for at least 5 years.
(4) The seller must either be selling all of his shares in the company or at least be substantially reducing his percentage shareholding to no more than 30 per cent of the issued share capital of the company. A 'substantial' reduction in the shareholding is a reduction of at least 25 per cent.

The question of whether the CGT basis or the income tax basis will apply to the sale of shares back to the company may be very important to the seller in that a significant difference in his liability to tax may be involved. If the CGT basis applies, the availability of reliefs (such as retirement relief), taper relief and the annual exemption may mean that he is not liable to tax. On the other hand, if the income tax basis applies, the tax credit of 10 per cent will mean that the maximum amount of tax which the seller will be left to pay under Schedule F (his 'excess liability') is 22.5 per cent (and this is only where he is a higher rate taxpayer).

Which treatment is preferable will depend on the seller's own circumstances and it may be possible to structure the sale back to ensure the most favourable tax treatment is obtained.

21.4.6 Corporation tax on dividends received

If a company receives dividends from shares it holds in another UK company, these dividends (and the tax credit that attaches to them) will generally be classed as 'franked investment income'. The effect of such franked investment income on the company's corporation tax bill is discussed at **21.2.7**.

21.5 TAXATION OF DEBENTURE HOLDERS

21.5.1 Income tax under Schedule D, Case III

(1) Interest payments

Schedule D, Case III charges income tax on interest receivable. When paid interest, the debenture holder will receive a sum which is net of tax deducted at source by the paying company at the rate of 20 per cent. This means that, depending on the level of his taxable income for the year, the individual debenture holder will either be:

(a) entitled to reclaim tax from the Inland Revenue (if he is a non-taxpayer or only liable to tax at the starting rate);
(b) will have no further tax liability (if liable to basic rate tax but not higher rate tax); or
(c) will have excess liability at 20 per cent of the gross interest before deduction of tax (if liable to higher rate tax).

(2) Deductible expenditure

There are no provisions in Schedule D, Case III for expenditure of any description to be deducted in calculating the amount of income which is taxable. For example, a debenture holder cannot use his income from this source to obtain tax relief on any pension contributions which he may be making. However, if the debenture holder has borrowed the money which he is himself lending to a 'close company', his interest payments may be deductible from his statutory income generally (see **21.4.2**).

21.5.2 Corporation tax

If a company invests by making a loan to another company (or to an individual), the interest it receives on the loan will also be paid net of tax deducted at source of 20 per cent. The gross amount of the interest is included in the profits of the company for its accounting period (see **21.2.2**) and taxed in the usual way, with a credit for the tax deducted at source being given against the final corporation tax bill.

PART V

DISPOSING OF BUSINESS ASSETS OR BUSINESS INTERESTS

Where there is a disposal of a business asset by a sole trader, partnership, company or shareholder, there will be capital gains tax implications and, if the disposal is by way of gift (or sale at an undervalue), there will also be inheritance tax implications.

Where a sole trader or partnership wishes to dispose of the entire business, certain steps and documentation will be required, as considered in Part VIII of this book. If one partner wishes to leave a partnership and to dispose of his interest in the business to the other partners, this disposal may simply take place under an existing partnership agreement, the terms of which provide for the assignment of the outgoing partner's share in the assets to the others and for the fixing and payment of the price; in the absence of any such agreement, the partners may negotiate an agreement as to such matters. These points were considered in Part III. If a shareholder wishes to dispose of his shares in a company, there will be a transfer of his shares, as described in Part IV, and, if he owns an asset such as business premises used by the company, he may negotiate and effect a sale of that asset to the company.

This Part aims to consider the tax implications of all these disposals by describing the possible charge(s) to tax and the relief(s) which may be available.

Chapter 22

CAPITAL TAXATION ON DISPOSALS

22.1 INTRODUCTION

Capital taxation involves the application of capital gains tax (CGT) (or corporation tax where the disponer is a company) and/or inheritance tax (IHT). When dealing with these taxes, the starting point is to identify what it is that may give rise to a charge to tax by looking at what is disposed of and at the type of disposal (broadly, sale, gift or death). Having identified a possible charge to tax, the next step is to identify what (if any) reliefs and/or exemptions might be available.

22.2 THE SUBJECT MATTER OF A CHARGE TO TAX

22.2.1 Sole trader

A sole trader may dispose of his business (or a part of it) which will comprise not only his tangible assets such as premises and fixtures but also his intangible asset of goodwill; disposal of these assets may have capital gains tax implications. (The tangible assets will also include trading stock and perhaps machinery and plant, in relation to both of which a disposal may have income tax implications rather than capital gains tax implications; the disposal of trading stock will be relevant to calculation of the final trading profit and the disposal of machinery and plant may result in a balancing charge or allowance for income tax purposes under the capital allowances system (see **3.2.2**).) If the disposal is not a sale at full value, it may also lead to inheritance tax implications.

22.2.2 Partner

A partner may dispose of his interest in the partnership business, comprising his fractional share in each of the assets of the business (as in **22.2.1**). This is equally the case if the firm is selling its business in that every partner is then disposing of his interest in the business. In addition, a partner may dispose of a particular asset (most notably the business premises) which is owned by him individually although used by the firm. (The sale of a particular asset by the firm is dealt with in detail at **9.3**.)

22.2.3 Shareholder

A shareholder in a company may dispose of his shares in the company and, perhaps, a particular asset owned by him individually although used by the company.

22.2.4 Company

A company may dispose of its business (or a part of it) in much the same way as a sole trader will dispose of his business, although special provisions may apply when the disposal is not a sale at full value (see **22.3.3**).

Chapter 22 contents
Introduction
The subject matter of a charge to tax
When and how capital taxation applies: principles
Capital tax reliefs
Summaries and checklists

22.3 WHEN AND HOW CAPITAL TAXATION APPLIES: PRINCIPLES

22.3.1 Sale at full value by individual or by company

(1) Capital gains tax on a sale by an individual

Where there is a disposal of assets as in **22.2** (whether by a sole trader, an individual partner, or partners acting together to sell a partnership asset) and the disposal is a sale at full value, there may be a charge to capital gains tax insofar as there is a disposal of chargeable assets which have increased in value during the period of ownership. For full details of the steps involved in calculating capital gains tax, see the LPC Resource Book *Pervasive and Core Topics* (Jordans). In outline, the gain is established as follows:

(a) add together the acquisition value (or for an asset acquired before March 1982, its market value at that time if higher), any items of expenditure reflected in the asset's value and any incidental costs of acquisition and disposal (such as professional fees);

(b) to the total in (a), add an indexation allowance so that any increase in value purely reflecting inflation over the relevant period (judged by the increase in the retail prices index) is taken into account. Note that, in disposals by individuals for gains made after 5 April 1998, the allowance is given only for periods up to that date, and, where the assets are acquired on or after 1 April 1998, no indexation allowance is given;

(c) deduct the total of (a) and (b) from the sale price (assuming a sale at full value) to find the (indexed) chargeable gain. If the total of (a) and (b) exceeds the sale price there will be no gain and may even be a loss, but note that the indexation allowance cannot be used to create or increase a loss;

(d) having established the chargeable gain, the reliefs described at **22.4.1** should be considered;

(e) for disposals by individuals, taper relief may be available to reduce the amount of the chargeable gain, depending (broadly) on how long the individual has owned the asset for periods after 5 April 1998. A far more generous rate of taper relief applies if the asset is a business asset;

(f) the annual exemption may, if available, be deducted from the tapered gain to establish the taxable amount of the gain.

(2) Corporation tax on a sale by a company

The capital gains chargeable to corporation tax on the disposal of a chargeable asset by a company are calculated as described at **21.2.4**. The main differences to note in the method used, as compared to that for individuals, are that the indexation allowance is given to the date of disposal by the company, and that taper relief is not applicable.

(3) Inheritance tax

There is no possible liability to inheritance tax on a sale at full value because there has been no 'transfer of value' under which the value of the disponer's estate is reduced.

22.3.2 Gift by individual

(1) Capital gains tax

Where an individual makes a gift of a chargeable asset (or of his share in a chargeable asset in the case of a partner), this is a disposal which may give rise to a chargeable gain in the same way as a sale at full value except that in calculating the disponer's gain it is necessary to use the asset's market value at disposal (as opposed to sale price). The logic of this lies in the fact that the tax is imposed broadly on the increase in the asset's value during the period of ownership rather than on any gain in monetary terms that the disponer has actually realised.

(2) Inheritance tax

Where an individual makes a gift of an asset, at the same time as being a disposal for capital gains tax purposes, this is a disposition which reduces the value of his estate and hence is a transfer of value for inheritance tax purposes. For full details of the steps involved in calculating inheritance tax, see LPC Resource Book *Pervasive and Core Topics* (Jordans). Broadly speaking, unless the gift is into a discretionary trust or to a company (a chargeable transfer), the gift is likely to be a potentially exempt transfer so that there is no immediate charge to inheritance tax. The charge to inheritance tax will only arise if the transferor then dies within 7 years of the gift. If death does occur within the 7 years, then (in outline) the possible charge to inheritance tax on the gift is worked out as follows.

(a) The value transferred is calculated by establishing the loss to the transferor's estate resulting from the disposition.
(b) Any available exemption is applied to the value transferred.
(c) Following the application of available exemptions, the possibility of reliefs should also be considered (see **22.4.3**).
(d) The resulting figure is that on which inheritance tax will be calculated. The rate of inheritance tax is ascertained by cumulating this figure with any other chargeable transfers by the transferor within the 7 years prior to the gift in question. If the resulting total does not exceed £234,000 (2000/2001), the rate of tax is nil. Insofar as the gift represents any part of the resulting total exceeding £234,000 the rate of tax on that part is 40 per cent.
(e) When tax has been calculated as above, tapering relief will be applied if the transferor survived 3 years from the gift:
   (i) if death occurred between 3 and 4 years after the gift, the tax on the gift is reduced by 20 per cent (ie only 80 per cent of the tax is payable);
   (ii) if between 4 and 5 years, 40 per cent;
   (iii) if between 5 and 6 years, 60 per cent;
   (iv) if between 6 and 7 years, 80 per cent.

22.3.3 Gift by company

(1) Corporation tax on any gain

Principles similar to those described in **22.3.2** apply (where the gain on disposal of a chargeable asset will be calculated by reference to market value), except that if the disposal is from one company to another company within a group of companies (broadly where there is a prescribed degree of common ownership) the first company's disposal may be treated, in effect, as neutral for tax purposes so that the recipient company takes over the tax position of the first company on that asset.

(2) Inheritance tax – close companies (IHTA 1984, s 94)

A company cannot make a transfer of value for the purposes of inheritance tax because inheritance tax is imposed on transfers of value by individuals. In order to avoid a company being used as a vehicle for making transfers which would otherwise escape inheritance tax, there are special provisions applicable to close companies. These are complex but, broadly, a gift made by a close company (one which is controlled by five or fewer participators or by participators who are directors – see **21.2.10**) is treated as a set of gifts by the participators (broadly the shareholders) in that company. This is achieved by apportioning the gift amongst the participators in accordance with their proportionate shareholdings in the company; each participator is then treated as having made a transfer of value of the appropriate fraction of the company's gift. Unless covered by an exemption and/or a relief, this is a chargeable transfer rather than a potentially exempt transfer so that inheritance tax may become payable immediately. It is the company itself which is primarily liable for any tax arising. These provisions do not apply if the company's gift is charged to income tax in the hands of the recipient. The main examples of this would be:

(a) a dividend which is chargeable to income tax under Schedule F;
(b) a benefit in kind provided for a director or employee which is chargeable to income tax under Schedule E.

22.3.4 Sale at an undervalue by an individual or by a company

Where a sale is at an undervalue, there may be liability to capital gains tax as in **22.3.2** or corporation tax as in **22.3.3** on the net increase in the asset's value during the period of ownership and possible liability to inheritance tax on the loss to the disponer as a result of the gift element. The position is different if the disponer has sold at an undervalue merely as a result of making a bad bargain (eg through not recognising how much the asset is really worth). The implications of a sale at an undervalue with a gift element as distinguished from a bad bargain are considered separately below in relation to each of the possible charges to tax.

(1) Capital gains tax

The significance of the distinction between a gift and a bad bargain will lie in the calculation of the gain. If a sale is at an undervalue with a gift element, the gain, if any, will be calculated by reference to market value at disposal in the same way as with an outright gift; this prevents taxpayers avoiding capital gains tax by fixing an artificially low sale price which would correspondingly produce an artificially low gain. If the sale is a bad bargain, the gain, if any, will be calculated by reference to the actual sale price. The problem of distinguishing between the two is often avoided by provisions in the Taxation of Chargeable Gains Act 1992 on 'connected persons' (TCGA 1992, s 286). A disposal to a connected person will be deemed to be made at market value rather than at the actual sale price; 'connected persons' include the spouse of the disponer or other close relatives of the disponer (essentially parents, grandparents, children, grandchildren and siblings or his/her spouse (and the spouses of those people) but not, for example, aunts or uncles or nephews or nieces); business partners are also connected persons, but a disposal between partners which is negotiated on a commercial basis will be taken to be at the actual sale price.

(2) Corporation tax

The rules are similar to those described above for capital gains tax. A company is 'connected' with a person if that person controls the company (either alone or with others connected to him). A company is connected to another company if they are both controlled by the same person or by a combination of that person and others connected with him (TCGA 1992, s 286(5)).

(3) Inheritance tax

The Inheritance Tax Act 1984, s 10(1) provides that a disposition is not a transfer of value if the transferor had no intention to transfer a gratuitous benefit. Thus if the transferor can prove that he made a bad bargain, having no intention to confer a gratuitous benefit on another person, the loss to his estate resulting from that bad bargain will not have any inheritance tax implications. As with the equivalent capital gains tax point, there may be difficulty in establishing this distinction, although again the concept of a 'connected person' is used. For inheritance tax purposes, the definition of connected person is wider than that for capital gains tax as it is extended to include aunts or uncles or nephews or nieces (or their spouses) (IHTA 1984, s 270). If the transaction is with a connected person, the burden on the transferor of proving that there was no 'transfer of value' is heavier because he must show that there was no intention to confer a gratuitous benefit and that the transaction was on the same terms as if it had been made with a person with whom he was not connected.

Example 1

A, a sole trader, has decided to retire and to allow his son B to purchase the business from him. The net worth of the business is £100,000. B can only afford to pay £60,000 even by using all his savings and borrowing as much as he can. A sells to B at £60,000.

Capital gains tax: The fact that B is 'connected' to A is incidental on these facts because it is clearly a sale at an undervalue; A's gains must be calculated by reference to the market value of the chargeable assets of which he disposes.

Inheritance tax: Again the fact that B is 'connected' to A is incidental because A is clearly going to be unable to prove that this was merely a bad bargain; A suffers a loss to his estate of £40,000 so that he has made a potentially exempt transfer which will become chargeable to inheritance tax if A dies within 7 years (subject to exemptions and reliefs).

Example 2

C, a sole trader, receives an offer from D.E. Co Ltd (a company with which he has no connection) to purchase his business for £80,000. C accepts the offer and sells at this price without bothering to have the business professionally valued. In fact the business is worth at least £90,000.

Capital gains tax: The company is not 'connected' with C and therefore the transaction can be taken as being merely a bad bargain; the actual consideration will be used for calculation of C's gain.

Inheritance tax: Since the company is not a connected person, C should have no difficulty in establishing that he had no intention to confer any gratuitous benefit on the company so that there are no inheritance tax implications.

22.3.5 Death of individual

(1) Capital gains tax (TCGA 1992, s 62)

It is a fundamental principle of capital gains tax that there can be no charge to the tax on death; technically, this position is achieved by providing that on death there is no disposal of assets. Also significant is the fact that any increase in the value of assets during the deceased's ownership will not attract any charge to capital gains tax because the personal representatives (and eventually the person who inherits an asset) are deemed to acquire the deceased's assets at their market value at the date of death.

(2) Inheritance tax

On death, there is a deemed transfer of value by the deceased of his entire estate immediately before death (IHTA 1984, s 4(1)); also, any potentially exempt transfers made by the deceased in the 7 years preceding his death become chargeable transfers as a result of his death. The possible charge to inheritance tax is worked out broadly as described in **22.3.2**:

(a) inheritance tax will be assessed on any potentially exempt transfer which became chargeable as a result of the death within 7 years;
(b) the value of the estate immediately before death will then be added to the value of transfers in the previous 7 years which were, or have become, chargeable transfers in order to ascertain the appropriate rate of inheritance tax.

22.4 CAPITAL TAX RELIEFS

22.4.1 Capital gains tax – individuals

Having established the chargeable gain (after any indexation) on the disposal of a chargeable asset, the available reliefs should be considered. The reliefs relate to business assets of various kinds, and have been introduced over the years to encourage investment in business. The focus of the reliefs is on smaller businesses, hence the various conditions that have to be satisfied in order to qualify for relief.

(1) Retirement relief (TCGA 1992, ss 163–164)

Retirement relief was introduced over 20 years ago with the aim partly to enable the gift of family businesses intact, and partly to protect those who sold their business on retirement from having the sale proceeds reduced by tax to the extent that they could not support themselves financially in retirement. Following the introduction of taper relief in 1998, retirement relief is being phased out, but remains available until 5 April 2003.

(A) CONDITIONS FOR THE RELIEF

(i) Retirement relief is available to an individual who disposes of his 'business interest' when aged 50 or over (even if not actually retiring, despite the description 'retirement relief'), or when actually retiring below that age on the ground of ill health.
(ii) Retirement relief is only available on a disposal of a business interest (and not on the disposal of a single business asset without any disposal of an interest in a business) and only on any resulting gain which relates to chargeable business

assets. Business assets are assets which are used in the business (such as goodwill, premises occupied for the purposes of the business and plant and machinery) as opposed to assets owned as investments (such as premises which are let to another business). Applying this to the different types of person being considered, the disposal must satisfy the following conditions.

(a) If by a sole trader, the disposal must be a disposal of the business or of an interest in the business (such as when taking on a partner for the first time); relief may be available on gains on those assets making up the business which are chargeable business assets as above or, in the context of a sole trader taking on a partner, on the share therein of which he is disposing.

(b) If by a partner, the disposal must be a disposal of his interest in the business; relief may be available on gains on his fractional share in each of the chargeable business assets as above. Provided the partner is disposing of his interest in the business as described, relief may also be available on a gain on an associated disposal of a chargeable business asset which is used in the business but owned by him individually (such as the business premises), although the relief will be restricted if he has charged the firm a rent for its use.

(c) If by a shareholder, the disposal must be a disposal of his shares; relief may be available on a gain on his shares, although the relief can be claimed only on that percentage of his gain which reflects the percentage of the company's chargeable assets which are chargeable business assets as opposed to investments. Provided the shareholder is disposing of his shares, relief may also be available on a gain on an associated disposal of a chargeable business asset which is used in the business but owned by the shareholder individually, although the relief will be restricted if he has charged the company a rent for its use. Further conditions which must be satisfied (generally at the date of disposal and for one year before) if the shareholder is to qualify for retirement relief on his disposal are that the shareholder is a full-time working officer or employee and that the company is his 'personal company' whose income is derived, broadly, from trading activities as opposed to investment. A company is an individual's 'personal company' if he owns at least 5 per cent of the voting shares.

(B) AMOUNT OF THE RELIEF

The amount of retirement relief to which the individual is entitled depends on the length of time for which he has satisfied the conditions for relief:

(i) if they were satisfied for at least 10 years, the maximum relief will be available;
(ii) if they were satisfied for less than one year, no relief will be available;
(iii) if they were satisfied for between one and 10 years, the maximum relief must be scaled down according to the number of complete years during which the conditions were satisfied (eg someone who satisfied the conditions for 8 years would get $^8/_{10}$ of the maximum relief).

In ascertaining the length of time for which a business (or shareholding in a company) has been owned, it may be possible to add together the period of ownership of that business (or shareholding) and the period of ownership of a business previously carried on by the taxpayer, for example where a business run as a sole trader is converted into a company and the individual eventually disposes of shares in the company (TCGA 1992, Sch 6).

For the year 2000/2001, the maximum amount of retirement relief is:

(a) full exemption for gains up to £150,000; and
(b) 50 per cent exemption for gains between £150,000 and £600,000.

On a gain of £600,000 or more, this would provide relief for £375,000 of the gain, so that the taxpayer would be chargeable to capital gains tax (subject to any other available relief or exemption) on £225,000 plus the whole of the balance of the gain over £600,000.

The relief is given against qualifying chargeable gains calculated after indexation allowance (which is restricted to periods up to 5 April 1998) but before any of the other reliefs considered below and before any taper relief.

As mentioned above, retirement relief is being phased out over the next few years. It will no longer be available from 6 April 2003. The phasing-out is being effected by reducing, annually, the full exemption and the 50 per cent exemption limits.

The maximum retirement relief for each year during the phasing-out period is as follows:

Year	Full exemption on gains up to:	50% exemption on gains between:
1999/2000	£200,000	£200,001 – £800,000
2000/2001	£150,000	£150,001 – £600,000
2001/2002	£100,000	£100,001 – £400,000
2002/2003	£50,000	£50,001 – £200,000

Note that otherwise the rules for calculating this relief are unchanged.

(2) *Hold-over relief on gifts (and the gift element in sales at undervalue) of business assets (TCGA 1992, s 165)*

Hold-over relief on gifts is available to an individual who disposes of 'business assets' by way of gift or, to the extent of the gift element, by way of sale at an undervalue. Unlike retirement relief, hold-over relief does not exempt any of the chargeable gain, but instead acts to postpone any tax liability. The relief is designed to allow business assets to be given away without a tax charge falling on the donor (who would not otherwise have any sale proceeds to fund the tax).

(a) Only the gain relating to chargeable business assets can be held-over. 'Business assets' include the following.

  (i) Assets which are used in a business or the individual's interest in such assets. This applies to the assets of a sole trader or partnership.
  (ii) Shares in a trading company which are unquoted. (Shares on the AIM are unquoted for tax purposes.)
  (iii) Shares in a personal trading company even if dealt with on The Stock Exchange.
  (iv) Assets owned by the shareholder and used by his personal trading company.

  'Personal company' is defined as for retirement relief.

(b) To apply hold-over relief, the chargeable gain (after any indexation) must be calculated in the usual way (taking market value as the consideration for the disposal) and then this (indexed) gain will be deducted from the market value of

the asset in order to establish an artificially low 'acquisition cost' for the disponee. For the relief to apply, both disponer and disponee must so elect, as the disponee is taking on the liability for any capital gains tax that eventually arises.
(c) Taper relief is not applied before holding over the gain, and so is lost for the period of ownership of the disponer (this can be a serious drawback).
(d) When the disponee eventually disposes of the asset, the artificially low acquisition cost (plus any qualifying expenditure – see below) is deducted from the sale price (on a sale at full value) or market value (on a gift) to find the gain of the disponee. Thus the disponee's gain will include the held-over gain plus any gain attributable to his own period of ownership. Having calculated the disponee's chargeable gain, reliefs should be considered (including hold-over relief again if relevant) and taper relief may be available (for the period of ownership of the disponee only). If the disponee dies without having disposed of the asset, all gains then accumulated in respect of the asset will escape capital gains tax altogether.

Example 1

J gives M, his son, the family business at a time when the business' chargeable assets are worth £100,000 and the total (indexed) gains on those assets are £20,000. Eighteen months later M sells the business for £110,000 (he makes no other disposals in the same tax year).

(1) J and M elect to hold-over J's gain on the disposal to M, so that M's adjusted acquisition cost is £80,000 (£100,000 - £20,000). Any taper relief accrued during J's period of ownership is lost and J's annual exemption for the year cannot be deducted from the held-over gain.
(2) On the sale of the business by M, his gain is:

	£
Sale price	110,000
Less: adjusted acquisition cost	(80,000)
Gain	30,000

M will be able to claim 1 year's worth of business taper relief for his period of ownership, and his annual exemption for the tax year of the sale can be used to further reduce the tapered gain.

Note: In calculating the gain, as described in the previous paragraphs, there is one item which may be deducted as an expense which would not usually occur. Given that this relief is only relevant to gifts or sales at an undervalue, the original disposal may lead to eventual charges to both inheritance tax on the original disposal (if a potentially exempt transfer is followed by death within 7 years) and capital gains tax (on the disponee's eventual disposal) which will include the held-over gain from the original disposal. If a charge to inheritance tax does occur, the inheritance tax paid by the disponee can be treated as an expense which is deductible in calculating the gain on the disponee's eventual disposal.

As most business assets qualify for 100 per cent relief from inheritance tax (see **22.4.3**), such an inheritance tax charge will occur infrequently. An example of when it might occur is following a chargeable transfer of a minority holding of *quoted* shares (eg a gift followed by the donor's death within 7 years). This transfer may well qualify for hold-over relief for CGT purposes (as a shareholding of 5 per cent or more of the company's shares) but not for inheritance tax business property relief (as it is not a controlling shareholding).

Example 2

M gives her 5 per cent shareholding in B plc to her daughter D in September 2000 when the shares are valued at £100,000 (according to the price quoted on The Stock Exchange at the time). M acquired the shares several years previously – they were then valued at £20,000. There was no relevant expenditure to deduct in calculating M's gain and her indexation allowance was £10,000. M and D claim hold-over relief on M's gain. M dies in January 2001 and D has to pay IHT of £40,000 in relation to the gift of shares from M (the PET becomes chargeable as a result of M's death within 7 years and M's nil rate band had been exhausted by other gifts shortly before that to D).

In July 2001, D sells the shares for £110,000. She had no relevant expenditure to deduct in calculating her gain. Calculations for CGT purposes are as follows:

M's disposal (the gift to D)	£
Disposal value	100,000
LESS	
Acquisition value	(20,000)
LESS	
Indexation allowance	(10,000)
M's gain held over (no taper relief)	70,000

D's disposal (sale)	£
Disposal price	110,000
LESS	
Acquisition value as reduced by the gain held over on M's disposal (ie £100,000 less £70,000)	(30,000)
	80,000
LESS	
IHT paid by D as a result of M's PET becoming chargeable on the death of M	(40,000)
D's gain (no taper relief – asset held less than 1 year)	40,000

D will be able to use her annual exemption for 2001/02 to reduce the gain further.

(3) Roll-over relief on replacement of qualifying assets (TCGA 1992, ss 152–159)

The details of roll-over relief were described, and an example of its working was given, in **9.3.4**. It is important to remember that the definition of 'qualifying assets' for roll-over relief is narrower than that for either retirement relief or hold-over relief; the principal 'qualifying assets' are goodwill, land, buildings and fixed plant and machinery; the list does not include shares in a company.

If a person disposes (whether by sale or by gift) of a qualifying assets or assets (or an interest in them), whether or not he is disposing of his interest in the business as a whole, and, within the time-limits, buys other qualifying asset(s) to be used in his business, he may claim to roll over his gain into the acquisition cost of the 'new'

asset(s) in order to postpone any liability to capital gains tax at least until disposal of the 'new' asset(s). Any 'new' asset need not actually be a replacement, providing it is within the list of qualifying assets, and it need not be used in the same business.

This relief is not available to a company shareholder on disposal of his shares (because shares are not qualifying assets) but it is available if he disposes of a qualifying asset used by the company (provided that the company is his personal trading company as defined at **22.4.1**) and purchases a new qualifying asset for such use. It is also available to a partner in equivalent circumstances, although there is then no equivalent to the requirement of 'personal trading company'.

This relief is given after the (indexed) gain has been calculated but the gain is not tapered before it is rolled over and the relief cannot be used in addition to the annual exemption.

(*Note:* Although roll-over relief on the replacement of qualifying asstes can apply in theory when a qualifying asset is given away, it would be unusual in practice for a donor to be so generous as to both make a gift and retain the CGT liability relating to that gift. The hold-over relief described above is likely to be more relevant in these circumstances as liability for any future CGT passes to the donee under the terms of that relief.)

(4) Deferral relief on re-investment in EIS shares (TCGA 1992, s 150C and Sch 5B)

Unlimited deferral of capital gains arising on the disposal, by sale or gift, of *any* asset is available where an individual subscribes wholly for cash for shares in a company which qualifies under the Enterprise Investment Scheme (EIS). (As the shares must be acquired for cash, this relief will not usually be available to a partner or sole trader who transfers his business to a company, as the shares acquired following such a transfer are usually issued in return for the non-cash assets of the business.)

(a) The relief is complex but, in general terms, the individual's chargeable gain on the disposal of the asset (up to the subscription cost of the shares) is deferred until he disposes of the shares at which time taper relief is given against the deferred gain based on the period of ownership of the original asset. The deferred gain is taxed at the rate applicable to the taxpayer in the tax year of the disposal of the EIS shares. EIS relief operates as a pure deferral of the gain – this is different to the roll-over and hold-over reliefs which act to reduce the acquisition cost of the qualifying asset which is acquired.

(b) The relief is available where the EIS shares are acquired within one year before or three years after the disposal.

(c) This deferral relief is available where the shares acquired meet the requirements of the Enterprise Investment Scheme. As described at **21.4.3**, they must be unlisted shares in a trading company carrying on certain non-excluded activities. Activities which are excluded include, for example, share dealing, property development and farming. However, the requirement for EIS income tax relief (and for relief on the gain on the EIS shares themselves – see below), that the investor must not be 'connected' with the company, is not required for EIS CGT deferral relief.

(d) As regards the 'true gain' on the disposal of the EIS shares themselves, a slightly different relief applies. Such gains will be exempt from CGT if held for

3 years, but only if the investor is not 'connected' with the company (see LPC Resource Book *Pervasive and Core Topics* (Jordans)).

Example

Shares in X Co Ltd (not EIS) have been held by Andrew for 2 years. He sells them and realises a gain (untapered) of £60,000. This gain is deferred when he subscribes for shares in Y Co Ltd (an EIS company) for £100,000. Andrew holds the shares in Y Co Ltd for 4 years and then sells them for £120,000. His deferred gain of £60,000 is now chargeable to CGT but attracts taper relief applicable to the original 2 years' ownership. The 'true' gain of £20,000 on the disposal of the shares in Y Co Ltd will be exempt if all the qualifying conditions are met.

If the 'true gain' on the disposal of the EIS shares is not exempt, it will attract taper relief in the usual way depending upon the period of ownership. If such gains are postponed on re-investment in another EIS company then, on the ultimate disposal, taper relief is calculated for the entire (ie cumulative) period of EIS ownership.

(5) Deferral relief on re-investment in VCT shares (TCGA 1992, ss 151A, 151B and Sch 5)

A similar deferral relief to that described for EIS shares is available where the individual invests in VCT shares, though, in this case, the shares must be acquired within one year before or one year after the disposal.

(6) Roll-over relief on incorporation of a business (TCGA 1992, s 162)

Where a business is transferred by a sole trader or partners to a new or existing company in return for shares in the company, the untapered gain on disposal by the sole trader or partners *must* be rolled over into the acquisition cost of the shares in the company; liability to pay capital gains tax is thus postponed until a subsequent disposal of the shares.

Certain conditions must be satisfied and, if they are satisfied, the relief is mandatory.

(a) The business must be transferred as a going concern. This means that the business must essentially be carried on as the same business albeit with a change of owner; if, for example, the business premises are transferred but a different business is then carried on by the company, this is not a transfer as a going concern.

(b) The whole gain can be rolled over only if the consideration is all in shares issued by the company. If, for example, the company 'pays' for the business as to 50 per cent by an issue of shares but as to the other 50 per cent by an issue of debentures (ie this amount is treated as a loan to the company), then roll-over relief can only apply to 50 per cent of the gain.

(c) The business must be transferred with all of its assets (although cash is ignored for this purpose). If, for example, a sole trader's business is transferred to a company as a going concern but ownership of the business premises is retained by the sole trader who will allow the company to use them, then roll-over relief will not apply.

Note: although this relief is applied automatically by the Inland Revenue, retirement relief may be taken first so that only the balance of any gain has to be rolled over. However, the rolled-over gain cannot be tapered and so the taper relief for the ownership of the original asset(s) is lost. Nor can the annual exemption be used to reduce the rolled-over gain.

(7) Enhanced taper relief for business assets (TCGA 1992, s 2A and Sch A1)

In addition to considering the various reliefs described above, thought must be given to whether the enhanced taper relief for business assets applies and, if so, whether it can be used in conjunction with the other reliefs or whether it must be treated as an alternative.

When taper relief was introduced in 1998, it was designed to fulfil a dual function; it replaced the indexation allowance as a method for (broadly) excluding gains caused by inflation from the charge to tax.

In addition, the relief was made more attractive for gains realised on business assets to encourage longer term investment in business by individuals. Originally, maximum relief was given if assets were held for at least 10 years, but in his March 2000 Budget the Chancellor reduced the period for business assets to 4 years. The range of qualifying business assets was also increased so that it now includes:

(a) assets used in the trade or an individual's interest in such assets. This covers assets used by sole traders and partners for their business;
(b) all shares in unquoted trading companies;
(c) all shares owned by employees in quoted trading companies;
(d) voting shareholdings of 5 per cent or more in quoted trading companies (whether or not the shareholder is an employee);
(e) assets owned by an individual and used in a trade by a company whose shares qualify as business assets in relation to the owner (see (b), (c) and (d) above).

(Special rules exist to apportion the chargeable gain when an asset has qualified as a business asset for part of the period of ownership but not the whole period.)

The conditions applying to the application of taper relief are described in the LPC Resource Book *Pervasive and Core Topics* (Jordans). It should be noted that taper relief cannot be used at the time a chargeable gain is rolled-over or held-over under the reliefs described above. Given the relatively generous rates of the enhanced taper relief, it will be important for a taxpayer think carefully before opting to use any relief which involves losing accumulated taper relief entitlement (see (10) below for further details).

(8) Annual exemption

In each tax year, a prescribed amount (the first £7,200 for 2000/2001) of an individual's net gains (after any taper relief) is exempt from capital gains tax. If the exemption is unused (in whole or in part) for any year, there is no provision for it to be carried forward and so any unused exemption is lost.

As mentioned above, the annual exemption cannot be used on a gain which is being rolled over or held over.

(9) Instalment option (TCGA 1992, s 281)

In limited circumstances, payment may be made by ten annual instalments, the first being on the usual date for payment of capital gains tax (31 January following the tax year of the disposal), with interest being charged on the outstanding tax.

The conditions are:

(a) the disposal giving rise to the capital gains tax must have been a gift; and
(b) hold-over relief must not be available (as opposed to merely not claimed); this means that the instalment option will rarely be relevant to disposal of business interests by sole traders, partners or shareholders in private companies except in relation to assets of the business which are investments; and
(c) the property disposed of must have been either land, a controlling shareholding in any company, or any shareholding (whether controlling or otherwise) in a company whose shares are unquoted.

(10) Interrelation between reliefs and exemption

On a disposal it is possible that more than one relief could apply and that the disponer's annual exemption has not been used (on other disposals) so that it is necessary to consider whether a choice as to which relief(s) to claim must be made by the taxpayer.

(A) RETIREMENT RELIEF

Where retirement relief is available this can be applied to the chargeable gain first, and other reliefs, and/or the annual exemption, can then be considered in relation to any balance of the gain so far as the available retirement relief was insufficient fully to absorb the gain.

(B) ROLL-OVER RELIEF ON THE REPLACEMENT OF QUALIFYING ASSETS

In certain (restricted) circumstances, this relief can be used in conjunction with any available retirement relief. The rolled-over gain cannot be tapered before being rolled-over and nor can the annual exemption be set against it. The relief cannot generally be used in conjunction with hold-over relief, roll-over relief on incorporation, or EIS/VCT deferral.

(C) HOLD-OVER RELIEF ON GIFTS OF BUSINESS ASSETS

This relief can be used after any available retirement relief has been applied to the gain. The gain cannot be tapered before being held-over and nor can the donor's annual exemption be set against it. The relief cannot generally be used in conjunction with the roll-over reliefs or EIS/VCT deferral.

(D) ROLL-OVER RELIEF ON THE INCORPORATION OF A BUSINESS

Although this relief, if it applies, is mandatory, the Inland Revenue does allow any retirement relief available to be deducted prior to rolling over the gain.

To the extent that shares are received in consideration for the transfer of the business, taper relief cannot be applied to the gain prior to the roll-over, and nor can the annual exemption. The relief in these circumstances cannot be used at the same time as roll-over relief on replacement of qualifying assets (shares do not qualify) nor hold-over relief (there is usually no gift) nor EIS/VCT deferral (the consideration for the shares is not in cash).

If, however, part of the consideration is in cash and part in shares it might, in certain circumstances, be possible to use the roll-over relief on incorporation for that proportion of the gain attributable to the part of the business exchanged for shares, leaving taper relief and the annual exemption to be used on the proportion of the gain attributable to the part of the business sold for cash (EIS deferral may also occasionally be available where cash is received in this way and used to buy shares in an EIS qualifying company).

(E) EIS/VCT DEFERRAL

This relief can be used after any available retirement relief has been claimed. Taper relief is given on the deferred gain for the *original* period of ownership of the 'old' asset when the gain is eventually taxed (see below). The deferred gain cannot be reduced by the annual exemption but, as the entire sale proceeds from the 'old' asset do not have to be reinvested in the EIS/VCT shares, it should be possible to hold back sufficient cash from the sale to leave a small amount of the gain 'undeferred' and the annual exemption can be set against this. The interrelation of this relief and the hold-over and roll-over reliefs is set out above.

(F) TAPER RELIEF

From the above it can be seen that taper relief is deductible after any retirement relief has been given, but that any accrued taper relief is lost if the hold-over or roll-over reliefs are used. If a chargeable gain is deferred using EIS/VCT relief, the taper relief is 'frozen' so that when the gain is eventually charged to tax, taper relief is given for the period of ownership of the original asset on which the deferred gain was made. The annual exemption, if available, can be used to reduce tapered gains which are being taxed in any given tax year.

(G) THE ANNUAL EXEMPTION

This is the final point to consider when looking at the various reliefs and exemptions, and its interrelation with each of the other reliefs is set out above.

Example

A, aged 55, is a higher-rate taxpayer and has run a manufacturing business as a sole trader for 10 years; he retires in June 2000 and gives the business including some land held as an investment to his daughter. His accountant advises that his chargeable (indexed) gain on the chargeable business assets is £500,000; he will also make a chargeable (indexed) gain on the land held as an investment of £50,000.

A qualifies for the maximum retirement relief relevant to his gain on the chargeable business assets. His relief will be £325,000 (made up of full relief on the first £150,000 of his gain and 50 per cent relief on the balance of his gain (ie on £350,000)). He and his daughter can claim hold-over relief on the balance of his indexed gain on the chargeable business assets (£175,000). Alternatively, A could (having claimed retirement relief) claim 2 years' worth of enhanced taper relief (2 complete years from 6 April 1998 – the 'bonus' year is not relevant for business assets) so that 75 per cent of the gain of £175,000 is chargeable. The tapered gain of £131,250 could be further reduced by A's annual exemption of £7,200 leaving a taxable amount of £124,050 to be taxed at 40 per cent.

Regarding the £50,000 gain on the investment land, neither retirement relief nor hold-over relief is available, but A can taper the gain on this non-business asset (based on 2 complete years' of ownership plus the 'bonus' year) so that 95 per cent of the gain will be chargeable. If not already used, the tapered gain can be reduced by his annual exemption, and the tax on the balance may be paid by instalments over a 10-year period.

22.4.2 Corporation tax

Of the capital gains tax reliefs and exemption described in **22.4.1**, only roll-over relief on replacement of qualifying assets is applicable to a company's chargeable gains, as described in **21.2.4**. For companies that acquire, and later dispose of, shares in certain other companies there is a relief similar to EIS relief known as the 'Corporate Venturing Scheme'. The details of the relief are beyond the scope of this book but, in essence, the relief is designed, like EIS, to encourage investment in small 'enterprise' companies.

22.4.3 Inheritance tax

As described in **22.3.2**, a relief may be available to reduce the value transferred by a non-exempt transfer of value for inheritance tax purposes. The reliefs should be considered after applying any available exemptions (see the LPC Resource Book *Pervasive and Core Topics* (Jordans)). The reliefs are designed to try and ensure that businesses are not unnecessarily broken up by the burden of inheritance tax following gifts made during the donor's life or on his death.

(1) Agricultural property relief (IHTA 1984, ss 115–124)

(A) SOLE TRADERS AND PARTNERS

This relief operates to reduce the agricultural value of agricultural property (as defined) by a certain percentage. The 'agricultural value' is the value of the property if it were subject to a perpetual covenant prohibiting its use other than for agriculture. This will be significantly less than its market value if, for example, the land has development potential (eg for housing). That part of the property's value which is over and above its 'agricultural value' will not qualify for any agricultural property relief, but may qualify for business property relief (see below). A reduction of 100 per cent is allowed where either (broadly) the transferor had the right to vacant possession immediately before the transfer or where the property was subject to a letting commencing on or after 1 September 1995. A reduction of 50 per cent is allowed in other cases. Further conditions which must also be satisfied for any relief are either that the property was occupied by the transferor for the purposes of agriculture for the 2 years prior to the transfer or that it was owned by him for the 7 years prior to the transfer and was occupied by someone throughout that period for the purposes of agriculture.

(B) SHAREHOLDERS

This relief is also available where the agricultural property is held by a company in which the transferor of shares had control. The value of the shares may be reduced by the appropriate percentage (100 per cent or 50 per cent) where the value of the shares is attributable to the agricultural value of the company's agricultural property. The company's occupancy or ownership of the land (for 2 years or for 7 years (see above)) is treated as that of the transferor of shares and the transferor must also have held the shares for the qualifying 2- or 7-year period (as the case may be).

(C) RELATIONSHIP WITH BUSINESS PROPERTY RELIEF

Agricultural property relief is given in priority to business property relief (see below), but any of the value transferred not reduced by agricultural property relief may qualify for business property relief.

(2) Business property relief (IHTA 1984, ss 103–114)

This relief operates to reduce the value transferred by a transfer of value of relevant business property by a certain percentage.

(a) A reduction of 100 per cent of the value transferred is allowed for transfers of certain assets; this will mean that there will be no charge to inheritance tax. They are:

    (i) a business or an interest in a business (eg a partnership share);

    (ii) shares which are not quoted on The Stock Exchange (shares quoted on the AIM are treated as unquoted for tax purposes).

(b) A reduction of 50 per cent of the value transferred is allowed for transfers of any other assets which qualify for business property relief. They are:

    (i) shares which are quoted on The Stock Exchange itself and where the transferor had voting control immediately before the transfer;

    (ii) land, buildings, machinery or plant owned by the transferor personally but used by a partnership of which he is a member or by a company of which he has voting control.

Note: 'voting control', for these purposes, means the ability to exercise over 50 per cent of the votes on *all* resolutions.

(c) A number of further points must be considered as to the availability of business property relief, some of which are illustrated below:

    (i) To attract any relief the asset or assets in question must have been owned by the transferor for 2 years at the time of the transfer, or broadly must be a replacement for relevant business property where the combined period of ownership is 2 years. This would include the situation where a sole trader or partner incorporated his business; the shares he received would be relevant replacement property.

    (ii) The transfer need not be of the transferor's entire interest in the business or his entire shareholding.

    (iii) Where the charge to inheritance tax arises as a result of a potentially exempt transfer which is followed by death of the transferor within 7 years, the transferee must still own the asset (or a replacement asset which qualifies as relevant business property) at the date of the transferor's death (or if earlier, the transferee's own death).

    (iv) 'Control' for the purposes of qualifying for relief at 50 per cent may be denied by a provision in the company's articles of association (eg, a *Bushell v Faith* clause) which gives weighted voting rights on certain matters (notably dismissal of a director); the purpose and effect of such an article will be to prevent, for example, a majority shareholder from exercising his normal voting control on those matters and thus to deprive him of 'control'. For example, business property relief on assets owned personally by the shareholder may be defeated by the *Bushell v Faith* clause because of the absence of control.

    (v) In assessing whether or not a person has control (and for that purpose only), separate shareholdings of husband and wife can be taken as one so that if the combined percentage of the votes gives the couple control then the test will be satisfied.

(vi) Where a person has entered into a contract for the sale of his interest in a business (or his shares) his interest is then taken to be in the proceeds of sale; since cash is not relevant business property, no relief will be available where there is a binding contract for sale. This may arise particularly under the terms of a partnership agreement which provides that on a partner's retirement or death, for example, the continuing partners will buy and the former partner (or his PRs) will sell the share of the former partner. Where this is a binding contract to buy and sell (as opposed to a mere option to buy) then no business property relief will be available in relation to the partner's interest in the business. A similar situation could arise in respect of a shareholders' agreement in the company context.

Example 1

A is a 60 per cent shareholder in XY plc (a quoted company on The Stock Exchange) which he established many years ago. He gives half of his shares to his daughter on her twenty-first birthday. Three years later he gives the other half of his holding to his son on his twenty-first birthday. A dies in the following year.

Providing A's daughter still owns the shares on A's death (when the potentially exempt transfer becomes chargeable), the value transferred will be reduced by 50 per cent. The gift to B will not qualify for any business property relief because a 30 per cent holding in a quoted company is not relevant business property.

Example 2

For many years A and B have owned 55 per cent and 25 per cent respectively of the shares in a private company whose articles are in the form of Table A; they have also owned the business premises in equal shares as tenants in common. They are both killed in a road accident and their entire estates are inherited by A's son and B's daughter respectively.

A's shareholding and B's shareholding both qualify for 100 per cent business property relief. A's interest in the premises qualifies for business property relief at 50 per cent because his shareholding gave 'control'; B's interest in the premises does not qualify for business property relief at all.

Example 3

For many years A, B and C have been partners, sharing profits and losses equally; they have also owned the business premises in equal shares as tenants in common. There is no provision in their partnership agreement dealing with the purchase and sale of assets on the death or retirement of a partner. A and B are both killed in a road accident and their entire estates are inherited by A's son and B's daughter respectively.

The interest in the business of each partner qualifies for 100 per cent business property relief and also each partner's interest in the premises qualifies for business property relief at 50 per cent. (No business property relief at all would have been available if there was a partnership agreement under which there was a binding contract for the purchase and sale of the partners' interests.)

It can be seen that more favourable treatment is given to partners who own assets used by their business than to shareholders who own assets used by their company.

(3) Instalment option (IHTA 1984, ss 227–228)

Provided the requirements described below are met, payment of IHT can be made by ten annual instalments, the first being due when the tax would normally be due.

The instalment option is only available in relation to tax on the following assets:

(a) land;
(b) shares which gave the transferor control;
(c) in certain circumstances, non-controlling shares which are not quoted on The Stock Exchange, for example: (i) where the shares are worth over £20,000 and at least 10 per cent of the nominal value of the company's issued share capital; or (ii) where the Inland Revenue are satisfied that payment of tax in a lump sum would cause undue hardship; or (iii) the IHT attributable to the shares and any other instalment option property in the estate amounts to at least 20 per cent of the IHT payable on the estate;
(d) a business or an interest in a business.

The instalment option is only available in certain circumstances, primarily:

(a) Where the recipient of a PET is paying the tax. The instalment option applies where a PET becomes chargeable as a result of the transferor's death within 7 years of the transfer, the transferee pays the inheritance tax and the transferee still owns the original asset (or a qualifying replacement) at the date of the death. If the asset is later sold, the outstanding tax must then be paid.
(b) Where personal representatives are paying the tax. The instalment option applies where the transfer of value was the deemed transfer on death.

Interest is only charged on the outstanding tax if the asset in question is land which is not business or agricultural land, or is shares in an investment company, except that if an instalment is in arrears interest then becomes chargeable on the overdue instalment.

22.5 SUMMARIES AND CHECKLISTS

(1) The occasions for a capital tax charge against an individual are:

CGT	IHT
Disposal by sale	Lifetime chargeable transfer
Disposal by gift	PET where death occurs within 7 years
[NOT death]	Death

(2) The possible business reliefs or exemptions include:

CGT	IHT
Retirement relief	Agricultural property relief
Hold-over relief (gifts)	Business property relief
Roll-over relief on replacement of qualifying assets	Instalment option
Roll-over relief on incorporation of a business	
Deferral relief on reinvestment in EIS or VCT shares	
Business taper relief	
Annual exemption	
Instalment option	

PART VI

INSOLVENCY

This Part first considers the implications of the insolvency of an individual (a 'debtor'). The debtor who is unable to pay his debts is faced with the possibility of bankruptcy whereby virtually all his assets are taken and shared between his creditors. At the end of the bankruptcy, the debtor is largely freed from outstanding claims and able to start afresh. As an alternative to bankruptcy, a debtor may succeed in making a 'voluntary arrangement' with creditors whereby they will accept payment which is delayed or which is less than their entitlement.

Secondly, the insolvency of a company is considered. An insolvent company may be put into liquidation whereby all assets are taken and shared between the creditors; this is broadly equivalent to the bankruptcy of an individual. However, liquidation differs fundamentally from bankruptcy in that at the end of the liquidation the company ceases to exist. Consideration is also given to alternative processes applicable to companies which may enable the company to survive the insolvency.

Chapter 23

INDIVIDUAL INSOLVENCY: BANKRUPTCY

23.1 INTRODUCTION

The term 'bankruptcy' applies to individuals, not to companies. In the context of a business, which is probably the most common situation leading to bankruptcy, an individual may be declared bankrupt because an unincorporated business has failed (ie either the business of a sole trader or of a partnership, neither of which has the advantage of limited liability), or because he has carried on his business through the medium of a limited company but nevertheless has incurred personal liability in some way. This could happen, for example, where directors are forced personally to guarantee a loan to their company, or where they are guilty of wrongful acts, such as wrongful or fraudulent trading. Equally, bankruptcy could arise through unwise personal extravagance and could be unrelated to the individual's business interests.

Chapter 23 contents
Introduction
What is bankruptcy?
The bankruptcy process
Effect of bankruptcy on the bankrupt
Increasing the bankrupt's estate
Avoiding bankruptcy: individual voluntary arrangements
Summaries and checklists

23.2 WHAT IS BANKRUPTCY?

Bankruptcy is a judicial process by which a person (a debtor) is found to be unable to pay his debts from his resources. A debtor may be unable to do this because he has cash-flow problems. He could pay all his debts eventually but does not have sufficient available resources to pay those debts which are due to be paid now or in the near future. Alternatively, the debtor may be insolvent because, although he can pay all his short-term debts as they fall due, taking a long-term view he has insufficient assets to cover his liabilities. If a debtor is unable to pay his debts in either of the two ways described above, he is insolvent. If the court makes a bankruptcy order, that debtor will become a bankrupt and his property will vest in his trustee in bankruptcy and be distributed among his creditors. Eventually, even if all of his debts have not been paid in full, the bankrupt may be discharged and he is then free from almost all of his previous debts.

23.3 THE BANKRUPTCY PROCESS

Bankruptcy is commenced by the presentation of a petition, and is governed principally by the Insolvency Act 1986 as amended by the Insolvency Act 1994.

23.3.1 The petition

Creditor's petition

A creditor can present a petition to the court (IA 1986, s 264) if the debtor owes him £750 or more (the amount owing being a liquidated sum which is an unsecured debt) and he claims that the debtor is unable to pay the debt or has little prospect of being able to pay it, as evidenced by the fact that he has failed either to comply with a 'statutory notice' (a demand for payment formally served on the debtor by the creditor) or to satisfy execution of a judgment debt. Any creditor who is owed less than £750 cannot present a petition on his own but can join together with other creditors to present a petition, provided the total amount owed to all the petitioners is not less than £750. The petition should be presented to the High Court (if the debtor either lives or carries on business in London) or the county court with bankruptcy jurisdiction for the area where the debtor resides or carries on business (not all county courts have bankruptcy jurisdiction).

Debtor's petition

A debtor may petition for his own bankruptcy. In his petition, he must allege that he cannot pay his debts, and this must be accompanied by a statement of affairs, ie details of all his creditors, debts, liabilities and assets.

A debtor may petition for his own bankruptcy in order to escape the inevitable pressure from creditors. By doing so, he places responsibility for his financial affairs in the hands of another, his trustee in bankruptcy. Any existing creditors should then claim from the trustee rather than dealing with the debtor. This can be an enormous relief to the debtor, as can the fact that, once he is discharged as a bankrupt, he is free from virtually all of his current debts, even if such of his assets as are available to his trustee are insufficient to pay them all in full.

23.3.2 The order

Where there is a creditor's petition before the court the bankruptcy order will usually be granted if all the necessary conditions are satisfied.

Where the petition is a debtor's petition, in certain circumstances the court will appoint an insolvency practitioner to investigate the possibility of a voluntary arrangement before reaching a final decision as to whether to make a bankruptcy order.

An insolvency practitioner is licensed either by the Department of Trade and Industry or by his own professional body. In the case of solicitors, insolvency practitioners are authorised by The Law Society. An individual will only be licensed as an insolvency practitioner if he has sufficient experience of insolvency work.

23.3.3 The trustee in bankruptcy

When a bankruptcy order is made by the court, the Official Receiver initially takes control of the debtor's property and he may continue to supervise the sale and distribution of the debtor's assets if he assumes the role of trustee in bankruptcy. The debtor must submit a statement of affairs to the Official Receiver within 21 days of the order, who will then decide whether it is necessary to call a meeting of creditors to enable them to appoint an insolvency practitioner of their choice as trustee in bankruptcy. Any creditor can demand that such a meeting be called if he and any other creditors supporting him comprise one quarter in value of the bankrupt's creditors (IA 1986, s 294). This will depend upon the complexity of the debtor's financial affairs and the size and number of his debts. If the creditors do not appoint their own trustee in bankruptcy, or if the Official Receiver decides that a creditors' meeting is unnecessary, then the Official Receiver will continue to conduct the bankruptcy as trustee in bankruptcy.

23.3.4 The debtor's property

Virtually all of the debtor's personal property vests in his trustee in bankruptcy (IA 1986, s 306). All property owned by the debtor on the date of the bankruptcy order and any property acquired after that date (where the trustee serves written notice claiming this property) will pass to the trustee and he can also take any income of the bankrupt in excess of what is considered 'reasonable' if the court makes an income payments order (IA 1986, s 310). The debtor is entitled to retain only the tools of his trade. This could include a vehicle, if he needs one for his employment or trade, although he may have to replace a luxury vehicle with something more functional. He may also retain clothing, furniture and bedding belonging to him and his family, although, as before, valuable items may have to be sold and replaced with something more utilitarian.

For many debtors, the most valuable asset they own is the house in which they live. If the debtor owns his own home, his interest in that home passes to the trustee in bankruptcy. However, there may be other legal or equitable interests in the house, and therefore frequently the trustee is not free to realise the value of this major asset immediately. The house may be held in joint names with the spouse of the bankrupt or, even where the house is in the sole name of the debtor, the spouse may have an equitable interest arising from an implied, resulting, or constructive trust (for example where that spouse contributed to the purchase price). The spouse may also have a right of occupation under the Matrimonial Homes Act 1983 and, where minor children (under 18) live with the bankrupt in his home, that may give the debtor himself a right of occupation. In these situations, the debtor cannot be evicted from his home, so the trustee cannot sell it without a court order. When deciding whether to make such an order, the court will consider the interests of creditors, the financial resources of the bankrupt, the needs of the children (if any) and all relevant circumstances.

After one year the needs of the creditors outweigh all other considerations. This means that, although the trustee in bankruptcy is unlikely to be able to obtain an order for possession within the first year, after that time the debtor and his family will almost certainly be evicted by court order.

If no spouse or minor children live in the house with the bankrupt (ie where the bankrupt lives alone, with a cohabitee or with adult children), the trustee can sell immediately. When the house is sold, the trustee in bankruptcy can only claim whatever the bankrupt would have been able to claim had he been the seller, ie the trustee can only claim the amount of the debtor's interest in the property.

23.3.5 Distribution of assets

The task facing the trustee in bankruptcy is to convert the debtor's property into money, and to use that money to pay the bankrupt's debts.

Secured creditors may not be dependent upon the trustee for repayment of the debt due to them. A secured creditor can realise the asset over which he has a charge as security for the debt. If the sale does not produce funds equivalent to the full amount of the debt, the creditor will have to claim the balance as an unsecured creditor. If the proceeds of sale are greater than the sum due to the secured creditor, he must pay over the excess to the trustee in bankruptcy for distribution among other creditors.

The trustee must pay the bankrupt's debts in the order set out below.

The cost of the bankruptcy

The first item to be paid is the expense incurred as a result of the bankruptcy, including the professional charges of the trustee in bankruptcy himself.

Preferential debts

The Insolvency Act 1986 creates a long and rather arbitrary list of debts which are designated as 'preferential debts'. They include:

(1) PAYE income tax and national insurance contributions due in the last 12 months before the bankruptcy order;
(2) VAT due in the 6 months prior to the order;
(3) accrued holiday pay owed to employees; and
(4) wages of employees due in the last 4 months before the bankruptcy order (subject to a current maximum amount of £800 per employee).

If there is insufficient money available to pay all preferential debts, they rank and abate equally. This means that each creditor will receive only a percentage of the amount due to him, that percentage being the same for each creditor.

Ordinary unsecured creditors

Ordinary unsecured creditors can only be paid once both of the above categories of debt have been paid in full. If funds are insufficient to pay all debts in this category, they rank and abate equally.

Postponed creditors

Certain debts can only be paid once all the ordinary creditors' debts have been paid in full. The main example of a 'postponed debt' is a loan between spouses.

23.3.6 Discharge

When the bankruptcy order is discharged, the bankruptcy comes to an end. The effect of this is that the bankrupt is released from most of his previous debts (IA 1986, s 281) and freed from most of the disqualifications which affect a bankrupt (see **23.4**).

A bankruptcy order is normally discharged automatically 3 years after the date of the bankruptcy order, unless the trustee in bankruptcy opposes this, which he would do, for example, if the bankrupt had failed to co-operate in the administration of his estate (IA 1986, s 279). At this point, the realisation and distribution of the assets of the bankrupt may not be complete. Any property which has vested in the trustee in bankruptcy remains so, and is not returned to the debtor, and the debtor is still required to assist the trustee with his task. Any property acquired by the debtor after the discharge of the bankruptcy order does not vest in the trustee in bankruptcy but belongs to the ex-bankrupt.

A brief summary of bankruptcy procedure is given at **23.7.2**.

23.4 EFFECT OF BANKRUPTCY ON THE BANKRUPT

When a bankruptcy order is made, the individual who is the subject of that order is subjected to a number of restrictions and disabilities.

23.4.1 Restrictions on business activities

If the bankrupt has been running an unincorporated business as a sole trader, the trustee in bankruptcy will probably encourage him to continue trading, so earning income and enabling the court to make an income payments order, which will swell the fund available to pay his creditors. He is allowed to retain the tools of his trade and a vehicle, but it is a criminal offence for a bankrupt to obtain credit of more than a prescribed amount (currently £250 in total) without disclosing his bankruptcy and, practically, this may make it extremely difficult for him to carry on his business. It is also a criminal offence for the bankrupt to trade under any name other than that in which he was declared to be bankrupt by the court, unless he discloses to all persons with whom he enters into any business transaction the name in which he was declared bankrupt (IA 1986, s 360).

If the bankrupt has previously been running a business in partnership with others, his bankruptcy will automatically cause the dissolution of that partnership (Partnership Act 1890, s 33), unless the partnership agreement provides otherwise. The bankrupt's share in the partnership will have to be realised. It is common to find a provision in the partnership agreement by which the bankrupt immediately and automatically ceases to be a partner and the other partners have an option to buy him out, rather than completely dissolving the firm.

If a director of a company is declared to be bankrupt, the articles usually provide that he immediately ceases to hold office as a director (Table A, art 81), as a bankrupt is prohibited from acting as a director or being involved directly or indirectly in the management of a company (Company Directors Disqualification Act 1986, s 11).

23.4.2 Personal disabilities

Various jobs and positions are barred to an individual who is an undischarged bankrupt. These include:

(1) solicitor;
(2) barrister;
(3) insolvency practitioner;
(4) justice of the peace;
(5) Member of Parliament (in either House);
(6) member of a local authority.

23.5 INCREASING THE BANKRUPT'S ESTATE

The trustee has a duty to creditors to increase the fund available to pay them, if possible, and to do nothing which would diminish whatever money is available. The following provisions are designed to enable him to do so.

23.5.1 Onerous property

The trustee can disclaim onerous property (IA 1986, s 315), such as land burdened with onerous covenants or unprofitable contracts. A disclaimer ends all the bankrupt's rights and liabilities in respect of the property in question and discharges the trustee from any personal responsibility for that property. Any person who suffers loss as a result of a disclaimer by the trustee in bankruptcy may claim their loss from the bankrupt's estate. To prevent third parties from having to wait a long time to find out whether a trustee intends to disclaim, any person who has an interest in property previously owned by the bankrupt is entitled to serve written notice on the trustee in bankruptcy requiring him to disclaim the property within 28 days, failing which he loses the power to do so (IA 1986, s 316).

23.5.2 Legal action by creditors

The trustee must ensure that such funds as are available from the realisation of the bankrupt's estate are distributed fairly among his creditors in the prescribed order. Therefore, even though creditors may have commenced legal action against the debtor prior to his bankruptcy, they cannot necessarily pursue this once the bankruptcy order has been made. A judgment creditor can retain the money realised from enforcement of the judgment only if the process is completed (which means the goods have been seized and sold) before the date of the bankruptcy order (IA 1986, s 346), and, if a landlord distrains on the goods of the bankrupt for rent due, he can only keep the proceeds equivalent to 6 months' arrears and must prove in the bankruptcy as an ordinary unsecured creditor if he is owed more (IA 1986, s 247).

23.5.3 Disposals between date of presentation of the petition and appointment of the trustee in bankruptcy

Any disposition by the bankrupt of any of his property between the date of the presentation of the petition and the appointment of the trustee is void unless the court gives its consent or subsequently ratifies that disposition (IA 1986, s 284).

23.5.4 Transactions at an undervalue (IA 1986, s 339)

A transaction is at an undervalue where the bankrupt has made a gift, or has received consideration significantly lower in value than that which he provided (see **22.3.4**). If the bankrupt was party to any such transaction in the 5-year period prior to the petition, the trustee can apply to the court to have the transaction set aside, provided he can show that the debtor was insolvent at the time of the transaction at an undervalue or became insolvent as a result of it (IA 1986, s 341). If the transaction at an undervalue took place within 2 years before the bankruptcy, insolvency of the debtor at the time or as a result of the transaction is not a requirement.

Where the transaction at an undervalue is in favour of an 'associate' (broadly, a close relative), the debtor's insolvency at the time is presumed unless the associate can rebut this presumption (IA 1986, ss 341 and 435).

Any transaction at an undervalue, for whatever purpose, is caught by this provision, including, for example, a property adjustment order on divorce, nullity or judicial separation.

23.5.5 Preferences (IA 1986, s 340)

An arrangement is a preference if it places a creditor or surety in a better position than he would have been in otherwise and the debtor intended (at least partly) to do this (IA 1986, s 340). For example, if the debtor has borrowed money from a friend and, facing imminent bankruptcy, repays that friend in order to ensure that the friend does not lose money, that would be a preference. The trustee must prove that the debtor was insolvent at the time or became insolvent as a result of the preference being granted. The trustee in bankruptcy can make an application to set aside any 'preference' made within the 6 months prior to the petition, or within 2 years prior to the petition if the preference is in respect of an associate (IA 1986, s 341).

Where the preference is in favour of an associate, there is a presumption that the debtor intended to prefer that person, unless the contrary can be proved.

Generally, a preference must be a voluntary act of the debtor; a payment made under threat of bankruptcy is usually not thought to be a preference. A debtor who pays a creditor simply to avoid his own bankruptcy is generally not considered to have the necessary intention to benefit that creditor.

23.5.6 Transactions defrauding creditors

Where a transaction has been made at an undervalue for the purpose of making the debtor's property unavailable to pay creditors, the trustee or the supervisor of a voluntary arrangement (see **23.6**) can apply to have such a transaction set aside. This provision has no time-limit, so even a transaction which took place many years ago could be set aside on this basis, although the greater the time that has elapsed between the transaction and the bankruptcy, the weaker is the evidence that the aim of the transaction was to avoid the asset in question being used to pay creditors (IA 1986, s 423).

For example, a person might undertake a risky business venture and immediately prior to doing so put his house in the name of his spouse. This would be a transaction defrauding creditors if the necessary intention could be proved. However, since it is extremely difficult to establish such intention, proceedings under this provision are rare.

23.6 AVOIDING BANKRUPTCY: INDIVIDUAL VOLUNTARY ARRANGEMENTS

If a debtor is in financial difficulties, he may attempt to make a voluntary arrangement in order to avoid a bankruptcy order. To do this, he requires professional assistance, so he must find an insolvency practitioner who is willing to assist him in drawing up proposals and to supervise their implementation if they receive the approval of creditors. The insolvency practitioner is known as the debtor's 'nominee'.

Once he has found someone willing to be his nominee, the debtor must prepare a statement of affairs for that nominee, and should immediately apply to the bankruptcy court for an interim order (IA 1986, s 252), which has the effect of stopping any other proceedings being taken against him while his creditors consider his proposals. While the interim order is in force (usually for 14 days but it can be extended), no bankruptcy petition can be presented or proceeded with unless the leave of the court is obtained, and no other proceedings, execution or other legal process can be commenced or continued against the debtor or his property; it creates a moratorium.

The nominee will prepare a report for the court advising whether there are any realistic proposals to be made and therefore whether it is worth calling a meeting of creditors. If a meeting of creditors is called and the meeting approves the proposals (by more than three-quarters majority in value), every ordinary, unsecured creditor who had notice of the meeting and was entitled to attend and vote is bound by the decision of the meeting, whether or not he actually did so. Preferential and secured creditors are bound by the voluntary arrangement only if they agree to it (IA 1986, s 260).

If the creditors approve the proposed voluntary arrangement, the nominee (now called a 'supervisor') will implement the proposals. If the debtor fails to comply with the arrangement, or if it transpires that the creditors were persuaded to accept his proposal by means of false or misleading information, the supervisor or any creditor who is party to the voluntary arrangement can petition for the debtor's bankruptcy. This is particularly relevant where it is discovered that the debtor has made transactions at an undervalue (see **23.5.4**) or preferences (see **23.5.5**) immediately prior to the voluntary arrangement, as only a trustee in bankruptcy has the power to set aside these transactions and recover the money which can be used to pay creditors; a supervisor has no power to do this.

23.6.1 Advantages for the debtor in a voluntary arrangement

If a debtor manages to reach a voluntary arrangement with his creditors, he avoids the stigma of bankruptcy, the accompanying bad publicity, and the trauma of, possibly, a public examination in open court. He also avoids the various disabilities and disqualifications which follow from being declared bankrupt (see **23.2**).

23.6.2 Advantages for the creditor

If the debtor is insolvent (as he frequently will be) then creditors, particularly ordinary unsecured creditors, will have to accept that they are unlikely to be paid the amount due to them in full. They may feel that if they accept a voluntary arrangement proposed by the debtor they will recover a higher percentage of the debt due to them (because the costs involved in a voluntary arrangement may be lower than in a full bankruptcy) or that they will be paid sooner (because the full bankruptcy process can be extremely lengthy). Creditors will also need to judge for themselves whether the debtor can be relied upon to honour the arrangement, although they can always instigate bankruptcy proceedings should the debtor prove to have deceived them in the information he has provided or to be untrustworthy.

23.7 SUMMARIES AND CHECKLISTS

23.7.1 The home

- If house is in joint names of bankrupt and co-owner:
  - if co-owner had legal and beneficial interest, trustee needs court order for sale

- If house is in sole name of bankrupt:
  - an occupier may have beneficial interest (eg by contribution to purchase price)
  - a spouse may have right of occupation under Matrimonial Homes Act 1983
  - if so, trustee needs court order for sale

- If infant children live with the bankrupt in the house:
  - gives bankrupt a right of occupation against the trustee
  - trustee needs court order for sale
- Trustee needs no court order for sale where house in sole name of bankrupt and either:
  - he lives alone, or
  - he lives with a cohabitee and/or adult children who have no equitable interest in the property

23.7.2 Summary of bankruptcy procedure

- petition – creditor's or debtor's
- court hearing – bankruptcy order made
- Official Receiver appointed
- statement of affairs submitted to Official Receiver within 21 days (unless already done with debtor's petition)
- creditors' meeting held – at discretion of Official Receiver or if sufficient creditors demand it
- trustee appointed by creditors or Official Receiver continues to act
- bankrupt's property vests in trustee
- trustee distributes assets
- bankrupt discharged (usually 3 years after bankruptcy order made)

Chapter 24

CORPORATE INSOLVENCY: LIQUIDATION

24.1 INTRODUCTION

Liquidation is the process by which the existence of a company is brought to an end and its property administered for the benefit of creditors and members. A liquidator is appointed to take control of the company, collect in all its assets, pay all its debts and distribute any surplus between members. When all this has been done, the company is dissolved and will be struck off the register.

24.2 WHAT IS LIQUIDATION?

The terms 'liquidation' and 'winding-up' are synonymous, both describing the process by which the existence of a company is brought to an end and its property administered for the benefit of its creditors and members. There are three types of liquidation: compulsory, members' voluntary and creditors' voluntary.

The distinction between 'compulsory' and 'voluntary' liquidations lies in the fact that a compulsory liquidation is imposed on the company by a court order, whereas a voluntary liquidation is commenced by the company's own resolution.

The relevant procedure is set out in the Insolvency Act 1986 and detailed Insolvency Rules 1986 (SI 1986/1925).

24.3 COMPULSORY LIQUIDATION

24.3.1 Commencement

Compulsory liquidation of a company is begun by the presentation of a petition to the Chancery Division of the High Court. The Insolvency Act 1986 lists seven grounds upon which a petition may be based (ss 122 and 123) but the most commonly used ground is that the company is unable to pay its debts.

The petitioner is assisted by a presumption that the company is unable to pay its debts if it fails to comply with a 'statutory notice' (a demand for payment made in a particular form) from a creditor or creditors owed more than £750, or fails to satisfy enforcement of a judgment debt. If neither of these events has occurred, the petitioner must prove to the satisfaction of the court that the company is unable to pay its debts, taking into account prospective and contingent liabilities. (For the meaning of insolvency, see **23.2**.)

Any creditor may petition for the liquidation of the company (IA 1986, s 124). The court has a complete discretion as to whether to make the order for winding up the company, even if the grounds on which the petition is based have been satisfactorily

Chapter 24 contents
Introduction
What is liquidation?
Compulsory liquidation
Voluntary liquidation
The company's property
Distribution of assets
Dissolution
Increasing company assets
Alternatives to liquidation
Summaries and checklists

established (IA 1986, s 125). When exercising its discretion, the court will have regard to the wishes of the creditors. In particular, where the company is in the process of being wound up voluntarily, the court will not normally make an order for compulsory liquidation where the majority of creditors want the voluntary winding up to continue.

The company may petition for its own liquidation. This may be a necessary course of action, for example, where the members will not pass the necessary resolution at general meeting to put the company into voluntary liquidation, but the directors realise the financial position of the company is insecure and are required to take action to avoid liability for wrongful trading (see **24.8.4**).

24.3.2 Who is the liquidator?

If the court makes an order for compulsory liquidation of the company, the winding up is deemed to have begun on the date the petition was presented to the court, not the date of the order (IA 1986, s 129). The Official Receiver will become the liquidator, and will remain in that position unless the creditors of the company decide to appoint an insolvency practitioner of their choice to be the liquidator. The Official Receiver must officially advertise the winding up in the *London Gazette* and in a local newspaper, and must notify the registrar of companies and the company itself.

When the court makes an order for compulsory liquidation, most powers of the directors are withdrawn from them in favour of the liquidator, who is then empowered to manage the company. All company papers must state that the company is in liquidation. All employees of the company are automatically dismissed when such an order is made and employees dismissed in this way may be entitled to a redundancy payment, although claims for wrongful dismissal and unfair dismissal are not normally relevant. Wrongful dismissal may occur where a fixed term contract is prematurely terminated or where insufficient notice is given

The Official Receiver may require the directors to prepare a statement of affairs, giving details of the company's assets and liabilities, the names of creditors and details of any security they may have (IA 1986, s 131). The Official Receiver must prepare a report for the court dealing with the company's financial position, the cause of its failure and whether there are any suspicious circumstances surrounding the liquidation. He will then call separate meetings of creditors and members and must do so if one quarter in value of the company's creditors demand it (IA 1986, s 136). Although both the members' meeting and the creditors' meeting can nominate someone other than the Official Receiver to act as liquidator, if there is any disagreement over the appointment, the creditors' nominee takes precedence.

24.4 VOLUNTARY LIQUIDATION

24.4.1 Types

There are two types of voluntary winding up of a company. The distinction lies in whether or not the majority of the directors are prepared to make a statutory declaration that the company is solvent and will be able to pay all its debts in full, plus interest, within a specified period not exceeding 12 months (IA 1986, s 89). If they do make such a declaration, then the winding up is known as a members' voluntary winding up. However, if they are not prepared to make such a declaration, usually either because the company is insolvent or facing insolvency, then it will be a creditors' winding up (IA 1986, s 90).

Any director who makes a declaration of solvency without reasonable grounds is liable to criminal sanctions. If the company is wound up and all the debts are not paid in full within the period specified in the declaration, then the directors are presumed not to have had reasonable grounds (IA 1986, s 89).

24.4.2 Commencement

A voluntary winding up of the company is begun by the members passing a resolution in general meeting (IA 1986, s 86).

In the case of a **members'** voluntary winding up, a special resolution is required to wind up the company, but the wording of the resolution need not state the reasons. The resolution must be passed within 5 weeks of the making of the statutory declaration.

A **creditors'** voluntary winding up is initiated by the members passing an extraordinary resolution to the effect that the company cannot continue because of its liabilities and that it is advisable to wind up (IA 1986, s 84).

24.4.3 Procedure

In the case of a **members'** voluntary winding up, the members appoint a liquidator of their own choice, often as part of the special resolution to wind the company up (rather than by a separate ordinary resolution). No meeting of the creditors is required. The statutory declaration, together with the special resolution, need to be filed with the registrar of companies within 15 days of the resolution being passed. Both the resolution and the notice of the liquidator's appointment must be published in the *London Gazette* within 14 days (IA 1986, ss 85 and 109). In addition, the liquidator must file notice of his appointment with the registrar of companies.

In a **creditors'** voluntary winding up, there must be a meeting of the creditors, in addition to the general meeting at which the extraordinary resolution to wind up the company is passed. The creditors' meeting must be held within 14 days of the general meeting (IA 1986, s 98) and notice must be sent by post to the creditors not less than 7 days before the meeting and also advertised in the *London Gazette* and two local newspapers in the vicinity of the company's principal place of business.

At the creditors' meeting, the directors must present a full statement of affairs listing the company's assets and liabilities, the creditors and details of any security they may have (IA 1986, s 99). Both the creditors and the members can nominate an insolvency practitioner of their choice to act as liquidator, but if there is any disagreement, the creditors' choice of liquidator takes precedence. The extraordinary resolution and the statement of affairs must be filed with the registrar of companies. As in the case of a members' voluntary winding up, the resolution to wind up the company and the appointment of the liquidator must also be published in the *London Gazette* and the appointment notified to the registrar.

In either type of voluntary winding up, the powers of the directors cease on the passing of the resolution and are assumed by the liquidator.

Where the company is insolvent, employees of the company are automatically dismissed on the appointment of the liquidator. However, where the company is solvent, it is unclear whether employees are automatically dismissed, but the liquidator will usually take action to effect their dismissals.

24.5 THE COMPANY'S PROPERTY

Although the property of the company does not vest in the liquidator (unlike the property of a bankrupt which does vest in the trustee in bankruptcy), the liquidator is required to take all company property into his possession. He must then realise all company assets and use the proceeds to satisfy the debts and liabilities of the company in the proper order. Any surplus can be distributed among the members (IA 1986, s 143). Neither property held by the company on trust for another nor property subject to a retention of title clause can be used by the liquidator in this way, as such property does not really belong to the company.

24.6 DISTRIBUTION OF ASSETS

Once the liquidator has details of all company debts, he must distribute such funds as he has realised in the proper order. A creditor with security in the form of a fixed charge over company assets will usually enforce his security and will therefore not be paid by the liquidator. If a sale of the asset charged produces insufficient funds to discharge the debt, the creditor will prove for the balance in the liquidation as an ordinary unsecured creditor. If the proceeds of the sale are greater than the sum owed to the creditor, he must pay over the excess to the liquidator for distribution among other creditors. The proceeds must be distributed in the order set out below.

24.6.1 Expenses of winding up

The expenses of winding up include the cost of collecting in the company's assets, the cost of the petition (if a compulsory liquidation) and the remuneration of the liquidator. The total amount can be substantial.

24.6.2 Preferential creditors

Preferential creditors are the same as for bankruptcy (see **23.3.5**); if insufficient funds are available to pay all these debts in full, they rank and abate equally.

24.6.3 Creditors with floating charges

Creditors who have secured their debt by way of a floating charge cannot enforce their security until all preferential creditors have been paid in full, even if the floating charge crystallised before the commencement of the liquidation. Floating charges rank for priority in the order of creation, ie those created first are paid off first.

24.6.4 Ordinary unsecured creditors

If there is insufficient money to pay all ordinary unsecured creditors, these debts rank and abate equally.

24.6.5 Members

If there is any money remaining after paying all the previous categories of creditors in full, the company is solvent and the members can be repaid all or part of their capital investment in the company.

24.7 DISSOLUTION

24.7.1 Compulsory liquidation

Once the liquidator has completed his task of winding up the company, he summons a meeting of the creditors and reports on the winding up (IA 1986, s 146). He then sends the final return to the court and the registrar of companies and the company will be automatically dissolved 3 months later.

24.7.2 Voluntary winding up

If there has been a **members'** voluntary liquidation, only a meeting of members will be held. In the case of a **creditors'** voluntary winding up, separate meetings of members and creditors will be necessary. The liquidator will produce a final return and accounts to the meeting(s), showing how the winding up has been conducted and how the assets have been distributed. The final return will then be sent to the registrar of companies and the company will automatically be dissolved 3 months later.

A summary of the basic procedure on winding up a company is given at **24.10.3**.

24.8 INCREASING COMPANY ASSETS

Like a trustee in bankruptcy, the liquidator is under a duty to preserve the property of the company and, if possible, to increase it in order to swell the fund which will be available to pay the company's creditors. The following provisions are designed to enable him to do so.

24.8.1 Onerous property (IA 1986, s 178)

A liquidator may disclaim onerous property in the same way as a trustee in bankruptcy (see **23.5.1**). There is no time-limit within which he must disclaim, but any third party who has an interest in the property in question can serve a notice on the liquidator requiring him to decide whether or not to disclaim the property within 28 days. If he fails to disclaim the property within this time-limit, the liquidator loses the power to do so.

24.8.2 Legal action by creditors

If the court makes an order for compulsory liquidation, no legal action against the company or its property can be commenced or proceeded with unless the leave of the court is obtained (IA 1986, s 130). Where the company is in voluntary liquidation the court may order a stay of any such proceedings, unless there is a dispute as to liability which could turn out to be to the company's advantage.

Only if execution against the company has been completed before either the presentation of the petition or the passing of the members' resolution will the creditor be able to keep the proceeds he obtains as a result. If execution has not been completed (ie the goods seized and sold) before commencement of winding up, the sheriff will hand over any proceeds to the liquidator (IA 1986, s 183). Once liquidation of the company has begun then, in a compulsory liquidation any attempt to levy execution against the company is void and, in a voluntary winding up, although the execution is not void, the liquidator may apply to the court to exercise its discretion to stay the proceedings and the court will usually do so to ensure that any assets are fairly distributed among all creditors.

24.8.3 Fraudulent trading (IA 1986, s 213)

Anyone found to have been participating in fraudulent trading can be required to contribute to the assets of the company such amount as the court decides (IA 1986, s 213). Only those who are knowingly party to fraudulent trading incur such liability. Some positive steps are necessary; mere omission is not sufficient. Fraudulent trading involves continuing to trade and incur debts at a time when there is, to the knowledge of the person concerned, no reasonable prospect of those debts being paid either at the time they are due or shortly thereafter. By action of this type, the fraudulent trader is deceiving creditors into believing that they will be paid on the agreed date, when there is little chance of that happening. Only the liquidator of a company can make application to the court for such an order. If the necessary intention and participation can be established, anyone exercising some kind of controlling or managerial function in a company (not just the directors) could be found liable for fraudulent trading.

Fraudulent trading is also a criminal offence (CA 1985, s 458).

24.8.4 Wrongful trading (IA 1986, s 214)

A director (or shadow director) of an insolvent company may be found liable for wrongful trading if he knew or ought to have known that there was no reasonable prospect of the company avoiding insolvent liquidation and, from that point, failed to take every step to minimise the loss to creditors. Dishonesty is not necessary here; a director can be liable for wrongful trading where he ought to have known the situation, even if he did not. When judging whether a director should have been aware of the risk, the court will expect every director to have at least the general knowledge, skill and experience which could be expected of someone in their position. If a particular director actually has greater expertise than would generally be expected (eg if he is the managing director, the finance director or has a relevant professional qualification), the court will require a higher standard of awareness. It is no defence for a director to do nothing. He is required to take action to protect creditors as soon as he becomes aware, or should have been aware, of the risk of insolvency; the court will take an objective view of the action which the director(s) ought to have taken. If a director is found to have been wrongfully trading, he can be required to contribute to the assets of the company, the amount being decided by the court. Only the liquidator of a company can apply to the court for such an order.

24.8.5 Transactions at an undervalue (IA 1986, s 238)

The liquidator can make application to the court to set aside any transaction at an undervalue (see **22.3.4**) which the company entered into within the 2 years prior to the commencement of the liquidation, provided the company was insolvent at the time of such a transaction or became insolvent as a result. A transaction at an undervalue is one in which the company receives no consideration, or receives significantly less consideration than it is providing. A transaction will not be set aside if there were genuine commercial reasons for it at the time, even though it later proves to be a bad bargain. For example, a company with cash flow problems may sell some of its stock at a discounted rate in order to obtain the cash it desperately needs. This type of transaction will not be set aside provided the court is satisfied that the directors of the company were acting in good faith for the benefit of the company.

24.8.6 Preferences (IA 1986, s 240)

A transaction is a 'preference' if it benefits a creditor or surety in some way, and it was the intention of the company that this should happen (see **23.5.5**). A transaction is therefore usually only a preference if it is a voluntary act of the company, rather than being done under threat of liquidation. A preference may be set aside by the court on the application of the liquidator if made within the 6 months prior to the commencement of the winding up. If the preference is in favour of a person connected with the company (a director or close relative of a director (IA 1986, s 249)) such a transaction which has taken place within the 2 years prior to the liquidation can be set aside, and in such a case there is a presumption that the company was influenced by the desire to prefer the connected person. As with transactions at an undervalue, it is necessary for the liquidator to show that the company was insolvent at the time or became insolvent as a result of the transaction.

24.8.7 Transactions defrauding creditors (IA 1986, s 423)

If the liquidator can establish to the satisfaction of the court that a transaction at an undervalue has taken place, and the aim of that transaction was to place the assets of the company beyond the reach of creditors, the court will make an order that such a transaction be set aside. There is no time-limit for such transactions, although clearly more recent transactions are more likely to have been intended to defraud creditors than those which took place when the company was more successful. Insolvency of the company at the time or as a result is not necessary. The liquidator is the most likely applicant for such an order, although application is also possible by creditors, shareholders, an administrator or the supervisor of a voluntary arrangement.

24.8.8 Company charges: fixed and floating

A fixed or floating charge created by the company must be registered at Companies House within 21 days (CA 1985, ss 395–397). If this is not done the charge in question is void as against a liquidator. Late registration is only permitted with leave of the court and the court may order that the charge take subject to any charges registered in the meantime (see **18.7.2**).

24.8.9 Floating charges

A floating charge may be set aside because it has been granted as a preference to one creditor (see **24.9.6**), or it may be set aside because it has been given in exchange for prior consideration (IA 1986, s 245). Any floating charge created within the 12 months prior to commencement of winding up is invalid security for any company debt which existed prior to the creation of the floating charge, but is valid security for any fresh consideration advanced to the company on or after the granting of the floating charge.

For example, if a company has an unsecured bank loan of £10,000 but, in exchange for extending that loan to £15,000, it grants the bank a floating charge as security, that floating charge is not valid security for the pre-existing £10,000 loan, but will serve to secure the new £5,000 advance if the company goes into insolvent liquidation within 12 months following the date of that floating charge.

A floating charge can only be set aside on this basis if the company was insolvent at the time or became insolvent as a result. It is for the company to prove that it was solvent at the time and did not become insolvent as a result of granting the floating charge. If the floating charge in question is granted in favour of a director or close relative of a director, the time-limit is extended to 2 years, and it is not necessary to establish the existing or resulting insolvency of the company. If a floating charge is set aside under this provision, the debt still remains as an unsecured debt.

24.9 ALTERNATIVES TO LIQUIDATION

24.9.1 Defunct companies

If a company is declared to be 'defunct' it can be struck off the register; this is a much cheaper way of terminating the existence of a company than winding up. A director of a company which has ceased trading might ask the registrar of companies to strike the company off the register or the registrar might do so on his own initiative if he believes that this is so, for example, where no documents have been filed for a lengthy period. The registrar must advertise widely his intention to strike a company off the register but, if the company itself, any member or creditor is aggrieved by this action, application may be made at any time within the next 20 years for the company to be returned to the register.

24.9.2 Voluntary arrangement

A voluntary arrangement for a company is similar to a voluntary arrangement for an individual except there is no interim order (see **23.6**) and has the same aim, namely, to avoid insolvency proceedings. The directors must draw up proposals, assisted by an insolvency practitioner (a 'nominee'), who will report to the court as to whether meetings of members and creditors should be called to consider the proposals.

The arrangement is approved if a simple majority of members are in favour and more than three-quarters in value of the creditors (excluding secured creditors) agree to it. If the members and creditors approve the proposed scheme, the nominee will implement it, and it is then binding on any person who had notice of the meeting and was entitled to attend and vote, whether or not he actually did so. The rights of secured and preferential creditors are unaffected unless they agree to the voluntary arrangement (IA 1986, s 5).

The basic procedure for a voluntary arrangement is as follows:

- the directors appoint a nominee and devise proposals
- nominee reports to court
- meetings of members and creditors approve proposals – arrangement becomes binding (except for secured and preferential creditors)
- approval reported to court
- nominee becomes 'supervisor' and implements scheme
- at any stage creditors may challenge the supervisor's decision in court and the supervisor may ask the court for directions.

24.9.3 Administration order

The aim of an administration order is to postpone or even completely avoid the liquidation of a company which is in financial difficulties.

The process is begun by presentation of a petition to the court by the directors, the company or a creditor (IA 1986, s 9). From the date such a petition is presented:

(1) the company may not be wound up although a petition for compulsory liquidation may still be presented (IA 1986, s 10). (This will be dismissed if an administration order is subsequently made.);
(2) a fixed chargee cannot enforce his security (although a floating chargee can still appoint an administrative receiver, which effectively gives him a veto over this attempt to rescue the company) (IA 1986, s 10(2));
(3) goods in the company's possession but not its ownership may not be repossessed;
(4) any existing legal actions against the company are stayed; and
(5) no new proceedings can be commenced (IA 1986, s 11).

Presentation of a petition for an administration order therefore creates a moratorium; a breathing space in which an administrator can be appointed. He will then try to save the company from liquidation.

The court will make an administration order if it is satisfied that the company is likely to become insolvent and that by making the order either the company's survival as a going concern, in whole or in part, could possibly be achieved or there would be a more advantageous realisation of the company's assets than could be achieved on a winding up (IA 1986, s 8). It is possible for the directors of a company to petition for an administration order in order to achieve a moratorium to prevent the company being wound up while they try to put together a voluntary arrangement. If an order is made, all company stationery must state that the company is subject to an administration order and give the name of the administrator. Any petition for compulsory liquidation will be dismissed by the court. Any administrative receiver will be required to vacate office, as the order can only be made with the consent of the debenture holder who appointed the administrative receiver. The moratorium on enforcement will continue until such time as the administration order is discharged.

The directors of the company must submit a statement of affairs to the administrator (an insolvency practitioner), who will base his subsequent recommendations on this information (IA 1986, s 22). He will manage the company's affairs generally and will take charge of its business and property. He has power to carry on the company's business, to deal with or dispose of its assets and to borrow money in the company's name (IA 1986, s 14). He can also apply to have transactions at an undervalue, transactions defrauding creditors and preferences set aside in the same way as a liquidator could (see **24.8.5**, **24.8.7** and **24.8.6**). Unregistered and late registered charges are void against the administrator in the same way as they would have been void against a liquidator (see **24.8.8**). The directors of the company will, however, remain in office unless the administrator removes them. Within a 3-month time-limit, his task is to make proposals which may save the company from liquidation, either by reorganisation of the company or by realising company assets in such a way as to gain maximum benefit and, if his proposals gain the approval of the company's unsecured creditors by simple majority in value, to supervise their implementation.

The administrator may apply to the court for the administration order to be discharged or varied if either the purpose for which the order was made has been achieved or that purpose has proved incapable of achievement (IA 1986, s 18).

The basic procedure is as follows:

- petition
- moratorium
- court makes administration order (which states purpose for which it is made) and appoints administrator – moratorium continues
- statement of affairs made by directors to administrator
- administrator makes proposals
- creditors' meeting held to approve proposals
- administration ends when court discharges the order.

An administration order has a number of advantages for the company. By creating a moratorium it provides a breathing space during which the administrator may be able to save the business or at least to consider the possibility of a voluntary arrangement. By preventing other creditors from petitioning for winding up, it may lead to a better realisation of assets in the long term.

24.9.4 Administrative receivership

If the company is in financial difficulties and has defaulted under the terms of a debenture, the debenture holder may appoint a receiver to enforce his security rather than making application for compulsory liquidation of the company.

A receiver is an administrative receiver if the debenture holder who has appointed him had a floating charge over the whole or substantially the whole of the company's undertaking. An administrative receiver must be an insolvency practitioner. He must notify the company itself, all known creditors and the registrar of companies of his appointment. If an administrative receiver is appointed, that appointment does not create a moratorium, but it does cause the floating charge to crystallise, which means that the company can no longer continue to deal with the assets which are subject to the floating charge.

The powers and duties of the administrative receiver will usually be specified in the debenture. As an administrative receiver, he would need to have power to manage the company until such time as his task is completed. He can require the directors to deliver to him a statement of affairs, and he will take possession of all assets which are the subject of the floating charge. His aim is to recover for the debenture holder who appointed him the debt owed, plus interest and the costs of his appointment (IA 1986, s 240) but he must allow for creditors with priority to the floating chargee who appointed him (ie fixed chargees and preferential creditors) to be paid off first.

He also has power to apply to court for any transactions defrauding creditors to be set aside.

Once the administrative receiver has recovered everything due to his appointor, then he may resign from office. The debenture holder who appointed the administrative receiver does not have the power to remove him. Only the court can remove him prior to the completion of his task (IA 1986, s 45).

The basic procedure is as follows:

- debenture holder appoints administrative receiver
- administrative receiver formally accepts office
- administrative receiver sends notice forthwith to the company and to all known creditors within 28 days
- directors prepare statement of affairs
- administrative receiver sends report to registrar of companies and to creditors within 3 months giving his views on why the company defaulted and setting out its current financial position
- meetings of creditors held to consider report
- administrative receiver submits various reports and accounts before leaving office.

It could be advantageous to a creditor to appoint an administrative receiver rather than take some other action against the company in default (eg administration order or winding up petition). The creditor chooses the insolvency practitioner who acts as the administrative receiver; there is no fixed moratorium and so the creditor is not prevented from enforcing any fixed charges he may have; and as the court is not involved the costs will usually be lower.

24.10 SUMMARIES AND CHECKLISTS

24.10.1 Factors influencing choice between administration order and administrative receivership

- Administrator – chosen by the court
  Administrative receiver – chosen by debenture holder

- Administration order – moratorium
  Administrative receivership – no delay

- Administration order prevents petition for liquidation by other creditors
  Administrative receivership does not

- Administrator – can apply to set aside various transactions (defrauding creditors, preferences and undervalue transactions)
  Administrative receiver – can only apply to set aside transaction to defraud creditors

- NB An administration order can only be made with the consent of any debenture holders – they are mutually exclusive remedies.

24.10.2 Comparison of provisions relating to company and individual insolvency

LIQUIDATION		BANKRUPTCY	
Commencement		**Commencement**	
(a)	by petition from creditor(s) on ground that company is unable to pay its debts (compulsory liquidation)	(a)	by petition from creditor(s) owed £750 or more on ground that debtor is unable to pay his debts
presumption of inability to pay where:			
– non-compliance with statutory demand			
– unsatisfied enforcement of judgment debt			
(b)	by resolution at GM – 'members' if declaration of solvency by directors – creditors' in other cases (voluntary liquidation)	(b)	n/a
Winding up order		**Bankruptcy order**	
(a)	liquidator takes possession of assets	(a)	bankrupt's property vests in the trustee in bankruptcy
(b)	– all actions stayed (compulsory) – actions may be stayed (voluntary)	(b)	all actions stayed
(c)	n/a	(c)	bankrupt becomes subject to certain disabilities
(d)	n/a	(d)	spouse/children in occupation may refuse order for sale of home, but normally not for more than 12 months
(e)	liquidator may seek court order that certain persons contribute to the assets of the company: – any person, for fraudulent trading – directors, for wrongful trading	(e)	n/a

Corporate Insolvency: Liquidation

Liquidator may apply to court to set aside certain transactions	Trustee may apply to court to set aside certain transactions
(a) transactions at an under value – if within 2 years of commencement of winding up where company insolvent at time or as a result	(a) transactions at an under-value – if within 2 years of petition or 5 years where debtor insolvent at time or as a result

(b)   preferences
 	
     –   if within 6 months of commencement of winding up (2 years with 'connected person')
 	
         where company insolvent at time or as a result
	(b) preferences
	
	     – if within 6 months of petition (2 years with 'an associate')

	– must show 'influenced by desire' to prefer
	(c) transactions defrauding creditors
	– no time-limit but must show undervalue and intention of putting assets where debtor insolvent at time or as a result beyond the reach of claimants
	(d) disclaim onerous property
Charges	
(a) all charges must be registered at Companies House	n/a

(b)   floating charges may be ineffective to secure an existing debt without fresh consideration
 	
     –   if created within 12 months of commencement of winding up
 	
     –   if company insolvent at time or as result
 	
     –   (time period is 2 years if in favour of 'connected person' and not necessary to show insolvency)
	n/a

Assets distributed in statutory order	Assets distributed in statutory order
• debts secured by fixed charge	• debts secured by fixed charge
• costs of winding up	• costs of administration
• preferential debts	• preferential debts
• debts secured by floating charge	• n/a
• ordinary debts	• ordinary debts
• members	• n/a
• n/a	• postponed debts |//
Voluntary arrangements – companies	**Voluntary arrangements – individuals**
(a) Proposed by directors who appoint insolvency practitioner as nominee	(a) Proposed by debtor who appoints insolvency practitioner as nominee
(b) n/a	(b) debtor seeks interim order from court – stay on proceedings for limited period
(c) if proposals approved, all creditors bound except non-assenting secured and preferential creditors	(c) if proposals approved, all creditors bound except non-assenting secured and preferential creditors
(d) nominee/supervisor cannot apply to set aside transactions at an undervalue or preferences or transactions defrauding creditors nor invalidate floating charges	(d) nominee/supervisor cannot apply to set aside transactions at an undervalue or preferences or transactions defrauding creditors

24.10.3 Basic procedure

(a) Compulsory liquidation

- petition court and advertise petition in *London Gazette*
- hearing – court makes order
    - Official Receiver becomes liquidator
    - Official Receiver advertises order in *London Gazette* and local newspaper, notifies registrar and company
- statement of affairs
- meetings of members and creditors to nominate liquidator of their choice (creditors' choice takes precedence)
- assets collected in and distributed in required order
- final meeting of creditors held
- final return filed with court and registrar
- company dissolved 3 months later

(b) Creditors' voluntary winding up
- directors prepare statement of affairs
- extraordinary resolution passed by members – members can nominate liquidator at GM

Both filed with registrar
- resolution advertised in *London Gazette* within 14 days
- creditors' meeting held within 14 days of GM
  - NB notice requirements
  - creditors' choice of liquidator takes priority over that of members
- appointment of liquidator published in *London Gazette* and notified to registrar
- assets collected in and distributed in required order
- final meetings of creditors and members held
- final return filed with registrar
- company dissolved 3 months later

(c) Members' voluntary liquidation
- statutory declaration of solvency by directors
- special resolution passed by members within 5 weeks of statutory declaration – members appoint liquidator at GM

Both filed with registrar
- resolution and notice of liquidator's appointment advertised in *London Gazette* and notice of appointment to registrar
- assets collected in and distributed in required order
- final meeting of members held
- final return filed with registrar
- company dissolved 3 months later

PART VII

CHOOSING THE FORM OF BUSINESS ORGANISATION

Where a single person decides to set up a business, consideration should be given to whether to trade as a sole trader or as a limited company. Similarly, where two or more persons decide to set up a business, they should consider whether to trade as a partnership or as a limited company.

This Part begins by considering these questions by reference to taxation, both in terms of the business profits and in terms of capital taxation. There are many differences between the treatment of an unincorporated business (sole trader or partnership) and that of a company and its directors and shareholders, some of which favour the former while others favour the latter. Consideration is then given to the significant differences other than in the context of taxation between trading as an unincorporated business and trading as a limited company.

Chapter 25

THE TAX CONSIDERATIONS

25.1 INTRODUCTION

In order to compare the tax treatment of different forms of business organisation, it will be necessary to consider not only the year-by-year treatment of the income profits generated by the business but also the longer-term possibilities of capital taxation. Taxation of income profits requires a comparison between taxation of the self-employed (ie sole trader or partners) and taxation of the incorporated business where profits may be taxed in the hands of the company, its directors and employees and/or its shareholders. Possible future taxation invites a comparison between the reliefs available for sole traders or partners on the one hand and for a company and/or its shareholders on the other hand.

25.2 INCOME PROFITS

Although the income profits of a company are calculated under the same rules as the income of a partnership or a sole trader (applying Schedule D, Case I), significant differences arise from the fact that the company is a taxpayer in its own right, quite separate from its directors, employees and shareholders.

25.2.1 Comparing Schedules

If *all* of the company's income is withdrawn as directors' fees/employees' salaries, no corporation tax will be chargeable because the company is left with no taxable profit; the directors'/employees' salaries will suffer income tax under Schedule E. If the same business were run by a partnership or a sole trader, income tax would be charged on the income of the partners or the sole trader under Schedule D, Case I. It follows therefore that a comparison of the tax treatment of the income of these businesses becomes a comparison between the application of Schedule E in the context of the company and the application of Schedule D, Case I, in the context of the partnership or sole trader. Particular differences are:

(1) the rules on deductible expenditure are more generous under Schedule D, Case I ('wholly and exclusively for the purposes of the trade') than under Schedule E ('wholly, exclusively and necessarily in the performance of the employee's duties');

(2) there are rules under Schedule E (but not under Schedule D, Case I) for charging income tax on fringe benefits provided by the company, so that if a director/employee uses assets of the company (eg a dwelling) without payment to the company, there is a charge to income tax;

(3) the timing of payment of tax is more favourable under Schedule D, Case I (tax in two instalments where calculation is based on profits of the accounting period which ends in the tax year) than under Schedule E (tax on a current year basis collected at source under the PAYE system).

Chapter 25 contents
Introduction
Income profits
Income loss reliefs
Pension arrangements
National insurance contributions
Relief for interest paid
Available reliefs for capital gains
Possibility of double taxation of a company's income and capital profits
Available reliefs for inheritance tax
Conclusion

25.2.2 Rates of tax

If a business is run by a company and only *some* of the company's income is withdrawn as salaries, the business profits are split so that the company's portion may attract corporation tax while the salaried portion may attract income tax. If the same business were run by a partnership or a sole trader, income tax would be charged on the entire profits irrespective of whether or not they were withdrawn from the business as opposed to being 'ploughed back'. It follows, therefore, that a comparison of the tax treatment of the income of these businesses becomes a comparison between, on the one hand, the payment of corporation tax under Schedule D, Case I and income tax under Schedule E and, on the other hand, the payment of income tax under Schedule D, Case I. Apart from differences (as above) under the rules of the Schedules, differences would arise as to rates of tax payable.

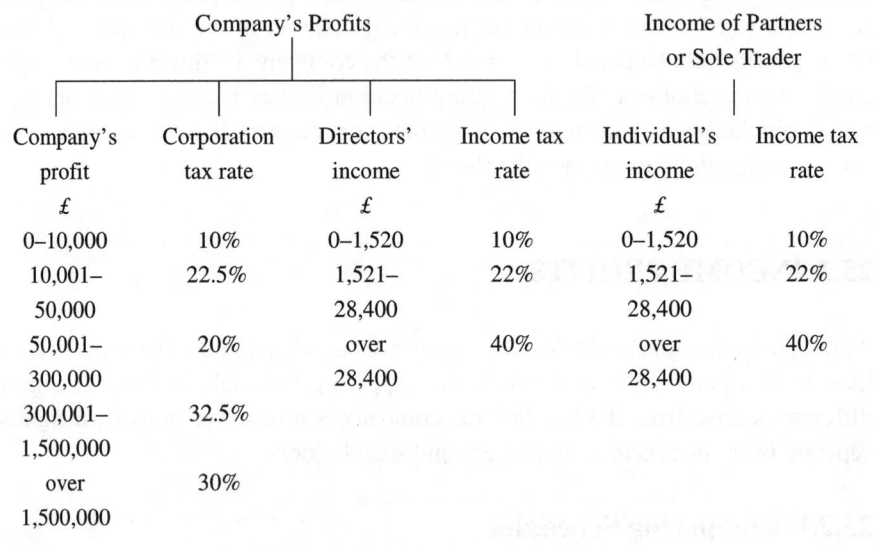

Company's Profits				Income of Partners or Sole Trader	
Company's profit £	Corporation tax rate	Directors' income £	Income tax rate	Individual's income £	Income tax rate
0–10,000	10%	0–1,520	10%	0–1,520	10%
10,001–50,000	22.5%	1,521–28,400	22%	1,521–28,400	22%
50,001–300,000	20%	over 28,400	40%	over 28,400	40%
300,001–1,500,000	32.5%				
over 1,500,000	30%				

A company can retain profits of up to £10,000 before starting to pay tax at a rate higher than 10 per cent and up to £300,000 before starting to pay tax at a rate higher than 20 per cent; even above that figure the overall rate of corporation tax will never exceed 30 per cent. Apart from this, the directors may enjoy taxable incomes of up to £28,400 (in addition to personal allowances) before starting to pay tax at 40 per cent. Partners (or sole traders) will pay income tax on all of the business profit without the advantage of being able to split the income between the two taxes (although they will also have their personal allowances to set against the income). This is more likely to be significant when, in a profitable business, the profits are being ploughed back to finance growth; in a company, the retained profits may well be taxed at no higher rate than 20 per cent while for an equivalent partnership or sole trader the top rate of income tax (40 per cent) may be applicable.

25.3 INCOME LOSS RELIEFS

Although most loss-relieving provisions applicable to companies have an equivalent provision applicable to partnerships and sole traders, there are three particular points worth noting.

25.3.1 Start-up relief (ICTA 1988, s 381)

Start-up relief, which permits trading losses assessable in the first 4 tax years of a business to be carried back and deducted from the income of the taxpayer for the preceding 3 tax years, is only available to partners and sole traders (see **3.4.1**).

25.3.2 Carry across reliefs – setting losses against other income or gains

A company's trading losses relieved under s 393A of ICTA 1988 cannot be set against the income or gains of the persons running the company, whereas the trading losses of a partner or a sole trader can be set against that person's other income and, possibly, gains under ICTA 1988, s 380 (see **3.4** and **21.2.3**).

25.3.3 Terminal loss relief by carry-back

When a company ceases to carry on a trade, a trading loss sustained in its final 12 months may be carried back against its profits of any description (income or capital) for the previous 3 years (ICTA 1988, s 393A). The position is more restrictive for sole traders or partners; for these taxpayers, a trading loss made in the final 12 months' trading has a 3-tax-year carry back, but the loss can only be set against previous profits of the same trade – ICTA 1988, s 388 (see **3.4.2** and **3.4.4**).

25.4 PENSION ARRANGEMENTS

The detail of the rules relating to pension payments is outside the scope of this book. However, the ability to make pension arrangements with the benefit of tax relief is greater for a company and its directors/employees through an occupational pension scheme or through the company contributing to the individual's personal pension scheme because two parties are contributing, both with the benefit of tax relief. Where a partner or sole trader is making pension arrangements, he is the only person contributing, albeit with tax relief.

25.5 NATIONAL INSURANCE CONTRIBUTIONS

National insurance contributions are subject to complex rules, and thresholds are adjusted each year. In general, however, the burden of national insurance contributions in the company context, where both the company and its employees make contributions, will be greater than that in the partnership context. Although the company will get tax relief on its contributions, the employees will not get tax relief; a self-employed person (a partner or a sole trader) will get some tax relief on his contributions.

25.6 RELIEF FOR INTEREST PAID

A person who pays interest on a loan to enable him to buy a share in a partnership or to lend to a partnership will obtain income tax relief for that interest (see **9.2.4**). A person who pays interest on a loan to enable him to buy shares in a company or to lend to a company in which he is a shareholder will only obtain income tax relief if certain conditions are met; these conditions are that the company must be a close company and that the shareholder must either own more than 5 per cent of the ordinary share capital or work for the greater part of his time in the management or conduct of the company (however few shares he holds – see **21.4.2**).

25.7 AVAILABLE RELIEFS FOR CAPITAL GAINS

25.7.1 Comparing companies with partners and sole traders

(1) Roll-over relief on replacement of qualifying assets

The roll-over relief on replacement of qualifying assets is available on disposals by companies, partners and sole traders.

(2) Other business reliefs

Other business reliefs discussed in Chapter 22 are restricted to disposals by individuals and are therefore not available where a company is the disponer. The following are therefore not available to a company:

(a) retirement relief;
(b) hold-over relief on a gift of business assets;
(c) deferral relief on reinvestment in EIS and VCT shares (although the Corporate Venturing Scheme offers a broadly similar relief to companies).
(d) Roll-over relief on incorporation of an unincorporated business.

By definition, this relief is only available to individuals.

(3) Taper relief and indexation

Companies continue to benefit from the indexation allowance throughout the period of ownership of a chargeable asset, whereas for gains made by individuals this has been superseded from 6 April 1998 by taper relief. Which is more favourable will depend on a number of factors including the amount of the gain, the rate of inflation and the length of ownership of the asset in question.

(4) The annual exemption

The annual exemption is not available to companies.

25.7.2 Comparing shareholders with partners and sole traders

The details of the available reliefs were considered in Chapter 22. A general difference between the treatment of a shareholder on the one hand and partners or sole traders on the other lies in the fact that, for the shareholder to obtain relief, additional conditions must be satisfied which do not have to be satisfied by a partner or a sole trader.

(1) For retirement relief where a shareholder disposes of his shares (and perhaps makes an associated disposal of an asset such as premises which is used by the company), the company must be the personal trading company of that shareholder and the shareholder must have been a full-time working officer or employee of the company.

(2) For roll-over relief on replacement where a shareholder disposes of a qualifying asset (such as premises, fixed plant and machinery or goodwill) used by the company and purchases another qualifying asset, the company must be the personal trading company of that shareholder. A further major difference is that shares do not count as qualifying assets for the purposes of roll-over relief on replacement, whereas a sole trader or partner will have an interest in qualifying assets (such as premises, fixed plant and machinery and goodwill).

(3) For hold-over relief where a shareholder makes a disposal other than at arm's length of a business asset (eg premises) used by the company, the company must be the personal trading company of that shareholder. If the disposal is of the shares themselves, the company need only be the shareholder's personal company if the shares are quoted on The Stock Exchange (see **22.4.1**).

(4) In contrast with the other reliefs, deferral relief when investing in EIS/VCT shares favours the shareholder as it is not available where the reinvestment is in an unincorporated business as the investment must be in company shares.

(5) Enhanced business taper relief is available for all shareholdings in unquoted trading companies, but if the company is quoted the shareholder must either be an employee or hold 5 per cent or more of the company's voting shares to qualify. Assets held by the individual and used by the company will only qualify for the relief if the company's shares qualify as business assets in relation to the owner.

25.8 POSSIBILITY OF DOUBLE TAXATION OF A COMPANY'S INCOME AND CAPITAL PROFITS

25.8.1 Distributions

Every pound of profit a company makes is charged to corporation tax at effective rates of 10 per cent, 22.5 per cent, 20 per cent, 32.5 per cent and 30 per cent (see **21.2.7**). When that profit, net of tax, is distributed as a dividend to its shareholders, it is received as their Schedule F income (see **21.4.1**). The same profit is thus capable of attracting a double charge.

The effect of the double charge will depend upon the rate of corporation tax payable by the company and the circumstances of the individual taxpayer. For a small company whose shareholders pay income tax only at the starting rate or the basic rate, there is no further liability to pay tax beyond that paid by the company, but, in a large company, the company will pay 30 per cent corporation tax and the shareholders may pay income tax at the higher rate and therefore suffer the Schedule F upper rate beyond the amount of the tax credit.

25.8.2 Capital gains tax

Because the company has a separate legal personality and therefore is a taxpayer separate from the individuals who are the directors/employees and shareholders, there is a possibility that capital gains on the company's assets may give rise to charges to corporation tax on the company and capital gains tax on the individuals concerned. Suppose, for example, that a company owns some land as an investment. The land has increased in value by £100,000 (after allowable expenditure and indexation) and correspondingly the shares in the company have increased in value by £80,000 (after allowing for a potential corporation tax charge of £20,000). If the company were to sell off the land and the shareholders were to sell some shares, the company would be liable to pay corporation tax on its gain and the shareholders would be liable to pay capital gains tax on their gains; even though the shareholders' gains are at least partly attributable to the gain on the premises which is charged to corporation tax, the shareholders are chargeable to capital gains tax without credit for the corporation tax paid by the company. If, on the other hand, the land in the above situation was owned by a partnership, the partners might pay capital gains tax on their disposal of the land, but there would be no equivalent of the second charge to tax which occurred in the company context.

25.8.3 Avoiding the double charge

To avoid the possibility of this double charge to taxation suffered by a company and its shareholders, it may be advisable for an appreciating asset, such as premises, to be owned by a shareholder or shareholders individually rather than by the company; the company may be allowed to use the premises under the terms of a lease or a licence. The advantage of individual ownership of assets used by the company is that, although the individual owner may suffer capital gains tax on a disposal, there can be no second charge to tax as might occur if the company owned and disposed of the asset. There are, however, potential problems with such an arrangement from a tax perspective. For retirement relief, the shareholder must be a full-time working officer or employee in his 'personal company' and no relief will be available if he has charged the company a full market rent for the use of the asset (see **22.4.1**). For inheritance tax business property relief, a maximum 50 per cent relief will be available and then only if the shareholder has voting control of the company (see **22.4.3**).

25.9 AVAILABLE RELIEFS FOR INHERITANCE TAX

The details of the available reliefs were considered in Chapter 22. The essential differences between the treatment of a shareholder on the one hand and the treatment of partners or a sole trader on the other hand lie in the fact that, as with capital gains tax reliefs, there are additional conditions imposed on shareholders which may result in their receiving less favourable treatment.

25.9.1 Agricultural property relief

For a shareholder to qualify in respect of his shareholding, he must have had control of the company at the time of the transfer; for a sole trader or partner, there is no equivalent of this condition.

25.9.2 Business property relief

For a shareholder, relief at 100 per cent is available on the transfer of unquoted shares and at 50 per cent on the transfer of quoted shares which give the shareholder a controlling interest. For a partner or sole trader transferring an interest in the business or the business, 100 per cent relief is available.

Assets such as land, buildings, machinery or plant used by a partnership but owned by a partner will qualify for 50 per cent business property relief. This relief is only available in the company context if the owner is a shareholder whose holding yields control of the company.

25.9.3 Instalment option for payment of IHT

A business or an interest in a business held by a sole trader or partner always qualifies as property in relation to which the instalment option may be available, but a shareholding will only qualify if it is a controlling shareholding or, failing that, if further conditions are satisfied (see **22.4.3**).

25.10 CONCLUSION

Whether it is preferable to trade as a sole trader, in a partnership, or via a company will depend, from a tax viewpoint, on the exact circumstances of the client's business and the tax regime in force at the time of consideration. It is not possible to say that one way of conducting business will always be more tax efficient than another. In addition the non-tax considerations set out in Chapter 26 must be taken into account before a final decision can be taken.

Chapter 26

CONSIDERATIONS OTHER THAN TAX

26.1 INTRODUCTION

Often, the differences in tax treatment of the self-employed and of the incorporated business have a significant bearing on the choice of the form of business organisation. Where these differences are not critical, a number of other factors are significant. This chapter considers, first, the factor which is likely to be the most important in practice: the scope for the individuals involved to be shielded from the risk of personal insolvency by the limited liability enjoyed through trading as a limited company. The main examples of other factors are then discussed, in outline, although the significance of any of these factors will vary according to particular circumstances.

Chapter 26 contents
Introduction
Liability for debts
Raising finance
Management structure
Status
Formality in setting up
Publicity of information
Statutory obligations and control

26.2 LIABILITY FOR DEBTS

26.2.1 Directors

In a number of circumstances, directors are personally liable for what they have done or failed to do. Examples include the following.

Personal guarantees

Personal guarantees may be required, for example, for repayment of the company's overdraft in the event of the company's failure or for satisfying the company's obligations under a lease. In theory, anyone dealing with the company might seek guarantees from the directors in this way but these two examples are the main ones.

Fraudulent trading or wrongful trading (IA 1986, ss 213 and 214)

Directors may be ordered to make a contribution to the company's assets in the company's liquidation.

Penalties under the Companies Acts

Penalties under the Companies Acts are imposed, for example, for default in filing returns and documents with the registrar of companies or in maintaining the company's own records (CA 1985, Sch 24).

Breach of duty to the company

Directors may be liable to their company for damages and/or an account for profit if they are in breach of their fiduciary duties (see **13.10**).

Signature of certain documents

A person who signs a document (including cheques) on which the company's name is not correctly stated can be sued personally on that document.

However, these are exceptional circumstances and the general position is that directors are agents of the company and as such are not normally liable for their actions or for the company's debts.

26.2.2 Shareholders

The liability of a shareholder in a limited company is limited to paying the agreed price for his shares and usually this is paid in full at, or within a short time after, allotment by the company. The main, albeit unusual, example of possible personal liability for a shareholder is where he has been a party to fraudulent trading.

26.2.3 Partners and sole traders

Partners and sole traders are fully liable for all the debts of the business. A partner has a right of contribution from his fellow partners but if they are unable to contribute he is liable without limit.

26.3 RAISING FINANCE

26.3.1 Loans

A person lending to any business will usually seek security for repayment of the loan. Companies, partnerships and sole traders can all create fixed charges over their assets as security. However, only a company is able to create a floating charge. Although the floating charge is an inferior form of security compared with a fixed charge, nevertheless it affords the company the opportunity to use, for example, its stock-in-trade and future assets as security for its borrowing. Therefore, a company has greater scope than a partnership or a sole trader for raising loan finance.

26.3.2 Capital

A limited company which asks a person to introduce capital by becoming a shareholder has the benefit of being able to assure the investor of limited liability. A partnership which asks a person to introduce capital and become a partner is asking that person to accept unlimited liability for all the debts of the partnership incurred after he becomes a partner.

26.4 MANAGEMENT STRUCTURE

A company has a prescribed structure which facilitates the separation of management functions from capital investment in the company. Management functions are exercised, broadly, by the directors and relatively few (albeit major) functions are reserved to the shareholders in general meeting. It follows that shareholders have no authority (actual or apparent) to act in the management of the company's business.

A partnership is at liberty to organise itself in such a way that certain partners exercise management functions and the other partners are only consulted on major issues (as identified in their agreement). However, so far as an outsider is concerned, any partner may have apparent authority to act in management and may therefore bind the firm.

26.5 STATUS

There may be a feeling on the part of persons dealing with the business that a company is a more substantial business medium than a partnership or a sole trader. Such persons may therefore be more willing to deal with a company.

26.6 FORMALITY IN SETTING UP

A partnership can be set up without any formality (or expense) since it is simply a question of applying the definition of a partnership to a business relationship in order to discover whether or not a partnership exists. By contrast, the Companies Act 1985 imposes formalities on the formation of a company in that prescribed documents must be lodged with the registrar of companies.

This difference between companies and partnerships may have less substance than at first appears, because it will always be advisable for persons entering into partnership to have an agreement drawn up which provides comprehensive treatment of all present and future aspects of their relationship. Failure to do this may lead to problems sooner or later. It follows therefore that, in practice, there may well be a similar degree of formality involved in the formation of both a partnership and a company.

26.7 PUBLICITY OF INFORMATION

A company must make public a range of information about its affairs, its directors and its shareholders by filing returns and documents with the registrar of companies. This information includes information as to its year-end accounts, although many companies will qualify as 'small companies' which need only file an abbreviated balance sheet and need not file a profit and loss account.

A partnership is entitled to maintain privacy in all of its affairs, except that the identity of all partners and an address for service of documents must be revealed.

26.8 STATUTORY OBLIGATIONS AND CONTROL

Throughout its life, a company must comply with statutory obligations as to maintenance and filing of records and information. Examples include the completion of minutes of meetings and statutory registers, and the filing of an annual return and the year-end audited accounts. These obligations represent both an administrative inconvenience and some expense in professional fees. The Companies Act 1985 also imposes controls on certain activities; for example, a dividend can only be paid out of 'available profit' and the company can only purchase or redeem its own shares if detailed conditions and procedures are observed.

A partnership is not subject to any such controls and is free to organise its affairs as it pleases.

PART VIII

CONVERTING THE FORM OF AN EXPANDING BUSINESS

Part VII considered the question of choosing the form of business organisation by a general comparison of the tax and other considerations as they affect the organisation. These considerations can be applied to the specific context of an expanding business in identifying possible reasons for converting the form of organisation. A sole trader might take someone into partnership with him in order to attract capital from that person or to make that person more committed to the business by having a stake in it. A partnership or a sole trader might convert into a limited company in order to benefit from limited liability for the member(s), to benefit from the different tax treatment or to facilitate the raising of finance. A private limited company might convert into a public limited company in preparation for applying to The Stock Exchange for a full listing or to be quoted on the Alternative Investment Market.

Chapter 27

CONVERSION AND THE IMMEDIATE IMPLICATIONS

27.1 INTRODUCTION

This chapter considers the steps and documentation which would be required to effect the conversion from sole trader to partnership, from unincorporated business to limited company and from private limited company to public limited company; the tax implications that might ensue as a direct result of the transactions are also considered. For the individuals involved, the possible implications of being a partner rather than a sole trader or of being a director/shareholder rather than being a partner or sole trader may be appreciated from the topics covered earlier in this book.

Chapter 27 contents
Introduction
Converting from sole trader to partnership
Converting from unincorporated business to limited company
Converting from private to public limited company

27.2 CONVERTING FROM SOLE TRADER TO PARTNERSHIP

27.2.1 Formalities

In law, the creation of a partnership is simply a question of whether or not the statutory definition of partnership under PA 1890, s 1 is satisfied. It follows that there is no necessary formality to be observed in converting from sole trader to partnership. Nevertheless, certain questions should be considered.

To whom will the business assets belong?

It is inevitable that certain assets, particularly stock-in-trade and perhaps goodwill, will belong to the partners jointly. In relation to other assets, it will be necessary for the partners to reach agreement as to ownership of assets. Ownership of assets can simply be dealt with by means of a clause in the partnership agreement which declares which assets are partnership assets and which assets used by the partnership belong to a partner individually. In relation to premises, for example, this clause would operate as a declaration of trust, where legal title is to remain in the name of one partner alone but the beneficial ownership is to be shared by all the partners. The partners may prefer a formal transfer of title from the original owner to the partners jointly, in which case a conveyance or transfer of the title will be required.

Will there be a formal partnership agreement?

Partners should always have a formal partnership agreement prepared, not only to deal with the question of ownership of assets but also to deal with all other aspects of the relationship as described in Chapter 5.

Will the Business Names Act 1985 apply?

If the name of the business is to differ from those of the partners, it will be necessary to set out the names of the partners, together with an address for each partner for service of documents, on all business stationery and on the business premises.

27.2.2 Income tax implications

The incoming person will be assessed to income tax under the rules described in **3.3.1** and **3.3.2**.

27.2.3 Capital gains tax implications

Where the sole trader agrees to share ownership of the business assets with his new partner, he will be disposing of a share in those assets. If the assets are chargeable assets for capital gains tax purposes (such as premises, fixed plant and machinery, and goodwill), there will be a possible charge to capital gains tax on the disponer. Reliefs and exemptions that might be available include:

(1) retirement relief if the disponer is aged at least 50 and has owned the business for at least one year;
(2) hold-over relief if the disposal is by way of gift to the incoming partner;
(3) enhanced business taper relief; or
(4) the annual exemption.

27.2.4 Employees

Since the former sole trader continues as an employer, there are no necessary implications so far as the positions of employees are concerned.

27.3 CONVERTING FROM UNINCORPORATED BUSINESS TO LIMITED COMPANY

27.3.1 Formalities

Because the conversion from unincorporated business to limited company involves a sale of the business by the present owners (partners or sole trader) to a new owner (the company), there are many more formalities attached to this conversion than to that described in **27.2**.

(1) The present owners will need to form, or purchase off the shelf, a company of which, normally, they will be the sole directors and shareholders and to which they will sell the business. The consideration for the sale will normally consist exclusively of shares in the company but some of the consideration may be in the form of debentures (under which part of the agreed price is left outstanding as a loan to the company) or cash.
(2) Once the company is ready, it will buy the business from the present owners and it will be necessary for the company to observe the usual formalities on decision-making within the company, on filing returns with the registrar of companies and on maintaining the company's own records (see, generally, Chapters 12 and 13).
(3) The sale of the business will be effected under the terms of a contract (a sale agreement); typically this will:

   (a) describe the assets being sold to the company;
   (b) describe the price and the way in which it will be paid by the company, normally wholly in shares;

(c) apportion the price to show the value attributed to the various assets or groups of assets comprised in the business and being sold to the company;

(d) contain covenants on the part of the company designed to indemnify the sellers in respect of any liability for the existing debts, liabilities and obligations connected with the business;

(e) contain the company's acceptance of the seller's title to the premises, for example, to ensure that no claim could be brought by the company against the sellers for a defective title (this might otherwise have been a possibility should the company eventually change hands, eg in liquidation); and

(f) contain the company's acceptance of the equipment and stock in its current condition so that no claim can be brought by the company against the sellers on the basis of these items being defective or in poor condition.

The contract so far described is designed to ensure not only that ownership of the business and assets changes hands effectively, but also that the sellers (who will run the company but who will in future be protected by limited liability) obtain maximum protection from the company for any present or future liability. This differs significantly from a contract for the sale of a business to a person with whom the sellers are not connected. In such a situation (an arm's length sale), the buyer will be anxious to obtain maximum protection for its own position, including obtaining from the sellers warranties as to assets (eg that they are in a satisfactory state of repair and unencumbered state), employees (terms of their employment and the existence of any disputes), possible litigation (liabilities revealed to the buyer) and environmental matters (compliance with legislation on environmental matters).

In pursuance of the sale agreement, title to certain assets (notably the business premises) will, if appropriate, be transferred to the company by separate document, whilst the title to other assets may pass under the sale agreement (eg goodwill) or by physical delivery (eg stock).

If, as is common, the company takes over the previous name of the business and this is not the same as the company's name, it will be necessary for the company's stationery and a notice at the company's place of business to state the company's name and address (BNA 1985, s 4).

27.3.2 Income tax implications

(1) General

When the unincorporated business is sold to the company, this is a discontinuance of the business so far as the partnership (or sole trader) is concerned, so that the partners (or sole trader) will be assessed to income tax under the rules for the closing tax year of a business (see **3.3.4**) up to the date of the transfer of the business, and the company must pay corporation tax on profits thereafter.

(2) Capital allowances

Insofar as the partnership (or sole trader) sells to the company assets on which capital allowances have been claimed (eg machinery and plant), there may be a balancing charge to income tax on any profit identified by comparing the sale proceeds with the assets' value as written down by capital allowances from cost. Suppose, for example, that some machinery cost £16,000 when purchased 3½ years ago and capital allowances have been claimed totalling £9,250, so that the written down value is £6,750. If the value attributed to this machinery on the sale was

£8,000, there could be a balancing charge to income tax on the £1,250 'profit'. In other words, this 'profit' would be taxed as part of the Schedule D, Case I income in the closing tax year. Conversely, if there is a loss calculated on the same basis, there will be a deduction from profits for the final year for income tax purposes, known as a balancing allowance. If the company is controlled by the sellers of the business, the company and the sellers can elect within 2 years that the company shall take over the position of the sellers so that no balancing charge occurs (CAA 1990, s 77).

(3) Trading losses

If the unincorporated business has made trading losses which have not been relieved when the business is transferred to the company, these losses can be carried forward and deducted from income which the former partners (or sole trader) receive from the company, such as a salary as director or dividends as shareholder. This relief is available only if the business is transferred to the company wholly or mainly in return for the issue of shares in the company (see **3.4.5**).

(4) Interest on a qualifying loan – income tax relief for partners

Details of this relief are given at **9.2.4**. If a partnership is incorporated as a close company and the loan remains outstanding following incorporation, relief will continue to be given if the conditions for the relief that apply to close companies continue to be met (see **21.4.2**).

27.3.3 Capital gains tax implications

When the business is transferred to the company there will be a disposal to the company by the partners (or sole trader) of any of the assets of the business which do not remain in their personal ownership. Insofar as these assets are chargeable assets for capital gains tax purposes, there may be a charge to capital gains tax. Reliefs which may be available include:

(1) Roll-over relief on incorporation of a business (TCGA 1992, s 162)

The details of this relief were considered at **22.4.1**. The conditions for the relief to apply include the condition that the business must be sold to the company as a going concern with all of its assets (although cash may be ignored for this purpose). Transferring all the assets may present certain disadvantages including:

- possible stamp duty on the transfer of assets (see **27.3.4**);
- various other expenses incurred in transferring assets, such as professional fees;
- possible double charge to taxation in relation to future gains on those assets transferred (see **25.8**);
- availability of those assets transferred for payment of the company creditors.

Note: this relief is mandatory and, strictly, therefore, it will apply to the disposal of assets on incorporation of a business unless conditions are not satisfied, rather than being a matter of choice for the taxpayer(s). However, the partner or sole trader will be permitted to claim retirement relief, if eligible prior to rolling over any balance of the gain (see **22.4.1**).

(2) Other reliefs

The taxpayer may not wish to roll-over his gain on incorporation of the business. By retaining assets in his own name or receiving all or part of the consideration for the business in cash rather than shares, the relief can be disapplied in whole or part. This may be advantageous if the taxpayer wishes to use one or more of the following reliefs (if available – see **22.4.1**):

(a) EIS deferral relief;
(b) Enhanced business taper relief;
(c) The annual exemption.

27.3.4 Stamp duty implications

Stamp duty is chargeable on the purchase of assets, ownership of which passes to the company by document (eg contract or conveyance); these are dutiable assets. Where ownership of assets passes by delivery (eg stock-in-trade, machinery and plant which is not fixed to the premises), the assets are not dutiable.

It is necessary to ascertain the combined total value of all dutiable assets passing to the company. If that combined total does not exceed £60,000 and this fact is certified in the document(s), no stamp duty will be payable. If the value does exceed that figure, but is not more than £250,000, then stamp duty is chargeable on all these assets at 1 per cent of their value. If the value exceeds £250,000 but is not more than £500,000, stamp duty is chargeable on all assets at 3 per cent of their value. If their value exceeds £500,000, stamp duty is chargeable at 4 per cent of the value. Likely examples of dutiable assets are goodwill, book debts and the benefit of pending contracts (ownership passing under the sale agreement) and premises and fixed plant and machinery (ownership passing by conveyance or transfer). Any stamp duty payable is charged on the document by which ownership passes and is the responsibility of the purchaser. Transfers of certain 'intellectual property' rights (eg patents and copyright) are exempt from stamp duty.

27.3.5 VAT implications

If the company is not registered for VAT purposes before the sale to the company takes place, the sellers must charge VAT on the transaction; this is avoided by ensuring that the company is registered for VAT before the sale takes place.

27.3.6 Employees

As a result of the sale of the business, the owner of the business and therefore the employer will change. Under the Transfer of Undertakings (Protection of Employment) Regulations 1981, the new employer (the company) is taken to stand in the shoes of the old employer and the rights of the employees are automatically transferred. If no change is made affecting the employees, then there will be no immediate implications of the change of employer. The company should provide the employees with a formal notice under s 1 of the Employment Rights Act 1996 of the change in the identity of their employer.

27.4 CONVERTING FROM PRIVATE TO PUBLIC LIMITED COMPANY

27.4.1 Procedural requirements

The company must pass one special resolution to re-register as a public limited company which will cover altering its memorandum of association (so that it states that the company is to be public), the name (which must end with the words 'public limited company' or the abbreviation 'plc'), and possibly the capital clause to comply with the following requirements.

The company must satisfy the financial criteria applicable to public limited companies, including the requirement that the company's issued share capital must be at least £50,000 in nominal value and that each share must be paid up at least as to 25 per cent of its nominal value and the whole of any premium.

The company must submit to the registrar of companies (CA 1985, s 43):

(1) an application to be re-registered as a public company;
(2) the new memorandum and articles;
(3) a copy of the latest balance sheet;
(4) an unqualified auditor's report on the latest balance sheet;
(5) a further report from the auditors that the company's net assets are not less than its capital as shown in the balance sheet; and
(6) a statutory declaration from a director or the secretary that the company's net asset position as reflected in the report of the auditors is still maintained and that the requirements of the Companies Act 1985 as to re-registration have been complied with.

If satisfied, the registrar of companies will issue a certificate of incorporation stating that the company is a public limited company.

27.4.2 Implications

Since the company remains the same person, there are no implications for the company in terms of taxation or in terms of the employees. The real implications for the company lie in the realm of the company's ability to raise finance by inviting the public to purchase its shares and by applying to have its shares dealt in on The Stock Exchange.

For the shareholders in the company there may be implications as to the availability or otherwise of capital tax reliefs. For example, some inheritance tax reliefs (such as business property relief and the instalment option) operate less favourably for shareholdings in quoted companies than for shareholdings in unquoted companies and some capital gains tax reliefs (such as retirement relief) are dependent on the company being a 'personal trading company' which is less likely to be established in a company whose shares are quoted on The Stock Exchange.

PART IX

FORMS OF TRADING

Part IX considers the legal and practical aspects of establishing relationships with suppliers and customers, and of preparing suitable documentation for dealings with those persons.

Chapter 28 introduces some general principles which will help in the effective drafting of commercial contracts.

Chapter 29 takes as an example one type of commercial contract (the sale of goods contract) and outlines the statutory framework provided by the Sale of Goods Act 1979 (SGA 1979). A fuller discussion of this framework can be found in the Appendix.

Chapter 30 deals briefly with contracts for the supply of services.

Chapters 31–33 examine agency and distribution agreements and Chapter 34 considers the impact of competition law.

Chapter 28

DRAFTING COMMERCIAL AGREEMENTS – BASIC PRINCIPLES

28.1 INTRODUCTION

The basic principles of drafting are dealt with in the LPC Resource Book *Skills for Lawyers* (Jordans). This chapter looks at some of the particular problems posed by commercial contracts. There are two main problem areas:

(1) how to ensure that the terms form part of the contract;
(2) how to ensure that they give the rights and protection needed.

A further point is how far the terms of the contract may be controlled by statute (particularly by the Unfair Contract Terms Act 1977 (UCTA 1977)). Most of these points should already be familiar from the study of contract law.

28.2 WHAT ARE THE TERMS OF THE CONTRACT?

In commercial situations, there will usually be no doubt that a contract actually exists. The key elements of offer and acceptance (or agreement), consideration and contractual intention will be clearly established. Sometimes, it may be more difficult to establish what the terms of that contract are; in other words, what promises form part of the offer and acceptance. This is a particular problem where there have been protracted pre-contractual negotiations during which both parties have said many things.

28.2.1 Guidelines for determining the parties' intentions

As usual in contract, the parties' intentions are paramount. If these intentions are not obvious, the court considers various factors in trying to establish what they are, for example, the time lapse between the statement and the contract (*Routledge v McKay* [1954] 1 All ER 855), the relative expertise and knowledge of the supplier and the customer (*Dick Bentley Productions Ltd v Harold Smith (Motors) Ltd* [1965] 2 All ER 65: cf *Oscar Chess Ltd v Williams* [1957] 1 All ER 325), and the obvious importance placed on the statement by the customer (*Bannerman v White* (1861) 10 CBNS 844).

28.2.2 Written contracts

Generally, it is much easier to decide on the parties' intentions when they have put their agreement in writing. The court assumes that the document is intended to be a complete and exhaustive record of the terms and a party who signs a written contract will generally be bound by any term in that contract even if he has not read it (*L'Estrange v Graucob* [1934] 2 KB 394) unless the other side has been guilty of

---

Chapter 28 contents
Introduction
What are the terms of the contract?
Are the terms clear?
Statutory control of contract terms under UCTA 1977
Statutory control of contract terms under the Unfair Terms in Consumer Contracts Regulations 1999
An exemption clause checklist
Two examples of exemption clauses

fraud or misrepresentation in relation to the existence or scope of the term. This rule is particularly significant in relation to exemption clauses (see **28.2.3**).

By the same token, the court will not usually allow outside evidence to add to, vary or contradict the written document (the 'parol evidence rule'). As always, however, this is subject to the parties' contrary intentions and the court, applying the guidelines in **28.2.1**, may decide that the parties intended the contract to be partly oral and partly written or that an oral promise forms the basis of a collateral contract standing outside the main contract.

28.2.3 Some problems with written standard terms

Often a contracting party (eg a seller) will draw up a document setting out the standard terms on which he is prepared to do business. If the buyer signs a written contract containing those terms, the buyer will normally be bound by them (see **28.2.2**). But what if the terms are in an unsigned document (eg on the back of an invoice or in a notice up on the wall of the seller's office)? Will those terms form part of any resulting contract?

The seller must show that the buyer had reasonable notice of the terms and that he accepted them without qualification.

(1) Did the buyer have reasonable notice of the terms?

If the buyer had actual knowledge of the term before the contract was entered into, he is clearly bound by it. If not, he will still be bound by it if he ought to have known of it. The court will consider various factors.

(a) Was the document containing the term one which a reasonable person would consider as likely to contain contractual terms? A ticket may well satisfy this condition, but a receipt may not. A document which might not normally qualify may do so if there is a clear statement on the face of it that there are conditions on the back.

Where the document is 'contractual,' the buyer will normally be bound by any 'usual' terms in that type of contract. This will also be the result if the buyer knows there are terms in the document but not what they are (*Thornton v Shoe Lane Parking* [1971] 2 QB 163; *Interfoto Picture Library v Stiletto Visual Programmes* [1988] 1 All ER 348).

(b) How prominent was the term? If the clause is at all unusual or onerous, then greater steps may have to be taken to bring it to the buyer's attention.

(c) Was the buyer given a reasonable opportunity to see the term before the contract was entered into? If the term is contained in an invoice which arrives when goods are delivered, this will normally be too late, unless the seller can show a sufficient regular and consistent course of dealings between himself and the buyer.

Although the above rules apply to all contractual terms, they are particularly important in relation to exemption clauses (see below).

(2) Has the buyer accepted the seller's terms without qualification?

Even if the buyer has had reasonable notice of the seller's terms, he won't be bound by them if he attempts to insert contradictory terms of his own, as he will then be making a counter-offer rather than accepting the seller's terms. This becomes a particular problem where the buyer has standard written terms of his own. (This presupposes that the buyer has sufficient bargaining power to impose his own terms.)

Example

(A) THE 'BATTLE OF THE FORMS'

A manufacturer offers to sell some of his products to a wholesaler at a particular price but makes it clear that the deal is to be on his (the manufacturer's) written standard terms. The wholesaler 'accepts' the offer but specifies that his (the wholesaler's) written standard terms are to apply. The manufacturer acknowledges the order but again emphasises that his own conditions are to apply. This is the so-called 'battle of the forms' which was illustrated in the case of *Butler Machine Tool v Ex-cell-o* [1979] 1 All ER 965.

(B) ANALYSIS

In the above example, there is as yet no contract. Assuming the manufacturer's first communication was a genuine offer, the wholesaler's reply was not an acceptance but merely a counter-offer, since it introduced different terms. The manufacturer's acknowledgment was not an acceptance as the acknowledgment was on different terms.

(C) WHO WINS?

There is no easy answer to this problem. The situation is often resolved by one party making a mistake. In the *Butler* case, the seller made the error of acknowledging the buyer's order without specifying that it was subject to his own terms and thereby ended up being bound by the buyer's terms. In other cases, no contract at all will come into existence under the normal analysis of offer and acceptance and any claims which the parties may have will be in quasi-contract.

28.3 ARE THE TERMS CLEAR?

To take full advantage of a contractual term, the person seeking to rely on it must show that it is clear and unambiguous.

28.3.1 Rules of interpretation

In interpreting contracts, the courts will adopt the normal rules of interpretation, for example words are to be understood in their ordinary and literal meaning. If the term in question is an exemption clause, however, the rules are stricter. This means that clarity of drafting is even more important than usual.

28.3.2 Exemption clauses and the 'contra proferentem' rule

If there are two interpretations of a term, one which protects the party in breach and one which does not, the court will construe the clause strictly against the person trying to rely on it (who is sometimes referred to as the 'proferens'). This is often known as the 'contra proferentem' rule.

28.3.3 Clear words needed to exclude liability for negligence

In addition to the contra proferentem rule, case-law has established that very clear words are needed to exclude negligence. On the other hand, it is not necessary to use the word 'negligence' in the clause as long as the other side should reasonably interpret the words to cover negligence. In *Gillespie Brothers v Roy Bowles Transport* [1973] QB 400, the defendant agreed to 'keep the carrier indemnified against all claims and demands whatsoever ...'. This wording was held to be sufficiently clear to cover negligence.

The courts are likely to be stricter in a consumer contract and have even gone so far as to suggest that a clause could not cover negligence even though negligence was the only liability which could arise. In *Hollier v Rambler Motors* [1972] 2 QB 71, one of the judges suggested an 'intelligent layman' test should be applied, ie would the intelligent layman have assumed that the wording in question would cover a negligent breach of contract by the other side?

28.3.4 Limitation clauses

Some clauses do not exclude liability altogether, but merely limit it to a certain figure. In a supply contract, this will usually be an attempt to avoid liability for anything but the repair or replacement of the goods or services provided, or the return of any money paid. For instance, the supplier will normally wish to avoid liability for loss of profits arising from the breach.

(1) Example

A seller agrees to sell some machinery to a buyer for £5,000 and to deliver it to the buyer's factory on a certain date, knowing that the buyer intends to use the machinery to expand his business. The seller fails to deliver the goods and as a result the buyer has to buy the machinery from another supplier for £6,000. It takes several days for the buyer to obtain the alternative machinery and in the meantime he loses £2,000 worth of profits. The buyer decides to claim damages for the seller's breach.

(2) A reminder of the basic contractual principles relating to damages

The aim of contractual damages is purely compensatory, to put the innocent party in the same position he would have been in had the contract been properly performed. This is a forward-looking test rather than the backward-looking test in tort (where the court tries to put the innocent party back into the position they would have been in had the tort never been committed). This is why contract damages may compensate the plaintiff for loss of bargain and tort damages will not. As a result, the buyer would normally be able to claim the extra cost of buying substitute machinery and loss of profits. This is subject to various limitations, ie the breach must have caused the loss being claimed, the loss must not be too remote and the buyer must have taken reasonable steps to mitigate his loss.

(3) The principles applied to the example

In the above example, there is no problem with causation. As to remoteness, the extra cost of buying a replacement machine will presumably fall within limb one of the test in *Hadley v Baxendale* (1854) 9 Exch 341, being loss which arises naturally (ie according to the usual course of things) from the breach. The buyer should get damages for this as long as the seller cannot show that the buyer failed to mitigate by paying over the odds for the replacement.

In addition to actual knowledge, the seller is deemed to have 'imputed knowledge', ie the knowledge which any reasonable person in his position would have had (*Victoria Laundry (Windsor) Ltd v Newman Industries Ltd* [1949] 2 KB 528). Armed with this knowledge at the contract date, the seller should have contemplated that the loss of £2,000 worth of profit was a 'serious possibility' (see *The Heron II* [1969] 1 AC 350), unless it derived from the loss of a particularly lucrative contract in which case the seller would need special knowledge at the contract date to be liable (see the *Newman* case).

It seems clear from the case-law that 'unusual' loss of profits (eg from the loss of a particularly lucrative contract) will fall within the second limb of *Hadley v Baxendale*, being such loss as may be reasonably supposed to have been within the contemplation of the parties at the contract date as a probable result of the breach. It is less clear which of the two limbs is relevant for 'usual' loss (ie loss which is within a contractor's imputed knowledge). There is some evidence for suggesting that it was also originally intended to fall within limb 2 (see, eg, s 51 of the Sale of Goods Act 1979) but later cases have tended to place it within limb 1 (see, eg, *The Heron*, mentioned above, and the *British Sugar* case, below).

(4) Use of a limitation clause

If the seller does not want to be liable to pay these damages, one option would be to include a clause in the contract limiting his liability to the price of the machine. The courts have been prepared to show more lenience in the construction of limitation clauses, on the basis that a party is much more likely to have accepted a limitation of liability than a complete exclusion.

Presumably, this approach would only be taken if the limitation sum was reasonably substantial. There seems little distinction between a clause limiting damages recoverable to £1 and a clause excluding liability altogether.

(5) Excluding 'consequential loss'

Sometimes, draftsmen seek to exclude liability for loss of profits by providing that the supplier is not to be liable for 'consequential loss'. Unfortunately, the Court of Appeal decision in *British Sugar plc v NEI Power Projects Ltd,* (1997) unreported, 8 October, has rendered this a risky enterprise. Whilst accepting that 'consequential loss' could be used in different and varying senses so that 'it may be difficult to be sure in some contexts precisely what it does mean', Waller LJ went on to hold that a rather oddly drafted clause stating that 'the Seller's liability for consequential loss is limited to the value of the contract' did *not* cover loss of profits. Instead, the court affirmed the trial judge's interpretation that 'consequential loss' in this case only covered loss which required special knowledge under the second limb of *Hadley v Baxendale*.

The Court of Appeal relied on a slender thread of authority (arguably based on a misapplication of an earlier case called *Millar's Machinery v David Way* (1935) Com Cas 204 and a misunderstanding of s 51 of the Sale of Goods Act 1979) but obviously the expression 'consequential loss' needs to be handled with great care. Where it is used in a contract, it seems prudent to put in a non-exhaustive list of illustrations to make it clear that the phrase includes loss of profits. Alternatively, use a straightforward limitation clause and leave the expression out altogether.

28.4 STATUTORY CONTROL OF CONTRACT TERMS UNDER UCTA 1977

28.4.1 Clauses affected

UCTA 1977 covers a wide variety of different clauses. All the relevant sections of UCTA 1977 talk about attempts to 'exclude or restrict' liability so the Act clearly covers limitation clauses as well as strict exclusion clauses. Section 13 of UCTA 1977 provides that exclusion or restriction of liability also encompasses other less direct attempts to cut down liability. For example, a clause which makes enforcement of the liability subject to restrictive or onerous conditions (eg by insisting on strict time-limits for bringing a claim) will be covered by UCTA 1977 as will a clause which excludes or restricts any right or remedy in respect of the liability.

For example, where the seller of goods breaks a strict condition of the contract, this gives the buyer the right to reject the goods and terminate the agreement. A clause seeking to prevent a buyer returning defective goods and ending the contract for breach of the implied condition of satisfactory quality (see **29.4.6**) will be covered by UCTA 1977. Where a supplier of services breaks his implied duty to provide those services with reasonable skill and care, the customer has the right to terminate if the breach is serious enough (if it 'goes to the root of the contract' or deprives him of substantially the whole benefit of the contract). UCTA 1977 will control a clause which attempts to exclude or restrict his right to do this.

UCTA 1977 goes so far as to control attempts to exclude or restrict rules of evidence or procedure. In addition, the most important sections also prevent the exclusion or restriction of liability by reference to terms and notices excluding or restricting the relevant obligation or duty.

In the discussion which follows, any reference to an attempt to exclude liability includes an attempt to restrict or limit liability unless otherwise specified.

28.4.2 Some basic definitions

Where UCTA 1977 applies to a clause, it will either render it void or subject it to the so-called 'reasonableness test'. Although there are some clauses which will be void in all circumstances (eg attempts to exclude liability for personal injury or death caused by the contractor's negligence or to exclude liability for breaking the implied conditions relating to title in goods contracts), others will be void only if they attempt to exclude liability as against someone who 'deals as consumer' (see Flow charts 2 and 3 at **28.6.3**). The concept of dealing 'as consumer' is also important in other ways. For example, s 3 applies only where one party deals as consumer or on the other's written standard terms. However, the expression 'standard terms' should not be construed too narrowly, eg *South West Water v ICL* (1999) unreported, where even a negotiated contract was held to be on standard terms and therefore UCTA 1977, s 3 was held to apply.

(1) Dealing 'as consumer'

Section 12 states that a party 'deals as consumer' if:

'(a) he neither makes the contract in the course of a business nor holds himself as doing so; and

(b) the other party does make the contract in the course of a business; and

(c) in the case of a contract governed by the law of sale of goods or hire-purchase, or by section 7 of this Act, the goods passing under or in pursuance of the contract are of a type ordinarily supplied for private use or consumption.'

(2) The reasonableness test

(A) THE BASIC TEST AND BURDEN OF PROOF

Section 11(1) of UCTA 1977 states that:

'In relation to a contract term, the requirement of reasonableness ... is that the term shall have been a fair and reasonable one to be included having regard to the circumstances which were, or ought reasonably to have been, known to or in the contemplation of the parties when the contract was made.'

Notice that the test is a 'reasonableness of incorporation' test, not a 'reasonableness of reliance' test. The court is supposed to consider whether, taking into account the parties' knowledge (actual and constructive) at the contract date, it was reasonable to include the clause in the contract at that time, not to look at whether it was reasonable for the guilty party to rely on the clause in the light of the events which actually happened (note the significance of this point in *Thomas Witter Ltd v TBP Industries Ltd* [1996] 2 All ER 573).

It is always up to the person seeking to rely on an exemption clause to show that it satisfies the reasonableness test in UCTA 1977. Indeed, a defendant who raises an exemption clause as a defence will be taken to have raised the question of reasonableness without the plaintiff having to plead it specifically (*Sheffield v Pickfords Ltd* (1997) 16 Tr LR 337).

(B) THE SCHEDULE 2 GUIDELINES

Section 11(2) refers to Sch 2 to UCTA 1977 which sets out various 'guidelines' for applying the reasonableness test. Strictly speaking, the guidelines apply only to cases within ss 6 and 7 (attempts to exclude implied terms in goods contracts; see **28.4.3**) but the courts will apply them by analogy whenever a clause must satisfy the reasonableness test. The list in Sch 2 is not exhaustive and the court may take into account any relevant factor in deciding whether the clause is reasonable.

The first two guidelines seem to be aimed at ensuring that a party agrees to the terms freely and voluntarily. The court must consider:

(i) the relative bargaining strengths of the parties (taking into account other ways in which the customer's requirements could have been met);

(ii) whether the customer received any inducement to agree to the term (eg by being offered a 'two-tier' contract whereby he could have paid more for greater protection) and also what opportunity he had of entering into a similar contract with somebody else without having to accept this type of term.

The next two guidelines seem to be aimed at ensuring that the party enters the agreement with his eyes open. Here, the relevant considerations are:

(iii) whether the customer knew or should have known that the term existed and what it covered. (This obviously overlaps to a certain extent with the incorporation point above but does allow the court to invalidate a clause in a signed contract where that clause is in 'regrettably small print'. It also allows the court to strike out a clause because of the obscurity of its drafting);

(iv) if the term excludes or restricts liability on the non-occurrence of some condition, whether it was reasonable at the contract date to expect that it would be practicable to comply with the condition.

The final guideline is a bit different. This covers the situation where the goods were manufactured, processed or adapted to the customer's special order. If the customer lays down the specification for the goods, it is usually going to be reasonable for the supplier to exclude liability for the fact that the resulting product does not work or is not reasonably fit for the customer's purpose.

28.4.3 The main provisions

(1) Goods contracts – attempts to exclude statutory implied terms

As will be seen (**29.4.2**, **29.4.5** and **29.4.6**), SGA 1979 implies various provisions into sale of goods contracts and similar provisions are implied into other types of goods contracts by the Supply of Goods (Implied Terms) Act 1973 (SOGITA 1973) and the Supply of Goods and Services Act 1982 (SGSA 1982). Attempts to exclude these implied terms are governed by ss 6 and 7 of UCTA 1977.

The implied terms relating to title (**29.4.2**) cannot be excluded in any contract. The implied terms relating to description, satisfactory quality, reasonable fitness for the buyer's purpose and sample cannot be excluded against a party who 'deals as consumer'. In non-consumer cases, the clause will only be valid insofar as it is reasonable.

(2) Services contracts – attempts to exclude the duty to exercise reasonable care and skill

Section 1 of UCTA 1977 makes it clear that this is an attempt to exclude liability for negligence. There is no distinction between consumer and non-consumer contracts here. In both cases, the clause will be ineffective to exclude liability for personal injury or death caused by negligence (s 2(1)). Other negligently caused loss can only be excluded insofar as the clause in question is reasonable (s 2(2)).

(3) Attempts to exclude other terms

Section 3 of UCTA 1977, which mainly covers attempts to exclude express terms, applies in two situations:

(1) where the party in default is trying to exclude his liability as against someone who 'deals as consumer'; and
(2) where the party in default has imposed its own written standard terms of business on the other.

As a result, s 3 is by no means limited to consumer contracts. A clause to which the section applies will be valid only insofar as it is reasonable.

Section 3 not only applies to straightforward exclusion or restriction of liability for breach. It also covers any claim by a party to be entitled:

  (i)   to render a contractual performance substantially different from that which was reasonably expected of him; or
  (ii) in respect of the whole part or any part of his contractual obligation, to render no performance at all' (s 3(2)(b)).

28.5 STATUTORY CONTROL OF CONTRACT TERMS UNDER THE UNFAIR TERMS IN CONSUMER CONTRACTS REGULATIONS 1999

Since this book deals mainly with commercial contracts, we will make only passing reference to the Unfair Terms in Consumer Contracts Regulations 1999, SI 1999/2083 (previously UTCCR 1994, SI 1994/3159). These Regulations apply to any term in a contract concluded between a seller or supplier and a consumer where the term has not been individually negotiated (other than certain 'core terms' phrased in plain, intelligible language). Schedule 1 excludes some contracts from the scope of the Regulations (eg employment contracts).

Regulation 8 provides that a consumer will not be bound by any term which is an 'unfair term' (a term which 'contrary to the requirement of good faith causes significant imbalance in the parties' rights and obligations under the contract to the detriment of the consumer – reg 5). Schedule 2 contains a non-exhaustive illustrative list of terms which may be regarded as unfair (eg terms excluding or limiting the supplier's liability for a consumer's death or personal injury caused by the supplier's act or omission).

Since a consumer is defined as 'a natural person who, in making a contract to which these Regulations apply, is acting for purposes which are outside his business', a company cannot get the benefit of the Regulations and a commercial agreement will almost by definition fall outside their ambit. In the following discussion, we will assume that the agreement is a commercial one and that the Regulations do not apply.

28.6 AN EXEMPTION CLAUSE CHECKLIST

A party who wishes to claim the protection of an exemption clause must prove three things:

(1) that the clause forms part of the contract (incorporation) (see Flow chart 1);
(2) that the clause is clear enough to cover the breach (construction); and
(3) that the clause is not invalidated by UCTA 1977 (see Flow chart 2).

In the following flow charts, assume that party D is in breach of contract and is trying to rely on an exclusion clause in the contract to defend a claim by party P.

28.6.1 Incorporation

The relevant factors may be illustrated by a flow chart:

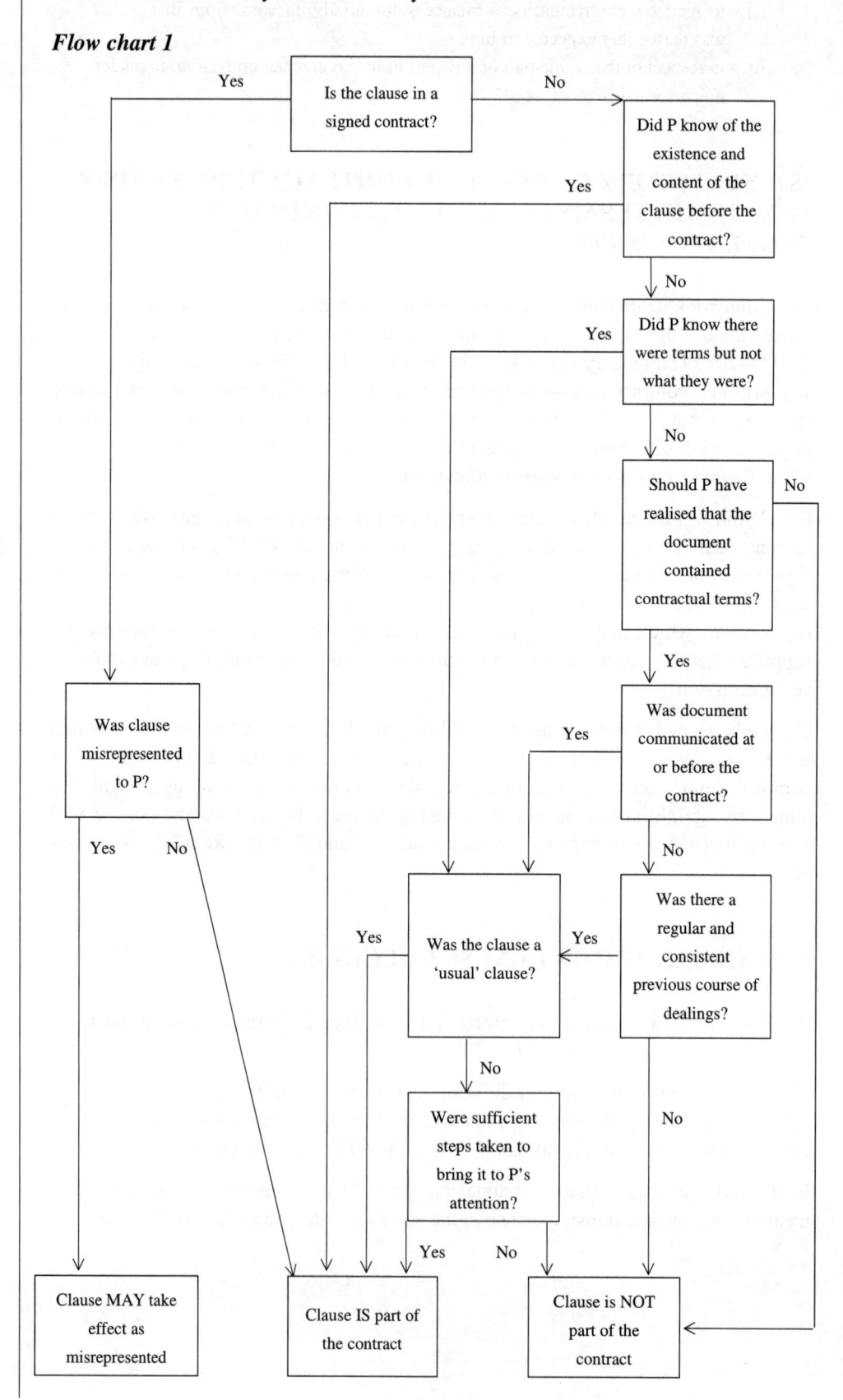

Flow chart 1

```
                               ┌──────────────────┐
                    Yes        │ Is the clause in │        No
         ┌─────────────────────│   a signed       │────────────────┐
         │                     │   contract?      │                │
         │                     └──────────────────┘                ▼
         │                                              ┌────────────────────┐
         │                                         Yes  │ Did P know of the  │
         │                            ┌─────────────────│ existence and      │
         │                            │                 │ content of the     │
         │                            │                 │ clause before the  │
         │                            │                 │ contract?          │
         │                            │                 └────────────────────┘
         │                            │                           │ No
         │                            │                           ▼
         │                            │                 ┌────────────────────┐
         │                            │            Yes  │ Did P know there   │
         │                            │    ┌────────────│ were terms but not │
         │                            │    │            │ what they were?    │
         │                            │    │            └────────────────────┘
         │                            │    │                      │ No
         │                            │    │                      ▼
         │                            │    │            ┌────────────────────┐
         │                            │    │            │ Should P have      │    No
         │                            │    │            │ realised that the  │──────┐
         │                            │    │            │ document contained │      │
         │                            │    │            │ contractual terms? │      │
         │                            │    │            └────────────────────┘      │
         │                            │    │                      │ Yes             │
         │                            │    │                      ▼                 │
         │                            │    │            ┌────────────────────┐      │
         │                            │    │       Yes  │ Was document       │      │
         │                            │    │  ┌─────────│ communicated at    │      │
         │                            │    │  │         │ or before the      │      │
         │                            │    │  │         │ contract?          │      │
         │                            │    │  │         └────────────────────┘      │
         │                            │    │  │                   │ No              │
         ▼                            │    │  │                   ▼                 │
┌────────────────┐                    │    │  │         ┌────────────────────┐      │
│ Was clause     │                    │    │  │         │ Was there a        │      │
│ misrepresented │                    │    │  │         │ regular and        │      │
│ to P?          │                    │    │  │         │ consistent         │      │
└────────────────┘                    │    │  │         │ previous course of │      │
   Yes     No                         │    │  │         │ dealings?          │      │
    │       \                         │    │  │         └────────────────────┘      │
    │        \                        │    ▼  ▼                    │                │
    │         \               Yes  ┌────────────────┐  Yes         │                │
    │          \              ┌────│ Was the clause │◄─────────────┤                │
    │           \             │    │ a 'usual'      │              │                │
    │            \            │    │ clause?        │              │                │
    │             \           │    └────────────────┘              │                │
    │              \          │            │ No                    │                │
    │               \         │            ▼                       │                │
    │                \        │   ┌────────────────┐               │                │
    │                 \       │   │ Were sufficient│               │ No             │
    │                  \      │   │ steps taken to │               │                │
    │                   \     │   │ bring it to P's│               │                │
    │                    \    │   │ attention?     │               │                │
    │                     \   │   └────────────────┘               │                │
    │                      \  │     Yes      No                    │                │
    ▼                       ▼ ▼      ▼        ▼                    ▼                ▼
┌────────────┐         ┌─────────────────┐              ┌────────────────┐
│ Clause MAY │         │ Clause IS part  │              │ Clause is NOT  │◄────────
│ take effect│         │ of the contract │              │ part of the    │
│ as misrep- │         │                 │              │ contract       │
│ resented   │         │                 │              │                │
└────────────┘         └─────────────────┘              └────────────────┘
```

28.6.2 Construction

D must show that the clause unambiguously covers the situation which has arisen for the courts to construe exclusion clauses strictly against those who wish to rely on them (the 'contra proferentem' rule).

If D is seeking to exclude negligence, particularly clear words must have been used. The word 'negligence' need not appear but P must reasonably have understood the words to have that effect. This is more of a problem in consumer contracts.

28.6.3 UCTA 1977

Again, flow charts may be useful:

Flow chart 2
Sale of Goods

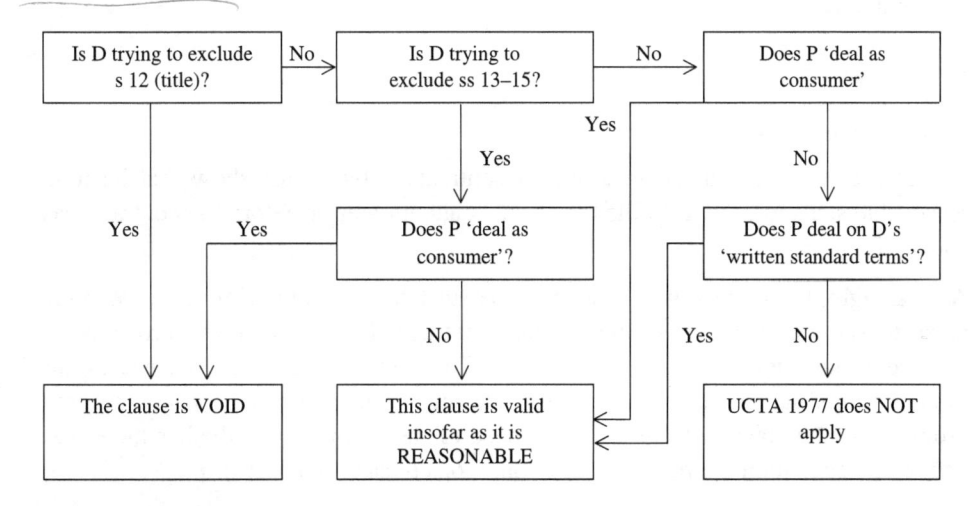

```
[Is D trying to exclude s 12 (title)?] --No--> [Is D trying to exclude ss 13–15?] --No--> [Does P 'deal as consumer']
         |                                              |                                        |
        Yes                                            Yes                                      No
         |                                              v                                        v
         |          Yes         [Does P 'deal as consumer'?]                         [Does P deal on D's 'written standard terms'?]
         v                              |                                                       |
  [The clause is VOID]                 No                                            Yes                No
                                        v                                             v                  v
                            [This clause is valid insofar as it is REASONABLE]   [UCTA 1977 does NOT apply]
```

Flow chart 3
Supply of Services

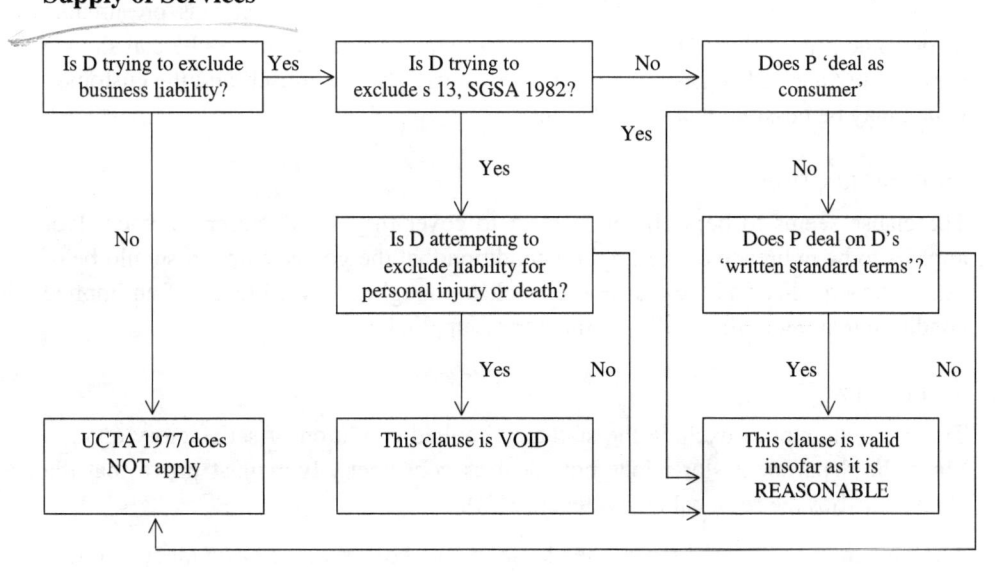

```
[Is D trying to exclude business liability?] --Yes--> [Is D trying to exclude s 13, SGSA 1982?] --No--> [Does P 'deal as consumer']
         |                                                          |                                            |
        No                                                         Yes                                          No
         |                                                          v                                            v
         |                                    [Is D attempting to exclude liability for                [Does P deal on D's 'written standard terms'?]
         |                                             personal injury or death?]                                 |
         v                                                  |          |                                    Yes        No
  [UCTA 1977 does NOT apply]                               Yes        No                                     v          v
                                                           v                                    [This clause is valid insofar as it is REASONABLE]
                                                  [This clause is VOID]
```

28.7 TWO EXAMPLES OF EXEMPTION CLAUSES

28.7.1 Example 1

(1) The facts

Ivor Lathe, a sole trader involved in the manufacture of furniture, is looking for outlets for his products. He does some market research and targets various department stores. He contacts one such store, offers his range of furniture to them which the store accepts.

Ivor delivers a three-piece suite to the store but the suite proves defective and collapses when a customer sits on it. The department store angrily demands compensation from Lathe, who wishes to rely upon a clause appearing on the back of the invoice which was delivered with the furniture. The clause reads:

> **The manufacturer is not liable for breach of any condition, warranty or other term relating to the quality of the goods supplied, whether express or implied.**

(2) Analysis

(A) INCORPORATION

The clause is not contained in a signed contract so Ivor must show that he took reasonable steps to draw it to the other side's attention at or before the contract was entered into.

At first sight, the invoice would seem to be sufficient. Commercial parties may be taken to know that invoices often contain contractual terms so would probably be deemed to have notice of any 'usual terms'. The clause in question does not appear to be that unusual in a commercial contract, but it would be worth examining how prominently the clause appeared on the back of the invoice and whether there was any reference to it on the front (eg 'For conditions of sale, see back').

A more difficult problem for Ivor is timing. Reasonable steps must normally be taken to draw the clause to the other side's attention before the contract is made. In this case, the invoice arrived with the furniture and the contract was presumably made some time earlier. This may be fatal to Lathe's argument unless he can show a previous regular and consistent course of dealings between himself and the customer, which may be possible in a case like this.

(B) CONSTRUCTION

The clause seems to be sufficiently clear to cover the manufacturer's breach. Ivor appears to be in breach of the implied condition that the goods supplied should be of satisfactory quality and the clause seems clear enough to cover breach of an implied condition relating to the quality of the goods supplied.

(C) UCTA 1977

This is an attempt to exclude the statutory implied condition of satisfactory quality. Since the department store does not 'deal as consumer', Ivor must prove that the clause satisfies the reasonableness test (s 6(3)).

Applying the Sch 2 guidelines to the clause, it may be that Lathe has a much stronger bargaining position than the department store and that the store can only obtain this particular range of furniture from him. These factors would point away from reasonableness. As the department store is denying all knowledge of the term, there can hardly have been any inducement offered to them to accept it. The clause was contained in an unsigned document so the court must already have come to the conclusion that a reasonable person in the department store's position should have known of the existence of the term. However, if the term is very obscurely drafted, it is open to the court to decide that the department store should not necessarily have grasped the extent of the term. If that is so, the court may decide that Ivor Lathe has not proved that the clause is reasonable.

28.7.2 Example 2

(1) Facts

Drafto Ltd, a company involved in the business of installing air-conditioning in office premises, agrees to install air-conditioning in a customer's office block. Unfortunately, the work is done so badly that the air-conditioning breaks down on the hottest day of the year. Working conditions become impossible and the customer has to vacate the office premises, thereby losing a great deal of money.

Drafto is trying to rely upon a clause in the written contract (signed by the customer) which reads as follows:

> **Should the Customer suffer any loss or damage whatsoever to its premises or its business, Drafto's liability is limited to the sum of £1,000, howsoever such loss or damage may have been caused.**

(2) Analysis

(A) INCORPORATION

Can Drafto prove that the clause is part of the contract? The clause is contained in a signed contract so (in the absence of fraud or misrepresentation) Drafto should have no problems in proving that the clause in question is incorporated.

(B) CONSTRUCTION

Drafto has an implied duty to provide its services with reasonable care and skill (see **30.2.1**). Its failure to do this is effectively a negligent breach of contract and remember that particularly clear words are needed to exclude liability for negligence. However, following the reasoning in the *Gillespie Brothers* case (**28.3.3**), the words 'any loss or damage whatsoever' and 'howsoever such loss or damage may have been caused' may be considered clear enough to cover Drafto's negligence. This result is all the more likely as the agreement is between two commercial parties.

In addition, Drafto's clause is not an exclusion clause but a limitation clause. It does not exclude liability altogether, but merely limits it to £1,000. As mentioned above (**28.3.4**), the courts have been prepared to show more lenience in the construction of limitation clauses.

(C) UCTA 1977

Since Drafto is attempting to limit its liability for failure to exercise reasonable care and skill, this will be treated as an attempt to exclude 'negligence' (UCTA 1977, s 1). The breach has caused financial loss. There is no question of death or personal injury being involved (s 2(1)). Therefore, Drafto must prove that the clause satisfies the reasonableness test (s 2(2)).

Although the Sch 2 guidelines do not apply specifically to attempts to exclude negligence under s 2(2), the courts have on many occasions taken the obvious step of deciding to apply them by analogy. So again, it will be a question of deciding the relative bargaining strengths of the parties, whether the customer had been offered an inducement to accept the clause etc. In particular, if the clause in the written contract was in very small print, the court might decide that it was not reasonable to include it in the contract.

Chapter 29

INTRODUCTION TO SALE OF GOODS

29.1 INTRODUCTION

Chapter 29 concentrates on one particular type of commercial contract (perhaps the most simple and common) – the sale of goods contract. This chapter asks what a sale of goods contract actually is and why Parliament has deemed it necessary to provide a statutory framework in the Sale of Goods Act 1979 (SGA 1979).

The chapter goes on to examine in outline the main points to be considered in drafting a sale of goods contract. A much fuller account of the SGA 1979 framework and its impact on drafting can be found in **Appendix 1**.

Chapter 29 contents
Introduction
What is a sale of goods contract?
The statutory framework
Drafting sale of goods contracts – an outline

29.2 WHAT IS A SALE OF GOODS CONTRACT?

The whole idea behind a sale of goods contract (as explained by s 2(1) of SGA 1979) is that it is 'a contract by which the seller transfers or agrees to transfer the property in goods to the buyer for a money consideration, called the price'.

The contract of sale may take place some time before ownership is actually transferred. SGA 1979 calls this 'an agreement to sell' (s 2(5)), as opposed to an agreement where ownership passes at once, which is called 'a sale' (s 2(4)). SGA 1979 contains complex and wide-ranging provisions to govern both sales and agreements to sell. Some of these provisions will be outlined in this chapter.

29.3 THE STATUTORY FRAMEWORK

29.3.1 Why do we need a statutory framework?

Sale of goods contracts are very common. People are selling and buying goods all the time and often with the minimum of formality. The parties will rarely think through all the repercussions of what they are doing. SGA 1979 therefore lays down a whole series of statutory presumptions about transfer of ownership, payment of the price, delivery and so on which will cover the situation in the absence of express agreement between the parties.

29.3.2 The SGA 1979 provisions usually take effect subject to the parties' intentions

If the seller and buyer have considered a particular area and come to specific agreement (eg as to time and place of delivery), this agreement will oust the provisions of SGA 1979. Section 55(1) specifically allows the rights, duties and liabilities arising under the Act to be negatived or varied by express agreement. In addition, the provisions may be affected by any previous course of dealings between the parties or any trade usage which binds them both.

However, the power of the parties to exclude some of the SGA 1979 provisions is controlled by UCTA 1977 (see **28.4.3**).

29.4 DRAFTING SALE OF GOODS CONTRACTS – AN OUTLINE

29.4.1 Introduction

There follows a brief summary of the main points to consider in drafting a sale of goods contract. For a fuller discussion of the principles involved, turn to **Appendix 1**.

Although SGA 1979 will imply terms to cover most eventualities in a sale of goods contract, it is usually a good idea to make express provision for important areas, since this creates certainty and also allows a party to tailor the agreement for his or her own protection.

In the following outline, we will generally assume that we are advising the seller of the goods.

29.4.2 Transfer of ownership

(1) When should ownership pass?

The parties will want to decide when the ownership of the goods will pass. Will ownership pass when the goods leave the warehouse, or when they arrive at the buyer's premises, or at some later date? This decision will be very much bound up with the question of whether the seller delivers the goods or the buyer collects them (see **29.4.4**).

Most goods which are the subject matter of commercial contracts are 'unascertained' rather than 'specific', ie they are not 'goods identified and agreed on at the time a contract of sale is made' (SGA 1979, s 61(1)). They are often generic goods, for example '100 tons of iron'. Neither party knows at the contract date which 100 tons will be delivered.

If the seller is going to use an independent carrier to deliver such goods to the buyer, and the parties have not agreed to the contrary, ownership will normally pass when the seller delivers the goods to the carrier (SGA 1979, s 18, Rule 5). Whatever the parties agree, ownership of unascertained goods cannot pass to the buyer until the goods are 'ascertained' (SGA 1979, s 16), ie when the seller irrevocably earmarks a particular set for that particular buyer.

There are special rules where the buyer's goods are mixed in with a larger consignment of the same goods. These rules are discussed further in **Appendix 1**.

(2) Retention of title

Section 19 of SGA 1979 envisages that a seller may 'reserve the right of disposal of goods until certain conditions are fulfilled'. This means that a seller who is providing his buyer with a period of credit may retain the ownership of the goods until the buyer pays the price. Such a clause is sometimes known as a *Romalpa* clause (from the case of *Aluminium Industrie Vaassen BV v Romalpa Aluminium* [1976] 2 All ER 552 (CA) where such clauses were first held valid).

If the buyer becomes insolvent before paying, the theory is that the seller may reclaim the goods themselves (as he still owns them) rather than getting involved in the hazardous business of claiming as an unsecured creditor in the buyer's insolvency.

That is the theory. Unfortunately, attempts by sellers to enforce these clauses have been fraught with difficulty. The contract has to contain a whole series of supplementary provisions to ensure that the seller can enforce his rights, for example the right to enter onto the buyer's premises to recover the goods and a duty on the buyer to store the goods separately from goods bought from other suppliers so that the seller can identify his own particular goods. Often the buyer fails to comply with the provisions, so the seller will be well advised to mark his goods with some form of identification. This may be difficult with 100 tons of gravel.

Even more problematical is the situation where the buyer no longer has the original goods, or not in their original form. What if he has sold them? Or used them in a manufacturing process? Attempts to extend retention of title to the proceeds of sale or the resulting manufactured product have usually failed, however carefully the relevant clause was drafted.

What if the seller is delivering a whole series of instalments of goods to the buyer and allowing a period of credit on each? Can the seller retain ownership on all of them until all of them have been paid for? A clause which attempts to achieve this is sometimes called an 'all monies' clause and will generally be effective. Even here there are circumstances where the seller may lose his protection.

For further discussion of these points, see **Appendix 1**.

(3) Risk

Another matter which the parties should expressly agree upon is who bears the loss of accidental damage to the goods. This is particularly important where the goods are to be delivered by an independent carrier. What happens if the carrier is involved in an accident and the goods are destroyed? Must the seller deliver other goods to satisfy the contract or is the risk on the buyer who therefore has no redress?

The seller will presumably wish the risk to pass as soon as possible. The buyer will want the opposite. It will be a matter of negotiation. If seller and buyer do not agree, risk normally passes at the same time as ownership (SGA 1979, s 20). Where the goods are subject to a retention of title clause, this will be the last thing the seller wants.

(4) The right to sell

Unsurprisingly, SGA 1979 makes it a condition of the contract that the seller has the right to sell the goods (s 12). If the seller breaches this condition, the buyer can terminate the contract and get any money paid back under a total failure of consideration. The buyer will normally have no option but to do this, as the seller will not be able to confer any ownership of the goods on him (unless the case falls into one of the exceptions to the 'nemo dat' rule – see **Appendix 1** for further discussion).

Any attempt to exclude this condition will be void (UCTA 1977, s 6).

29.4.3 Price and payment

(1) Calculation of the price

The price of the goods is the one term which the parties will usually remember to specify! If the price is to be determined by reference to the supplier's price lists and the seller issues new versions regularly, make sure that it is clear which price list is the relevant one.

The price can be left to be fixed by a third party, but remember to provide for what happens if he fails to do the necessary valuation or the agreement will be rendered void by SGA 1979 (s 9).

If nothing is expressed, the price may be inferred (eg by a previous course of dealing) or, in the last resort, the court may imply a reasonable price (s 8).

(2) Payment date

Again, the parties must agree whether cash is payable on delivery (implied by the SGA 1979 in the absence of contrary agreement) or whether the seller is to allow the buyer a period of credit. Alternatively, a seller in a strong bargaining position may stipulate payment of all or some of the price in advance.

(3) Effect of non-payment

If the buyer fails to pay on the due date, the seller can usually bring an action for the price. If the seller wants to claim interest on late payment, he should specify this in the contract as the courts determining such cases have traditionally been reluctant to award anything other than the debt owed.

Help may now be on the way for the seller in this position. The Late Payment of Commercial Debts (Interest) Act 1998 basically provides for the payment of 'statutory interest' where payment is late in the case of most commercial contracts for the sale of goods, hire and services. The parties may substitute another 'substantial contractual remedy' for the right to statutory interest but may not agree that late payment will not carry any remedy at all. At present, the Act only gives rights to 'small businesses' (defined as having 50 or fewer employees) against 'large businesses' (over 50 employees) and the UK public authorities, but the government plans to extend the Act's protection over the next few years and eventually it will apply in all circumstances.

If the seller has not yet delivered the goods, he may wish to terminate the contract. To do this, he must specify that the payment date is a strict condition of the contract, as the SGA 1979 provides that time for payment is usually 'not of the essence' (s 10(1)).

In any case, an 'unpaid seller' (as defined in the SGA 1979) need not part with the goods until he is paid (s 41) and indeed, where the buyer is insolvent, may stop the goods in transit and repossess them (ss 44–46).

The seller may want to make further express provisions to cover the eventuality of the buyer's insolvency (eg the right to terminate the contract and refuse further deliveries, the right to repossess the goods under a retention of title clause – see **29.4.2**).

29.4.4 Delivery

(1) Time and place of delivery

'Delivery' has a technical meaning under SGA 1979, ie 'voluntary transfer of possession from one person to another' (SGA 1979, s 61(1)). The parties will normally specify when and where the goods will be delivered.

If the buyer wants the seller to deliver the goods to him, he must stipulate this in the contract otherwise he will generally have to collect the goods from the seller's place of business (SGA 1979, s 29(2)) and if no date and time are agreed he must collect them at a reasonable hour.

If the parties agree that the seller is to deliver the goods, is he to do it himself or will he be using an independent carrier? In the first case, it may be sensible to provide that delivery takes place when the seller delivers the goods to the buyer. In the second, the seller will probably want to provide that delivery takes place when he delivers the goods to the carrier (this will be implied anyway, in the absence of contrary intention, under SGA 1979, s 32). Where the seller is to deliver and the parties do not agree a date and time, the seller must send the goods within a reasonable time and tender them at a reasonable hour (SGA 1979, s 29(5)).

If the seller wants to be able to deliver the goods in instalments, he must specify this in the contract (SGA 1979, s 31(1)).

(2) Effect of late delivery

Time for delivery is generally assumed to be 'of the essence' in a commercial sale of goods contract, so if the goods are delivered late the buyer will usually be able to reject them and terminate the contract.

Sellers often try and prevent this by stipulating that time for delivery is not 'of the essence' thereby limiting the buyer to an action for damages. The clause may go on to limit the seller's liability even further, for example by attempting to exclude consequential loss (such as profit lost by a factory owner as a result of late delivery of essential machinery), but be very careful when using the expression 'consequential loss' in the contract itself (see the discussion at **28.3.4**). Sellers sometimes go even further and try to avoid liability altogether by stating that the time for delivery is not a term at all but merely a statement of intention. If any of these clauses appears in written standard terms, it will be controlled by UCTA 1977 and will only be effective if it satisfies the reasonableness test (UCTA 1977, s 3: see **28.4**).

For further discussion of the buyer's rights on late delivery and also the seller's rights when the buyer wrongfully refuses to accept the goods, see **Appendix 1**.

29.4.5 Description

(1) What is a sale by description?

Where there is a sale by description, there is an implied condition that the goods will correspond with the description (SGA 1979, s 13). There will be a sale by description where the buyer is reasonably relying on the seller's description to identify the goods which are the subject matter of the contract. The usual (though by no means the only) situation is where the buyer has not seen the goods at the time of the contract. As mentioned above (at **29.4.2**) commercial sale of goods contracts very often involve unascertained goods and these are almost always sold by description since the buyer has not seen the goods at the contract date.

(2) When will the condition be breached?

Traditionally, the courts have taken a very strict view of description. Not only have they interpreted the term widely to cover weight, measurements, volume and packaging of goods, but they have usually demanded that the goods must correspond precisely with any description applied to them. Where the sale is by sample as well, the goods must correspond with the description and the sample (SGA 1979, s 15).

(3) Effect of breach

As the term relating to description is a condition, the buyer will normally be able to reject the goods, terminate the contract and claim damages if there is a breach. The buyer can always choose to keep the goods and claim damages. He may be forced to do this if the seller proves that the breach is so slight it would be unreasonable for him to terminate (SGA 1979, s 15A) or if he has accepted the goods or part of them (SGA 1979, s 11(4)) unless he has managed to negotiate an exclusion of these provisions in the contract. For further discussion of these points, see **Appendix 1**.

The seller may try to mitigate the harshness of the description rules by making express provision for tolerance in the contract. The buyer may be happy to agree to this in the case of weight, measurement, etc, as long as the resulting goods are still usable for his purpose.

Any clause in a commercial contract which attempts to exclude or limit the buyer's rights on the seller's breach of s 13 will be valid only if it satisfies the reasonableness test (UCTA 1977, s 6).

29.4.6 Quality

(1) What terms are implied?

Although s 14 of SGA 1979 begins by stating that the general rule in sale contracts is 'caveat emptor' ('let the buyer beware'), the section then goes on to imply two important conditions where the seller sells in the course of a business.

First, the goods must generally be of 'satisfactory quality' (substituted for the previous concept of 'merchantable quality' by the Sale and Supply of Goods Act 1994 (SSGA 1994)), ie they must 'meet the standard that a reasonable person would regard as satisfactory taking account of any description of the goods, the price (if relevant) and all the other relevant circumstances' (SGA 1979, s 14(2A)). Section 14(2B) goes on to give a non-exhaustive list of factors to be taken into account in deciding whether the goods are of satisfactory quality (eg fitness for all the common purposes, appearance, safety and durability).

Secondly, where the buyer has made the purpose of the goods known (either expressly or by implication), the goods must generally be reasonably fit for that purpose (SGA 1979, s 14(3)).

For further discussion of these conditions, see **Appendix 1**.

(2) Effect of breach

Both the terms implied by s 14 are conditions, so breach will normally allow the buyer to reject the goods, terminate the contract and claim damages, subject to the qualifications mentioned above in relation to s 13 (see **29.4.5**).

Again, any attempt in a commercial contract to exclude or limit the buyer's rights on a breach by the seller will only be effective if the clause satisfies the reasonableness test (UCTA 1977, s 6).

Chapter 30

SUPPLY OF SERVICES

30.1 INTRODUCTION

This chapter looks at contracts for the supply of services. In particular, it considers:

(1) what terms are implied into services contracts; and
(2) how far the supplier can exclude or restrict these terms.

It then goes on to have a brief look at contracts that combine goods and services.

Chapter 30 contents
Introduction
Services contracts
Supply of goods and services

30.2 SERVICES CONTRACTS

Let us take an example. An office cleaning business may have contracts with several different companies for the cleaning of their premises. These contracts will be contracts for the supply of services.

Section 12(1) of SGSA 1982 defines a contract for the supply of a service as:

> 'a contract under which a person ("the supplier") agrees to carry out a service.'

This is not very helpful! Contracts of service (ie employment contracts) and apprenticeship contracts are both excluded from this definition (s 12(2)). The Secretary of State may make regulations exempting certain services from the provisions of Part II of SGSA 1982 and advocates and company directors, inter alia, have been exempted in this way.

30.2.1 Terms implied into services contracts

Because there is such a wide variety of possible services which may be provided, there is really no such thing as a typical services contract in the same way that there could be said to be a typical sale of goods contract. As a result, in the case of services, there is no equivalent to the comprehensive statutory framework which was mentioned in Chapter 29 in relation to sale of goods contracts. However, where SGSA 1982 applies, it implies one or more of three terms into the contract.

(1) Implied term about care and skill

Section 13 of SGSA 1982 provides that where there is a contract for the supply of a service where the supplier is acting in the course of a business: 'there is an implied term that the supplier will carry out the service with reasonable care and skill'.

Unlike the implied terms about quality in SGA 1979, this term is not a condition but an innominate term or intermediate stipulation. This means that not every breach of the term will allow the innocent party to terminate the supply contract. The breach must 'go to the root of the contract' or deprive the innocent party of substantially the whole benefit of it.

The cases decided under the old common law duty which preceded the statute are still important in ascertaining the standard of the duty. In one case (*Bolam v Friern Hospital Management Committee* [1957] 2 All ER 118), McNair J stated that the person providing the service was required to exercise 'the ordinary skill of an ordinary competent man exercising that particular art'. If the 'buyer' of the service does not rely on the skill of the supplier, then it seems that this will imply a lower standard of care than if there was substantial reliance.

(2) Implied term about time for performance

Again, this term will only be implied if the supplier is acting in the course of a business. It will not apply if the time for the service to be carried out is fixed by the contract, left to be fixed in a manner agreed by the contract or determined by a course of dealing between the parties. In other words, it will only apply when a time for performance cannot be inferred in any other way. In such a case, there is an implied term (again innominate) that the supplier will carry out the service within a reasonable time (s 14(1)). What is a reasonable time is a question of fact (s 14(2)).

(3) Implied term about consideration

The implied term relating to consideration only applies if the court can find no other way of assessing the parties' intention about price (s 15(1)). The implied term is that the party contracting with the supplier will pay a reasonable charge. What is reasonable is a question of fact (s 15(2)).

30.2.2 Exclusion of implied terms

Section 16 provides that the implied terms may be negatived or varied expressly or impliedly by the parties. This is subject to the provisions of UCTA 1977. Attempts to exclude liability for s 13 of SGSA 1982 will count as attempts to exclude negligence and the effectiveness of the clause will depend on what loss has been caused by the negligence. If it is personal injury or death, liability cannot be excluded (UCTA 1977,
s 2(1)). Liability for other loss may be excluded insofar as the clause satisfies the reasonableness test (UCTA 1977, s 2(2)) (see **28.4.3**).

Sections 16(3) and (4) of SGSA 1982 make it clear that the duties imposed by Part II are additional to any other duties imposed by the contract or by other statutes.

30.3 SUPPLY OF GOODS AND SERVICES

Example 2 at **28.7.2** looked at the case of Drafto, the air-conditioning company. When Drafto contracts with a particular customer to install the air-conditioning, it will obviously be providing a service (the work involved in installing the system) but that is not all. There will be considerable materials involved in the project, materials which will become incorporated in the customer's premises.

A goods and services contract is in effect a hybrid contract.

As far as the workmanship is concerned, the fact that there are materials involved will not prevent it from being a 'contract for the supply of a service' under Part II of the SGSA 1982 (s 12(3)).

However, it will also be a 'contract for the transfer of goods' as defined in Part I of the SGSA 1982 (s 1(1)). It does not matter that services are also provided under the contract (s 1(3)). As a result, SGSA 1982 will imply terms relating to title, description and quality in respect of the materials provided. These terms are similar to those implied in sale of goods contracts.

A contract for the supply of goods and services is sometimes known as a contract for work and materials. It obviously has characteristics of both the sale of goods and the services contracts and if something goes wrong with the air-conditioning in the above example it will be important to establish whether this is due to the workmanship or the materials used.

Chapter 31

INTRODUCTION TO AGENCY AND DISTRIBUTION AGREEMENTS

31.1 INTRODUCTION

This chapter will look at differences between agency and distribution agreements and comparing them with other types of commercial contract, such as licensing and franchising agreements. Chapter 32, will consider the basic principles behind agency contracts. Chapter 33 will examine which factors are relevant in deciding whether to go for an agency or a distribution agreement.

Chapter 31 contents
Introduction
Agency
Distribution agreement
Other types of marketing agreement

31.2 AGENCY

Suppose Ivor Lathe, the furniture manufacturer in Example 1 at **28.7.1** decides to sell his furniture in France. He knows nothing about the market conditions in France and therefore any marketing exercises he might undertake over there would be, at best, ill-informed. One solution is to find someone who does know the market in question, and enter into an arrangement whereby that person sells the furniture on Lathe's behalf.

One way of marketing the goods would be to appoint a French company as the manufacturer's agent for the selling of the furniture. The agency agreement is likely to be one of two main types.

31.2.1 'Sales' agency

The agent (the French company) may be authorised to enter into contracts with customers on behalf of Lathe (called 'the principal'). As a result, Lathe will be in a direct contractual relationship with the French customers through the agent's actions. This is sometimes called a 'classical sales agency'.

31.2.2 'Marketing' agency

However, Lathe may not be very happy with the idea of being bound into a contractual relationship with a buyer whom he has never met. He may therefore prefer a more limited type of agency authority, where the agent is merely authorised to find potential buyers, carry out preliminary discussions and put them directly in touch with Lathe. This agent is sometimes known as a 'marketing', 'solicitation' or 'introducing' agent.

31.2.3 'Del credere' agency

This describes the situation where the agent agrees to guarantee the customer's performance of the contract in return for an additional commission. This is exceptional since the agent is usually not liable at all on any contract which he negotiates (see Chapter 32).

31.3 DISTRIBUTION AGREEMENT

Another marketing possibility for Lathe would be to sell the furniture to the French company, to enable them to sell on to customers in France.

However, Lathe wants to control the way in which the French company markets the product in France. He wants to ensure that the French company exercises its best endeavours to sell as many of the products as possible and uses advertising material which is appropriate to the product and accords with his image. He also wants to ensure that the distributor will carry enough sets of furniture to satisfy customer demand lest his goodwill in that country be damaged. The French company agrees to all these conditions in return for the exclusive right to sell Lathe's furniture in France. In other words, the parties enter into a distribution agreement.

31.3.1 The nature of a distribution agreement

In a distribution agreement, one party (the distributor) buys goods from the other (the supplier) in order to resell them to its own customers. Thus, there is a contract between Lathe and the distributor, and a contract between the distributor and its customers, but no contract between Lathe and the distributor's customer.

When goods are being marketed, there may be a number of levels of distribution between the producer of the goods and their ultimate consumer. For example, a manufacturer of goods enters into a distribution agreement with a wholesaler. The wholesaler then enters into a distribution agreement of its own with one or more retailers. A supplier at any level of distribution may enter into a number of separate but identical agreements with different distributors, so that the goods can be marketed as widely as possible. The number of distributors appointed by each supplier is likely to increase as the goods move down the 'marketing chain'.

31.3.2 Distribution contrasted with pure sale of goods

The relationship of supplier and distributor depends on the law of contract. A supplier and distributor will normally enter into a formal distribution agreement, which sets out the terms of their relationship. Central to this will be the terms on which the supplier sells the goods to the distributor (compare this to an agency agreement, where the principal is not selling the goods to the agent but there may be similar provisions relating to the terms upon which the agent contracts). These terms will cover matters such as the goods to be sold, price, payment, delivery and quality. Unlike an agent, a distributor will not receive commission for goods sold. A distributor makes its profit from the margin between the price it pays for the goods and the price at which it sells them.

Although a distribution agreement is essentially a sale of goods contract, it is much more than that. Of equal importance with the transfer of ownership in the furniture, is the 'umbrella' agreement under which the French company accepts certain obligations and restrictions in relation to its advertising and selling of the products and Lathe agrees to give it exclusive rights to sell in the relevant territory.

31.3.3 Types of distribution agreement

The form and substance of distribution agreements can vary considerably, depending on the nature of the products being marketed and the level of distribution which has been reached.

Despite this variety, however, agreements tend to fall into a number of broad categories (especially from the competition law point of view). For example, some are classified as 'selective distribution' agreements. In this case, the supplier attempts to control the sales which its distributor makes. A classic example of this is a manufacturer putting a term into its agreement with a wholesaler that the wholesaler can only sell the goods to persons who meet the manufacturer's suitability criteria, eg where the goods are luxury items and the manufacturer wants to ensure that any retail outlets have the appropriate ambience, or where the goods are highly technical and retailers need properly trained staff both to sell the goods and to provide effective after-sales service. In either case, the agreement must provide a set of clear and objective criteria for suitability (and even then, there may be problems with competition law – see Chapter 34).

Another significant category of agreement is 'exclusive distribution'. Usually, this means that the supplier appoints a distributor as its only authorised representative in a certain area (eg in the UK), agreeing not to appoint any other distributors and also not to supply customers in the area itself. Contrast a 'sole' agency agreement which usually allows the manufacturer to supply customers direct. (It is probably a good idea to avoid these terms in the drafting of an agreement as their meaning is not always precise!)

31.3.4 Distribution agreements and competition law

Great care has to be taken in drafting distribution agreements as they can easily fall foul of the competition provisions in the EC Treaty. These will be considered further in Chapter 34.

31.4 OTHER TYPES OF MARKETING AGREEMENT

Agency and distribution agreements are not the only types of marketing agreement available. This section will briefly consider:

(1) licensing agreements;
(2) franchising agreements; and
(3) joint ventures.

The agreements are by no means mutually exclusive. For example, a distributor may also need some access to the intellectual property rights of the manufacturer to enable him to demonstrate the product to potential customers. The distribution agreement may therefore include a licence of some of the manufacturer's rights to the distributor. This can cause problems of competition law (see Chapter 34).

31.4.1 Licensing

Example

An inventor has come up with a revolutionary new product with great sales potential. There may be various reasons why he does not want to manufacture and distribute that product himself:

(1) he may not have the facilities to manufacture or distribute the product. He may not be a manufacturer at all or he may be a small manufacturer with insufficient resources to meet the costs involved in developing, advertising and supplying sufficient quantity of the product in question;

(2) he may want to market the product in a particular territory and be compelled or encouraged by local laws in that territory to arrange for the product to be manufactured in the territory itself rather than to manufacture it himself and sell it to a distributor in the usual way.

In such cases, the inventor may consider granting a licence to a third party to manufacture and market the product on his behalf.

31.4.2 Franchising

The essence of a franchising agreement is that the franchisor establishes what is usually known as 'a uniform business format' and then authorises the franchisee (the satellite business) to use it.

Example

A restaurateur opens up an American-style restaurant in a large provincial town. The food is good, the atmosphere is agreeable and the decor distinctive. Before long, he is so busy he is turning customers away.

He begins to have a vision of many other similar restaurants in other large provincial towns, all with the same name, the same decor, the same menu and the same ambience. However, he does not want to run these restaurants himself and he does not want to employ managers to run them. He feels that someone with a financial stake in such a business is more likely to make a go of it.

The dilemma is one of control. The restaurateur does not want to be responsible for the satellite restaurants but he does want to be able to control them, in the sense of ensuring that they retain the same format as the original restaurant. One solution to this problem would be to grant franchises of the new restaurants.

(1) Advantages of a franchise

The restaurateur benefits since he can extend his business system without having to raise capital to do so. Also, since the franchisee is an independent owner operator, the restaurateur:

(1) can usually count on a higher level of performance and profitability; and
(2) incurs less risk of legal liability to customers and staff.

The franchisee benefits because:

(1) he can use a business format or product already tested in the market which carries a name familiar to customers and suppliers;

(2) he can usually count on the franchisor's assistance and training during the risky start-up period (eg advice on the provision of equipment and stock); and
(3) he will often find it easier to raise the necessary bank and other finance to get the business off the ground.

(2) Disadvantages of a franchise

The restaurateur may find it difficult in practice to maintain consistently high standards in the franchise and this may damage his reputation with third parties.

The franchisee may find the franchise frustrating because:

(1) the uniform business format leaves little room for individual initiative;
(2) the goodwill of the business remains in the franchisor (however hard the franchisee works to build up clientele); and
(3) the sale of the business therefore remains within the franchisor's control.

(3) Conclusion

In practice, many shops, restaurants and other outlets are franchised, including many fast-food restaurants (eg Kentucky Fried Chicken). Franchise agreements may be affected by EC competition rules (see Chapter 34).

31.4.3 Joint ventures

The joint venture agreement commonly occurs where two or more businesses collaborate on a particular project or business enterprise. They may be similar businesses which are, in effect, pooling their resources. Alternatively, they may operate in different spheres and be combining on a project which involves the application of both their areas of expertise.

Often, the parties involved will form a joint venture company and much thought will need to be given as to what powers each party has in respect of that company. The validity of a joint venture agreement may be affected by EC competition rules (see Chapter 34). However, there are other structures for joint ventures.

31.4.4 Other forms of agreement

There are many other forms of commercial agreement which are outside the scope of this book.

The next chapter looks back to the agency agreement and considers some of the basic principles underlying the relationship between an agent and his principal.

Chapter 32

THE BASIC PRINCIPLES OF AGENCY

32.1 INTRODUCTION

Agency is frequently encountered in everyday life, for example A asks B to do something on his behalf. This can occur both in the domestic and in the business context. Indeed, a solicitor acting on behalf of a client is acting as an agent for the client.

Example 1

Two friends, Phil and Andy, are working in an office in town. Phil says to Andy, 'I'm too busy to take a lunch hour today. Would you go down the road to the sandwich shop and buy a sandwich for me?' Andy obliges. This is a simple example of agency. Andy buys the sandwich on Phil's behalf. If he pays for the sandwich out of his own pocket, he will be entitled to claim reimbursement from Phil.

Example 2

Parapluie Ltd is a limited company involved in the manufacture of luxury umbrellas and parasols. Alison is the sales director. She enters into a contract on the company's behalf to supply certain of the company's products to a chain of department stores. Alison is acting as the company's agent. Indeed, a company (being an artificial legal personality) has no option but to operate through the medium of agents.

Example 3

Augusta, Boadicea and Cato are partners in a business which specialises in the provision of unusual vehicles for weddings and other occasions. They trade under the name of 'Chariot Begins at Home'. Boadicea drives the vehicles, Cato maintains them, and Augusta is in charge of advertising and contracting with the customers. Augusta enters into a contract on behalf of 'Chariot Begins at Home' with Hereward for the supply of an oxcart for his wedding. Augusta is acting as agent for herself and the other partners and all three will be liable under the contract. (For further discussion of agency in the partnership context, see Chapter 7.)

Example 4

Albert works as a travelling sales representative for Paramount Double Glazing. His job is to persuade householders to sign contracts with Paramount for the installation of Paramount's products in their houses. Although it is Albert who conducts all the pre-contract negotiations and hands over the agreement for signature, the contract is made between the householder and Paramount. Albert is merely acting as an agent.

Example 5

Primahosen MbH is a German company which designs, makes and sells sensible underwear for the older customer. It appoints Acmewear Ltd, an English company, to be its sole selling agent in England. Acmewear advertises the goods in the target

Chapter 32 contents
Introduction
The normal agency contract
Agents acting without actual authority
Undisclosed principals
Payments to agents
Termination of agency

territory and enters into contracts on Primahosen's behalf with English customers. All the relevant agreements are governed by English law.

32.1.1 Express and implied agency

(1) Express agency

Agency can arise either expressly or by implication. In the majority of cases, the agency is express. It is express in all the cases mentioned above. Phil expressly asked Andy to buy him the sandwich. Alison has been expressly appointed as Sales Director. The partners of 'Chariot Begins At Home' expressly agreed that Augusta should be in charge of contracting with customers.

(2) Implied agency

Agency can be implied, but only in very unusual circumstances. These cases (such as agency of necessity and agency by cohabitation) are outside the scope of this book and reference should be made to the standard textbooks on the subject.

32.1.2 Contractual and non-contractual agency

(1) Non-contractual agency

Most agencies arise out of some contractual relationship between the parties but this is not always the case. When Andy went to buy Phil's sandwich, he wasn't acting under any contractual obligation. Phil could not have sued him if he had come back and said, 'I didn't have time to go to the sandwich shop'. There was no contractual intention and Phil provided no consideration for Andy's promise.

(2) Contractual agency: agency as the whole point of the contract

Contractual agencies can be of several different types. The agency may be the whole point of the contract, as in the case of Albert and Paramount: the sole purpose of the agreement between them is for Albert to get customers to sign contracts with Paramount. The same is true for Primahosen and Acmewear: the whole point of the arrangement is for Primahosen to sell lots of their products to English customers through the efforts of the agent. In cases like this, the agent will normally be rewarded by some sort of commission on the sales.

(3) Contractual agency: agency merely as a by-product of the contract

The agency may sometimes be just a by-product of the contract. Alison's job as Sales Director of Parapluie involves a lot more than just negotiating contracts with retail outlets. The agency is only part of her responsibilities under her contract. This is often the case with senior employees and directors of companies. Such agents are usually rewarded with a salary for the job as a whole rather than with commission.

Augusta's position as a partner is similar. The partnership agreement she has entered into with the other two imposes many obligations apart from entering into contracts on the firm's behalf. Her most likely reward will be a share of the firm's profits. (For further discussion of the typical financial arrangement of a partnership, see Chapter 5.)

32.1.3 The form of the agreement

Agency authority can generally be given without any formality at all. If there is an agreement, it may be in writing but it does not have to be. It can be purely oral. The only exception to this is where the agent is being given authority to sign a deed. This type of authority must be given by deed. A deed which bestows agency authority is usually known as a power of attorney.

32.2 THE NORMAL AGENCY CONTRACT

32.2.1 Defining terms

A person who gives another person authority to act on his behalf is usually known as 'the principal'. The person who acts on the principal's behalf is known as 'the agent'. There is one other person involved in the normal agency situation: the person with whom the agent is negotiating on the principal's behalf. In the examples which follow, this character is referred to as 'the third party'.

32.2.2 The effect of the agency

(1) The normal rule: agent not liable under any contract negotiated by him

Where a properly authorised agent negotiates a contract with a third party on behalf of his principal, the normal rule is that the agent is not liable in any way under the resulting contract. He cannot be sued by the third party if the principal defaults. He cannot be sued by the principal if the third party defaults. By the same token, the agent has no rights under the contract and he cannot sue under it.

Therefore, if Parapluie Ltd provides defective umbrellas to one of its retail outlets, the shop will be able to sue Parapluie but will generally not be able to sue Alison. In the same way, if the shop fails to pay for goods delivered, the correct claimant for the money is Parapluie, not Alison. If a householder complains that double glazing has been badly installed in his house by Paramount, then it is Paramount who is liable. Albert is not liable under the contract merely because he negotiated it (although he might be liable in tort if he spoke fraudulently or negligently in the negotiations). In the same way, Acmewear will not be contractually liable for defective underwear supplied by Primahosen to a customer which the agent has introduced.

In other words, the contract is between the principal and the third party. They can sue and be sued. The agent, however, drops out of the picture altogether.

(2) Cases where the agent is liable

This normal rule can be excluded expressly, for example the agent may guarantee the third party's performance to the principal in return for increased commission (a 'del credere' agency) or conversely guarantee the principal's performance to the third party in return for the latter entering the main contract (this will usually be by means of a collateral contract).

The agent may also incur liability by implication, for example through trade custom or usage in the relevant business (see *Fleet v Murton* (1871) LR 7 QB 126).

32.2.3 Actual authority

Before a valid contract can arise between the principal and the third party, the agent must generally have actual authority to enter into the contract on the principal's behalf.

(1) Express actual authority

Actual authority includes authority to do all those things which have been expressly authorised by the principal. However, it will usually be impracticable for the principal to list every single action which the agent may have to carry out in order to achieve the main purpose of the agency.

(2) Implied actual authority

Alison's authority to act as sales director of Parapluie will normally be expressed in general terms. The company will not specifically authorise her to telephone potential customers or send out mailshots. This will be implied from her position as sales director. In other words, an agent has implied authority to do all those acts which are incidental to the performance of the main purpose of the agency. An agent also has implied authority to do all those acts which are customary in the particular trade or place in which he or she is employed. This authority, though not express, is still actual authority.

32.3 AGENTS ACTING WITHOUT ACTUAL AUTHORITY

What happens if an agent negotiates a contract with a third party on the principal's behalf but has no actual authority to do it? Suppose Acmewear enters into a contract with a customer for the sale of underwear but at a price substantially lower than that prescribed by Primahosen. Or suppose that Albert is sacked from his job with Paramount but in a fit of spite goes round to a large number of householders purporting to sell them double-glazing on Paramount's behalf at knock-down prices.

32.3.1 The general rule

(1) The principal is not liable to the third party

The general rule is that a principal is not liable to a third party under a contract entered into by an agent without actual authority. To hold otherwise would be to invite absurdity. Parties would find themselves bound to third parties they had never met through the actions of agents they had never authorised.

(2) The agent is liable to the third party

If the principal is not liable, the third party may find himself in an unfortunate situation. The English customer in the example above may have expended a considerable amount of money in preparing to perform the expected contract only to discover that the contract does not exist.

However, all is not lost. The agent has in effect misled the third party as to the extent or existence of his authority and the third party can sue the agent for this breach of warranty of authority. This is in effect another example of a collateral contract. The agent guarantees that he is authorised to act on the principal's behalf in return for the third party entering into the proposed contract and will therefore be liable to the third party for any loss of bargain or wasted expenditure.

32.3.2 Apparent or ostensible authority

A third party may not be adequately compensated by suing an unauthorised agent for breach of warranty of authority. The householders in the example mentioned above may not be able to find Albert and, if they do, he may not have any money. Is there any way that the third party can hold a principal liable under a contract negotiated by an unauthorised agent?

An agent may not have actual authority but he may have 'apparent' (sometimes known as 'ostensible') authority. For this type of authority to apply, the principal must have held out the agent as having authority to the third party and the third party must have entered into the contract relying on this holding out.

This holding out may be:

(1) by means of a specific representation by the principal, for example Primahosen tells customers that Acmewear is authorised to sell its underwear but does not mention that the agent is not authorised to sell below a certain price or fails to inform them when the agency is terminated; or
(2) by status, for example Alison will have certain apparent authority as sales director even if her actual authority has been restricted by the company – see further Chapter 13 (apparent authority of company officers) and also Chapter 7 (apparent authority of partners); or
(3) by statute, for example see the provisions of s 2(1) of the Factors Act 1889 relating to mercantile agents.

Contrast apparent authority with the so-called 'usual authority' established in the far from usual case of *Watteau v Fenwick* [1893] 1 QB 346 where an unauthorised agent bound his principal even though he did not disclose the agency and contracted as if he himself was the principal.

32.3.3 Ratification

It is clear that a third party may in appropriate cases sue a principal on a contract negotiated by an agent without actual authority. But what if the principal actually wants to proceed with the contract but the third party (having discovered the agent's lack of authority) wants to back out? Can the principal enforce the contract against an unwilling third party?

If, for example, Acmewear negotiates a contract for the sale of Primahosen underwear to an English customer, but at a lower price than the minimum set out in the agency contract. Primahosen finds out but, because of the bad financial situation, decides that a contract at this price is better than nothing. The customer in the meantime has discovered the lack of authority and considers that this is a good excuse for getting out of the contract since it has found cheaper goods elsewhere. Can the customer use the agent's lack of authority as a pretext for escaping its bad bargain?

(1) The effect of ratification

The answer to the above question is 'No', provided that the principal effectively 'ratifies' the contract. If this occurs, the ratification relates back to the date of the agent's unauthorised act (unless the act is expressed to be 'subject to ratification') and the third party who tries to withdraw from the contract will put himself into breach of it (see, eg, *Bolton Partners v Lambert* (1889) 41 Ch D 295).

(2) The four conditions for ratification

Four conditions have to be satisfied, however, before the principal can ratify the agent's unauthorised act:

(1) the principal must be identifiable at the contract date (usually by name but some other unequivocal description will do);
(2) the principal must have contractual capacity both at the contract date and the date of ratification (eg a principal cannot ratify if he was still a minor when the agent entered the unauthorised contract);
(3) the act must be capable of ratification (eg not a forgery or contract void for mistake); and
(4) the principal must ratify within a reasonable time, usually at the latest by the date when the third party must perform his obligations under the potential contract (otherwise the third party will not know whether to perform or not) although the court will allow a later ratification if this is to the third party's benefit (see *Bedford Insurance Co Ltd v Instituto de Resseguros do Brazil* [1985] QB 966).

32.4 UNDISCLOSED PRINCIPALS

Sometimes, an agent will negotiate a contract with a third party without disclosing that he is acting for someone else. In a case like this, as might be expected, the agent may sue on the contract as if he was the principal but in most cases the principal may also disclose himself and sue on the contract.

The main exception to this is where the terms of the contract are incompatible with agency, for example where the wording expressly or impliedly rules out agency (contrast *Humble v Hunter* (1848) 12 QB 310 and *Fred Drughorn Ltd v Rederiaktiebolaget Transatlantic* [1919] AC 203) or the personality of the agent is a material element in the contract (see *Collins v Associated Greyhound Racecourses Ltd* [1930] 1 Ch 1 where a contract for underwriting shares in a company was held to depend too much on the integrity of the underwriter to allow the principal to intervene).

Where 'personality' is not material, it seems that the principal may intervene even if the principal knew that the third party would never have contracted with him direct (contrast *Said v Butt* [1920] 3 KB 497 and *Dyster v Randall & Sons* [1926] Ch 932).

In undisclosed principal cases, the third party generally has a choice as to whether to sue the agent or the principal. Once he has shown a clear decision to go for one or the other, he is generally bound by it, but the courts are very slow to infer an irrevocable election in such a case.

32.5 PAYMENTS TO AGENTS

It is generally unwise for a third party to pay an agent money which is owed to the principal. The payment will only discharge his debt if the agent has actual or apparent authority to receive payment (and an agent who is authorised to sell goods will not necessarily be deemed to have authority to take the money).

Where the principal owes money to a third party, it is obvious that he will normally not be able to discharge his debt by paying his own agent. The only exception is where the third party misleads the principal into thinking that he (the principal) is merely reimbursing the agent for money which the agent has already paid to the third party (an estoppel which is very difficult to prove in practice).

32.6 TERMINATION OF AGENCY

32.6.1 Termination by the parties

The parties can agree to terminate the agency in the same way as they agreed to create it (eg Primahosen and Acmewear agree to end a 5-year agency agreement after 2 years because the relationship is not working).

Either party can unilaterally terminate the agency at any time. This will bring the agent's actual (though not necessarily his apparent) authority to an end, but, where the agency is contractual, unilateral termination may well be a breach of that contract, rendering the terminating party liable to pay damages to the other (see *Martin-Baker Aircraft Co Ltd v Canadian Flight Equipment* [1955] 2 QB 556).

In some cases, a debtor will give his creditor authority to sell his (the debtor's) goods in order to reimburse himself out of the proceeds. This type of agency (sometimes known as an authority 'coupled with an interest') is really a form of security for a pre-existing debt and is irrevocable without the creditor's consent while the debt is still owing (contrast *Greer v Downs Supply Co* [1927] 2 KB 28 and *Smart v Sandars* (1848) CB 895).

32.6.2 Termination by operation of law

Agency authority conferred by a fixed-term contract will normally end automatically when the term expires.

The death of either party will bring an end to both the actual and apparent authority of the agent, who may find himself liable to a third party for breach of warranty of authority (see **32.3.2**) although he and the third party may obtain a certain measure of protection where the authority is given under a power of attorney (Powers of Attorney Act 1981, s 5(1)).

Serious mental illness affecting the principal will terminate the actual (although not the apparent) authority of the agent. Again, the Powers of Attorney Act 1981 may rescue an agent who would otherwise be in breach of his warranty of authority. Serious mental illness of the agent will terminate all types of authority. Note the provisions of the Enduring Powers of Attorney Act 1985, which allow a person suffering from a progressively debilitating mental disorder such as Alzheimer's disease to make arrangements for someone to manage his affairs when he is no longer capable of doing so himself.

The agency will also terminate if either party becomes bankrupt or if the relationship becomes illegal (eg where one of the parties becomes an enemy alien).

Chapter 33

CHOOSING A MARKETING AGREEMENT

33.1 INTRODUCTION

Chapter 33 contents
Introduction
Commercial factors
Overseas operations
UK taxation
Competition law
Making a choice

This chapter looks in outline at the various factors which might be relevant in choosing between an agency or a distribution agreement.

A commercial client may not always require outside assistance in marketing its goods. For example, a large manufacturer intending to market a new line of goods may already be established (eg in the form of a subsidiary company) in its chosen market. It may then be appropriate to let the subsidiary handle the marketing (this can have competition law advantages; see Chapter 34).

However, where a client does need a 'trading partner' to help it find buyers and make sales, both agency and distribution agreements are potentially suitable. The client will naturally wish to market the goods as cheaply and efficiently as possible, as well as to promote demand for the goods in the chosen market. The best way of doing this will have to be assessed individually in each case, but the factors described in the following paragraphs should always be considered. Some of these factors may suggest whether an agency or distribution agreement is more suitable; others should always be borne in mind when considering marketing agreements generally.

33.2 COMMERCIAL FACTORS

Commercial factors play an important part in making the right choice of marketing agreement for a client. They may vary from case to case, but certain points are always worth considering.

33.2.1 Size and organisation of the client's business

A large business with considerable resources may be able to use existing subsidiaries, or set up new ones to handle marketing. In this way, it may be able to create an integrated marketing system which runs more efficiently than one in which goods are sold on down the marketing chain between different, independent businesses.

This may, however, not be possible for many clients; setting up a subsidiary (especially overseas) may be too expensive and time-consuming, in which case the client should consider appointing an independent agent or distributor. Bear in mind that a sales agency will need more supervision than a marketing agency or distribution agreement, because a sales agent binds its principal. A client which lacks the time or resources to keep a close check on its marketing operations should choose either a marketing agency or a distribution agreement.

33.2.2 Location and nature of proposed market

If the client is trying to penetrate an unfamiliar market (especially overseas), a distribution agreement is likely to be preferable to an agency agreement. Under a distribution agreement, the client does not have the risk of operating in the market itself, and can rely on the distributor's knowledge of local trading conditions and rules. This may be particularly helpful if there is a language barrier to be overcome. As an independent entrepreneur, a distributor may also have more incentive to exploit the market to the full (a distributor is acting for itself, and keeps the profit it earns).

33.2.3 Nature of goods to be marketed

If the client's goods are relatively easy to market (eg they are standard in specification, do not vary greatly according to customer requirements and do not require repackaging before they can be sold to customers) a distribution agreement is particularly suitable. If, however, it is essential for the client to be in touch with customers to give them the products they need (eg tailor-made goods, or goods requiring substantial modifications to suit individual customers) an agency agreement is more appropriate.

33.2.4 Client's responsibility to customers

In an agency agreement, the principal will have a contractual relationship with customers (ie the ultimate buyers of the goods); the agent will have either made the contract on the principal's behalf (sales agency) or found and introduced the customers to the principal (marketing agency). In a distribution agreement, the supplier is only liable in contract to the distributor, not to the ultimate customers. If the goods are defective, customers sue the distributor. The supplier's liability to the distributor will be subject to the terms of their agreement and the law governing that agreement, but it may be possible to define and control this liability more strictly than liability to customers. A supplier may, however, be liable to the distributor's customers in other ways (eg in certain circumstances under the Consumer Protection Act 1987 in the UK or parallel provisions in other Member States of the European Union (EU)).

33.3 OVERSEAS OPERATIONS

If the parties to a marketing agreement are to be based in different countries (eg a UK supplier appoints a French distributor to market the supplier's goods in France), they should consider a number of points concerning the law which applies to the agreement.

33.3.1 Governing law

If the parties to an agency or distribution agreement are in different countries, they will have to decide what law they wish to govern the agreement. For example, the UK supplier and French distributor are likely to choose either English law or French law. If, however, they cannot agree on the law of one of the parties, they should find an acceptable compromise, such as the law of a neutral third country.

As far as the UK and most of the countries of Western Europe are concerned, contracts made on or after 1 April 1991 are governed by the 1980 Rome Convention relating to contractual obligations. Under the Convention, the general principle is that the parties have complete freedom to decide which law governs their contract. However, this will not prevent certain mandatory rules applying to the contract.

For instance, where all the elements of the contract apply to one country only, the mandatory rules of that country cannot be excluded by merely choosing the law of a different country. For example, if both parties were resident in England and the contract were to be performed in England, the parties could not avoid the impact of English law on, for example, restraint of trade, by opting for Swiss law. Even where some of the elements of the contract apply to a different country, certain mandatory rules protecting consumers and employees may be non-excludable.

The best advice must be to examine the terms of the Convention before committing the client to a particular choice of law.

33.3.2 How will local law affect the agreement?

Local law (ie the law of the place where the agreement is performed) may be relevant even if the parties have chosen a different law to govern the agreement. Although detailed consideration of this aspect of the parties' relationship is beyond the scope of this chapter, the solicitor should be aware that, in some jurisdictions, provisions of local law may purport to exclude or override parts of the agreement.

33.3.3 Agency agreements

In drafting an agency agreement which is to operate within the EU, it is important to be aware of the impact of the Directive on the Co-ordination of the Laws of Member States relating to Self-Employed Commercial Agents (Directive 86/653). The Directive attempts to harmonise national laws on commercial agency, and in particular provides for the way in which agents are to be remunerated and for the compulsory payment of sums of money by way of compensation or indemnity to an agent on termination of an agency agreement in certain circumstances. The UK has implemented the Directive by the Commercial Agents (Council Directive) Regulations 1993, SI 1993/3053, which came into force on 1 January 1994. Detailed consideration of the Regulations is beyond the scope of this chapter, but it is important to note that their provisions on remuneration, termination and compensation considerably strengthen the agent's position under an agency agreement. Although the Regulations are still relatively new, there is some evidence that businesses which might in the past have appointed agents are now choosing other forms of marketing arrangements, as they are concerned about the high level of protection which the Regulations give to agents. In this sense, the Regulations must now be counted as a factor in the choice between agency and distribution. (The full text of the Regulations is reproduced in the *Business Law and Practice: Legislation Handbook* (Jordans).)

33.3.4 Specialist advice

If the client's agreement has an overseas element, it will usually be necessary to take the advice of a local lawyer. Local factors may affect the choice of agreement (eg in some countries, foreign businesses are not permitted to act as principals; they can trade only through a locally-run office). Specialist advice may also be needed on other matters, including the effect of local taxation. In addition, if the proposed agent is an individual, local employment or social security laws may apply to the agreement.

33.4 UK TAXATION

If both parties to an agency or distribution agreement are based in the UK, there are no particular tax advantages or disadvantages to either type of agreement. However, it may be important to advise a client on taxation when the principal or supplier is based overseas, with the agent or distributor in the UK, because the principal or supplier could in some circumstances be liable to pay UK corporation tax.

The detailed rules in this area are beyond the scope of this chapter; broadly speaking, however, if an overseas business trades in the UK through a branch or agency, it can be liable to UK corporation tax. For example, if a sales agent makes regular contracts on its principal's behalf here, the principal may become sufficiently established in the UK for tax purposes and the agent may have to account to the Revenue for tax on the principal's profits on the principal's behalf. In a distribution agreement, the important factor in deciding whether a non-resident supplier can be liable for corporation tax is whether the supplier has established a sufficient business presence within the UK.

Other features of the agreement between the parties may also require special care from the tax point of view; in particular, whether there is any liability on either party to pay VAT. It may be necessary to take specialist advice on this matter.

33.5 COMPETITION LAW

The impact of EC competition law on both agency and distribution agreements is dealt with in Chapter 34.

For the purposes of this chapter, it is sufficient to note that agency agreements are often unaffected by EC competition law. This means that Article 81 (Article 85 prior to the re-numbering of the EC Treaty by the Treaty of Amsterdam: for more detail on the re-numbering, see Chapter 34) of the European Community Treaty (often still referred to as the Treaty of Rome) cannot apply to the agreement (see further **34.8.2**).

Distribution agreements may run into difficulties with EC competition law. Many distribution agreements contain terms which could adversely affect trade and competition (eg the supplier appoints the distributor to be its distributor for a defined territory, and then agrees to appoint no other distributors for that territory: see further **34.4.2**). It is often possible, however, to arrange matters so that the practical effect of competition law on the agreement is minimal. The EC competition law authorities are relatively sympathetic in their treatment of distribution agreements (especially those between smaller businesses), believing that such agreements may facilitate trade between Member States and help reinforce the single market.

English competition law has recently changed substantially as a result of the Competition Act 1998, which received its Royal Assent in November 1998. Section 2 of the Act (which came into force on 1 March 2000) contains a general prohibition on agreements and certain other business arrangements which may affect trade within the UK and have as their object or effect the prevention, restriction or distortion of competition within the UK. This is known as the 'Chapter I prohibition', and is almost identical in its wording to Article 81 (85) of the EC Treaty. It is unlikely that this provision will apply to agency agreements, but it may affect some distribution agreements. The Act's precise impact in this area will not be fully worked out for some time; however, most vertical agreements have been excluded from the Act's scope by the Competition Act 1998 (Land and Vertical Agreements Exclusion) Order 2000, SI 2000/310. It is nevertheless important to note that agreements which contain price-fixing terms fall outside this exclusion. See **34.4.1** for a reminder about vertical agreements.

33.6 MAKING A CHOICE

The choice of marketing agreement must depend on the circumstances of each case. However, the following examples show how the choice might work in practice:

Example 1: Distribution agreement

Tea Time Ltd was set up 5 years ago. It is a small company which manufactures jams and pickles. The directors believe that the company's products will sell very well in France, but are not confident about conducting business abroad and in a foreign language. They can spend some time on developing their overseas business, but feel that they do need to concentrate on manufacturing. The jams and pickles can be easily exported in a form suitable for immediate resale.

These facts strongly suggest that a distribution agreement is the right choice. The company needs a trading partner, and wants to trade overseas in an unfamiliar market. The expertise of a local trading partner will help to overcome the language barrier, but the company will not be able to spare the time or resources to supervise that partner very closely. The goods can easily be marketed in the form in which they leave the company. One possible disadvantage of a distribution agreement when compared to an agency agreement is that EC competition law is more likely to apply, but if the trading partner is also a small business, this is unlikely to be a major problem (see **34.8.3**).

Example 2: Agency agreement

Wood Magic Ltd is a medium-sized company based in Chester. It has traded successfully for nearly 20 years, making luxury fitted furniture from woods such as yew and cherry. Its operations have so far been confined to northern England, but it now wishes to expand into the rest of the UK (and possibly into Europe). The company has up to now handled its own marketing, because of the need to make each piece of furniture to exact customer requirements. However, its directors feel that they will require outside marketing assistance in making the planned expansion. They are happy to spend time working with and supervising their chosen trading partner; they feel that this will be necessary to maintain the excellent reputation of their products.

These facts suggest that an agency agreement is appropriate. The company is experienced in running its business, but needs a trading partner. Customer contact is absolutely vital. It may be a case where agency is appropriate for the projected overseas operations as well as those in the UK; the factor of customer contact may outweigh the drawbacks of operating an agency agreement abroad. Either sales or marketing agency may be suitable, although marketing agency does have the advantage of requiring less supervision. This may not, however, be crucial if Wood Magic Ltd is prepared to set aside plenty of time to keep a check on the agency.

Chapter 34

COMPETITION LAW

34.1 INTRODUCTION

This chapter builds on and develops the basic principles of EC competition law which were introduced in the LPC Resource Book *Pervasive and Core Topics* (Jordans), placing particular emphasis on the application of EC competition law to individual commercial agreements. In order to prepare for this, a reminder of those basic principles is likely to be helpful.

34.2 PRINCIPLES AND SOURCES OF EC COMPETITION LAW

34.2.1 Direct effect

Articles 81 (formerly 85) and 82 (formerly 86) of the European Community Treaty (known as the Treaty of Rome; this chapter will refer to the Treaty as the 'EC Treaty') have direct effect and are directly applicable in all Member States. EC law takes precedence over the law of Member States where there is a conflict between the two. Thus, if the law of a Member State permits a trading practice, but EC competition law prohibits it, the practice is unlawful.

As noted briefly in the previous chapter, the Articles of the EC Treaty were re-numbered by the Treaty of Amsterdam, which came into force on 1 May 1999. The remainder of this chapter uses the new numbers for these Articles.

34.2.2 Sources

There are four main sources:

(1) the relevant Articles of the EC Treaty (see **34.5**);
(2) secondary legislation issued under the authority of the Treaty by the Council of Ministers or European Commission (eg Regulation 17/62 on enforcement of competition law: see **34.6.2**);
(3) case-law (created by decisions of the Commission and judgments of the Court of First Instance and the European Court of Justice);
(4) notices issued by the Commission indicating policy (eg the Notice on Agreements of Minor Importance: see **34.8.3**).

34.2.3 Operation of EC competition law: the institutions

The European Commission

The Council of Ministers has delegated power to the Commission to supervise the operation of EC competition law. The Commission, through its Competition Law Directorate General, is therefore responsible for developing competition policy, investigating suspected infringements of competition law, issuing Decisions on most

Chapter 34 contents
Introduction
Principles and sources of EC competition law
Other systems of competition law
EC competition law and commercial agreements
The relevant Articles of the EC treaty
The Commission's powers of investigation and enforcement
Consequences of infringement
Avoiding infringement of Article 81
Applying the Articles to specific commercial agreements

points of competition law and taking action against infringements if necessary. It also vets individual agreements to assess compliance with the law.

The European Court of Justice and Court of First Instance

The European Court of Justice gives preliminary rulings on points of competition law referred to it from national courts under Article 234 (formerly 177) of the EC Treaty. However, as far as appeals against Decisions of the Commission are concerned, it is the Court of First Instance which hears the initial appeal. Appeal from the Court of First Instance is to the European Court of Justice.

34.3 OTHER SYSTEMS OF COMPETITION LAW

34.3.1 Systems of Member States

It is important to note that most Member States have their own domestic systems of competition law, which will apply to agreements as well as EC law (assuming that the two systems do not clash: see **34.2.1**). Competition law in the UK (as noted at **33.5**) has recently undergone major changes. The Competition Act 1998 repeals a number of existing UK competition law statutes (notably the Restrictive Trade Practices Act 1976 and the Resale Prices Act 1976), and replaces them with a system much closer to Articles 81 and 82 of the EC Treaty. The emphasis in future will therefore be on prohibiting agreements which have the object or effect of preventing or distorting competition in the UK and on prohibiting abuse of a dominant position. The new legislation came into force (for the most part) on 1 March 2000.

34.3.2 US competition law

It is worth noting that probably the most developed system of competition law in the world is that of the USA. Like EC competition law, it shows the strong influence of political theory (although it obviously lacks the EC dimension of being used as a means of creating the single market) and has been even more heavily influenced by economic theory. The competition authorities of the USA and EC frequently liaise together, and so developments in US policy may influence EC thinking. Briefly, US competition law began with the Sherman Act 1890. This was designed to combat the anti-competitive practice by which trustees took control of independent companies, and then used that control to eliminate competition. US competition law is therefore known as 'anti-trust' law, although the term has come to refer to any action taken against anti-competitive practices. Its development has seen a number of different approaches to regulating the struggle between small and large businesses; each type of business has had periods of being in and out of favour with the law. By contrast, EC competition policy has always favoured smaller businesses.

34.4 EC COMPETITION LAW AND COMMERCIAL AGREEMENTS

34.4.1 Vertical and horizontal agreements

For competition law purposes, agreements are often classified as either 'vertical' or 'horizontal'. As a general principle, the EC competition authorities are likely to treat vertical agreements more leniently than horizontal agreements; the same principle applies to English competition law following the advent of the Competition Act 1998.

As noted briefly at **33.5**, most vertical agreements have been excluded from the scope of the Act by statutory instrument (Competition Act 1998 (Land and Vertical Agreements Exclusion) Order 2000, SI 2000/310). By reg 3, vertical agreements (as defined in reg 2) are excluded from the Act's Chapter I prohibition, but by reg 4, this exclusion does not apply where price-fixing is involved.

Vertical agreements

Broadly speaking, a vertical agreement is an agreement between parties at different levels of the marketing 'chain', although it is now important to note that both English and EC law have their own precise definitions of 'vertical agreement' (see previous paragraph and **34.8.7** below). Examples include supply, distribution, agency and franchising agreements. The parties to a vertical agreement may wish to use terms in that agreement which potentially restrict competition. Assume, for example, that a manufacturer and a wholesaler entering into a distribution agreement agree that the wholesaler will buy all its goods for resale from the manufacturer, and that the manufacturer will sell to the wholesaler and no one else. This ties them to one another, and potentially reduces competition in the market in which the parties operate (eg other potential wholesalers may find it harder to break into the market because they cannot easily acquire suitable goods for resale). However, it is arguable that the potential restriction of competition may be beneficial to consumers of the goods in question, rather than harmful. The parties are secure in their relationship, which may encourage greater availability of the goods and more efficient supply.

In 1996, the Commission issued a Green Paper on vertical restraints to encourage a detailed discussion and review of current EC policy on dealing with this type of arrangement. These discussions led, at the end of 1999, to the adoption of a new block exemption covering vertical agreements. See further **34.8.6** below.

Horizontal agreements

A horizontal agreement is one between parties at the same level of supply; for example, where competing manufacturers agree to fix the prices at which they will sell their products, or to share out product markets between themselves. This type of agreement (often referred to as a 'cartel') is likely to operate in a way which seriously reduces competition and harms consumers (eg prices are kept artificially high). EC law rarely permits such restriction of competition; the same is true of the Competition Act 1998.

34.4.2 Drafting vertical agreements: likely problem areas

Competition law may have a considerable effect on commercial agreements. It may, for example, influence the choice of agreement, as an agency agreement is less likely to infringe Article 81(1) or the Chapter I prohibition than a distribution agreement (see **34.8.2**). This chapter is, however, primarily concerned with the effect of competition law on the drafting of an agreement. The following examples are based on the application of EC competition law: the position should be the same in each case under the Chapter I prohibition where an agreement is capable of affecting trade and competition within the UK.

Grant of territory

Assume that a UK company ('the supplier') is appointing a distributor to sell its goods in France. In order to get the distributorship firmly established, the supplier is prepared to offer the distributor some protection from competition. What the distributor wants in this respect is for the supplier not to appoint any other distributors to sell in France, and not to sell direct to French customers itself. Will it cause competition law problems if the supplier agrees to this? The term which the parties are contemplating (often referred to as the grant of 'exclusive territory') is a potential restriction on competition. It cuts down the sources from which consumers can buy the goods and, as a result, may keep the price artificially high. It may stop other sellers coming into the market. However, although this is a potential infringement of Article 81(1), it should be permissible under the vertical agreements block exemption (see **34.8.7**).

Export ban

Assume that the grant of territory which has just been described is lawful. In return for giving this concession, the supplier wants to ensure that the distributor concentrates on the French market by providing that the distributor will sell the goods only in France and not export them to Belgium. Because one of the aims of EC competition law is to ensure that goods can circulate freely around the entire common market, a term in the agreement which restricts or bans exports will cause problems. It will artificially partition the common market along national lines. It may prevent consumers from being able to buy goods more cheaply in other Member States than they can at home, by impeding 'parallel imports'. Typically, these happen when a trader buys goods in a part of the EU where those goods are cheap, and resells in higher-priced areas, undercutting the higher prices and making them difficult to maintain. The Commission encourages parallel imports as a means of consolidating the single market; an export ban is therefore seen as a serious infringement of Article 81(1) and is unlikely to be permitted.

Unsolicited requests from outside the territory

Assume that the supplier wants to include a term in the agreement forbidding the distributor from selling the goods in response to sales requests from Italy, believing that the distributor should concentrate its efforts on exploiting its exclusive territory (ie France). The term is likely to impede the free flow of goods around the common market, and potentially cuts off a source of goods for parallel imports. It is a potential restriction of competition and infringement of Article 81(1). However, EC law will probably allow some compromise. The client may be able to stop the distributor actively seeking orders from outside France (making 'active' sales), but may not be able to stop it meeting unsolicited requests (making 'passive' sales). The point is considered further at **34.8.7**.

34.5 THE RELEVANT ARTICLES OF THE EC TREATY

34.5.1 Articles 2 and 3: general principles

Article 2 sets out the Community's general aims of establishing a common market and approximating the economic policies of Member States. Article 3 lists activities of the Community which are intended to achieve this, including at Article 3(g), 'the institution of a system ensuring that competition in the common market is not distorted'. The Commission and Courts often refer to Articles 2 and 3 in their decisions on Articles 81 and 82, using the general principles as a starting point for the interpretation of the specific Articles.

34.5.2 Articles 28–30: free movement of goods

Articles 28–30 (formerly 30–36) deal with import and export restrictions on the free flow of goods around the common market, and so are indirectly relevant to competition. Broadly, Article 28 prohibits measures enacted by Member States which impose total or partial restraint on imports (eg rules requiring import licences or inspection of imports). Article 29 does the same thing for export restraints (eg export licences). The emphasis is therefore on government restrictions on trade, rather than on arrangements between businesses. Article 30, however, sets out circumstances in which such controls may be permitted. For a more detailed discussion of how the Articles operate, see the LPC Resource Book *Pervasive and Core Topics* (Jordans).

34.5.3 Article 81: principle, effect and exemption

Article 81(1) prohibits as incompatible with the common market agreements between undertakings, decisions by associations of undertakings or concerted practices which may affect trade between Member States and, which have as their object or effect the prevention, restriction or distortion of competition within the common market. It also sets out a non-exhaustive list of business operations which infringe this general principle (eg an agreement to share markets or to fix prices). By Article 81(2), such agreements, decisions or practices are void. Article 81(3), however, allows the Commission to grant individual exemption (see **34.8.11**). Article 81 is reproduced in full in *Business Law and Practice: Legislation Handbook* (Jordans) and discussed in detail in the LPC Resource Book *Pervasive and Core Topics* (Jordans).

34.5.4 Article 81: a brief reminder of the key points

Agreements between undertakings

'Agreements' may be formal or informal, written or oral; for example, a formal written contract between two companies for one to distribute the other's products would be an 'agreement', but this would also be the case if nothing were put into writing. This chapter is largely concerned with the effect of Article 81 on agreements.

Decisions by associations of undertakings

A common example of this is where a trade association (ie an 'association of undertakings') makes a decision to fix the prices of products sold by its member businesses, instead of those businesses fixing their own prices in individual agreements with buyers. The price-fixing is likely to be well-organised and widespread, and so may be a potentially serious restriction of competition.

Concerted practices

'Concerted practices' can cover virtually any type of co-operation between undertakings. The concerted practice is most often found in relation to manufacturers (the basic test is whether the undertakings involved have knowingly substituted co-operation for competition), but possible examples in relation to vertical agreements include:

- INFORMAL CO-OPERATION

    Two undertakings draft an agreement which does not infringe Article 81(1), then abide by different, informally agreed, terms which do restrict competition (in practice, this sort of situation may constitute an informal agreement rather than a concerted practice; however, the precise classification is not usually significant for the purposes of Article 81(1)).

- NETWORKS

    In a network of distribution agreements, one supplier enters into a number of agreements with different distributors. Even if none of these agreements contains any terms which directly restrict competition, the effect of the network of agreements may be to close off a market to new businesses trying to enter; it may mean that no new suppliers or distributors are required for that market.

Undertakings

The term 'undertakings' covers any entity which is engaged independently in economic activity, including (in the UK) sole traders, partnerships and companies.

May affect trade between Member States

The basic test is whether the relevant agreement, decision or practice alters or has the potential to alter the natural flow of trade between Member States. The effect on trade must be appreciable, but the agreement does not necessarily have to be between undertakings based in different Member States. An agreement between parties based in the same Member State and which appears at first sight only to concern that domestic market can 'affect trade' in the way required by Article 81(1). For example, two large UK-based businesses which enter into a distribution agreement relating only to the UK market may be able to close off that market so that competitors based elsewhere in the EU find it difficult to enter. It is also possible that an agreement where one party is based outside the EU (or European Economic Area) and one within it may affect trade within the EU, especially where there is a strong trading relationship between the EU and the non-EU country involved.

Object or effect

'Object' means that Article 81 applies to agreements deliberately designed to restrict competition (eg price-fixing agreements) whether they succeed or not. 'Effect' means that it also applies to agreements which were not necessarily intended to restrict competition, but which do in practice have that effect. This gives the Commission an enormously wide discretion when applying Article 81.

Prevention, restriction or distortion of competition within the common market

The Commission gives these words their natural meaning. If an agreement has already been found to affect (or have the potential to affect) trade, it will normally be straightforward for the Commission to demonstrate the necessary effect on competition.

Article 81(2)

As far as individual commercial agreements are concerned, Article 81(2) may render the whole agreement void if it contains provisions which infringe Article 81(1). However, it may be possible for a national court applying Article 81 to sever the offending provisions (in accordance with the severance rules of the national law governing the agreement) leaving the rest of the agreement valid. It may be difficult for the court to do this in a distribution agreement, where the offending provisions (eg those relating to exclusive territory) are often part of the consideration offered to induce the potential distributor to accept the agreement (see **34.4.2**), and are therefore so central to the agreement that they cannot be severed.

Article 81(3)

Article 81(3) applies where an agreement, decision or practice infringes Article 81(1) but the Commission decides that it is worthy of an individual exemption (so Article 81(2) does not apply). Individual exemption will be given only if the agreement etc is essentially pro-competitive (broadly, it must promote or improve trade, give consumers some benefit and not contain unnecessary restrictions of competition).

34.5.5 Article 82: the principle

Broadly, Article 82 prohibits as incompatible with the common market the abuse by one or more undertakings of a dominant position within the common market or a substantial part of it in so far as that abuse may affect trade between Member States. The Article is reproduced in full in *Business Law and Practice: Legislation Handbook* (Jordans).

34.5.6 Article 82: key points

One or more undertakings

The activities of one undertaking can infringe Article 82. Unlike Article 81, it is not necessary to have an agreement between undertakings (this would normally also be covered, although exactly when two or more unconnected undertakings can be 'jointly dominant' in a market is still to some extent unclear; for guidance, see *Re Italian Flat Glass* [1990] 4 CMLR 535). There have been some interesting recent developments in this area, however: see the judgment made by the Court of First Instance in *Irish Sugar* Case T-228/97 [2000] All ER (EC) 198 for the principle that collective dominance can be exercised by parties to a vertical agreement.

Dominant position

Broadly speaking, an undertaking enjoys a dominant position in a market when it is able to behave independently of its competitors and customers, to stop effective competition against itself and to maintain that state of affairs. There is no conclusive arithmetical test of 'dominance'; it all depends on the conditions of the relevant market.

Market

The word 'market' includes both product and geographic markets. See the LPC Resource Book *Pervasive and Core Topics* (Jordans) for a discussion of how to recognise these markets.

Substantial part

Each Member State of the EU is likely to be a 'substantial part' of the common market. Smaller divisions may be possible.

Abuse

Abuse is essentially behaviour by a dominant undertaking which is not normal market behaviour and which is detrimental to competitors or consumers. Examples include:

(1) a dominant undertaking exploiting its customers by charging very high prices, or charging very low prices in order to drive competitors out of the market ('predatory pricing');
(2) a dominant undertaking refusing to supply a customer for no commercially justifiable reason.

May affect trade

This is the same requirement as in Article 81 (see **34.5.4**).

34.5.7 Application of the Articles

Article 81 is more likely than Article 82 to be relevant to an individual commercial agreement (eg a distribution agreement). However, both Articles can apply to the same set of facts; equally, the fact that Article 81 does not apply will not rule out the application of Article 82 (and vice versa).

34.6 THE COMMISSION'S POWERS OF INVESTIGATION AND ENFORCEMENT

34.6.1 Attitude of the Commission

Both Articles 81 and 82 are expressed in wide terms, and the Commission is prepared to interpret them flexibly. It is unsafe to assume that the Commission will be unable to discover an infringing agreement or practice; it takes enforcement of the competition law rules very seriously and is endowed with considerable powers to track down infringements.

34.6.2 Regulation 17/62

The Commission's Competition Law Directorate-General carries out the administration and enforcement of both Articles principally under Regulation 17/62 (adopted by the Council of Ministers under Article 87 (now renumbered as 83) of the EC Treaty). Regulation 17/62 confers a wide range of powers on the Commission, including power to obtain information, to investigate suspected infringements of the Articles and to make Decisions about the effect of individual agreements.

34.6.3 Obtaining information

The Commission receives a considerable amount of unsolicited information about possible infringements. For example, information may come from a party to an agreement which feels that it is being unfairly treated by the other party, or from a business claiming that a competitor is abusing a dominant position and driving it out of business. The Commission can also obtain information by request under Article 11 of Regulation 17/62. Most requests are informal: the Commission can make a formal request, but this is uncommon. In both cases, the Commission can fine any undertaking which refuses to supply the information requested.

34.6.4 Investigations

When representatives of the Competition Law Directorate-General investigate an undertaking, they have power to inspect its premises, examine its books and records, and demand immediate explanations of 'suspicious' material or practices. Investigators can seek out information which they believe to be useful but which was not previously known to them (subject to the rules of privilege). Under Article 14 of Regulation 17/62, the Competition Law Directorate-General can make both informal and formal investigations (the latter is usually known as a 'dawn raid'). An undertaking must submit to a dawn raid, which usually happens unannounced and at all the undertaking's premises; refusal to comply will usually result in a fine. Before the Commission makes a decision on the merits of a case, the undertakings concerned have the right to a hearing (the details of the procedure are outside the scope of this chapter).

34.7 CONSEQUENCES OF INFRINGEMENT

34.7.1 Fines

The Commission can impose heavy fines in respect of infringements of both Articles 81 and 82. Undertakings involved can be fined up to 1 million euros, or a greater sum not exceeding 10 per cent of their turnover in the preceding business year. In deciding on the appropriate level of fines, the Commission will take into account matters such as the size of the undertakings involved, their market share, the seriousness and duration of the infringement and (if relevant) how much the parties to the infringement have profited by keeping others out of their market. Note that the Commission can and will fine in respect of unintentional infringements or behaviour which the Commission has not previously punished, although such fines are likely to be smaller than for deliberate infringements. Co-operation with the Commission during an investigation may be a mitigating factor.

34.7.2 Actions in national courts

It is possible for undertakings to bring actions in their national courts if they have suffered loss due to infringement of either Article 81 or 82 (both Articles are directly effective). The remedies available for infringement will vary between different Member States because they will be national remedies. In the UK, this area is still not entirely clear. There is authority suggesting that it may be possible to claim damages for breach of statutory duty or obtain an injunction (*Garden Cottage Foods*

Ltd v Milk Marketing Board [1984] AC 130: an Article 86 case). An injunction was obtained in *Cutsforth and Others v Mansfield Inns Ltd* [1986] 1 All ER 577, giving the applicant a remedy in circumstances where he would have had none under English law.

34.7.3 Other consequences

Infringement can also have less tangible consequences. For example, a large manufacturer may impose an agreement which it knows to be suspect under Article 81 on a small distributor. If the distributor realises that the agreement may infringe Article 81, it may be able to win concessions from the manufacturer by threatening to notify the Commission of the potential infringement. The manufacturer may then be forced to renegotiate the agreement from a position of weakness. Obviously, any undertaking which notified the Commission in these circumstances would itself be running risks, but it is possible that the distributor would be prepared to use the threat as a bargaining counter, significantly altering the normal balance of bargaining power.

34.8 AVOIDING INFRINGEMENT OF ARTICLE 81

34.8.1 Difficulty of avoiding infringement

Subject to what is said at **34.8.8** below, infringement of Article 81 cannot be avoided simply by using a particular form of agreement. The ways in which Article 81 may apply can be difficult to predict, and it may be impossible to advise a client with certainty on whether a particular agreement or practice is likely to amount to an infringement. However, depending on the nature of the agreement, it may be possible to take steps to minimise the risk.

34.8.2 Article 81(1) does not apply

It is sometimes possible to argue that an agreement containing potentially restrictive terms falls outside Article 81 altogether. This is particularly likely where the parties to an agreement cannot be described as two separate undertakings; in such a situation, any agreement between them cannot be anti-competitive. There are two important examples of this: agreements between parent and subsidiary companies, and agency agreements.

Parent and subsidiary companies

An agreement between a parent and a subsidiary company is unlikely to infringe Article 81; the Commission normally regards this sort of agreement as nothing more than allocation of business within a group of companies. The parties would never have been potential competitors, and so an agreement between them cannot have an effect on competition.

Agency agreements

Agency agreements often fall outside Article 81 as a result of the Commission's Notice (sometimes described as an 'Announcement') of 24 December 1962 on exclusive dealing contracts with commercial agents. Broadly speaking, this provides that if an agent is economically at one with its principal, and does not act as an independent trader in relation to the goods which are the subject of the agreement, the agreement between agent and principal cannot infringe Article 81(1) even if it contains potential restrictions of competition. Whether the agent is independent depends not on its legal status, but on which party has the financial risk under the agreement. The Commission considers that an agent which accepts risk (eg by keeping large stocks of goods as its own property on its premises, or having the ability to determine prices under the agreement) is independent and therefore not covered by the Notice. It can be difficult to apply the Notice in practice, but it should always be considered when drafting an agency agreement. Note that the Commission is proposing to change the way in which agency agreements are dealt with. The 1962 Notice is to be replaced by a section of the new Guidelines on the vertical agreements block exemption (see **34.8.7** below). However, at the time of writing (May 2000), the Guidelines are only in draft, and it is unclear when they will come into force. The Commission is aiming for a date of 1 June 2000, the day on which the new block exemption itself starts to apply, but there is no guarantee that this date will be met.

34.8.3 The Notice on Agreements of Minor Importance

Even if an agreement is made between two independent undertakings, and could affect trade between Member States, its effects may in practice be so small that the Commission will ignore the existence of the agreement. There are two main reasons for this. The Commission has the resources to investigate only the most seriously anti-competitive arrangements; in addition, it is prepared to encourage comparatively small undertakings by allowing them to make agreements which may in theory restrict competition, but which do not have an appreciable impact on market conditions. The Notice on Agreements of Minor Importance sets out guidelines for these 'small' agreements. Broadly, the Notice can apply to all types of agreement as long as the agreement satisfies an appropriate guideline (the 'thresholds').

These are expressed in such a way that agreements between undertakings which produce or distribute goods (or provide services) will not fall within Article 81(1) if the aggregate market shares of all participating undertakings do not exceed, on any of the relevant markets:

(a) a 5 per cent threshold, where the agreement is a horizontal agreement;
(b) a 10 per cent threshold, where the agreement is a vertical agreement.

(Where the agreement is 'mixed' horizontal and vertical, or where it is difficult to classify as being of either type, it is the 5 per cent threshold which is relevant.)

The Notice goes on to provide some guidance on the difficult question of how to define the market(s) for this purpose; it is clear that both the relevant geographic and relevant product markets must be investigated, and that, as far as product market is concerned, substitutability is the important point (compare Article 82 of the EC Treaty).

Interestingly, para 19 of the Notice contains a general statement to the effect that agreements between small and medium-sized undertakings will generally not fall within Article 81(1) anyway, because they are rarely capable of affecting trade as the Article requires, and that the Commission will not start Article 81 proceedings against these types of undertaking even if their market shares exceed the thresholds. However, by para 20, the Commission does reserve the right to intervene if they do significantly impede competition.

34.8.4 Effect of the Notice

If the Notice applies, the Commission is unlikely to find that an agreement infringes Article 81(1), even if it contains terms which potentially restrict competition. It is important to realise that the Notice only provides guidance and does not bind the Commission, the European Courts or national courts. For example, para 11 of the Notice makes it clear that the applicability of Article 81(1) cannot be ruled out in, for example, a price-fixing agreement, even where the parties satisfy the thresholds noted above. However, if the parties to an agreement do rely on it, genuinely believing that it applies to them when in fact it does not, they will not be fined unless the mistake was due to 'negligence' (para 5 of the Notice). It is not necessary to notify an agreement to the Commission to obtain the benefit of the Notice.

34.8.5 Agreements likely to infringe Article 81(1)

In the case of an agreement between substantial independent undertakings which is likely to have an appreciable effect on trade within the common market, there is a serious possibility that it will infringe Article 81(1). This is particularly likely with distribution agreements, which often contain provisions (eg exclusive territory) considered by the parties to be essential to the workings of the agreement, but which have the potential to restrict competition. At this stage, the parties should consider whether the agreement could be re-drafted to get the benefit of a block exemption.

34.8.6 Block exemptions

Block exemptions are in the form of Commission Regulations, and have been designed to ensure that the Commission does not have to investigate agreements which potentially infringe Article 81(1), but do not in fact impose serious restrictions on competition, and which may actually benefit consumers. Currently, there are block exemptions covering a variety of commercial agreements, including vertical agreements (see **34.8.7** below) and agreements for the transfer of technology (eg the transfer of certain types of intellectual property, such as patents). Although there are some differences in format and presentation, block exemptions tend to follow a similar pattern; first, the Regulation states, in a preamble, the Commission's policy in allowing block exemption for the type of agreement concerned and then outlines terms which the parties to such agreements commonly wish to use. Traditionally, block exemptions have contained at least two lists of terms: the so-called 'white' and 'black' lists. However, the most recent block exemption to be adopted departs from this approach to some extent (see **34.8.7**).

'White-listed' terms

A 'white list' sets out terms which may restrict competition, but which the parties may nevertheless use without infringing Article 81(1). It may also set out terms which are unlikely to infringe Article 81(1) anyway, but which are expressly stated to be permissible for the avoidance of doubt.

'Black-listed' terms

A 'black list' contains terms or describes situations which will prevent the block exemption from applying. Terms which fall within a black list are likely to infringe Article 81.

34.8.7 An example of a block exemption in outline: Regulation 2790/99

As previously noted, the Commission's review of how EC competition law operates has generated a new block exemption, granted by Regulation 2790/99 (commonly known as the 'vertical agreements' or 'vertical restraints' block exemption). It was adopted by the Council on 22 December 1999, and has applied to vertical agreements (as defined in Article 2) since 1 June 2000.

The 'old' block exemptions

Regulation 2790/99 replaces three earlier block exemptions: Regulation 1983/83 on exclusive distribution agreements, Regulation 1984/83 on exclusive purchasing agreements, and Regulation 4087/88 on franchising agreements. Article 12.2 gives transitional relief, in the sense that agreements which were already in force on 31 May 2000, and which satisfied the provisions of one of the old block exemptions, but not the new block exemption, are still safe from the prohibition in Article 81(1) of the Treaty until 31 December 2001.

The 'new' block exemption (in outline)

It is important to note that the new Regulation takes a different approach from its predecessors. There is no 'white list' of permitted terms: instead, the new block exemption simply 'black-lists' terms which are not permissible (see Article 4). Anything not listed in Article 4 will (normally) be permissible. In addition, the new block exemption is subject to a market share threshold; by Article 3, the block exemption only applies to an agreement if the supplier's share (or in some cases the buyer's share; see Article 3.2) of the relevant market does not exceed 30 per cent; this could be seen as an attempt to bring some economic reality into the operation of the block exemption. The main provisions of the Regulation are as follows.

Preamble:	explains the philosophy behind the grant of block exemption to vertical agreements.
Article 1:	defines various important phrases (eg 'non-compete obligation', 'exclusive supply obligation').
Article 2:	grants exemption to vertical agreements (as defined in Article 2.1).
Article 3:	sets out the market share threshold above which the block exemption will not apply.
Article 4:	black-listed terms; notably most forms of price-fixing (Article 4(a)) and certain territorial restrictions (Article 4(b)). Use of such terms will prevent the block exemption applying to the agreement at all.
Article 5:	provides further restrictions of the exemption in certain cases of selective distribution or non-compete clauses.

Note that by Articles 6–8, the block exemption may be withdrawn; either selectively by the Commission or Member States (Articles 6 and 7) or by the Commission in relation to particular markets (Article 8).

34.8.8 Advantages of block exemption

It is desirable to use block exemptions wherever possible, as this is likely to be cheaper, quicker and safer for the parties concerned. If an agreement is drafted in a way which closely follows any relevant block exemption, it is unlikely that the Commission will take an interest in the agreement unless circumstances change. In addition, there is no need to notify the agreement to the Commission in order to get the benefit of a block exemption. It may not, however, always be clear that an agreement could benefit from a block exemption; if that is the case, it is possible to ask the Commission for its opinion.

34.8.9 Notification to the Commission

Whether or not to notify an agreement to the Commission is an important tactical decision. The parties do not have to notify simply because they suspect that the agreement may infringe Article 81. However, if they want the Commission's formal opinion that there is in fact no infringement, or that the agreement deserves an individual exemption under Article 81(3), they must apply for it using Form A/B. This means revealing a considerable amount of information to the Commission, not only about the agreement itself but also about the parties' business operations. Once an agreement has been notified, the Commission may react in the following ways.

34.8.10 Negative clearance

If the Commission gives an agreement negative clearance, this means that the agreement as notified does not infringe Article 81 at all. The parties often apply for negative clearance and individual exemption in the alternative, so that the immunity from fines which covers an application for individual exemption (see **34.8.11**) also extends to the application for negative clearance.

34.8.11 Individual exemption

Individual exemption is a declaration by the Commission that the agreement as notified does infringe Article 81(1), but in the circumstances is worthy of exemption under Article 81(3). Very few individual exemptions are granted, the process often takes several years to run its course, and, inevitably, the agreement is brought to the Commission's attention. Individual exemption does, however, have several advantages. It binds the Commission, the European Courts and national courts. Note that, as a result of amendments which Regulation 1216/99 made to the enforcement Regulation (17/62), it is no longer necessary to notify agreements in advance to gain individual exemption.

34.8.12 Comfort letters

The Commission's standard response following notification is to send the parties a 'comfort letter', which pronounces informally on the effects of the agreement. There are different types of comfort letter. For example, the letter may state that the agreement does not infringe Article 81(1) at all. Although this is not a binding opinion, it would be good evidence in proceedings concerning the agreement before a national court. Alternatively, it may state that the agreement falls within a block exemption, or that the agreement deserves exemption, but that the Commission is closing its file on the matter.

34.8.13 Other methods

The Commission can also deal with agreements in certain other ways. For example, it may negotiate with the parties and try to persuade them to delete offending or doubtful provisions from the agreement, so that Article 81 will no longer apply or exemption will be possible. The Commission can also agree not to pursue an investigation in return for the parties modifying their behaviour.

34.8.14 Avoiding infringement of Article 82

The Commission can grant negative clearance under Article 82 in the same way as it can under Article 81. However, none of the other methods of avoiding infringement of Article 81 is relevant to Article 82. In particular, there are no block exemptions, and no possibility of individual exemption, because conduct which amounts to abuse of a dominant position does not deserve exemption.

34.9 APPLYING THE ARTICLES TO SPECIFIC COMMERCIAL AGREEMENTS

Although it is not always easy to predict the operation of Articles 81 and 82 in relation to a commercial agreement, it is worth considering certain points when drafting or reviewing an agreement. In particular, the solicitor should try to establish two important points: are the Articles likely to apply, and how, if at all, can this be prevented? Bear in mind, however, that the answers may not be clear-cut, and that the following paragraphs provide guidance only on the points to consider.

34.9.1 Article 81: agency agreements

When drafting or reviewing a client's agreement, consider the following points.

(1) Article 81(1) may not apply at all because one or more of the following statements is true.

　(a) The agreement is within the Notice of 24 December 1962 because the agent is not acting independently in relation to the contract goods and, for example, accepts no financial risk under the agency agreement (or, when the Guidelines to the vertical agreements block exemption reach their final form, the agreement falls within the section relating to agency agreements).

　(b) The principal and agent are parent and subsidiary companies and therefore count as one undertaking.

　(c) The agreement is otherwise incapable of affecting trade and competition within the common market (eg it does not contain any restrictive terms).

(2) The parties' market shares may be small enough to fall within the Notice on Agreements of Minor Importance. If so, the Commission is unlikely to take an interest in the agreement.

If neither (1) nor (2) is relevant, the agency agreement will probably have to be treated in the same way as a distribution agreement (see below). Bear in mind, however, that there are no block exemptions which apply to agency agreements.

34.9.2 Article 81: distribution agreements

When drafting or reviewing a client's distribution agreement, consider the following points.

(1) Article 81(1) may not apply because either (or both) of the following statements are true.

    (a) The parties are parent and subsidiary companies and therefore count as one undertaking.

    (b) The agreement is otherwise incapable of affecting trade and competition within the common market (eg it does not contain any restrictive terms).

(2) Does the Notice on Agreements of Minor Importance apply? (See (2) at **34.9.1** above.)

(3) If neither (1) nor (2) is relevant, consider the terms which the client wants to include in the agreement. If they are likely to restrict competition, it is probably best to assume that Article 81(1) applies, and then decide if it is possible to avoid infringement.

(4) (a) If drafting a new agreement, draft to get the benefit of the relevant block exemption (Regulation 2790/99) wherever possible.

    (b) If reviewing an existing agreement, consider whether it could be redrafted to bring it within the block exemption.

(5) If none of the above is appropriate, consider notifying the agreement to the Commission for negative clearance or an individual exemption.

34.9.3 Article 82

Article 82 is far less likely to apply to individual commercial agreements than Article 81. However, it must not be ignored, especially if one of the parties has a large market share (eg if a supplier with a large market share refused to supply a distributor, it could in certain circumstances be abusing a dominant position). Bear in mind that if Article 82 does apply, there is no way of avoiding infringement. Consider the following questions.

(1) Does the agreement involve one or more undertakings?
(2) Does the agreement involve an undertaking with a dominant position in the relevant markets?
(3) Is that dominant position within the common market or a substantial part of it?
(4) Does the conduct of the dominant undertaking amount to abuse of a dominant position?

If the answer to all these questions is yes, Article 82 prohibits the abuse insofar as it may affect trade between Member States.

Appendix 1

DRAFTING A SALE OF GOODS TRANSFER

Chapter 29 contained a summary of the main points to be considered in drafting a sale of goods contract. This Appendix contains a much more detailed discussion of these points against the background of the relevant provisions of the SGA.

In considering the impact of the statutory framework in the SGA, we will refer to the standard example given at the beginning of this Appendix.

THE STANDARD EXAMPLE

Supawave is a small company involved in the manufacture of microwave ovens. One of its main customers is a large department store called Bumpa-store with many branches around the country.

The way the business arrangement between buyer and seller works is as follows. Supawave provides a demonstration model of each of its microwaves to the relevant Bumpa-store. Bumpa-store does not pay for the demonstration models at this stage. Customers of Bumpa-store who select Supawave microwaves are given an approximate delivery date. Bumpa-store then puts in an order to Supawave together with a 10 per cent deposit on the value of the goods ordered and Supawave sends the relevant number of microwaves to the shop via an independent carrier. Bumpa-store pays the balance owing on each microwave on delivery. Bumpa-store then delivers the microwave to the customer using its own van and driver.

When a demonstration model has been in the shop for some time, Bumpa-store sells it off at a knock-down price and, at that stage, the price becomes payable to Supawave. The same thing happens when a particular model is about to be superseded by a more modern one.

Part 1

TRANSFER OF OWNERSHIP

A1.1 INTRODUCTION

This chapter looks at the concept of ownership in SGA 1979. It considers:

(1) the significance of ownership passing to the buyer;
(2) the effect of the seller having no right to sell;
(3) the rules for deciding when ownership passes;
(4) the limits on how far the seller can retain ownership of the goods after delivery; and
(5) the relationship between ownership and risk.

Part 1 contents
Introduction
Significance of the transfer of ownership
Seller with no right to sell
When does ownership pass?
Retention of title
Ownership and risk

A1.2 SIGNIFICANCE OF THE TRANSFER OF OWNERSHIP

Section 2(1) of SGA 1979 makes it clear that transfer of ownership is the whole point of a sale of goods contract (although SGA 1979 refers to the 'transfer of property' and the 'transfer of title' rather than the 'transfer of ownership' which is used in the following paragraphs).

The time when ownership passes may be important for various reasons. If ownership passes at the contract date and the seller goes bankrupt before delivering the goods, the buyer will have an action in rem for the goods themselves rather than having to claim in the bankruptcy for damages or the return of the price (but see SGA 1979, s 25 at **A1.3.2**). Whether the ownership has passed also has some bearing on a seller's right to claim the unpaid price for goods (see SGA 1979, s 49 at **A2.3.2**). Who bears the risk of accidental damage to goods in transit may also depend on who owns them at the time of the damage (see **A1.6**).

A1.3 SELLER WITH NO RIGHT TO SELL

The above paragraph presupposes that the seller either owned the goods or at least had the right to sell them on behalf of the person who did own them. What happens if the seller does not have that right? How does this affect the buyer?

First, the buyer may be able to sue the seller for breach of the contract. Secondly, the buyer will not obtain ownership of the goods, unless he can show certain exceptional circumstances.

A1.3.1 The seller is in breach of contract

(1) Implied condition that the seller has the right to sell

The seller will be in breach of contract where he has no right to sell the goods. Section 12(1) of SGA 1979 provides that, subject to one exception:

'there is an implied condition on the part of the seller that in the case of a sale he has a right to sell the goods, and in the case of an agreement to sell he will have such a right at the time when the property is to pass.'

Thus, where ownership passes at once under the contract, the seller must have the right to sell at the contract date. When the ownership is to pass at a later stage (under an agreement to sell) the seller must have obtained the right to sell by the time ownership passes.

Breach of this implied condition allows the buyer to terminate the contract (in most cases, the contract will be emptied of all content if the seller cannot pass ownership of the goods) and claim back any money paid under a total failure of consideration. Since transfer of ownership is the whole point of the sale of goods contract, the whole price will be recoverable even if the buyer has had considerable use of the goods before the seller's lack of ownership is discovered (see *Rowland v Divall* [1923] 2 KB 500).

The seller may agree to transfer a more limited title in certain circumstances (s 12(3)–(5)).

(2) Other terms implied by s 12

Section 12(2) implies various warranties relating to the buyer's enjoyment of the goods.

(3) Seller's duties under s 12 are non-excludable

The seller's duties as laid down in s 12 of SGA 1979 cannot be excluded by any contractual term. This is the effect of UCTA 1977, s 6(1) and is one of the few instances where an exclusion clause is void even in a non-consumer case (see **28.4.3**).

A1.3.2 Generally no ownership will pass to the buyer – 'nemo dat quod non habet'

(1) The general rule

Section 21(1) of the SGA 1979 provides that, subject to certain exceptions:

'where goods are sold by a person who is not their owner, and who does not sell them under the authority or with the consent of the owner, the buyer acquires no better title to the goods than the seller had, unless the owner of the goods is by his conduct precluded from denying the seller's authority to sell.'

This rule embodies the principle 'nemo dat quod non habet' – nobody can give what they have not got.

Thus, if a car dealer purports to sell a car to a customer and it transpires that the car has been stolen, the seller has no ownership and therefore cannot pass ownership to the customer. The original owner, from whom the car was stolen, remains the owner and may reclaim the car from the customer. If the customer refuses to return the car, the original owner may sue him in conversion. The customer can sue the dealer for breach of s 12(1) and recover his money but this will be little consolation if the dealer has disappeared or gone bankrupt.

The nemo dat rule does not apply where the goods are sold by an agent with the owner's authority (which may be either actual or apparent: see Chapter 32).

(2) Exceptions to the nemo dat rule

Sections 22–25 of SGA 1979 contain various exceptions to the rule. Perhaps the most important in a commercial context is s 25 which provides that a buyer, who has possession of the goods but does not yet own them, may in certain circumstances give good title to someone who buys the goods off him. This is particularly relevant where the buyer possesses the goods under a retention of title clause (see **A1.5**).

Private purchasers of motor vehicles may also be protected under Part III of the Hire Purchase Act 1964 (as amended by the Consumer Credit Act 1974).

A1.4 WHEN DOES OWNERSHIP PASS?

We will now turn to SGA 1979 provisions for establishing when ownership passes. These provisions vary according to whether the goods which are the subject matter of the contract are 'specific' or 'ascertained' goods.

A1.4.1 Passing of ownership in 'specific' goods

(1) What are 'specific' goods?

Specific goods are defined as 'goods identified and agreed on at the time a contract of sale is made' (SGA 1979, s 61(1)). In other words, the buyer must be able to point to some specific goods and say, 'Those are mine.' This will happen when a customer selects particular goods in a shop or self-service supermarket and takes them to the cash desk. The subject matter of the contract is those goods and those goods alone. Another example would be the case where someone sees a second-hand car advertised in the local paper and buys that car.

In the standard example, the purchase by Bumpa-store customers of the reduced-price demonstration models is a purchase of specific goods. The actual microwave in question is there in front of him. The customer knows exactly which microwave he is buying. The goods are identified and agreed upon at the time of the contract.

(2) Ownership passes when the parties intend it to pass

There is very little problem working out when ownership passes in 'specific' goods. The ownership passes when the parties intend it to pass (SGA 1979, s 17). This intention can be discovered from looking at 'the terms of the contract, the conduct of the parties and the circumstances of the case' (SGA 1979, s 17(2)). For example, if the seller reserves a right of disposal under a retention of title clause (see **A1.5**), this will show a clear intention that the ownership is not to pass until certain conditions are satisfied.

If no intention can be discovered in this way, s 18 lays down various rules to help.

(3) Where no intention appears, ownership normally passes at the contract date

Normally, ownership passes when the contract is made (s 18, Rule 1) 'and it is immaterial whether the time of payment or the time of delivery, or both, be postponed'. However, the contract must be unconditional (eg not subject to any condition precedent like the approval of a third party) and not require the seller to do anything to the goods to ascertain the price. The contract must also be for the sale of specific goods 'in a deliverable state', ie the seller has not got to do anything to the goods before they are delivered to the buyer. (Goods are in 'a deliverable state' when they are 'in such a state that the buyer would under the contract be bound to take delivery of them' (SGA 1979, s 61(5)).)

(4) What if the seller has to do something to the goods to put them in a deliverable state?

Suppose, for example, that a buyer is interested in buying a second-hand car from a car dealer but wants the dealer to convert the car so it can use unleaded petrol. Clearly, Rule 1 does not apply. The contract is not unconditional and the goods are not in a deliverable state. Ownership passes when the buyer receives notice that the required action has been carried out (s 18, Rule 2).

(5) What if the seller must weigh, measure, test or do something else to the goods to ascertain the price?

Ownership passes when the buyer receives notice that the price has been ascertained (s 18, Rule 3).

A1.4.2 Passing of ownership in 'unascertained' goods

(1) What are 'unascertained' goods?

In many cases, a buyer will not be able to identify a particular set of goods when the contract is entered into. When someone buys by mail order, he cannot say which particular set of extendable window cleaning brushes are going to be his. When a heavy engineering company orders 20 tons of iron, it does not know which 20 tons in the supplier's yard are going to be loaded on the lorry for delivery to its factory. These are unascertained goods. Although there is no definition of 'unascertained goods' in SGA 1979, it is generally accepted that the term covers any goods which are not specific.

All of the goods in the standard example (except the reduced-price demonstration models mentioned at **A1.4.1** above) are unascertained. When Bumpa-store orders demonstration models, they do not know which specific microwave they will receive of each type. The same is true at the later stage when the store puts in a larger order for particular models to satisfy their customers' requirements. When a customer orders a particular model of microwave from the store, the goods are again unascertained. The customer knows which model he is going to buy but not which specific set of goods. All of these are examples of goods being ordered generically.

(2) Ownership cannot pass until the goods are 'ascertained'

Whatever the parties intend, ownership cannot pass 'unless and until the goods are ascertained' (SGA 1979, s 16). So how do unascertained goods become ascertained? There is no actual definition in the SGA 1979 but it is generally accepted that the goods will become ascertained when a particular set is singled out as the one which is to go to that particular buyer by some irrevocable act of the seller (see *Wardar's (Import and Export) Co v W Norwood and Sons Ltd* [1968] 2 QB 663).

There are special rules when the contract is for a specified quantity of unascertained goods in a deliverable state and the buyer's goods are mixed in with an identified larger consignment of the same goods. This might occur when the seller has sold the same type of goods to a number of different buyers and delivers the correct global quantity to a carrier without separating them out.

Let us assume that the buyer is the last delivery point. At the previous delivery point, the carrier unloads a consignment of goods leaving the buyer's goods as the only ones left on the lorry. At this point, the goods will become ascertained and ownership will pass to the buyer (in the absence of contrary agreement). This is s 18, Rule 5(3) giving statutory effect to the old common law doctrine of exhaustion and inserted by the Sale of Goods (Amendment) Act 1995.

In fact, the buyer may become owner at an earlier stage, not of the goods themselves but of an undivided share in the bulk as a whole, and owner-in-common of the bulk itself (the new s 20A). This will occur only where the buyer pays the price for some or all of the goods, and the proportion of the bulk which he owns will depend on the proportion the price paid bears to the bulk as a whole.

(3) Once goods are ascertained, ownership passes when the parties intend it to pass

As with specific goods, the starting point is the parties' intentions and again this can be discovered from the express words of the agreement (eg where the seller makes use of a retention of title clause) or may be inferred from all the circumstances (SGA 1979, s 17(2)).

(4) What if the parties' intentions cannot be discovered?

If the parties' intentions cannot be discovered, the rules in s 18 may help.

Where there is a sale of unascertained goods by description (the normal situation), ownership passes when goods of the contract description and in a deliverable state are unconditionally appropriated to the contract either by the seller with the buyer's assent or (more unusually) by the buyer with the seller's assent (SGA 1979, s 18, Rule 5(1)). This assent may be given either before or after appropriation and will often have to be implied.

Delivery of the goods to the buyer or to an independent carrier for transport to the buyer will generally be taken to be an unconditional appropriation (Rule 5(2)).

As a result, ownership in unascertained goods normally passes to the buyer when they become 'ascertained' unless:

(1) the parties expressly or impliedly agree a later time; or
(2) the contract is conditional, for example on the approval of a third party; or
(3) something has to be done to the goods after they are ascertained to put them into a deliverable state, for example they have to be customised after they are taken out of the warehouse.

A1.4.3 Passing of ownership in 'future' goods

'Future goods' are 'goods to be manufactured or acquired by the seller after the making of the contract of sale' (s 61(1)), for example the case of the buyer who orders a special car from a dealer before the car has even been made by the factory. It is probably best to think of them as a particular type of unascertained goods.

Once the goods have been made or acquired, ownership passes when the parties intend it to pass (SGA 1979, s 17). If no intention can be inferred, the provisions of s 18, Rule 5 apply, ie ownership normally passes on unconditional appropriation unless the parties show an intention that it should be later.

A1.4.4 Passing of ownership in goods on approval or sale and return

Section 18, Rule 4 contains detailed provisions to cover this situation.

A1.4.5 Flow chart to illustrate passing of ownership

OWNERSHIP PASSES:

- Is the contract subject to some other condition? → **Yes** → Presumably when (the buyer is notified that?) the condition is satisfied
- ↑ **No**
- Does the seller have to do something to put the goods in the deliverable state or to ascertain the price? → **Yes** → When the buyer is notified that action has been carried out (s 18, Rules 2 and 3)
- ↑ **No**
- Is it an unconditional contract for goods in a deliverable state? → **Yes** → At the contract date (s 18, Rule 1)
- ↑ **No**
- Have the parties agreed (expressly or impliedly) when ownership is to pass? → **Yes** → When the parties agree (s 17)
- Are the goods specific? → **Yes** → (to above)
- **No** ↓
- Have the parties agreed (expressly or impliedly) when ownership is to pass? → **Yes** → Is agreed time after the goods have been ascertained? → **Yes** → When the parties agree (s 17)
  - **No** → When goods become ascertained (s 16)
- **No** ↓
- Is it a sale by description? → **Yes** → When goods are unconditionally appropriated to the contract (s 18, Rule 5)
  - **No** → ?

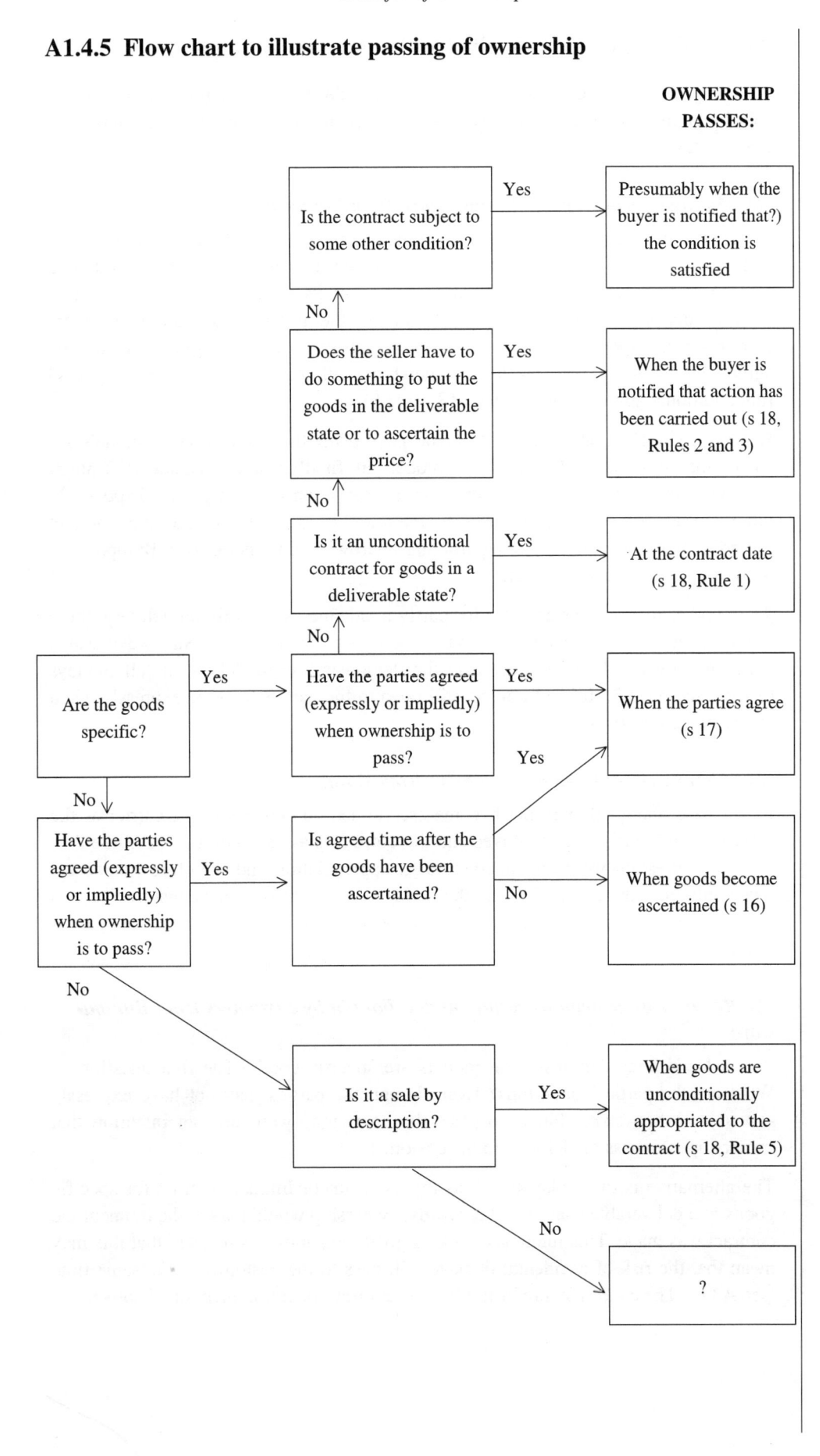

A1.4.6 The above rules applied to the standard example

All the goods in the example (apart from the reduced-price demonstration models sold by Bumpa-store) are unascertained goods so no ownership can pass until they are ascertained.

(1) Microwaves ordered by Bumpa-store from Supawave

In the case of microwaves ordered by Bumpa-store (both the demonstration models and those to satisfy customer orders) the goods will presumably become ascertained when Supawave sets aside particular goods from its warehouse to fulfil Bumpa-store's order or perhaps when Supawave delivers the microwaves to the independent carrier for transport to Bumpa-store. In the absence of any express or implied agreement between the parties, ownership will pass at this time as well (unconditional appropriation under s 18, Rule 5).

However, since Bumpa-store will not be paying for the demonstration models for some time (ie when the demonstration models are finally sold to customers), it might be appropriate for Supawave to insist on a reservation of the right of disposal. In other words, Supawave may insert a retention of title clause into the contract providing that the ownership of a particular microwave does not pass to Bumpa-store until they resell it to a customer.

As the other microwaves are paid for partly in advance and partly on delivery, there seems to be little justification for retaining title to them (unless Supawave wants extra security for the debts owed on the demonstration models – an 'all moneys clause', see **A1.5.3**). It is, of course, still open to the parties to agree expressly when the ownership is to pass.

(2) Microwaves ordered by customers from Bumpa-store

In this case, the goods will not become ascertained on delivery to the carrier as the carrier is the seller's own employee and therefore acts as its agent. In a case like this, there will presumably be no unconditional appropriation and therefore transfer of ownership until the carrier delivers the goods to the customer. In a consumer case, it seems likely that this would be taken to be the implied intention of the parties anyway.

(3) Reduced-price demonstration models bought by customers from Bumpa-store

The reduced-price demonstration models are specific goods. The first question is: What are the parties' intentions? Even though the parties may not have expressly agreed on when ownership is to pass, the court may well infer an intention that ownership is to pass on delivery to the customer.

The alternative is to invoke Rule 1 as this is an unconditional contract for specific goods in a deliverable state. In other words, ownership would pass at the moment the contract was made. This might seem like a good idea until it is realised that this may mean that the risk of accidental damage will pass to the customer at the same time (see **A1.6**). The court may prefer to infer the contrary intention mentioned above.

A1.5 RETENTION OF TITLE

It was suggested above that Supawave may wish to retain ownership of the demonstration models until they are paid for. Such a retention of title clause is expressly envisaged by s 19 of the SGA 1979 which provides that:

> 'Where there is a contract for the sale of specific goods or where goods are subsequently appropriated to the contract, the seller may ... reserve the right of disposal of the goods until certain conditions are fulfilled.'

If the seller does this, the ownership in the goods does not pass to the buyer until the relevant conditions are fulfilled. This is so, despite delivery to the buyer, or to a carrier or anyone else for the purpose of transporting them to the buyer. Of course, the most common condition which is imposed in a case like this is payment of the price for the goods.

A1.5.1 The *Romalpa* case

A retention of title clause was held to be valid in the case of *Aluminium Industrie Vaassen BV v Romalpa Aluminium* [1976] 2 All ER 552 (CA) where the sellers had reserved the title in aluminium foil until it had been paid for. Since that time, retention of title clauses have been known as *Romalpa* clauses.

In this case, the sellers had gone a couple of steps further than s 19 of SGA 1979. They had inserted a clause which stated that no title would pass until the buyers had paid for all goods supplied to them by the sellers. This is usually known as an 'all moneys' clause and is generally considered to be effective.

The sellers had also tried to stake a claim to the proceeds of sale of goods which had been sold on. The Court of Appeal allowed the sellers to 'trace' into the proceeds of sale on the grounds that there was a fiduciary relationship between the sellers and buyers. This argument, based on the idea that the buyers sold as agents for the sellers, is not without difficulty and its correctness has been doubted.

A1.5.2 Problems of enforcing a retention of title clause

(1) Right to recover the goods and enter premises

The idea of a *Romalpa* clause is that, if the buyer does not pay the seller and goes bust, the seller may reclaim the goods on the ground that they still belong to him. Therefore, it is important that the seller has the right to recover the goods and to enter the buyer's premises to do this. These rights should be written into the contract.

(2) Identifying the contract goods

If the buyer has bought the same type of goods from a variety of different sources, how can the seller tell which are the ones that he delivered? The seller will normally insert a clause in the contract requiring the buyer to store the goods separately but this can always be defeated by the buyer failing to carry out the instructions. The seller should therefore take all possible steps to ensure that his particular goods are identified in some way as belonging to him.

A1.5.3 How far can you go?

(1) Straight retention of title and 'all moneys' clauses

There seems little doubt that the basic *Romalpa* clause is effective provided that it makes it clear that the seller is reserving full legal title to the goods (an attempt to reserve 'equitable and beneficial ownership' will not be enough: see *Re Bond Worth Ltd* [1980] Ch 228).

The 'all moneys' clause seems to be accepted although there can be a problem where a seller makes consecutive deliveries of goods to the buyer and all the deliveries are stored together. If the buyer pays for all the goods delivered so that the retention of title clause ceases to operate in respect of those goods and then the buyer takes delivery of further goods, as yet unpaid for, it may be difficult to identify which of the goods are subject to retention of title and which are not.

(2) Tracing into the proceeds of sale

The sellers successfully traced into the proceeds of sale in the *Romalpa* case itself but subsequent attempts to do this have all failed. The courts have been unwilling to hold that there is a fiduciary relationship, preferring the more obvious interpretation that the buyer resells on his own account. It seems that even a very carefully worded clause will only create a charge (see *Compaq Computer Ltd v Abercorn Group Ltd* [1991] BCC 484) and this will usually be void for non-registration under the CA 1985 (see **18.7**).

(3) Trying to obtain ownership of mixed goods

Sometimes the goods are not resold but mixed with other goods, for example being physically bolted together with them (such as the components of an engine) or combined in a manufacturing process.

In the first case, a simple *Romalpa* clause should be perfectly effective, as long as the original product retains its identity and can be reasonably easily detached (see eg *Hendy Lennox Ltd v Graham Puttick Ltd* [1984] 1 WLR 485 where the sellers recovered diesel engines which were easily detached from the generating sets to which they had been attached).

In the second case, a normal retention of title clause may be ineffective, particularly if the original goods have lost their identity in the manufacturing process. Some sellers have tried to extend the *Romalpa* principle in order to obtain ownership rights over the finished product. Again, these attempts have been generally unsuccessful. (See the case of *Clough Mill Ltd v Martin* [1985] 1 WLR 111 for an interesting discussion of the practical problems involved.) The courts are prepared to accept retention of title clauses where the seller is retaining something which actually already belongs to him. They are not happy about the seller trying to assert ownership over something which he has never owned before. Such clauses are usually interpreted as charges over the buyer company's assets and therefore void for non-registration.

A1.5.4 The limitations of retention of title – s 25

A retention of title clause is generally only effective to protect the seller's rights while the buyer retains possession of the goods. Once the goods are sold, the advantage is lost. Usually the sale of goods contract will allow the buyer to resell the

Romalpa goods on to a customer and provide that ownership will pass to the buyer immediately before the resale.

Even if there is no such clause in the contract, the buyer will almost certainly be a 'buyer in possession' within s 25 of SGA 1979 and the sub-buyer will get good title (see **A1.3.2***(2)*). Section 25 may also apply to give a sub-buyer good title if the buyer goes into receivership or liquidation and the receiver or liquidator sells off the assets to pay the creditors.

A1.6 OWNERSHIP AND RISK

A1.6.1 The significance of risk

(1) Accidental damage

So far, we have been concentrating on ownership and the significance of when it passes to the buyer. However, the passing of ownership may also affect when the risk of the goods passes to the buyer. Risk becomes important when the goods are accidentally damaged (eg in transit). The party who bears the risk will bear the loss. If the buyer bears the risk of the journey, he cannot complain if the goods arrive damaged. If the seller bears the risk, he must either replace the goods or compensate the buyer. Commercial parties who have been properly advised will no doubt arrange appropriate insurance if they are to bear the risk in this way.

(2) Risk and breach of duty

These rules apply only to accidental damage or loss. They do not apply if the buyer is complaining of some inherent defect in the goods themselves, for example, that they are not of satisfactory quality or reasonably fit for the purpose which the buyer made clear (see **A5.3** and **A5.4**). These will be straightforward breaches of contract by the seller.

(3) Risk and bailment

A seller in possession of the goods will still have certain duties in respect of the goods even though the risk has passed to the buyer. This is because the seller is a voluntary bailee and therefore owes the buyer a duty to take reasonable care of the goods. Thus, if the goods are being transported to the buyer by a driver employed by the seller and the goods are damaged due to his negligent driving, the seller will be liable to the buyer for the damage.

In the same way, a buyer in possession of goods before risk has passed to him will be liable for damage to the goods caused by his failure to take reasonable care of them, as this is a breach of his duty as a voluntary bailee.

A1.6.2 Rules for ascertaining when risk passes

(1) Risk passes when the parties intend it to pass

The parties may expressly (or impliedly) agree that risk should pass at a particular time. If they do, their intention is conclusive.

(2) If no intention appears, risk usually passes with ownership

Section 20 of SGA 1979 provides that, as a general rule:

'the goods remain at the seller's risk until the property in them is transferred to the buyer, but when the property in them is transferred to the buyer the goods are at the buyer's risk whether delivery has been made or not.'

Risk therefore usually passes with ownership.

There are special rules where there is a delay due to the fault of one of the parties (s 20(2)) and where the goods suffer deterioration necessarily incident to the course of transit (s 33).

A1.6.3 Risk and frustration

The normal rules of frustration do not apply where the contract in question is an agreement to sell specific goods and the goods subsequently perish without fault on either side before the risk passes to the buyer (s 7 of SGA 1979 and the Law Reform (Frustrated Contracts) Act 1943).

A1.6.4 The above rules applied to the standard example

(1) Microwaves ordered by Bumpa-store from Supawave

It was decided above that, in the absence of any contrary intention, ownership in the above (both demonstration models and microwaves ordered to satisfy customer demand) passes to Bumpa-store when Supawave delivers the models to the independent contractor for transport to the store. If so, risk passes at the same time under s 20, unless the parties agree otherwise.

However, it was also suggested that Supawave may wish to retain title to the demonstration models until they are paid for, or at least until the store resells them. If so, risk will not pass until the resale and Supawave are responsible for any accidental damage which occurs during transit and also while the goods are in Bumpa-store's possession. For example, if the goods are damaged in a fire while they are in the shop waiting to be sold, Supawave cannot hold Bumpa-store responsible unless the fire is Bumpa-store's fault (in which case, Bumpa-store will be in breach of its duty as a voluntary bailee to take reasonable care of the goods). This is hardly satisfactory from Supawave's point of view, so they will almost certainly seek to provide in the contract that the risk will pass to the buyer on delivery to the carrier.

(2) Microwaves ordered by customers from Bumpa-store

It was suggested above that ownership will pass to the customers when Bumpa-store's driver delivers the goods to them. Risk presumably passes at the same time.

(3) Reduced-price demonstration models bought by customers from Bumpa-store

It was suggested at **A1.4.6** that the court may very well infer an intention that the ownership of these specific goods should pass on delivery. This is because a strict interpretation of s 18, Rule 1 may cause injustice. If ownership passes to the customer as soon as he agrees to buy the demonstration model in the shop then (according to s 20) the risk will pass at the same time. If the shop burns down before the microwave can be delivered, strictly speaking the customer bears the risk (unless Bumpa-store is to blame for the fire and therefore in breach of its duty as bailee to take reasonable care of the goods).

The same is true if there is accidental damage while the demonstration model is being delivered (unless that damage is caused by the negligence of the store or its driver).

The customer is very unlikely to have insured against any of these risks. On the other hand, Bumpa-store probably will have done so. As a result, the court may be willing to infer agreement that both property and risk pass when the goods are delivered and no earlier. It would be possible to decide that the parties intended ownership to pass at once and risk only to pass on delivery, but this way of giving the customer the best of both worlds is probably stretching the process of implication too far.

Part 2

PRICE AND PAYMENT

A2.1 INTRODUCTION

Part 2 contents
Introduction
Price
Payment
A seller's rights against the buyer
A seller's rights against the goods
The above principles applied to the standard example

This chapter will examine the SGA 1979 provisions relating to price and payment. It will consider:

(1) how the price is ascertained;
(2) when it has to be paid; and
(3) what the seller can do if the buyer fails to pay.

Section 27 states:

> 'It is the duty of the seller to deliver the goods, and of the buyer to accept and pay for them, in accordance with the terms of the contract of sale.'

Where the parties have not made the terms of the contract clear, SGA 1979 will imply certain provisions.

A2.2 PRICE

A2.2.1 Price agreed by the parties

Section 8(1) of SGA 1979 provides that:

> 'The price in a contract of sale may be fixed by the contract, or may be left to be fixed in a manner agreed by the contract, or may be determined by the course of dealing between the parties.'

Thus, the parties may agree the price:

(1) expressly (this will be the usual situation); or
(2) impliedly (eg the price may be inferred from a regular and consistent previous course of dealings between the seller and buyer).

The parties may leave the price to be fixed in a manner agreed by the contract, for example, by a third party's valuation (see s 9).

A2.2.2 No price agreed at all

It is very unusual for no price to be agreed at all. The absence of any agreement as to price may lead the court to decide that the parties have never got past the stage of negotiating (see, eg, *May and Butcher v R* [1934] 2 KB 17).

However, it may be quite clear that the parties have entered into a contract of sale of goods but yet have not decided on the price. In such a case, s 8(2) of SGA 1979 provides that the buyer must pay a reasonable price. What is a reasonable price is a question of fact depending on the circumstances of each particular case (s 8(3)).

A2.3 PAYMENT

A2.3.1 The general rule – cash on delivery

If the parties do not come to any specific agreement as to the time of payment, s 28 provides that 'delivery of the goods and payment of the price are concurrent conditions' that is, cash on delivery.

A2.3.2 The parties may agree otherwise

In practice, the parties will often make alternative arrangements. The seller may want to have all or some of the payment 'up front' in the form of a deposit or other pre-payment. The buyer may want some credit facility. It is very common for a seller to extend 'ordinary trade credit', perhaps allowing the buyer 30 days after delivery to pay for the goods. If so, the parties must obviously come to some clear agreement to vary the normal rule in s 28.

A2.4 A SELLER'S RIGHTS AGAINST THE BUYER

Where the buyer fails to pay the price on the due date, the seller may be able to:

(1) terminate the contract; or
(2) sue for the price (an 'action for an agreed sum').

In addition, the seller may be able to retain or recover possession of the goods and resell them. These are really rights against the goods themselves 'in rem' rather than rights against the buyer 'in personam' and will be considered in the next section.

In the following discussion, it is assumed that the buyer has no excuse for not paying, ie the price is due and the seller is not himself in breach of any of his obligations under the contract.

A2.4.1 Termination of the contract

To terminate, the seller will usually have to show that he has made the time for payment a strict condition of the contract, ie time of payment is 'of the essence'. This is because s 10(1) of SGA 1979 provides:

> 'Unless a different intention appears from the terms of the contract, stipulations as to time of payment are not of the essence of a contract of sale.'

Even if the seller has not made 'time of the essence' in the contract, he may be able to make it so by serving notice on the buyer, once the payment date has passed, requiring payment within a certain time. As long as this notice is reasonable, he may terminate if the buyer fails to pay by the specified date.

The seller will be able to terminate in two other circumstances:

(1) where the buyer's failure to pay amounts to a repudiation of the contract because the buyer is not merely saying 'I cannot pay on time' but 'I am never going to pay at all'; and
(2) where the buyer's delay is so long that the seller cannot be expected to wait any longer. Delay which robs the innocent party of substantially the whole benefit of the contract is sometimes known as 'frustrating delay'.

A2.4.2 An action for the price

Normally, ownership in the goods must have passed to the buyer before the seller can claim the price for them (s 49(1)). As usual, though, the parties can agree differently. If the price (or some of it) is due on a particular date, irrespective of whether the goods have been delivered or even appropriated to the contract, and the buyer fails to pay, the seller can claim the price (or part of it) whether ownership has passed or not (s 49(2)). In the meantime, the seller can retain the goods (see **A2.5.1**).

Even if the seller suffers extra loss due to late payment or non-payment, traditionally his loss is still taken to consist of the price and nothing else, although the court has awarded extra damages where the buyer had actual knowledge of the seller's potential loss (see *Wadsworth v Lydell* [1981] 1 WLR 598).

The court has a discretion to award interest where the claim is pursued to judgment provided a capital sum was owing at the date proceedings commenced (Administration of Justice Act 1982, s 15). However, the best solution for the seller is to provide expressly in the contract for the buyer to be liable for interest if the payment is late. The court has been known to imply such an agreement but nothing is as safe as a clear provision in the contract. However, care needs to be taken that the interest is not excessive since the provision may then be struck down as a penalty (see, eg, the discussion in *Lordsdale Finance plc v Bank of Zambia* [1996] 3 WLR 688). (Also now consider the Late Payment of Commercial Debts (Interest) Act 1998 discussed at **29.4.3**.)

A2.5 A SELLER'S RIGHTS AGAINST THE GOODS

In addition to personal rights against the buyer, the unpaid seller may have specific rights against the goods themselves (sometimes known as rights 'in rem', against the thing itself). This is particularly useful if the buyer is insolvent.

A seller will be an 'unpaid seller' when some or all of the price is still outstanding (s 38(1)). If all the price is paid, presumably the seller would not need these rights anyway.

There are three main rights and in exercising them the seller can usually ignore any sub-sale the buyer may have arranged unless the seller has assented to it expressly or impliedly (see s 47 for further exceptions).

A2.5.1 Right to retain the goods

Where the seller is still in possession of the goods, he can retain them until the price is paid. This right obviously does not apply if the seller has granted the buyer credit and the credit period has not yet expired (unless the buyer is insolvent (s 41(1)).

A2.5.2 Right to stop the goods in transit

If the buyer is insolvent, the seller may be able to recover the goods he has delivered to an independent carrier as long as they are still in transit (s 44). Sections 45 and 46 lay down detailed rules as to when transit ends and how stoppage is effected.

A2.5.3 The right to resell the goods

The seller may have provided himself with an express power in the sale contract entitling him to resell the goods in the event of non-payment. Even if there is no express power, s 48(3) of SGA 1979 gives the seller statutory powers to resell in two cases:

(1) where the goods are of 'a perishable nature'; and
(2) where the unpaid seller notifies the buyer of his intention to sell and the buyer does not pay or tender the price within a reasonable time.

Whether the seller resells under an express contractual power or under the statutory powers in SGA 1979, he may claim damages from the original buyer for any loss on the resale (eg where he cannot get such a good price or incurs extra expense) (s 48(3)).

A2.6 THE ABOVE PRINCIPLES APPLIED TO THE STANDARD EXAMPLE

A2.6.1 Price

Presumably the parties have expressly agreed on the price of the microwaves.

A2.6.2 Time for payment

The parties have altered the normal 'cash on delivery' rule in two ways:

(1) Supawave has allowed a credit period on the demonstration models – the price is not due until they are ultimately sold to customers;
(2) Supawave has stipulated a 10 per cent deposit on the general order models. The rest of the money is paid on delivery.

A2.6.3 Supawave's rights as an 'unpaid seller'

(1) Stage 1

(A) THE FACTS

Supawave is becoming concerned about Bumpa-store's financial position. Although Bumpa-store is not insolvent, it did not include the stipulated 10 per cent deposit with its latest order of general order models. In addition, Supawave has not received payment for several demonstration models which it believes Bumpa-store has sold on to customers.

Supawave is particularly worried as it has just despatched several consignments of demonstration and general order models by two lorries to various Bumpa-store shops and wonders if it will ever see the money. Another couple of consignments of demonstration models are waiting at the warehouse ready to be delivered to the independent carrier.

(B) ANALYSIS

(i) Models still at warehouse

Supawave need not despatch the general order models to Bumpa-store. Payment of the 10 per cent deposit is presumably a condition precedent to delivery. However, it cannot withhold delivery of the consignments of demonstration models still at the warehouse as it has granted Bumpa-store a credit period which has not expired.

(ii) Models already despatched

Supawave cannot stop these goods in transit as Bumpa-store is not insolvent.

(iii) Demonstration models sold by Bumpa-store to its customers

Supawave can sue Bumpa-store for the price of these goods.

(2) *Stage 2*

(A) THE FACTS

Supawave has now learnt that Bumpa-store is, in fact, insolvent.

(i) Demonstration models at warehouse

There are still two consignments of demonstration models ready for despatch at the warehouse.

(ii) Models already despatched

Supawave has tried to contact the carriers to recover the goods which have been despatched to Bumpa-store and has discovered that two of the consignments are still in transit but the rest have been delivered.

(B) ANALYSIS

(i) Demonstration models at warehouse

Supawave can withhold delivery of these models since the buyer is now insolvent.

(ii) Models already despatched

Supawave may stop and recover the two consignments which are still in transit. It is too late to recover the other consignments in this way (although Supawave may be able to recover some of them under retention of title clauses if relevant, see **A1.5**).

Part 3

DELIVERY

A3.1 INTRODUCTION

This chapter will examine the concept of delivery. It will consider:

(1) when and where delivery must take place;
(2) what the buyer can do if the seller does not deliver in accordance with the contract (and how far the seller can exclude his liability); and
(3) what the seller can do if the buyer wrongfully refuses to accept the goods.

A3.2 TIME AND PLACE OF DELIVERY

The seller has a duty to deliver the goods (SGA 1979, s 27) but delivery has a rather different meaning in SGA 1979 than in common speech. Section 61(1) defines it as:

> 'voluntary transfer of possession from one person to another.'

In other words, it does not necessarily involve the seller sending the goods. The buyer may have to collect them. This depends entirely on the parties' intentions. Section 29(1) provides:

> 'Whether it is for the buyer to take possession of the goods or for the seller to send them to the buyer is a question depending in each case on the contract, express or implied, between the parties.'

Usually the parties will express their intention in the contract but it may be inferred from the circumstances, for example by a regular and consistent course of dealings between them or a clear trade usage or custom which applies in their particular business. If an intention to send the goods can be found but no time is fixed for sending them, the seller must send the goods within a reasonable time (s 29(3)) and tender them at a reasonable hour (s 29(5)) or the buyer can refuse to accept them.

A3.2.1 Place of delivery agreed by the parties

There would appear to be two main options:

(1) the seller has to send the goods to the buyer either using his own driver or an independent carrier;
(2) the buyer has to collect the goods from the seller's premises or from the premises of a third party.

Where the seller is using an independent carrier to send the goods (whether nominated by the buyer or not), delivery to the carrier is treated as delivery to the buyer unless the parties agree otherwise (s 32(1)).

The seller must negotiate a reasonable contract with the carrier having regard to all the circumstances (in particular, the nature of the goods) and if the goods are lost or

Part 3 contents
Introduction
Time and place of delivery
Buyer's rights on incorrect delivery
Seller's rights on buyer's non-acceptance of the goods

damaged in transit as a result of the seller's failure to do this, the buyer may treat the goods as not delivered and sue for damages accordingly (s 32(2) and see **A3.3.1**).

A3.2.2 No agreement as to place of delivery

In the absence of anything express or implied in the contract:

(1) the place of delivery is the seller's place of business or, if none, his residence, except that
(2) where the goods are specific and both parties know at the contract date that they are in another place, the place of delivery is that other place (s 29(2)).

In other words, the buyer must collect the goods; there is no duty on the seller to send them. The buyer must collect at a reasonable hour

In the absence of express agreement, the buyer is under no obligation to accept delivery by instalments (s 31(1)). If the parties do agree on instalments to be separately paid for, the court may treat each delivery as a separate contract and this may affect the parties' rights and obligations on breach (see **A4.3.2**).

A3.2.3 Applied to the standard example

Supawave has agreed with Bumpa-store that it will send the goods to the buyer using an independent carrier. Unless they agree otherwise, delivery to the carrier is equivalent to delivery to the buyer. If no delivery date is specified, the goods must be sent within a reasonable time and tendered at a reasonable hour.

A3.3 BUYER'S RIGHTS ON INCORRECT DELIVERY

If the seller makes an incorrect delivery (whether he delivers the wrong quantity, late or not at all), the buyer may claim damages (as long as he has not waived the breach).

SGA 1979 attempts to codify the common law rules on damages. The measure of damages is usually the estimated loss directly and naturally resulting, in the ordinary course of events, from the seller's breach – a basic restatement of the first limb of *Hadley v Baxendale* (s 51(2), s 53(2)). Consequential loss coming within the second limb may also be claimed (s 54, which also allows the seller to recover money paid under a total failure of consideration).

A3.3.1 The seller delivers the wrong quantity

Section 30 of SGA 1979 contains detailed rules to cover this situation. Where the buyer does not 'deal as consumer' (see **28.4.2**), and the seller shows that the excess or shortfall is so slight that it would be unreasonable for the buyer to reject the goods, the buyer will have to accept the goods and claim damages for breach of warranty (s 30(2A) and (2B), as inserted by the SSGA 1994). Presumably, the buyer will not have to bring an action against the seller as he will obtain a perfectly adequate remedy by setting damages off against the price (reducing or extinguishing it) (s 53(1), (4)).

If the seller fails to prove this, the buyer may reject the goods and, where there is an 'available market' for the goods (ie the same or similar goods are readily available on the open market), he can prima facie claim the difference between the contract price of the goods and their market value at the date they should have been delivered (s 51(3)).

This rule envisages that the buyer will mitigate his loss by buying alternative goods on the market at a reasonable price but it is only a starting point and s 54 allows the buyer to claim other loss which is not too remote (eg reasonable expenses of buying elsewhere but usually not the loss of a sub-sale unless the seller knew about it at the time of the contract – *Williams v Agius* [1914] AC 510).

A3.3.2 The seller delivers late

If nothing is mentioned in the contract, time for delivery is usually 'of the essence' (ie a strict condition) of a commercial sale of goods contract (contrast time for payment – **A2.4.1**), so the buyer will normally have the option of rejecting the goods and claiming damages for non-delivery as in **A3.3.1** above. Even if time is not initially of the essence, it may become so by the buyer serving notice or by 'frustrating delay' (see **A2.4.1**).

Even if time of delivery is a strict condition, the buyer can always decide to treat it as a mere warranty and accept the goods (s 11(2)). Again, the buyer may avoid bringing an action against the seller for late delivery by setting any damages off against the price (see **A3.3.1**).

A3.3.3 The seller fails to deliver altogether

The buyer can obviously terminate the contract and claim damages for non-delivery in a case like this (see **A3.2.1**). Alternatively, he could keep the contract going by affirming it and hoping that the seller will deliver.

If the goods are specific and special in nature, the buyer may claim specific performance (or 'specific delivery' in this case – s 52) but this is discretionary and will be granted only if damages are an inadequate remedy, for example if the goods are not readily available elsewhere (see the case of *Cohen v Roche* [1927] 1 KB 169, where the judge refused to order specific delivery of a set of chairs as they were merely 'ordinary articles of commerce and of no special value or interest', even though the chairs were made by Hepplewhite!).

A3.3.4 How far can the seller exclude or restrict his liability?

Where the seller seeks to exclude or restrict the above liabilities by means of a clause in his 'written standard terms', this will be valid only insofar as it satisfies the requirement of reasonableness (UCTA 1977, s 3, see **28.4.3**). This will probably be the case even if the seller tries to get round the problem by stating that delivery dates are merely approximate or not legally binding, because of the provisions of s 3(2)(b) of UCTA 1977 (see **28.4.3(3)**).

A3.4 SELLER'S RIGHTS ON BUYER'S NON-ACCEPTANCE OF THE GOODS

The buyer has a duty to accept and pay for the goods (s 27). If he unjustifiably fails to do so (eg because he has found a cheaper source of supply or has refused late delivery when he is not entitled to do so), the seller may claim damages for non-acceptance (s 50(1)).

Where there is an 'available market' (ie the goods can be freely and readily resold), the starting point for damages is the difference between the contract price of the goods and their market price at the time when they should have been accepted (s 50(3) – compare s 51(3) at **A3.3.1**). In other words, the seller is expected to mitigate his loss by selling the goods to another buyer at a reasonable price. The seller can claim other loss which is not too remote (s 54).

Any attempt by the buyer to exclude or restrict liability for non-acceptance in his 'written standard terms' will be valid only insofar as it satisfies the requirement of reasonableness (UCTA 1977, s 3, see **28.4.3**).

Part 4

DESCRIPTION

A4.1 INTRODUCTION

This chapter will look at SGA 1979 implied term relating to description and what happens if the seller breaches it.

Part 4 contents
Introduction
The implied term relating to description
The buyer's rights if the seller defaults

A4.2 THE IMPLIED TERM RELATING TO DESCRIPTION

Section 13(1) of SGA 1979 provides that:

> 'Where there is a contract for the sale of goods by description, there is an implied condition that the goods will correspond with the description.'

A4.2.1 What is a sale by description?

A sale will be 'by description' where, in buying the goods, the buyer reasonably relies on the seller's description rather than on his own skill and judgement.

This occurs when the buyer has not seen the goods at the contract date (eg when he is buying goods in a distant warehouse identified by a generic description or through a mail-order catalogue) but may also apply where he has seen and examined the goods (see *Beale v Taylor* [1967] 1 WLR 1193 where the sale of a 'Herald, convertible, white, 1961' was held to be by description even though the buyer had looked at the car in question and failed to spot that it was the back half of a 1961 Herald welded onto the front of a much older model, since the buyer was not an expert and it was reasonable for him to rely on the seller's description).

Contrast the situation where the buyer is relying on his own knowledge (as in *Harlingdon & Leinster Enterprises Ltd v Christopher Hull Fine Art* [1990] 1 All ER 737, where the sale of a painting described by reference to a catalogue as being by the German artist, Munter, was held not to be by description since the buyer was an expert on German art and the seller was not).

A4.2.2 What is included in the description?

It is usually said that words of description are those which relate to the identity of the goods as opposed to their quality although this distinction is often difficult to draw. None the less, the courts have interpreted this concept widely to cover such things as the weight, measurements, volume and packaging of goods (see *Arcos Ltd v E A Ronaasen & Son* [1933] AC 470 and *Re an arbitration between Moore & Co Ltd and Landauer & Co* [1921] 2 KB 519).

A4.2.3 Must the goods correspond with their description exactly?

The above cases suggest that the goods must correspond precisely with the description applied to them. Microscopic deviations can be ignored but anything more allows the buyer to reject (even if his real reason for doing this is to get out of a bad bargain). In *Reardon Smith Line Ltd v Hansen Tangen* [1976] 3 All ER 570, Lord Wilberforce suggested that the courts might be prepared to take a more lenient line nowadays but the prudent seller can avoid the problem by making express provision in the contract for tolerance.

A4.2.4 What difference does it make if the goods are also sold by sample?

A contract will be by sample if the parties so agree (s 15(1)), either expressly, or by implication (eg by trade usage or custom, or through a regular and consistent previous course of dealing). Usually, it will be obvious, for example where a buyer wishes to buy a consignment of grain and the seller shows him a sample of the grain.

Three conditions are implied into sales by sample (s 15(2)):

(1) the bulk must correspond with the sample in quality (where the sale is by description, the goods must correspond with the description as well (s 13(2));
(2) the buyer must have a reasonable opportunity of comparing the bulk with the sample; and
(3) the goods must be free from any defect making their quality unsatisfactory (see **A5.3**), which would not be apparent on a reasonable examination of the sample.

A4.3 THE BUYER'S RIGHTS IF THE SELLER DEFAULTS

Since the implied term relating to description is a strict condition, the buyer may generally:

(1) reject the goods, terminate the contract and claim damages for non-delivery (s 52, see **A3.3.1**); or
(2) accept the goods, affirm the contract and claim damages for breach of warranty (s 11(2) and s 53, see **A3.3.2**).

There is a third alternative, ie to reject this delivery but affirm the contract, thereby leaving it open to the seller to make a correct delivery.

Where the buyer does not 'deal as consumer' (see **28.4.2**) and the seller can show that the breach is so slight that it would be unreasonable for the buyer to reject the goods, the buyer will have to treat the breach of condition as a breach of warranty and accept the goods (s 15A(1) and (3), as inserted by the SSGA 1994). This rule will not apply if the parties have expressed a contrary intention in the contract, or such an intention can be implied (s 15A(2)).

The buyer's rights will also depend to a certain extent on whether the contract is 'severable' or 'non-severable'. A 'severable' (or 'divisible') contract is one where goods are to be delivered in stated instalments and each instalment is to be separately paid for. We start by considering 'non-severable' (or 'indivisible') contracts.

A4.3.1 Non-severable contracts

(1) The effect of acceptance

The buyer may lose his right to reject all the goods and terminate the contract if he 'accepts' the goods or part of them (s 11(4)), although he will still be able to sue for damages. Where the contract is for the sale of goods making one or more 'commercial units', a buyer who accepts any goods included in such a unit will be taken to have accepted all the goods in the unit. A 'commercial unit' is defined as a unit, division of which would materially impair the value of the goods or the character of the unit (s 35(7), as inserted by the SSGA 1994). Section 11(4) is subject to the contrary agreement of the parties, so perhaps the buyer should seek to exclude it expressly in the contract.

The buyer may still have a right to reject part of the goods even though he may have lost his right to reject the whole lot. If he has a right to reject the goods by reason of a breach which means that some or all of them are not in conformity with the contract, but has accepted some of them, this will not stop him rejecting the rest (s 35A(1) and (4), inserted by the SSGA 1994) unless the parties have shown a contrary intention, expressly or by implication (s 35A(4)). The section is not free from difficulty – it seems to suggest that the buyer must have accepted all unaffected goods before he can reject the rest but it is not clear if this is the intention.

(2) When will acceptance take place?

The buyer will be deemed to have accepted the goods in three circumstances (s 35(1)).

(A) WHERE HE INTIMATES TO THE SELLER THAT HE HAS ACCEPTED THEM

Intimation can be express, implied or by conduct (eg by asking the seller to make alterations to the goods after delivery or even to repair them). The buyer can insist on the seller giving him a reasonable opportunity to examine the goods on delivery for the purpose of ascertaining whether they are in conformity with the contract and (where appropriate) of comparing the bulk with the sample unless the parties agree otherwise (s 34). The buyer will not be taken to have accepted the goods unless such an opportunity has been given (s 35(2), inserted by the SSGA 1994) and a buyer who 'deals as consumer' cannot agree to exclude this right (s 35(3)).

(B) WHERE AFTER DELIVERY OF THE GOODS THE BUYER DOES ANY ACT IN RELATION TO THE GOODS WHICH IS INCONSISTENT WITH THE SELLER'S OWNERSHIP

Again, there can be no acceptance until the buyer has had a reasonable opportunity of examining the goods (s 35(2)) and, again, a consumer cannot lose the protection of this subsection by agreement or waiver (s 35(3)).

Mere use of the goods does not seem to count as acceptance on its own – essentially the buyer must be unable to restore the goods to the seller in substantially the same condition as when they were received, perhaps because a third party now has rights over the goods (most of the cases relate to sub-sales) or because the buyer has done something to the goods physically (eg consumed them or built them into something else so that they lose their identity).

(C) WHEN HE RETAINS THE GOODS BEYOND A REASONABLE TIME WITHOUT INTIMATING REJECTION TO THE SELLER

What is a reasonable time is a question of fact to be decided from all the facts of the case (s 59). In deciding this, the court must consider whether the buyer has had a reasonable opportunity of examining the goods for the purposes mentioned in (A) above (s 35(5), inserted by the SSGA 1994).

As this is only one of the relevant questions, previous case-law will presumably still be relevant. This case-law makes it clear that in deciding whether a reasonable time has elapsed, particular consideration must be had to the nature of the goods. The time apparently starts running from the date of delivery and not from the date when the buyer discovers the defect or ought to have done so (contrast rescission for misrepresentation). All that the buyer is allowed is enough time to try out the goods in general terms. The buyer cannot expect to retain his right to reject long enough to find out every particular defect in the goods.

Under s 35(6) (as inserted by the SSGA 1994), a buyer will not be taken to have accepted goods merely because:

(1) he asks for, or agrees to, their repair by or under an arrangement with the seller; or
(2) because the goods are delivered to another person under a sub-sale or other disposition.

A4.3.2 Severable contracts

Where the goods are delivered by instalments and each instalment is separately paid for, there is no problem of acceptance. However, the question arises as to whether the delivery of one defective instalment entitles the buyer to reject all future instalments and terminate the contract or whether he must affirm the contract and merely claim damages for the instalment in question. Section 31(2) of SGA 1979 is unhelpful as it says this is 'a question in each case depending on the terms of the contract and the circumstances of the case'.

There will be no problem if the parties have made express provision in the contract (eg that the buyer cannot reject future instalments) or if some agreement can be inferred from a regular and consistent previous course of dealings. Fortunately, the courts have suggested certain factors to consider when it is impossible to discover the parties' intentions:

(1) the ratio which the breach bears quantitatively to the contract as a whole (see *Maple Flock Co Ltd v Universal Furniture Products (Wembley) Ltd* [1934] 1 KB 148);
(2) the degree of probability that the breach will be repeated (ibid); and
(3) how far the parties have proceeded in performing the contract (the more they have done, the less likely it is that the buyer can terminate; see *Cornwall v Henson* [1900] 2 Ch 298).

In the *Maple Flock* case, the Court of Appeal decided that one defective delivery of rag flock out of twenty did not justify the buyer terminating the whole contract.

Where the buyer accepts part of an instalment, he may still be able to reject the rest (s 54A(2), and see **A4.3.1** above).

A4.3.3 How far can the seller exclude or restrict his liability for breach of s 13?

Section 6(2) of UCTA 1977 prevents a seller from excluding or limiting his liability for breach of s 13 as against a buyer who 'deals as consumer'. In other cases, an exclusion clause will be effective only insofar as it satisfies the requirement of reasonableness (UCTA 1977, s 6(3) (see **28.4.3**)).

A4.3.4 Applied to the standard example

Supawave delivers a consignment of general order microwaves to Bumpa-store and Bumpa-store discovers that they are a different model from the ones which were ordered. Assuming that the seller cannot show that the breach is so slight that it would be unreasonable to reject the goods, Bumpa-store can:

(1) reject the goods, terminate the contract for breach of s 13 and sue for damages for non-delivery; or
(2) reject the goods but leave the contract open for Bumpa-store to deliver the correct models and sue for damages for any resulting loss; or
(3) accept the goods and claim damages for breach of warranty.

Bumpa-store may go for option (3) if it thinks it can resell these particular models easily (although it may then have problems satisfying existing customer orders for the other model). It will probably go for option (2) (particularly if it can only sell the models delivered for less than those originally ordered), rather than accept the goods and sue Supawave for the difference in price.

Bumpa-store may lose the right to reject the goods if it accepts them (eg by signing a delivery note after having had a reasonable opportunity to examine the goods or by keeping them beyond a reasonable time without notifying its intention to reject them). In that case, Bumpa-store can still sue Supawave for breach of warranty. If Bumpa-store accepts some of the microwaves, it may still be able to reject the remainder (unless the parties have agreed otherwise).

Part 5

QUALITY

A5.1 INTRODUCTION

This final chapter on sale of goods looks at what terms the SGA 1979 implies in respect of the quality of the goods and what rights the buyer has if the seller breaches them.

The starting point is s 14(1):

> 'Except as provided by this section and section 15 below [sales by sample] and subject to any other enactment, there is no implied term about the quality or fitness for any particular purpose of goods supplied under a contract of sale.'

In other words, 'caveat emptor' – let the buyer beware!

However, where there is a sale in the course of a business, s 14 provides two substantial exceptions to the general rule:

(1) the goods supplied under the contract must generally be of satisfactory quality (s 14(2)); and
(2) where the buyer makes his purpose for the goods known to the seller either expressly or by implication, the goods supplied under the contract must generally be reasonably fit for that particular purpose (s 14(3)).

Part 5 contents
Introduction
Common features of the two conditions
Satisfactory quality
Reasonable fitness for the buyer's particular purpose
The buyer's rights on the seller's breach

A5.2 COMMON FEATURES OF THE TWO CONDITIONS

A5.2.1 Strict liability

Both conditions in s 14 impose strict liability on the seller. It is no excuse for the seller to say, 'This defect is not my fault. The goods were defective when I received them from the manufacturer'. The buyer may still claim breach of s 14(2) or (3), leaving the seller to pursue a claim for indemnity from the manufacturer.

A5.2.2 Both conditions apply to 'goods supplied under the contract'

The courts have construed the phrase 'goods supplied under the contract' very widely. Thus, it includes any container in which the goods are supplied.

The goods must be looked at as a whole and if some foreign body has found its way into the rest of the goods rendering them dangerous then it is no defence to say that the goods themselves are satisfactory or reasonably fit for the purpose (see *Wilson v Rickett, Cockerell & Co Ltd* [1954] 1 QB 598).

Instructions supplied with the goods will be part of the 'goods supplied' (*Wormell v RHM Agriculture (East) Ltd* [1986] 1 WLR 336). Also note the interesting discussion in Sir Ian Glidewell's judgment in *St Albans DC v ICL* [1996] 4 All ER 481 as to how a defective computer program (not itself goods) can render the disk which carries it (which is goods) of unsatisfactory quality.

A5.2.3 There must be a sale 'in the course of a business'

Neither condition will be implied if the seller is selling privately. So, if Sam sells his car privately through an advertisement in the local paper and Bernadette buys it, she will not be able to claim the benefit of either condition. If the car is defective, she will be able to allege breach of contract only if Sam has made some express promise about its quality.

(1) What is a sale 'in the course of a business'?

In most cases, it will be easy to spot when a sale is 'in the course of a business'. Bill goes into a high street store and buys a hi-fi. The shop is in the business of supplying hi-fi. It is a sale 'in the course of a business'. Similarly, when Supawave sells a load of microwaves to Bumpa-store, this is a sale 'in the course of a business' since Supawave are in the business of making and selling microwaves. Note that there is still a sale 'in the course of a business' when the buyer is acting in the course of a business. There is no requirement that the buyer should be 'dealing as consumer' (see **28.4.2**).

Do the conditions apply if the seller, although acting in the course of a business, is not in the business of selling those particular goods? For example, if a firm of solicitors sells off its old typewriters, does the fact that selling typewriters is not the main object of the solicitor's business mean that the sale is not 'in the course of a business'? The general view is that this is still a sale 'in the course of a business'; the section does not limit the concept to sales of goods which it is the seller's business to sell.

(2) Special cases

There are special rules where the person selling the goods is acting as an agent for a private seller (s 14(5)).

Alternatively, a seller in the course of a business may be tempted to pretend that he is a private seller in order to mislead the buyer into thinking that s 14 does not apply to the sale. This is a criminal offence (the Business Advertisements (Disclosure) Order 1977, SI 1977/1918).

A5.3 SATISFACTORY QUALITY

As mentioned at the beginning of the chapter, where there is a sale in the course of a business, s 14(2) implies a condition that the goods supplied are of satisfactory quality. Until the SSGA 1994 came into force on 3 January 1995, the section required the goods to be of 'merchantable quality' but the law was changed at the recommendation of the Law Commission. Of course, this means that most of the case-law is based on the old concept, but many of the previous decisions will still be relevant in interpreting the new test.

The condition does not extend to any matter making the quality of goods unsatisfactory:

'(a) which is specifically drawn to the buyer's attention before the contract is made;

(b) where the buyer examines the goods before the contract is made, which that examination ought to reveal; or

(c) in the case of a contract for sale by sample, which would have been apparent on a reasonable examination of the sample' (s 14(2C), inserted by SSGA 1994).

Note that exception (b) applies only if the buyer actually examines the goods and then only to those defects which that actual examination ought to have revealed. If the buyer only makes a cursory examination, then only defects which a cursory examination ought to reveal will be excluded from the condition of satisfactory quality. It may still be hazardous for a buyer to examine the goods, particularly if he does not really know what he is looking for! It is not entirely clear what level of expertise the buyer will be credited with.

The rest of this section looks more carefully at what 'satisfactory quality' actually means.

A5.3.1 The statutory definition of satisfactory quality

Section 14(2A) (inserted by SSGA 1994) states that goods are of satisfactory quality:

> 'if they meet the standard that a reasonable person would regard as satisfactory taking account of any description of the goods, the price (if relevant) and all the other relevant circumstances.'

Section 14(2B) goes on to say that the quality of goods includes their state and condition and then gives a list of some relevant aspects of the quality of goods. These are:

(a) fitness for all the purposes for which goods of the kind in question are commonly supplied;
(b) appearance and finish;
(c) freedom from minor defects;
(d) safety; and
(e) durability.

Let us consider these factors in more detail.

A5.3.2 Description and price

Section 14(2A) mentions description and price specifically as factors to be taken into account in assessing satisfactory quality. Obviously, the more the goods cost, the better the quality which the buyer can expect.

(1) Second-hand goods

It is difficult to lay down a general rule about what constitutes satisfactory quality in the case of second-hand goods. If the seller describes a second-hand car as 'nearly new condition' and sells it for £10,000, the buyer can expect a much higher standard than if he buys a second-hand car for £50 which is described as 'good for parts only'.

(2) Sale goods

The reduction in the price of sale goods will usually be ignored in deciding satisfactory quality, unless they are specifically described as 'shop-soiled' or 'seconds' or something similar. Thus, the customers who buy demonstration models at sale prices from Bumpa-store can expect as good a quality as if they had paid the full price.

A5.3.3 The section 14(2B) factors

(1) Cosmetic defects

Merchantable quality was criticised for being too functional a test, based as it was on fitness for purpose. Although fitness for purpose is still important, the new test makes it clear that cosmetic defects are relevant (although the courts had already been moving in that direction in their interpretation of the old test in cases such as *Rogers and Another v Parish (Scarborough) Ltd* [1987] 2 WLR 353, where Mustill LJ suggested that merchantable quality, when applied to a passenger vehicle, would not just include the buyer's purpose of driving the car from one place to another but 'of doing so with the appropriate degree of comfort, ease of handling and reliability and, one might add, of pride in the vehicle's outward and interior appearance').

Suppose that Supawave delivers a consignment of microwaves to Bumpa-store and, although the microwaves work, the finish on them is poor, or a seller delivers a car to the buyer and the bodywork is scratched and the upholstery uncomfortable. The goods are clearly not of 'satisfactory quality'.

(2) Fitness for all the common purposes

The new definition makes it clear that the goods should be fit for all the common purposes, not just one. This reverses the decision in *Aswan Engineering Establishment Co v Lupdine Ltd* [1987] 1 WLR 1.

(3) What if defects can easily be put right?

The courts have generally rejected the argument that goods are of satisfactory quality if defects in them can easily be put right. This approach has now been confirmed by the reference to freedom from minor defects in s 14(2B).

(4) What if the goods can be easily rendered satisfactory by the buyer?

Sometimes, goods may not be satisfactory on delivery but could be rendered so very easily. There seems no reason why the old cases on merchantable quality should not be followed on this point. If so, the seller will still have no defence unless both parties anticipated that this would be done. Contrast *Heil v Hedges* [1951] 1 TLR 512, and *Grant v Australian Knitting Mills* [1936] AC 85.

A5.3.4 For how long must goods remain satisfactory?

Unlike under the old test, durability is specifically mentioned in s 14(2B). Presumably, the courts will still tend to look for guidance by analogy to the decision of the House of Lords in *Lambert v Lewis* [1982] AC 225 where their Lordships suggested that the implied condition in s 14(3) was a continuing one and that the goods must remain fit for a reasonable time after delivery. What is a reasonable time will depend on the circumstances and particularly on the nature of the goods.

A5.4 REASONABLE FITNESS FOR THE BUYER'S PARTICULAR PURPOSE

Where the buyer wants to use goods for a particular purpose, it may be as well for him to specify what this is, since the provisions of s 14(2) may not give the buyer sufficient protection. The buyer can make his purpose known:

(1) expressly (obviously the best way); or
(2) impliedly (eg by a regular and consistent previous course of dealing or by the usage of the particular trade (see s 14(4)).

Where the goods are single purpose goods, the particular purpose will be implied. There is no need for the buyer of a hot water bottle to tell the seller what he is going to use it for. In a case like this, there is an overlap between s 14(2) and (3).

No condition will be implied under s 14(3):

> 'where the circumstances show that the buyer does not rely, or that it is unreasonable for him to rely, on the skill or judgment of the seller ...'

So if the buyer clearly shows that he is relying on his own skill and judgement in buying the goods, he cannot complain if they are not reasonably fit for his particular purpose. The same is true if the buyer is more expert than the seller as it would then be unreasonable for the former to rely on the latter's skill and judgement.

A5.5 THE BUYER'S RIGHTS ON THE SELLER'S BREACH

Since s 14(2) and (3) imply strict conditions into the contract, breach of either will generally allow the buyer to reject the goods, terminate the contract and claim damages unless he does not 'deal as a consumer' (see **28.4.2**) and the seller can show that the breach is so slight that it would be unreasonable for the buyer to reject the goods (see **A3.3.1**). Basically, all the same points apply as with breach of s 13 (the buyer's choice, the problem of acceptance, the measure of damages etc (see **A4.3**)).

A5.5.1 Damages for breach of warranty of quality

Where the buyer chooses, or is forced, to accept the goods and claim damages for breach of warranty, s 53(3) lays down a prima facie rule for the measure of damages where the breach relates to quality:

> 'such loss is prima facie the difference between the value of the goods at the time of delivery to the buyer and the value they would have had if they had fulfilled the warranty.'

This is only a starting point for the damages and the court may apply a different basis of assessment if appropriate. For instance, in the case of *Bence Graphics International Ltd v Fasson UK Ltd* [1997] 3 WLR 205, the Court of Appeal held that, where both seller and buyer had contemplated a subsale, and the buyer had successfully sold the defective products on, it was appropriate to substitute the compensation that the buyer had actually had to pay to the sub-buyer.

A5.5.2 How far can the seller exclude or restrict liability for breach of s 14(2) or (3)?

As with s 13, s 6(2) of UCTA 1977 prevents a seller from excluding or limiting his liability for breach of s 14(2) or (3) as against a buyer who 'deals as consumer'. In other cases, an exclusion clause will only be effective insofar as it satisfies the requirement of reasonableness (UCTA 1977, s 6(3)).

A5.5.3 Applied to the standard example

Suppose that Supawave delivers a consignment of microwaves to Bumpa-store and Bumpa-store discovers that on some of the models the outside of the microwave is badly scratched. Bumpa-store's customers may justifiably protest if they are supplied with microwaves in this condition.

Assuming that the seller cannot show the breach is so slight that it would be unreasonable to reject the goods, Bumpa-store can:

(1) reject the goods for breach of s 14(2) and (3), terminate the contract and claim damages for non-delivery; or
(2) reject the goods, keep the contract open and sue for damages for any loss; or
(3) decide to keep the goods and sell them off at a discount (in other words, Bumpa-store can treat the breach of condition as a breach of warranty and claim damages, presumably the difference between the price it can charge its customers for perfect microwaves and the price it can charge for scratched ones).

If Bumpa-store accepts some of the goods, it may still be able to reject the rest under s 35(A) (see **A4.3.1**).

Appendix 2

SUMMARY SECTION OF THE CONSULTATION PAPER ON CHANGES ON COMPANY LAW

Issued by
The Department of Trade and Industry
March 2000

This paper is included to indicate to readers the areas of company law which are likely to change over the next couple of years or so, if the government accepts the suggestions. This appendix does **not** form part of the LPC course on Business Law and Practice.

Modern Company Law – For a Competitive Economy

Developing the Framework
A Consultation document from the Company Law Review Steering Group
March 2000

Executive Summary

Introduction

1   This is the second strategic consultation document issued by the Steering Group of the Company Law Review. The first, issued in February 1999 (*Strategic Framework Consultation Document*) set out the terms of reference and the principles on which the Review was to be based, and analysed and made proposals on a number of areas for initial consultation. That was followed by three more detailed documents in October 1999 on company general meetings and shareholder communication, formation and capital maintenance, and oversea companies.

2   This document analyses and makes proposals on the key areas of 'governance' of companies (ie the main rules governing their operation and control, including transparency rules) and on small and private companies. Responses are sought by 15 June on small and private companies and 28 July on the remainder.

3   Readers wishing to gain an overview of our approach and key proposals may like to focus on Chapter 2 (on governance) and Chapter 6 (on small and private companies). These two Chapters set the scene for the proposals which are set out in more detail in subsequent Chapters.

4   Readers who wish to take the subject one stage further without the need to assimilate all the detail might then like to read the sections on directors' duties (paragraphs 3.37 to 3.73); the reporting requirements for public and very large private companies (paragraphs 5.20 to 5.35 and 5.74 to 5.92); the summary of proposals for private companies (paragraphs 7.3 to 7.5); the 'default' regime for private companies (paragraphs 7.86 to 7.94); and the outline of the proposed accounting regime for small companies (paragraphs 8.18 to 8.31).

5   To guide readers through the document, the executive summary indicates where to find more information on each of the main proposals. These cross-references are not exhaustive. Rather they direct the reader to the main features of the proposals likely to be of most widespread interest. We hope that they will assist readers to identify where topics of particular interest to them are addressed in the document.

6   We would strongly encourage those readers with an interest or expertise in particular areas addressed in this document to respond on these issues without feeling constrained to answer the consultation questions on other topics.

Corporate Governance: Overview (Chapter 2)

7   We address first the 'scope' issue – 'in whose interests should companies be run?' We argue that the overall objective of wealth generation and competitiveness for the benefit of all can best be achieved through the twin components of:

- an 'inclusive' approach to directors' duties which requires directors to have regard to all the relationships on which the company depends and to the long, as well as the short, term implications of their actions, with a view to achieving company success for the benefit of shareholders as a whole; and

- wider public accountability: this is to be achieved principally through improved company reporting, which for public and very large private companies will require the publication of a broad operating and financial review which explains the company's performance, strategy and relationships (eg with employees, customer and suppliers as well as the wider community).

Directors (Chapter 3)

8   This Chapter:

- puts forward a legislative restatement of directors' duties in high level principles; it includes an 'inclusive' duty of compliance and loyalty and an objective duty of care, skill and diligence (see paragraphs 3.37 to 3.73);

- proposes amendments to Part X of the Act, on conflicted transactions by directors (paragraphs 3.86 to 3.89 and Annex C);

- examines the detailed rules on directors and their relationships with the company, including liability to third parties (paragraphs 3.92 to 3.104) and training, qualifications and terms and conditions (paragraphs 3.105 to 3.111);

- examines – primarily in the context of listed companies – the role of non-executive directors; and raises various issues on the function and content of the Combined Code on Corporate Governance (paragraphs 3.132 to 3.153);

- assesses economic evidence on the functioning of the governance system and the corporate control and capital markets (paragraphs 3.126 to 3.128 and 3.154 to 3.168).

Shareholder (Chapter 4)

9   We examine the role of shareholders in company governance. We make proposals for:

- strengthening the relationship between companies and beneficial holders of shares who are not registered as members (paragraphs 4.7 to 4.18);

- improvements in rules on notice, timing, agendas, voting and resolutions for general meetings; we conclude that to permit public companies to dispense with annual general meetings would be premature, but suggest there should be provision to relieve them of this requirement, where developing technology offers alternative mechanisms with comparable safeguards (paragraphs 4.24 to 4.64);

- reform of the remedies available to minority shareholders, including reform of the personal rights of shareholders under the company constitution, of section 459 (the 'unfair prejudice' remedy), and of the law on actions brought by shareholders on behalf of the company ('derivative actions') (paragraphs 4.65 to 4.139).

Reporting and Accounting for Large Companies (Chapter 5)

10 The proposed new accounting framework for listed and other large companies is summarised in paragraphs 5.21 to 5.35.

11 We propose that for listed companies the preliminary statement of results should become a statutory document distributed to all shareholders and published on a company website. The full report would then be filed within 90 days of the year end and published on the web. It would be available to shareholders on request. We invite views on whether listed companies should have the option of sending Summary Financial Statements to shareholders in place of the preliminary statement.

12 We propose that all the rules on the form and content of accounts and reports, including the statutory preliminary statement, should be delegated to an appropriate rule making body, reserving for legislation only the overall framework, essentially prescribing the documents to be provided, their purpose and the time limits for filing and laying before the General Meeting (paragraphs 5.40 to 5.73).

13 Under our proposals, public and very large private companies would include in their full annual report a new statutory operating and financial review, which would enable the user to assess the performance and prospects of the business, including its wider relationships (eg with employees and suppliers), its reputation and its impact on the community and the environment. The content of the review would be partly prescribed by statute, with the detailed requirements being laid down in standards. The directors' report would be replaced for large companies partly by the operating and financial review and partly by a supplementary statement, and for small ones by a cover sheet to the accounts. The statement or cover sheet would contain any public interest disclosures prescribed by the Secretary of State. (See paragraphs 5.74 to 5.92.)

14 We propose that both the scope of audit and the range of auditors' liability should be widened. This would be balanced by a removal of the bar on auditors agreeing a limit on their liability with the company and clarification of the law on contributory fault by companies (paragraphs 5.129 to 5.168).

Small and Private Companies: Introduction (Chapter 6)

15 Our approach here is based on principles set out in the *Strategic Framework Consultation Document*: that legislation should provide a coherent, self-contained statement of the law for the small and private company to which more detailed provisions could be added for larger and public companies ('think small first'); and that this should form part of the overall framework of the Act, thereby avoiding the legislative constraints and unexpected traps which might otherwise arise when a company ceased to be eligible for small company treatment (the 'integrated approach'). The emphasis is on simplifying the law for all private companies where possible. Within this overall simplified framework we then propose a set of provisions specially suited to the needs of small companies. The latter regime is to be the norm: ie it will apply to all private companies unless they positively opt out. While designed for smaller companies it will not be formally restricted to them: by avoiding rigid eligibility thresholds we aim also to avoid the consequent traps and inhibitions to growth.

Proposed Simplifications for the Private Company (Chapter 7)

16 We examine proposals for simplifying the law for private companies generally, by shortening minimum notice periods for meetings, allowing companies to relax the requirements for resolutions in writing, further simplifying the capital maintenance rules, relaxing the restrictions on the powers of directors to issue shares, removing the requirement to have a company secretary, making provision for arbitration of shareholder disputes and simplifying the model constitution (Table A). (See the summary in paragraphs 7.3 to 7.5.)

17 To this would be added a regime designed for small companies, which would apply automatically on formation unless excluded. This would include the existing 'elective' regime which currently enables private companies to opt out of certain requirements relating to meetings, but requires a specific decision to do so. There would also be more flexible provisions on notice of meetings, the appointment of auditors and written resolutions. (See paragraphs 7.86 to 7.94.)

18 We then consider whether the law can be simplified for 'owner-managed' companies (ie companies where the owners and directors are the same people) for whom a distinction between board and general meeting is arguably superfluous. Three options are considered: conferring the powers of the general meeting on the board, conferring the powers of the board on the general meeting, and relaxing the rules on general meetings for owner-managed companies so as to enable general meetings to take place as if they were board meetings. All three models have both benefits and drawbacks. We invite views on whether any of them would provide net advantages over the simplified regime we propose for all companies. (See the summary in paragraphs 7.95 to 7.107.)

Reporting and Accounting for Small Companies (Chapter 8)

19 We propose a simpler form of report and accounts, to be prepared and filed by small companies (ie those satisfying 2 of the following: turnover of less than £4.8 million; gross assets of less than £2.4 million; fewer than 50 employees). We suggest that the distinction between accounts prepared for shareholders and those filed at Companies House should be abolished: the abbreviated accounts presently filed by some companies save no costs and provide inadequate information for users. The accounts should be filed within 7 months of the year end (rather than 10 months as at present). The separate category of medium sized companies would be abolished. We propose exemption from audit for companies which satisfy 2 of the following: turnover of less than £1 million; gross assets of less than £500,000; fewer than 25 employees. A new form of independent assurance, substantially short of audit is proposed ('independent professional review') for small companies above this threshold. (See paragraphs 8.18 to 8.31 for a summary of the small company accounting framework, and paragraphs 8.41 to 8.48 for the proposals on audit.)

Alternative Vehicles and Access to Limited Liability (Chapter 9)

20 No change is proposed in the law on companies limited by guarantee. We suggest that charitable companies should have a separate form of incorporation, overseen by the Charity Commission (see paragraphs 9.14 to 9.22). We suggest that this regime should not extend to other not-for-profit companies, whether formed for a public purpose or not. We invite views on whether the new regime for charitable companies should be mandatory, so that new and existing charitable companies would be required to register, or reregister, under the new regime and be excluded

from registration under the Act. Following an examination of other legislative vehicles available to businesses we suggest that there is no case for adding to them. We oppose the introduction of new barriers to formation of limited companies, believing that the risks are better regulated in other ways, including transparency requirements and insolvency law (see paragraphs 9.61 to 9.71).

Registration and Information Provision (Chapter 10)

21   We examine the requirements for companies to disclose information, whether by maintaining and granting access to their own registers and records or by filing information at Companies House. We suggest some reform of the register of members, its maintenance and structure, access to that register by members and others and the use which may be made of the information it contains (paragraphs 10.11 to 10.24). We propose some other small changes to the maintenance of certain company records, and disclosure of company ownership and officers at Companies House. We examine the requirement for the registrar to publish certain information in the national gazette and propose a limited power for the registrar to rectify the public register.

22   We invite views on whether further regulation is needed to control company names which are misleading or registered for an improper purpose (paragraphs 10.77 to 10.89). We put forward proposals to simplify procedures for restoring dissolved companies to the register (including an administrative process which would remove the need to go to court in some cases) and to reduce the risks of inadvertent striking off (see paragraphs 10.90 to 10.135).

Research and Information (Chapter 11)

23   We summarise the research and information gathering work which we have undertaken so far.

Way forward (Chapter 12)

24   We set our plans for the remainder of the Review. These include working groups to consider Boundaries, Sanctions, Groups, Reconstructions and the Transitional Regime; and working parties to complete the work on more minor issues and on aspects which have already been well progressed. We plan a further major consultation document in November 2000, leading to our final report in Spring 2001.

© Crown Copyright
Reproduced with permission of the Controller of HMSO.

INDEX

References are to paragraph. Prefix A refers to paragraph numbers in Appendix 1 materials

Accommodation 21.3.3
Accounting for profits 13.10.1
Accounts 16.1–16.5
   abbreviated 16.2
   accounting reference date 10.6.7
   auditors 15.1
   balance sheet 16.4
   board of meetings 10.6.7
   contents of 13.11.3
   corporation tax 21.2.6
   directors 13.11.3, 16.5
   dividends 17.4
   filing, requirement to file 16.2
   formation of companies 10.7
   management 16.5
   profit and loss 3.2, 16.1, 16.3
   resolutions 12.5.6
   shareholders 12.5.6–12.5.7
   sole traders 3.2
   standards 16.2
   starting up businesses 2.3
   taxation 2.3
   time-limit 16.2
   true and fair view 15.1
Administration orders 24.9.3, 24.10.1
Administrative receivers 24.9.3, 24.9.4, 24.10.1
Advertisements of liquidation 24.3.2, 24.4.3
Agency 32.1–32.6
   agreements 31.2, 32.1–32.6
      competition 34.8.1, 34.9.1
      form of 32.1.3
      marketing 33.1, 33.2.4, 33.3.1, 33.3–33.6
   authority 31.1.3
      actual 20.2.2, 20.3.2, 32.2.3
      apparent 20.2.2, 32.3.2
      breach of warranty of 20.4.2
      exceeding 20.3.2
      express 32.2.3
      implied 32.2.3
      ostensible 32.3.2
      usual 32.3.2
      without actual 32.3
   commercial 33.3.3
   company secretaries 20.2.2
   competition 34.8.1, 34.9.1
   contractual 32.1.2, 32.2, 32.4
   definitions 32.2.1
   del credere 31.2.3
   directors 20.2.2, 20.3.2
   effect of 32.2.2
   examples 32.1
   express 32.1.1
   holding out 32.3.2
   implied 32.1.1
   liability 20.2, 20.3.2, 20.4.2, 32.2.2, 32.3.1
   marketing 31.2.2
   non-contractual 32.1.2
   objects clause 20.2
   partnerships 7.2.2
   payments 32.5
   ratification 32.3.3
      conditions for 32.3.3
      effect of 32.3.3
   sales 31.2.1
   taxation 33.4
   termination 32.6
      operation of law, by 32.6.2
      parties, by 32.6.1
   third parties 32.3.1, 32.3.2
   undisclosed principals 32.4
Agreements, *see also* Contracts, Drafting commercial agreements
   agency 31.2, 32.1–32.6, 34.4, 34.5.7
   commercial 34.4, 34.9
   competition 34.4, 34.5.7
      agency 34.8.2, 34.9.1
      commercial 34.4, 34.9
      distribution 31.3.4, 33.5, 34.9.2
      drafting 34.4.2
      horizontal 34.4.1
      infringements 34.8.5
      minor importance 34.8.3–34.8.4
      notification to Commission 34.8.9
      undertakings 34.5.4
      vertical 34.4.1–34.4.2
   distribution 31.3, 31.3.4, 33.5, 34.9.2
   drafting 34.4.2
   franchising 31.4.2
   horizontal 34.4.1
   joint venture 31.4.3
   licensing 31.4.1
   marketing 31.4, 33.1
   minor importance 34.8.3–34.8.3
   novation 7.3.5
   partnerships 4.2.1, 4.3, 5.1–5.18, 6.4
      conversion 27.2.1
      dissolution of 8.2–8.2.1, 8.2.6, 8.3.1–8.3.2
   shareholders 10.8
   undertakings 34.5.4
   vertical 34.4.1–34.4.2
Agricultural property relief 22.4.3. 25.9.1
AIM (Alternative Investment Market) 1.5.1

All monies clause A1.5.3
Alternative Investment Market 1.5.1
Annual general meetings 12.4
    agenda for 12.5.12, 12.7.1
    auditors 15.2
    checklist 12.8.2, 12.8.4
    directors 12.4.1, 12.4.3, 12.5.7, 13.15.1–13.15.2
    minority shareholders 12.7.1, 12.7.3
    minutes 12.5.8
    notice 12.4.1, 12.4.4, 12.5.2, 12.7.3
    power to call 12.4.3
    resolutions 12.4.4, 12.4.7–12.4.9, 12.4.14–12.4.16
    shareholders 12.4.1, 12.4.4, 12.5.2, 12.5.7–12.5.8, 12.5.12–12.5.14
        minority 12.7.1
Annual returns 13.11.4
Approval, goods on A1.4.4
Arbitration 5.18
Articles of association
    chairman 13.2.3
    change of 11.4.3, 12.6.2
    constitution of companies 10.2.2, 10.2.3, 10.5, 10.8.1, 11.1, 11.3, 11.4.3
    contractual status 11.3.1
    directors 11.3.3, 13.10.1
        delegation 13.8.1
        disqualification of 13.14
        removal of, prevention of 11.3.3
    formation of companies 10.2.2, 10.2.3, 10.5
    minority shareholders 12.6.2
    shareholders 12.6.2
        agreements 10.8.1
    shares
        allotment 11.3.3
        transfer, restrictions on 11.3.3
    special 11.3.3
    specimen 11.3.2
    Table A 11.3.2–11.3.3
Assets
    balance sheets 16.4
    bankruptcy 23.3.
    business property relief 25.9.2
    capital gains 21.2.4
    capital gains tax 22.3.2, 22.4.1, 25.7.1, 27.3.3
    charging orders 8.2.3
    conversion 27.2.1, 27.3.2–27.3.3
    corporation tax 21.2.4
    converting the form of an expanding business, 27.2.1, 27.3.2–27.3.3
    disposal of businesses 22.2.1–22.2.3, 22.3.2
    distribution of 23.3.5, 24.6
    fixed charges 18.4.3
    goodwill 22.2.1
    increasing 24.8
    inheritance tax 22.3.2

    liquidation 24.5, 24.8
    ownership of 5.9
    partnerships 5.7, 5.9, 22.2.2
        conversion 27.2.1
        dissolution of 8.2.3, 8.5
    private limited companies 1.4.3
    replacement of 22.4.1, 25.7.1
    roll-over relief 22.4.1, 25.7.1
    shareholders 22.2.3
    sole traders 22.2.1, 27.2.1
    stamp duties 27.3.4
Auditors 15.1–15.5
    accounts 15.1, 15.4
    annual general meetings 15.2, 15.4
    appointment 10.6.7, 15.2
    board of meetings 10.6.7
    directors 15.2
    exemption 15.1
    extraordinary general meetings 15.4
    formation of companies 10.7
    functions 15.4
    notice 15.4
    removal 12.4.9, 15.5
    remuneration 15.3
    resignation 15.5
    resolutions 12.4.9, 15.2, 15.4–15.5
    shareholders 15.1
    terms 15.3

Bailment A1.6.1
Balance sheets 16.4
Bank accounts 10.6.6
Bankruptcy 23.1–23.7
    assets, distribution of 23.3.5
    avoiding 23.6
    business activities, restrictions on 23.4.1
    checklist 23.7
    creditors
        fraud on 23.5.6
        judgment 23.5.2
        legal action, by 23.5.2
        meetings 23.3.3
        petitions 23.3.1–23.3.2
        postponed 23.3.5
        secured 23.3.5
        unsecured 23.3.5
    criminal offences 23.4.1
    definition 23.2
    debtors
        petitions 23.3.1, 23.3.4
        property 23.3.4
    directors 23.4.1
        disqualification of 13.14
    discharge 23.3.6
    disposals between date of petition and appointment of trustee 23.5.3

Bankruptcy cont
- effect on bankrupt 23.4
- expenses 23.3.5
- fraud 23.5.6
- houses 23.3.4, 23.7.1
- income payments orders 23.3.4
- increasing the estate 23.5
- individual voluntary arrangements 23.3.2, 23.6
- insolvency practitioners 23.3.2–23.3.3, 23.6
- jobs and positions debarred to undischarged bankrupts 23.4.2
- liquidation compared with 24.10.2
- matrimonial home 23.3.4, 23.7.1
- nominees 23.6
- Official Receiver 23.3.3
- onerous property 23.5.1
- orders 23.3.2, 23.3.6
- partnerships 23.4.1
  - dissolution of 5.13.3, 8.2.4
- petition 23.3.1
  - creditors' 23.3.1–23.3.2
  - debtors' 23.3.1–23.3.2
- preferences 23.5.5
- preferential debts 23.3.5
- process 23.3, 23.7.2d
- shares 17.7, 17.8.3
- sole traders 23.4.1
- statement of affairs 23.3.3
- trustees, in 17.7, 23.3.3–23.3.6, 23.4.1, 23.5
- undervalue, transactions at an 23.5.4, 23.5.6
- voluntary arrangements 23.3.2, 23.6

Battle of the forms 28.2.3
Bell Houses clause 11.2.3
Benefits
- directors 21.3.3
- employee 21.3.3
- income tax 25.2.1–25.2.2
- non-cash 21.3.3
- taxation 21.3.3

Block exemptions 34.8.6–34.8.8
Board meetings
- calling of 13.9
- checklist 13.16.2
- conduct of 13.9
- directors 13.9.1–13.9.6, 13.16.2
- disputes 13.9.4
- minutes 13.9.5
- notice 13.9.1
- partnerships, formation of 10.6.7
- quorum 13.9.3–13.9.4
- resolutions 13.9.2, 13.9.6
- voting 13.9.2, 13.9.4

Board of directors, *see also* Board meetings
- accounting reference date 10.6.7
- auditors, appointment of 10.6.7
- chairman 13.2.3, 13.8.3
- first 10.6.7
- formation of companies 10.6.7
- decision making 1.4.1
- delegation 1.4.1
- fees of formation, approving 10.6.7
- names, using 10.6.7
- seals 10.6.7
- service contracts, awarding 10.6.7, 13.6.1
- share allotment 10.6.7

Borrowings, *see* Loans
Brand names 2.8
Buildings, *see* Industrial buildings
Business names 4.4.1, 10.6.7, 11.2.1
Business property relief 22.4.3, 25.9.2
Businesses, *see* Disposal of businesses, Sale of businesses
Buy back of shares 17.6

Capital, *see also* Capital allowances, Capital gains
- balance sheets 16.4
- clause 11.2.5
- companies 21.1.3
- constitution of companies 11.4.4
- debentures 18.10.1, 18.10.2
- double taxation 25.8
- expenditure 3.2.2
- finance 19.1–19.2
- income tax 21.4.4
- increase in 11.4.4
- investments 18.10.1
- limited liability 26.3.2
- loans 19.1–19.2, 26.3.2
- losses 3.5
- maintenance of 17.2.9
- memorandum of association 11.2.5
- nominal 11.2.5, 11.4.4, 17.2.1
- partnerships 5.4
  - dissolution of 8.5
- profits 3.5, 21.1.3, 25.8
- repayment of 18.10.1, 18.10.2
- shareholders 21.4.4
- shares 17.2.1, 17.2.9, 19.1–19.2
- sole traders 3.2.2
- venture 19.2.4
- Venture Capital Trust 21.4.3, 22.4.1

Capital allowances 3.2.2, 27.3.2
Capital gains, *see also* Capital gains tax
- assets 21.2.4
- corporation tax 21.2.4
- set off 3.4.2
- sole traders 3.4.2

Capital gains tax
- annual exemption 25.7.1
- assets 22.3.2, 22.4.1, 25.7.1, 27.3.3
  - replacement of 22.4.1
- checklist 22.5
- companies 21.1.1, 25.7.1, 27.3.3

Capital gains tax *cont*
    conversion   27.2.3, 27.3.3, 27.4.2
    corporation tax   21.2.4, 25.8.2
    death   22.3.5
    deferral relief   25.7.2
    disposal of businesses   22.1, 22.3.2, 22.3.4–22.3.5, 22.4
    enhances business taper relief   25.7.2
    Enterprise Investment Scheme   22.4.1
    exemptions   22.4.1, 25.7.1
        reliefs and   22.4.1
    form of business organisations   25.7
    gifts by individuals   22.3.2
    holdover relief   22.4.1, 25.7.2
    incorporation of businesses   22.4.1, 27.3.3
    indexation   25.7.1
    individuals   22.3.2, 22.4.1
    instalment options   22.4.1
    partnerships   9.3.1, 9.4, 22.4.1, 25.7.1–25.7.2, 27.2.3
    reinvestment   22.4.1
    reliefs   9.3.4, 21.2.4, 22.4, 25.7
        exemptions and   22.4.1
    retirement relief   22.4.1, 25.7.2
    roll-over relief   9.3.4, 22.4.1, 25.7.1–25.7.2, 27.3.3
    sale of businesses   22.3.1
    shareholders   22.4.1, 25.7.1, 25.8.2
    shares, sale of   21.4.5
    sole traders   22.2.1, 22.4.1, 25.7.1–25.7.2, 27.2.3
    tapering relief   22.4.1, 25.7.1
    undervalue, sales at an   22.3.4
    unincorporated businesses   25.7.1, 27.3.3
    venture capital trusts   22.4.1
Carry across reliefs   3.4.2, 21.2.3, 25.3.2
Carry back relief   3.4.4, 21.2.3, 25.3.3
Carry forward reliefs   3.4.3, 3.4.4
Cash on delivery   A2.3.1
Certificates of incorporation   10.3
Chairmen
    annual general meetings   12.4.11–12.4.12
    articles of association   13.2.3
    board of directors   13.2.3, 13.8.3
    extraordinary general meetings   12.4.11–12.4.12
    resolutions   12.4.11–12.4.12
    role of   12.4.11
    voting   12.4.12
Charges
    administration orders   24.9.3
    assets   18.4.3
    crystallisation of   18.4.2–18.4.3
    debentures, 18.3.2, 18.4.1–18.4.3, 18.5.3–18.5.4, 18.7–18.8
    fixed   18.4.1, 18.4.3, 18.5.3, 18.7, 24.8.8, 26.3.1
    floating   18.3.2, 18.4.2, 18.5.3–18.5.4, 18.8, 24.6.3, 24.8.8, 26.3.1
    income, deduction of   21.2.5
    liquidation   24.6.3, 24.8.8–24.8.9
    loans   26.3.1
    priorities   18.4.3
    registration of   18.7
        failure to register   18.7.1
        late or inaccurate   18.7.1
Close companies   21.2.10, 21.4.1, 22.3.3
Commercial agreements, *see* Drafting commercial agreements
Companies, *see* Constitution of companies, Directors, Private limited companies, Public limited companies, Shareholders, Small companies
    capital allowances   27.3.2
    capital gains tax   21.1.1, 25.7.1, 27.3.3
    capital profits   21.1.3
    close   21.2.10, 21.4.1, 22.3.3
    contracts   27.3.1
    conversion of form   27.3
    corporation tax   21.1.1, 21.2
    defunct   24.9.1
    disposal of businesses   22.2.4, 22.3.3
    documents   26.8
    employees   27.3.6
    formalities   26.6, 27.3.1
    gifts by companies   22.3.3
    groups of companies   10.9
    holding   10.9
    income profits   21.1.2
    income tax   21.1.1, 27.3.2
    inheritance tax   22.3.3
    liability   20.1–20.4
    loans   27.3.2
    names   27.3.1
    parent   34.8.1
    partnerships, compared with   27.7.1, 26.6
    profits   21.1.2–21.1.3
    publicity   26.7
    reform   App 2
    sale   27.3.1–27.3.2
    sole traders, compared with   25.7.1
    stamp duties   27.3.4
    statutory obligations and control   26.8
    striking off   24.9.1
    subsidiaries   10.9, 34.8.2
    trading losses   27.3.2
    unincorporated business, conversion from   27.3.1
    VAT   27.3.5
Company law, changes in   App 2
Company secretaries   14.1–14.5
    agency   20.2.2
    appointment of   14.2
    authority of   14.4
    formation of companies   10.2.3

Company secretaries *cont*
    functions   14.3
    removal   14.5
    remuneration   14.3
    terms   14.3
Compensation, *see also* Damages   13.12.1
Competence   2.2.10
Competition   34.1–34.9
    abuse of a dominant position   34.5.6
    agency agreements   34.8.2
    agreements   34.4, 34.5.7
        agency   34.8.2, 34.9.1
        commercial   34.4, 34.9
        distribution   31.3.4, 33.5, 34.9.2
        drafting   34.4.2
        horizontal   34.4.1
        infringements   34.8.5
        minor importance   34.8.3–34.8.4
        notification to Commission   34.8.9
        undertakings   34.5.4
        vertical   34.4.1–34.4.2
    anti-trust law   34.3.2
    associations of undertakings, decisions by   34.5.4
    black listed terms   34.8.6
    block exemptions   34.8.6–34.8.8
    comfort letters   34.8.12
    commercial agreements   34.4, 34.9
    concerted practices   34.5.4
    Court of First Instance   34.2.3
    dawn raids   34.6.4
    direct effect   34.2.1
    distortion, prevention or restriction of   34.5.4
    distribution agreements   31.3.4, 33.5, 34.9.2
    dominant position   34.5.5–34.5.6
    EC Treaty   34.5
    enforcement   34.6
    European Commission   34.2.3
        attitude   34.6.1
        investigation and enforcement powers   34.6
        notification to   34.8.9–34.8.14
    European Court of Justice   34.2.3
    European Union   33.5, 34.1–34.9
    exemptions   34.5.3
    export bans   34.4.2
    fines   34.7.1
    free movement of goods   34.5.2
    grant of territory   34.4.2
    individual exemptions   34.8.11
    informal cooperation   34.5.4
    information, obtaining   34.6.3
    infringement   34.7
        avoiding   34.8
    institutions   34.2.3
    investigations   34.6
    joint venture   31.4.3
    marketing agreements   33.5
    minor importance, notice on agreements   34.8.3–34.8.4
    national courts, actions in   34.7.2
    negative clearances   34.8.10
    networks   34.5.4
    non-competition clause, drafting   5.17.2
    parent companies   34.8.2
    partnerships   5.17.1–5.17.2
    preliminary rulings   34.2.3
    principles   34.1–34.9
    restraint of trade   5.17.1–5.17.2
    sources   34.1–34.9
    subsidiary companies   34.8.2
    systems of   34.3
    trade, effect on   34.5.4
    trade associations   34.5.4
    United States   34.3.2
    unsolicited requests from outside territory   34.4.2
    white listed terms   34.8.6
Compulsory liquidation   24.2, 24.3, 24.7.1, 24.8.2
Concerted practices   34.5.4
Concessions   21.3.5
Conduct   2.2.10
Connected persons   22.3.4
Consequential loss   28.3.4
Constitution of companies   11.1–11.5
    articles of association   10.2.2–10.2.3, 10.5, 10.8.1, 11.1, 11.3
        changes of   11.4.3
    changing the   11.4, 11.5.2
    checklists   11.5
    extraordinary general meetings   11.4.5
    memorandum of association   10.2.1, 10.2.3, 10.5, 11.1–11.2, 11.4.2
    minority shareholders   11.4.2
    name changes   11.4.1
    nominal capital, increase in   11.4.4
    objects   11.2.3
        change of   11.4.2
    procedure   11.4.5
    shelf companies   11.4
Constructive dismissal   2.2.9
Consumer credit   2.6.1
Continuity of employment   2.2.10, 2.2.11
Contra proferentem rule   28.3.2
Contracts, *see also* Agreements, Contracts of employment, Drafting commercial agreements, Drafting transfer of ownership contracts, Implied terms, Sale of goods contracts
    articles of association   11.3.1
    breach   A1.3.1
    companies   27.3.1
    consumer   28.3.3
    conversion   27.3.1, 27.4.2
    debentures   18.3
    debts   7.1, 7.2.2–7.2.3, 7.5

Contracts *cont*
    directors   13.11.8
    fixed-term   2.2.9, 2.2.10, 13.6.2
    formation of companies   10.3.2
    frustration   A1.6.3
    partnerships   6.4, 7.1, 7.2.2–7.2.3, 7.3.1, 7.5
    pre-incorporation   10.3.2
    privity of   7.3.1
    responsibilities, under   6.4
    Rome Convention 1980   33.3.1
    services   28.4.3, 30.2
    sole members   13.11.8
    supply of services   30.2
    unfair   28.1, 28.4–28.6
    unincorporated businesses   27.3.1
    written   28.2.2–28.2.3
Contracts of employment
    employees   2.2.3
    fixed term   2.2.9, 2.2.10
    notice   2.2.9
    service contracts   10.6.7, 13.6, 13.11.2, 13.12.3, 13.16.3
    wrongful dismissal   2.2.9
Converting the form of an expanding business   27.1–27.4
    assets   27.2.1, 27.3.2–27.3.3
    capital allowances   27.3.2
    capital gains tax   27.3.3, 27.4.2
    companies
        private limited   27.4
        public limited   27.4
        unincorporated business, conversion from   27.3
    contracts   27.3.1, 27.4.2
    employees   27.2.4, 27.3.6
    finance   27.4.1
    formalities   27.2.1, 27.3.1
    income tax   27.2.2, 27.3.3
    inheritance tax   27.4.2
    loans, interest on qualifying   27.3.2
    names   27.2.1, 27.3.1
    partnerships
        agreements   27.2.1
        sole traders, conversion into   27.2
    private limited company, conversion into public limited company   27.4
    procedure   27.4.1
    public limited company, conversion into private limited company   27.4.1
    reliefs   27.3.2
    resolutions   27.4.1
    sale of businesses   27.3.1–27.3.2
    sole traders, partnerships, conversion from   27.2
    stamp duty   27.3.4
    trading
        forms of   27.4.2
        losses   27.3.2
    unincorporated business, conversion into company   27.3
    VAT   27.3.5
Corporate Venturing Scheme   22.4.2
Corporation tax   21.1.1, 21.2
    accounting periods   21.2.6
    assets   21.2.4
    calculation of   21.2.6, 21.2.8
    capital gains   21.2.1, 21.2.4–21.2.5
    capital gains tax   21.2.4, 22.4.2, 25.8.2
    close companies   21.2.10
    Corporate Venturing Scheme   22.4.2
    debentures   21.5.2
    disposal of companies   22.3.3–22.3.4, 22.4.2
    distributions   25.8.1
    dividends   21.2.9, 21.4.6
    double taxation   25.8.1
    gifts by companies   22.3.3
    income
        deduction of charges on   21.2.5
        profits   21.2.1–21.2.2, 21.2.5
    loss relief   21.2.3
    private limited companies   1.4.4
    profits   21.2.1–21.2.2, 21.2.5, 21.2.7, 25.8.1
    rates of   21.2.7
    relief
        capital gains   21.2.4
        carry across or carry back   21.2.3
        loss   21.2.3
        terminal   21.2.3
    remuneration   25.2.1–25.2.2
    sale of businesses   22.3.1
    shareholders   21.4.6, 21.5.2
    trading losses   21.2.3
    trading profit   21.2.2
    undervalue, transactions at an   22.3.4
Creditors
    balance sheets   16.4
    bankruptcy   23.3.1–23.3.3, 23.3.5–23.5.6
    debentures   18.8
    floating charges   24.6.3
    fraud   23.5.6, 24.8.7
    individual voluntary arrangements   23.6
    judgment   23.5.2
    legal action, by   23.5.2, 24.8.2
    liquidation   24.3.2, 24.4.1, 24.7.1, 24.8.2, 24.8.7
    meetings   23.3.3, 24.3.2, 24.4.3, 24.7.1
    postponed   23.3.5
    preferential   24.6.2
    secured   23.3.5
    shares   17.2.9
    undervalue, transactions at an   23.5.6, 24.8.7
    unsecured   23.3.5, 24.6.4
    winding up   24.4.1, 24.4.2–24.4.3, 24.7.2, 24.10.3

Criminal offences
    bankruptcy   23.4.1
    directors   20.4.1, 20.4.6, 24.4.1
    health and safety   2.2.5
    liquidation   24.4.1

Damages
    consequential loss   28.3.4
    delivery   A3.3.3, A3.4
    drafting commercial agreements   28.3.4
    health and safety   2.2.5
    limitation clauses   28.3.4
    loss of profits   28.3.4
    maximum amount of   2.2.9
    mitigation   2.2.9
    quality   A5.5.1
    redundancy   2.2.12
    unfair dismissal   2.2.10, 2.2.12
    wrongful dismissal   2.2.9, 2.2.12
Death
    capital gains tax   22.3.5
    disposal of businesses   22.2.5
    inheritance tax   22.3.5
    partnerships, dissolution of   5.13.3, 8.2.4
    personal representatives   17.7, 17.8.3
    shares   17.7, 17.8.3
Debentures   18.1–18.11
    administrative receivership   24.9.4
    advantages   18.10
    capital
        repayment of   18.10.1–18.10.2
        value   18.10.1
    charges   18.3.2, 18.4.1–18.4.3, 18.5.3–18.5.4, 18.7–18.8
    checklists   18.11
    corporation tax   21.5.2
    creditors   18.8
    directors   18.3.1–18.3.2, 18.4.4, 18.6
    disadvantages   18.10
    dividends   18.10.2
    expenditure   21.5.1
    fixed charges   18.4.1, 18.4.3, 18.5.3, 18.7
    floating charges   18.3.2, 18.4.2, 18.5.3–18.5.4, 18.8
    guarantees   18.4.4
    income   18.10.1, 18.10.2
    income tax   21.5.1
    interest   18.5.2, 18.10.2, 21.5.1
    investments   18.1, 18.10.1–18.10.2
    limited liability   18.4.4
    loans   18.2, 18.3.1–18.3.2, 18.4, 18.5.3, 18.6
        checklists   18.11
        redemption of   18.9
    meaning   18.2
    memorandum of registration   18.7.3
    power of sale   18.5.5
    pre contract considerations   18.3
    priorities   18.4.3
    procedure for issue of   18.6
    receivers   18.5.4–18.5.6, 18.8
    redemption of loans   18.9
    registration   18.7
    remedies   18.8
    repayment date   18.5.1
    sale restrictions   18.10.1
    Schedule D   21.5.1
    security   18.4, 18.5.2
    shareholders   18.10.1, 21.5.1
    shares, comparison with   18.10
    taxation   18.10.2
    terms, typical of   18.5
    ultra vires   18.3.1–18.3.2
Debts, *see also* Bankruptcy, Liquidation
    commercial, late payment of   29.4.3
    contracts   7.1, 7.2.2–7.2.3, 7.5
    directors   13.7, 26.2.1
    form of business organisations   26.2
    late payment   29.4.3
    liability   1.4.5, 13.7, 26.2
    limited liability   1.4.5
    partnerships   7.1, 7.2.2–7.2.3, 7.5, 26.2.3
    preferential   23.3.5
    private limited companies   1.4.5
    shareholders   26.2.2
    sole traders   26.2.3
Decision making
    boards of directors   1.4.1
    delegation   1.4.1
    directors   1.4.1
        board of   1.4.1
    partnerships   5.12
    private limited companies   1.4–1.4.1
    shareholders   1.4.2
Deductions
    expenditure   3.2.1, 21.3.5, 21.4.1, 21.5.1
    income tax   21.3.5, 21.4.1, 21.5.1
    shareholders   21.5.1
    sole traders   3.2.1
Deferral relief   25.7.2
Defunct companies   24.9.2
Del credere agency   31.2.3
Delivery
    agreement on   A3.2.1
        absence of   A3.2.2
    buyers' rights   A3.3
    damages   A3.3.3, A3.4
    description   A4.3.1
    drafting transfer of ownership contracts   A3.1–A3.4
    example   A3.2.3
    exemption clauses   A3.3.4, A3.4
    fault to deliver   A3.3.3
    incorrect   A3.3
    late   29.4.4, A3.3.2

Delivery cont
   limitation of liability   A3.3.3, A3.4
   non-acceptance   A3.4
   payments   A2.3.1
   quantity, wrong   A3.3.1
   sale of goods   29.4.4
   sellers' rights   A3.4
   specific performance   A3.3.3
   standard terms   A3.3.4, A3.4
   time and place of   29.4.4, A3.2
   unfair contract terms   A3.3.4, A3.4
Department of Trade and Industry. Consultation Paper on Changes in Company Law   App 2
Description
   acceptance   A4.3.1
   breach of condition   29.4.5
   buyers' rights   A4.3
   definition   29.4.5, A4.2.1
   delivery   A4.3.1
   drafting transfer of ownership contracts   A4.1–A4.3
   exact correspondence with   A4.2.3
   example   A4.3.4
   exemption clauses   A4.3.3
   implied terms   A4.2, A4.3
   inclusions   A4.2.2
   instalments   A4.3.2
   limitation of liability   A4.3.3
   non-severance   A4.3.1
   quality   A5.3.2
   rejection   A4.3.1
   sale of goods   29.4.5
   samples   A4.2.4
   severance   A4.3.2
   unfair contract terms   A4.3.3
Designs   2.8
Directors, 13.1–13.16 *see also* Board meetings, Board of directors
   accommodation   21.3.3
   accounting for profits   13.10.1
   accounts   13.11.3
   administration orders   24.9.3
   agency   20.2.2
   alternate   13.2.7
   annual general meetings   12.4.1, 12.4.3, 12.5.7, 13.15.1–13.15.2
   annual returns   13.11.4
   appointment   13.2–13.3, 13.16.1
   articles of association   11.3.3, 13.8–13.8.1, 13.10.1, 13.14
   auditors   15.2
   authority of   13.8.2
      breach of warranty of   20.4.2
   bankruptcy   13.14, 23.4.1
   benefits   21.3.3
   board meetings   13.9.1–13.9.6
   breach of duty   13.10.4, 26.2.1
      ratification of   20.3.2
   checklists   13.16
   Companies Act requirements   1.5.3
   compensation   13.12.1
   concessions   21.3.5
   connected parties   13.12.2
   consent to act as   13.2
   contracts   13.6.1, 13.11.8
   criminal offences   20.4.1, 20.4.6, 24.4.1
   debentures   18.3, 18.3.2, 18.4.4, 18.6
   debts   13.7, 13.7.2, 26.2.1
   decision making   1.4.1
   deductible expenditure   21.3.5
   delegation of powers   13.8.1
   disqualification   13.13–13.14, 13.16.4
      acting whilst   13.7.2, 20.4.6
   dividends   12.5.3, 17.4
   documents, signature of   26.2.1
   duties   13.10–13.11
   emoluments   21.3.2–21.3.3, 21.3.6
   employees, interests of   13.12.5
   executive   13.2.5
   expenses   21.3.3, 21.3.5
   extraordinary general meetings   12.4.3, 13.15.2
   fiduciary duties   13.10
   finance   19.2.1
   fixed-term contracts   13.6.2, 13.11.2, 13.12.3
   formation of companies   10.2.3, 10.5, 10.7
   fraudulent trading   13.7.4, 20.4.4, 24.8.3, 26.2.1–26.2.2
   good faith   13.10.2
   guarantees, personal   13.7.1, 18.4.4, 20.4.5, 26.2.1
   holding out   13.7.5
   income tax   1.4.4, 21.3.1–21.3.6
   liability of   13.7, 20.3.2–20.3.3, 20.4, 26.2.1
      disqualified, acting while   20.4.6
      outsiders, liability to   20.4
      shadow   13.2.6
   liquidation   24.3.2, 24.4.1, 24.4.3, 24.9.2
   loans   13.7.1, 13.12.4
      interest free or low interest   21.3.3
   managing   13.2.4
   minority shareholders   20.3.3
   non-cash benefits   21.3.3
   non-executive   13.2.5, 13.5, 13.15.1
   notepaper   13.11.7
   notice of removal   13.15.2
   notification to the Registrar   13.4
   number of   13.2.1
   penalties under Companies Act   26.2.1
   pensions   21.3.3, 21.3.5
   personal interests   13.6.1, 13.11.1
   powers of   12.6.3, 13.8
      exceeding or abusing   13.10.2
   private limited companies   1.4.1–1.4.2, 1.4.4
   property transactions, substantial   13.12.2
   records, failure to maintain   13.7.6

Directors *cont*
   register of   13.3, 13.11.5–13.11.6
   registrar, notification to the   13.4
   removal of   12.4.9, 12.5.1, 13.2.4, 13.12.1
      checklist   13.16.5–13.16.6
      prevention of   11.3.3
      resolution, by   13.15.2
      shareholders, by   13.15
   remuneration   13.5, 13.6.1
   resolutions   12.4.9, 13.2, 13.15.2
   restrictions   13.12
   retirement by rotation   13.15.1
   role   13.1
   Schedule E tax   21.3.2
      collection of   21.3.6
   secret profits   13.10.1
   service contracts   13.6, 13.11.2, 13.12.3, 13.16.3
      awarding   10.6.7, 13.10.1
      inspection of   13.6.3
   shadow   13.2.6
   share schemes   21.3.3
   shareholders   1.4–1.4.12, 12.2.2, 12.3, 12.5.1, 12.5.3, 12.5.7, 12.6.1, 12.6.3
      fiduciary duties   13.10
      removal from office   13.15
      service contracts, approval of   13.6.2
      sole members, as   13.11.8
   shares   17.2, 17.2.1–17.2.6
      allotment   11.3.3
      qualification   13.2.2
   signature on documents   26.2.1
   skill and care   13.10.3, 20.4.3
   statutory duties   13.11
   taxation   21.3
   termination payments   21.3.4
   travelling expenses   21.3.5
   trustees, as   13.10.1
   ultra vires   20.3.1
   voluntary arrangements   24.9.2
   voting   12.6.1
   warranties, breach of   13.7.5
   wrongful trading   13.7.3, 20.4.3, 24.8.3, 26.2.1
Disability discrimination   2.2.1, 2.2.7
Disclaimers   24.8.1
Discounts   17.2.8
Discrimination
   disability   2.2.1, 2.2.7
   marital status   2.2.1, 2.2.7
   race   2.2.1, 2.2.7
   sex   2.2.1, 2.2.7
Dismissal   2.2.8–2.2.13
   constructive   2.2.9
   discrimination   2.2.13
   fairness of   2.2.10
   liquidation   24.3.2, 24.4.3
   overlapping claims   2.2.12
   reasons for   2.2.10
   redundancy   2.2.11
   unfair dismissal   2.2.10
   wrongful dismissal   2.2.9, 24.3.2
Disposal of businesses, *see also* Sale of businesses
   agricultural property relief   22.4.3
   assets   22.2.1–22.2.3, 22.3.2
   business property relief   22.4.3
   capital gains tax   22.1, 22.3.2, 22.3.5, 22.4
   capital taxation   22.1–22.5
      principles   22.3
   charge to tax, subject matter of   22.2
   companies   22.2.4, 22.3.3
   corporation tax
      gains on   22.3.3
   death   22.3.5
   gifts
      companies, by   22.3.3
      individuals, by   22.3.2
   inheritance tax   22.1, 22.3.2–22.3.3, 22.3.5
   partners   22.2.2, 22.4.3
   shareholders   22.2.3, 22.4.3
   sole traders   22.2.1, 22.4.3
Disqualification of directors   13.7.2, 13.13–13.14, 13.16.4, 20.4.6
Dissolution of partnerships   8.1–8.6
   agreements   8.2–8.2.1, 8.2.6, 8.3.1–8.3.2
   assets   8.2.3, 8.5
   bankruptcy   5.13.3, 8.2.4
   capital   8.5
   charging order   8.2.3
   court orders   8.2.6
   death   5.13.3, 8.2.4
   disposal of the business   8.4.1
   distribution of proceeds   8.5
   enforcement of judgments   8.2.3
   express terms   8.3
   fixed term, expiry of   8.2.2
   going concerns   8.4.1
   goodwill   8.4.2
   illegality   8.2.5
   insolvency   8.5
   notice   5.13.1–5.13.2, 8.2.1, 8.2.3
   purchase of outgoing partners' share   8.3.2
   restrictions on   8.3.1
   sale of business   8.4.1–8.4.2, 8.5
   time for   8.2
   winding up the affairs   8.6
Distribution agreements   31.3, 33.1, 33.2.4, 33.3.1, 33.3–33.6, 34.9.2
Dividends   17.4
   accounts   17.4
   corporation tax   21.2.9, 25.8.1
   debentures   18.10.2
   directors   12.5.3, 17.4
   expenditure   21.4.1
   income tax   21.4.1
   profits available   17.4, 25.8.1

Dividends cont
    Schedule F   21.4.1
    shareholders   12.3, 12.5.2, 17.4, 21.4.1
    tax
        credit   21.4.1
        rates   21.4.1
Documents
    companies   26.8
    directors   26.2.1
    formation of companies   10.2, 10.4
    partnerships   26.8
    signature   26.2.1
    statutory obligations and control   26.8
Double taxation   25.8
Drafting commercial agreements   28.1–28.7
    battle of the forms   28.2.3
    clarity of terms   28.3
    consumer contracts   28.3.3
    'contra proferentem' rule   28.3.2
    damages   28.3.4
    evidence   28.2.1
    exemption clauses   28.3.1–28.3.3, 28.4–28.7
    intention, determining   28.2.1–28.2.2
    interpretation rules   28.3.1
    limitation clauses   28.3.4, 28.4–28.6
    negligence   28.3.3
    parol evidence rule   28.2.2
    standard terms   28.2.3, A3.3.4, A3.4
        acceptance without qualification   28.2.3
        notice of   28.2.3
    statute, control by   28.1, 28.4–28.6
    terms of contract   28.2
        clarity of   28.3
    unfair contract terms   28.1, 28.4–28.6
    written contracts   28.2.2
Drafting sale of goods contracts   29.4
Drafting transfer of ownership contracts   A1.1–A1.64, A2.1–A2.6
    approval, goods on   A1.4.4
    breach of contract   A1.3.1
    deliverable state, seller has to do something to put goods in   A1.4.3
    delivery   A3.1–A3.4
    description   A4.1–A4.3
    example   A1.4.6, A2.6
    flow chart   A1.4.5
    future goods   A1.4.3
    intention   A1.4.1, A1.4.2
    nemo dat quod non habet   A1.3.2
    no right to sell, seller with   A1.3
    payment   A2.3A–2.5
    price   A2.2, A2.4–A2.5
        ascertaining   A1.4.1
    quality   A5.1–A5.5
    retention of tile   A1.5
    risk   A1.6
    sellers' rights   A2.4–A2.5
        goods, against   A2.5
    significance of   A1.2
    specific goods   A1.4.1
    time for transfer   A1.2, A1.4
    unascertained goods   A1.4.2
Drawings   5.6

EIS (Enterprise Investment Scheme)   21.4.3, 22.4.1
Elective regime   10.7
Emoluments   21.3.2–21.3.3
Employees
    accommodation   21.3.3
    benefits   21.3.3
    companies   27.3.6
    contracts of employment   2.2.3
    conversion   27.2.4, 27.3.6
    directors   13.12.5
    disability discrimination   2.2.1, 2.2.7, 2.2.13
    dismissal   2.2.8–2.2.13, 24.3.2, 24.4.3
    emoluments   21.3.2–21.3.3
    equal pay   2.2.1
    expenses   21.3.3
    formation of companies   10.6.4
    future dealings with   2.2.7
    health and safety   2.2.5
    higher paid
    income tax   21.3.1–21.3.6
    insurance   2.2.6
    interest   21.3.3
    interests of   13.12.5
    liquidation   24.3.2, 24.4.3
    loans   21.3.3
    lower paid   21.3.3
    marital status   2.2.1, 2.2.7, 2.2.13
    national insurance   2.2.4
    partnerships   27.2.4
    pensions   21.3.3
    race discrimination   2.2.1, 2.2.7, 2.2.13
    recruitment   2.2.1
    redundancy   2.2.11
    restraint of trade   2.2.3
    Schedule E tax   21.3.2
        collection of   21.3.6
    sex discrimination   2.2.1, 2.2.7, 2.1.13
    share schemes   21.3.3
    sole traders   27.2.4
    starting up businesses   2.2
    statement of terms   2.2.2–2.2.3
    taxation   2.2.4, 21.3
    termination   21.3.4
    transfer of undertakings   27.3.6
    unfair dismissal   2.2.10
    unincorporated businesses   27.3.6
    working time   2.2.5
    wrongful dismissal   2.2.9
Enterprise Investment Scheme   21.4.3, 22.4.1

European Union
  commercial agency agreements   33.3.3
  competition   33.5, 34.1–34.9
  Court of First Instance   34.2.3
  distribution agreements   33.5
  European Commission   34.2.3, 34.6, 34.6.1, 34.8.9–34.8.14
  European Court of Justice   34.2.3
  institutions   34.2.3
  marketing agreements   33.3.3
Exclusion clauses, *see* Exemption clauses
Exclusive distribution agreements   31.3.3
Execution of judgments   24.8.2
Exemption clauses
  checklist   28.6
  consumer contracts   28.3.3
  'contra proferentem' rule   28.3.2
  delivery   A3.3.4, A3.4
  drafting commercial agreements   28.3.1–28.3.3, 28.4–28.7
  examples   28.7.1–28.7.2
  flow chart   28.6.1
  implied terms   30.2.2
  incorporation   28.6.1, 28.7.1–28.7.2
  interpretation   28.3.1–28.3.2, 28.6.2, 28.7.1–28.7.2
  negligence   28.3.3
  quality   A5.5.2
  reasonableness   30.2.2
  supply of services   30.2.2
Expenses
  bankruptcy   23.3.5
  capital   3.2.2
  debentures   21.5.1
  deductible   3.2.1, 21.3.5, 21.4.1, 21.5.1
  directors   21.3.3, 21.3.5
  dividends   21.4.1
  employees   21.3.3, 21.3.5
  income tax   21.3.3, 21.3.5
  liquidation   24.6.1
  receipts   3.2.1
  shareholders   21.5.1
  sole traders   3.2.1–3.2.2
  travelling   21.3.5
Export bans   34.4.2
Extraordinary general meetings   12.4
  actions after the   12.4.14
  chairman   12.4.11–12.4.12
  checklist   12.8.2, 12.8.4
  constitution of companies   11.4.5
  directors   12.4.3, 13.15.2
  formation of companies   10.7
  minority shareholders   12.7.7
  minutes   12.4.14, 12.5.8
  necessity to hold   12.4.15
  notice   12.4.2, 12.4.4–12.4.6, 12.5.2, 12.5.9
  power to call   12.4.3
  proxies   12.4.7, 12.4.10, 12.4.13
  quorum   12.4.7
  resolutions   12.4.4, 12.4.7–12.4.9, 12.4.14–12.4.16
  shareholders   12.4.4, 12.5.2, 12.5.8–12.5.10, 12.5.13
    minority   12.7.7
  sole members   12.4.16
  voting   12.4.10–12.4.13

Fiduciary duties   13.10
Finance
  capital   26.3.2
  conversion   27.4.1
  directors   19.2.1
  fixed-term loans   19.2.3
  form of business organisations   26.3
  investments   19.1–19.2
  loan capital   19.1–19.2
  loans   26.3.1
  partnerships   5.4
  share capital   19.1–19.2
  shareholders   19.2.1
  sources of   19.1–19.2
  venture capital   19.2.4
Financial assistance for purchase of own shares   17.2.10
Fines   34.7.1
Fitness for purpose   A5.1–A5.2, A5.3.3, A5.3
Fixed charges   18.4.1, 18.4.3, 18.5.3, 18.7, 24.8.8, 26.3.1
Fixed-term contracts   2.2.9, 2.2.10, 13.6.2
Fixed-term loans   19.2.3
Floating charges   18.3.2, 18.4.2, 18.5.3–18.5.4, 18.8, 24.8.8–24.8.9, 26.3.1
Form 10   10.2.3
Form 12   10.2.4
Formalities
  companies   26.6, 27.3.1
  conversion   27.2.1, 27.3.1
  form of business organisations   26.6
  partnerships   4.4, 26.6, 27.2.1
  setting up   26.6
  sole traders   27.2.1
  unincorporated businesses   27.3.1
Formation of partnerships   10.1–10.10
  accounts   10.7
  articles of association   10.2.2–10.2.3, 10.5
  auditors   10.7
  bank accounts   10.6.6
  board meetings   10.6.7
  certificate of incorporation   10.3
  checklists   10.10
  Companies Registry   10.4
  company secretaries   10.2.3
  directors   10.2.3, 10.5, 10.7
  documents needed   10.2, 10.4

Formation of partnerships *cont*
   elective regime   10.7
   employees   10.6.4
   extraordinary general meetings   10.7
   fees   10.6.7
   Form 10   10.2.3
   Form 12   10.2.4
   group of companies   10.9
   holding companies   10.9
   insurance   10.6.5
   law stationers   10.4
   memorandum of association   10.2.1–10.2.3, 10.4, 10.5
   national insurance   10.6.4
   nominees   10.5
   PAYE   10.6.4
   pre incorporation of contracts   10.3.2
   registered office, address of   10.2.3
   registers   10.6.1
   separate legal identity   10.3.1
   shareholders' agreements   10.8
   shares   10.7
   shelf companies   10.5
   small companies   10.7
   stationery   10.6.3
   statutory books   10.6.1
   subsidiary companies   10.9
   Table A   10.2.2
   VAT registration   10.6.2
Forms of business organisations   1.1–1.5
   choice of   25.1–25.10
      debts, liability for   26.2
      finance, raising   26.3
      formalities   26.6
      management structure   26.4
      publicity of information   26.7
      status   26.5
      statutory obligations and control   26.8
      taxation   25.1–25.10
   debts, liability for   26.2
   finance, raising   26.3
   formalities   26.6
   management structure   26.4
   publicity of information   26.7
   status   26.5
   statutory obligations and control   26.8
   taxation   25.1–25.10
Franchising agreements   31.4.1
Fraud
   bankruptcy   23.5.6
   creditors   23.5.6, 24.8.7
   directors   13.7.4, 20.4.4, 24.8.3, 26.2.1
   fraudulent trading   13.7.4, 20.4.4, 24.8.3, 26.2.1–26.2.2
   liquidation   24.8.7
   minority shareholders   12.6.2, 20.3.2
   undervalue, transactions at an   23.5.6, 24.8.7
Free movement of goods   34.5.2

Frustration   A1.6.3
General meetings, *see* Annual general meetings, Extraordinary general meetings
Going concerns   8.4.1
Goods, *see also* Sale of goods contracts
   approval   A1.4.4
   free movement of   34.5.2
   future   A1.4.3
   mixed   A1.5.3
   sale   A5.3.2
   second hand   A5.3.2
   services and, supply of   30.3
   specific   A1.4.1
   transit, in, stopping   A2.5.2
   unascertained   29.4.2, A1.4.2
Good faith   13.10.2
Goodwill
   assets   22.2.1
   name changes   11.4.1
   partnerships, dissolution of   8.4.1
   sale of businesses   8.4.2
   sole traders   22.2.1
Groups of companies   10.9
Guarantees
   debentures   18.4.4, 20.4.5
   directors   13.7.1, 18.4.4, 20.4.5, 26.2.1
   liability, 20.4.5, 26.2.1
   loans   19.2.2

Health and safety   2.2.5
Holding companies   10.9
Holding out   7.3.3, 32.3.2
Holdover relief   22.4.1, 25.7.2
Hours of work   2.2.5
Houses   23.3.4, 23.7.1

Illegality   8.2.5
Implied terms
   agency   32.2.1, 32.2.3
   description   A4.2, A4.3
   exemption   30.2.2
   sale of goods   29.4.6
   supply of services   30.2.1, 30.2.2
   unfair contract terms   28.4.3
In rem rights   A2.5
Income, *see also* Income tax
   charges on, deduction of   21.2.5
   companies   21.1.2
   corporation tax   21.2.1–21.2.2, 21.2.5
   debentures   18.10.1–18.10.2
   double taxation   25.8
   form of business organisations   25.8
   loss   25.3
   partnerships   5.5

Income *cont*
    profits   21.1.2, 21.2.1–21.2.2, 21.2.5, 25.2, 25.8
    relief   25.3
    set off   3.4.2
    sole traders   3.4.2
Income tax
    accommodation   21.3.3
    assessment basis   3.3
    benefits   25.2.1–25.2.2
    borrowings   9.2.4
    capital   21.4.4
    companies   21.1.1
        close   21.2.10, 21.4.1
        conversion   27.3.2
    concessions   21.3.5
    conversion   27.2.2, 27.3.2
    date for payment   3.3
    debentures   18.10.2, 21.5
    deductions   21.3.5, 21.4.1, 21.5.1
    directors   1.4.4, 21.3.1–21.3.6
    dividends   21.4.1—
    employees   21.3.1–21.3.6
    Enterprise Allowance Scheme   21.4.3
    expenses   21.3.3, 21.3.5, 21.5.1
    interest   21.5.1, 25.6
    loans   21.2.10
        interest free or low interest   21.3.3
        shareholders   21.4.2
        written off   21.4.1
    partnerships   9.2, 25.2.1–25.2.2, 27.2.2, 27.3.3
    pensions   21.3.3, 21.3.5
    profits   9.2, 21.4.1
    relief   21.2.10, 21.4.2–21.4.3
    Schedule D   21.5.1
    Schedule E tax   21.3.2, 25.2.1–25.2.2
        collection of   21.3.6
    Schedule F   21.4.1
    shareholders   1.4.4, 21.4.1–21.4.2, 21.5
    shares
        disposal of   21.4.4
        sale of   21.4.1
        schemes   21.3.3
    sole traders   3.2–3.2.1, 3.3, 3.4.2, 25.2.1–25.2.2, 27.2.2
    travelling expenses   21.3.5
    unincorporated businesses   27.3.2
    Venture Capital Trust   21.4.3
Incorporation
    businesses of   3.4.5, 22.4.1
    capital gains tax   25.7.1, 27.3.3
    carry forward relief   3.4.5
    exemption clauses   28.6.1, 28.7.1–28.7.2
    roll-over relief   25.7.1, 27.3.3
    sole traders   3.4.5
    unincorporated businesses   25.7.1
Indexation   25.7.1

Individual voluntary arrangements   23.3.2, 23.6
Industrial buildings   3.2.2
Inheritance tax
    agricultural property relief   22.4.3, 25.9.1
    assets   22.3.2
    business property relief   22.4.3, 25.9.2
    checklist   22.5
    close companies   22.3.3
    connected persons   22.3.4
    conversion   27.4.2
    death   22.3.5
    disposal of businesses   22.1, 22.3.2–22.3.5, 22.4.3
    form of business organisations   22.4.3
    gifts by individuals   22.3.2
    instalment options   22.4.3, 25.9.3
    partnerships   9.5, 22.4.3
    potentially exempt transfers   22.3.5
    reliefs   22.4.3, 25.9
    sale of businesses   22.3.1
    shareholders   22.4.3
    sole traders   22.3.4, 22.4.3
    undervalues, transactions at an   22.3.4
Insolvency, *see also* Bankruptcy, Liquidation
    partnerships   7.4.1, 7.5
        dissolution of   8.5
    practitioners   23.3.2–23.3.3, 23.6, 24.4.3, 24.9.2
Instalments   29.4.2, A4.3.2
Insurance, *see also* National insurance
    employees   2.2.6
    formation of companies   10.6.5
    starting up businesses   2.7
Intellectual property   2.8
Interest
    debentures   18.5.2, 21.5.1
    income tax   21.5.1, 25.6, 27.3.2
    partnerships   5.5.2
    price, action on the   A2.4.2
    reliefs   25.6, 27.3.2
    shareholders   21.5.1
Interpretation   28.3.1–28.3.2, 28.6.2, 28.7.1–28.7.2
Investments
    capital gains tax   21.4.1
    capital value   18.10.2
    debentures   18.1, 18.10.1–18.10.2
    Enterprise Investment Scheme   21.4.3, 22.4.1
    finance   19.1–19.2
    venture capital   19.2.4
    Venture Capital Trust   21.4.3, 22.4.1

Joint ventures   31.4.3
Judgments
    bankruptcy   23.5.2
    creditors   23.5.2

Judgments *cont*
    enforcement of   8.2.3, 24.8.2
    execution of   24.8.2
    liquidation   24.8.2
    partnerships, dissolution of   8.2.3

Late payment of commercial debts   29.4.3
Law stationers   10.4
Liability, 20.1–20.4 *see also* Limited liability
    agents   20.2, 20.3.2, 20.4.2, 32.2.2, 32.3.1
    authority
        actual, exceeding   20.3.2
        breach of warranty of   20.4.2
    breach of duty
        ratification of   20.3.2
    clause   11.2.4
    companies of   20.1–20.4
        officers of   20.3
    criminal penalties   20.4.1
    debts   7.1–7.5, 13.7, 26.2
    directors   13.7, 20.3.2–20.3.3, 20.4, 26.2
        disqualified, acting while   20.4.6
        outsiders, liability to   20.4
        shadow   13.2.6
    enforcement   7.3, 20.3.3
    fraudulent trading   20.4.4
    guarantees   20.4.5, 26.2.1
    holding over   7.3.3
    memorandum of association   11.2.4
    minority shareholders   20.3.2–20.3.3
    novation agreements   7.3.5
    objects clause   20.2
    officers of the company   20.3–20.4
    outsiders. liability to   20.4
    partnerships   7.1–7.5, 26.2.3
    personal   7.2.3
    remedies   20.4.2
    shadow directors   13.2.6
    shareholders   26.2.2
    skill and care   20.4.3
    sole traders   26.2.1
    strict   A5.2.1
    third parties   32.3.1
    tortious   7.2.4
    ultra vires   20.2.1, 20.3–20.3.1
    winding up   20.4.4
    wrongful trading   20.4.3
Licences
    agreements   31.4.1
    consumer credit   2.6.1
    starting up businesses   2.6
Limited liability   20.1
    capital   26.3.2
    drafting commercial agreements   28.1, 28.4–28.6
    debentures   18.4.4
    delivery   A3.3.4, A3.4
    quality   A5.5.2
    shareholders   12.3.1
    unfair contract terms   28.1, 28.4–28.6
Liquidation   24.1–24.10
    administration orders   24.9.3, 24.10
    administrative receivership   24.9.4, 24.10
    advertising of   24.3.2, 24.4.3
    alternatives to   24.9
    assets
        distribution of   24.6
        increase in   24.8
    bankruptcy, comparison with   24.10.2
    charges   24.6.3, 24.8.8–24.8.9
    checklist   24.10
    compulsory   24.2, 24.3, 24.7.1, 24.8.2
        commencement   24.3.1
        procedure   24.10.3
    creditors
        floating charges   24.6.3
        fraud   24.8.7
        legal action by   24.8.2
        meetings   24.3.2, 24.4.3, 24.7.1
        ordinary secured   24.6.4
        preferential   24.6.2
    criminal offences   24.4.1
    definition   24.2
    defunct companies   24.9.1
    directors   24.3.2, 24.4.1, 24.4.3, 24.8.4, 24.9.2
    disclaimers   24.8.1
    discretion   23.4.1
    dissolution   24.7
    employees   24.3.2, 24.4.3
    execution of judgments   24.8.2
    expenses   24.6.1
    fixed   24.8.8
    floating charges   24.6.3, 24.8.8–24.8.9
    fraud   24.8.7
    fraudulent trading   24.8.3
    grounds   24.3.1
    insolvency practitioners   24.4.3, 24.9.2
    liquidators
        appointment of   24.4.3
        identity of   24.3.2
    Official Receiver   24.3.2
    onerous property   24.8.1
    preferences   24.8.6
    preferential creditors   24.6.2
    procedure   24.4.3, 24.10.3
    property   24.5, 24.8–24.8.1
    resolutions   24.4.2–24.4.3
    security   24.6
    shareholders   24.6.5
    solvency declarations   24.4.1
    statement of affairs   24.3.2, 24.4.3
    statutory notice   24.3.1
    surplus   24.5

Liquidation *cont*
   types of   24.4.1
   undervalue, transactions at an   24.8.5, 24.8.7
   voluntary   24.2, 24.4, 24.7.2, 24.8.2
      arrangements   24.9.2
      checklist   24.10.3
      commencement   24.4.2
   wrongful trading   24.8.4
Listing Rules   1.5.1
Loans
   capital   19.1–19.2
   charges   26.3.1
   checklist   18.11
   close companies   21.2.10, 21.4.1
   companies   27.3.2
   conditions   21.4.2
   conversion   27.3.3
   debentures   18.2, 18.3.1–18.3.2, 18.4, 18.5.3, 18.6, 18.9, 18.11
   directors   13.7.1, 13.12.4, 21.3.3
   employees   21.3.3
   finance   19.1–19.2, 26.3.1
   fixed charges   26.3.1
   fixed-term loans   19.2.3
   floating charges   26.3.1
   guarantees   19.2.2
   income tax   21.2.10, 21.3.3, 21.4.1, 27.3.2
   interest   27.3.2
   low interest or interest free   21.3.3
   memorandum of satisfaction   18.7.3
   qualifying purpose   21.4.2
   redemption of   18.9
   relief   21.2.10, 27.3.3
   security   18.4, 26.3.1
   shareholders   21.4.1
   shares   17.2.10
   ultra vires   18.3.1–18.3.2
   unincorporated businesses   27.3.2
   written off   21.4.1
Loss of profits   28.3.4
Losses
   capital   3.5
   carry back/carry forward relief   21.2.3, 25.3.3
   companies   27.3.2
   conversion   27.3.2
   corporation tax   21.2.3
   income   25.3
   partnerships   5.5
   reliefs   3.4, 21.2.3, 25.3
   sole traders   3.4
   start up   3.4.1
   terminal   25.3.3
   trading   3.4, 9.2.2, 21.2.3, 27.3.2

Machinery and plant   3.2.2

Management
   accounts   16.5
   form of business organisations   26.4
   partnerships   26.4
Managing directors   13.2.4
Marital status   2.2.1, 2.2.7
Marketing
   advice   33.3.4
   agency   31.2.2, 33.1, 33.2.4, 33.3.1, 33.3–33.6
   agreements   31.4, 33.1–33.6
   choice of   33.6
   commercial factors   33.2
   competition   33.5
   customers, client's responsibility to   33.2.4
   distribution   33.1, 33.2.4, 33.3.1, 33.3–33.6
   European Union   33.3.3, 33.5
   goods, nature of   33.2.3
   governing law   33.3.1
   local law, effect of   33.3.2
   location and nature of proposed market   33.2.2
   overseas operations   33.3
   remuneration   33.3.3
   Rome Convention 1980   33.3.1
   size and organisation of client's business   33.2.1
   taxation   33.4
Matrimonial home   23.3.4, 23.7.1
Meetings, *see also* Annual general meetings, Board meetings, Extraordinary general meetings
   bankruptcy   23.3.3
   creditors   23.3.3, 24.3.2, 24.4.3, 24.7.1
   liquidation   24.3.2, 24.4.3, 24.7.1
Members of company. *See* Shareholders
Memorandum of association
   amendment of   11.4.2
   capital clause   11.2.5
   constitution of companies   10.2.1, 10.2.3, 10.5, 11.2
   formation of companies   10.2.1, 10.2.3, 10.5
   liability   20.2–20.2.1
      clause   11.2.4
   minority shareholders   11.4.2
   name clause   11.2.1
   objects clause   11.2.3
      Bell Houses clause   11.2.3
      change of   11.4.2
      independent main objects clause   11.2.3
      liability   20.2–20.2.1
   registered office clause   11.2.2
   shareholders   12.2.1
   shelf companies   11.2.3
   subscribers to   12.2.1
Memorandum of satisfaction   18.7.3
Minority shareholders
   annual general meetings
      items place on agenda for   12.7.1

Minority shareholders *cont*
    annual general meeting *cont*
        notice   12.7.3
    articles of association   12.6.2
    constitution of companies   11.4.2
    derivative actions   12.6.4
    directors   20.3.3
    extraordinary general meetings   12.7.7
    Foss v Harbottle rule   12.6.4
    fraud   12.6.2, 20.3.2
    liability to   20.3.2–20.3.3
    memorandum of association, changes of   11.4.2
    notice, right to refuse to consent to short   12.7.3
    resolutions   12.7.3–12.7.4
        special, right to block   12.7.9
    restrictions on   12.6.4
    rights of   12.7
    ultra vires acts, right to restrain   12.7.8
    unfair prejudice   12.7.5
    winding up   12.7.6
    written statements, right to circulate   12.7.2
Minutes   12.4.14, 13.9.5
Moratoriums   24.9.3

Names
    business   4.4.1, 10.6.7, 11.2.1
    board of meetings   10.6.7
    change of   11.2.1, 11.4.1
    companies   27.3.2
    constitution of company   11.4.1
    conversion   27.2.1, 27.3.2
    goodwill   11.4.1
    index of   11.2.1, 11.4.1
    memorandum of association   11.2.1
    partnerships   4.4.1, 5.3, 27.2.1
    passing off   11.2.1
    restrictions on   11.4.1
    sole traders   27.2.1
    trade marks   11.2.1
    unincorporated businesses   27.3.2
National insurance   2.2.4
    form of business organisations   25.5
    formation of companies   10.6.4
    reliefs   25.5
    starting up businesses   2.4
Negative clearances   34.8.10
Negligence   28.3.3
Nemo dat rule   A1.3.2
Networks   34.5.4
Nominees   10.5
Non-executive directors   13.2.5, 13.5, 13.15.1
Notepaper   13.11.7

Notice
    annual general meetings   12.4.1, 12.4.5–12.4.6, 12.5.2, 12.7.3
    auditors   15.4
    board meetings   13.9.1
    competition   34.8.3–34.8.4, 34.8.9–34.8.14
    contracts of employment   2.2.9
    directors, removal of   13.15.2
    extraordinary general meetings   12.4.3, 12.4.5–12.4.6, 12.5.2, 12.5.9
    invalid   12.4.
    liquidation   24.3.1
    minor importance, agreements of   34.8.3–34.8.4
    minority shareholders   12.7.3
    partnerships
        dissolution   5.13.1–5.13.2, 8.2.1
        leaving   7.3.4
    proxies   12.4.13
    reasonable   2.2.9
    resolutions   12.4.8
    shareholders   12.5.2, 12.5.9
        minority   12.7.3
    short   12.4.6, 12.7.3
    standard forms   28.2.3
    unfair dismissal   2.2.10
    wrongful dismissal   2.2.9
Novation   7.3.5

Objects clause
    Bell Houses clause   11.2.3
    change of   11.4.2
    independent main objects clause   11.2.3
    liability   20.2
    memorandum of association   11.2.3, 11.4.2, 20.2–20.2.1
    shelf companies   11.2.3
    sub clauses   11.2.3
    ultra vires   20.2.1
Official List   1.5.1
Official Receiver   23.3.3, 24.3.2
One person companies   12.2.3
Onerous property   23.5.1, 24.8.1
Ownership, *see* Drafting transfer of ownership contracts

Parent companies   34.8.2
Partnerships   4.1–9.6, *see also* Dissolution of partnerships, Taxation of partnerships
    actions which are authorised   7.2
    agency   7.2.2
    agreements   4.2.1, 4.3, 5.1–5.18, 6.4, 27.2.1
    agricultural property relief   22.4.3
    arbitration   5.18
    assets   5.7, 22.2.2

Partnerships *cont*
   assets *cont*
      conversion   27.2.1
      ownership of   5.9
      values, increases and decreases in   5.7
   authority
      actual   7.5
      actions which are authorised   7.2.1
      ostensible   7.2.2
   bankruptcy   5.13.3, 23.4.1
   capital   5.4
   capital gains tax   22.4.1, 25.7.1–25.7.2, 27.2.3
   characteristics   4.2.2
   commencement date   5.2
   companies, compared with   25.7.1, 26.6
   competition   5.17.1–5.17.2
   contracts
      debts   7.1, 7.2.2–7.2.3, 7.5
      privity of   7.3.1
      responsibilities, under   6.4
   converting the form of an expanding business   27.2
   court orders   5.13.4
   death   5.13.3
   debts   7.1–7.5, 26.2.3
   decision making   5.12
   defendants, potential   7.3.1
   definition   1.3, 4.2
   disposal of   22.2.2, 22.4.3
   disputes   5.1
   documents   26.8
   drawings   5.6
   duration   5.13
   employees   27.2.4
   expulsion   5.15
   financial input   5.4
   formalities   4.4, 26.6, 27.2.1
   holding out   7.3.3
   income   5.5
   income tax   9.2, 25.2.1–25.2.2, 27.2.2, 27.3.2
   inheritance tax   22.4.3
   insolvency   7.4.1–7.4.2
   interest   5.5.2
   liability
      debts, for   7.1–7.5, 26.2.3
         enforcement   7.3
         failure to notify of leaving   7.3.4
         holding out   7.3.3
         inability to pay   7.4
         novation agreement   7.3.5
         personal   7.2.3
         tortious   7.2.4
   location   5.8
   losses   5.5
   management structure   26.4
   names   4.4.1, 5.3, 27.2.1
   nature of business   5.8
   non-payment   7.4
   notice of leaving   7.3.4
   novation agreements   7.3.5
   outgoing partner's share, payment for   5.16
   pensions   21.3.3
   personal liability   7.2.3
   place of business   5.8
   privity of contract   7.3.1
   profits   5.5
   publicity   26.7
   reliefs   22.4.3, 27.3.2
   restraint of trade   5.17
   retirement   5.14, 7.3.4
   roles   5.11
   salaries   5.5.1
   setting up   4.3
   shareholders, compared with   25.7.2
   shares
      asset value increases and decreases   5.7
         income profits and losses   5.5
   sole traders
      compared with   25.7.1–25.7.2
      conversion from   27.2
   starting up a   4.1–4.4
   statutory obligations and control   26.8
   suing in the firm's name   7.3.2
   tortious liability   7.2.4
   work input   5.10
Patents   2.8
PAYE (Pay As You Earn)   2.2.4, 10.6.4
Payment
   agency   32.5
   agreements   A2.3.2
   cash on delivery   A2.3.1
   example   A2.6
   drafting transfer of ownership contracts   A2.3
   goods in transit, stopping   A2.5.2
   in rem rights   A2.5
   non-payment, effect of   29.4.3
   resale   A2.5.3
   retention of goods   A2.5.1
   sale of goods   29.4.3
   sellers' rights   A2.4–A2.5, A2.6.3
   termination of contract   A2.4.1
   time for   A2.6.2
   time of the essence   A2.4.1
Penalties   26.2.1
Pensions
   directors   21.3.3, 21.3.5
   employees   21.3.3, 21.3.5
   form of business organisations, choice of   25.4
   income tax   21.3.3, 21.3.5
   reliefs   25.4
   taxation   25.4
Performance, time for   30.2.1
Personal representatives   17.7, 17.8.3

Plant and machinery 3.2.2
Pre-emption rights 17.2.3–17.2.4
Preferences
   bankruptcy 23.3.5, 23.5.5
   creditors 24.6.2
   debts 23.3.5
   liquidation 24.6.2, 24.8.6
   shares 17.3
Pre-incorporation contracts 10.3.2
Prejudice
   minority shareholders 12.7.5
   shareholders 12.5.14
   minority 12.7.5
   voting 12.6.1
Price
   action for the A2.4.2
   agreement on A2.2.1
      without A2.2.2
   calculation 29.4.3
   drafting transfer of ownership contracts A2.2
   example A2.6
   goods in transit, stopping A2.5.2
   in rem rights A2.5
   interest A2.4.3
   quality A5.3.2
   resale A2.5.3
   retention of goods A2.5.1
   sale of goods 29.4.3
   sellers' rights A2.3–A2.4, A2.6.3
   termination of contract A2.4.1
   time of the essence A2.4.1
Priorities 18.4.3
Private limited companies 1.4, *see also* Directors, Formation of companies, Shareholders
   assets 1.4.3
   conversion 27.4
      implications 27.4.2
      procedure 27.4.1
   corporation tax 1.4.4
   debts 1.4.5
   decision making 1.4–1.4.1
   limited liability 1.4.5
   public limited companies, conversion into 27.4
   publicity 1.4.6
   taxation 1.4.4
Privity of contract 7.3.1
Profit and loss accounts 3.2
Profits
   capital 3.5, 21.1.3, 25.8
   companies 21.1.2–21.1.3
   corporation tax 21.2.1–21.2.2, 21.2.5, 21.2.7, 25.8.1
   distributions 25.8.1
   dividends 17.4, 25.8.1
   double taxation 25.8

   income 21.1.2, 21.2.1–21.2.2, 21.2.5, 25.2, 25.8
   income tax 9.2, 21.4.1
   partnerships 5.5, 9.2
   sale of shares 21.4.1
   sole traders 3.1–3.5
   taxation 3.1–3.5
   trading 21.2.2
Property
   bankruptcy, 23.3.4, 23.5.1
   business property relief 22.4.3
   directors 13.12.2
   disclaimers 24.8.1
   liquidation 24.5, 24.8.1
   onerous 23.5.1, 24.8.1
Proxies 12.4.7, 12.4.10, 12.4.13
Public limited companies 1.5, *see also* Directors, Shareholders
   Alternative Investment Market 1.5.1
   Companies Act requirements 1.5.2–1.5.3
   conversion 27.4
      implications 27.4.2
      procedure 27.4.1
   definition 1.5
   listing 1.5.1, 1.5.3
   share dealing 1.5.1
   private limited company, conversion into 27.4
   Yellow Book 1.5.1
Publicity
   companies 26.7
   form of business organisations 26.7
   partnerships 26.7
   private limited companies 1.4.6
Purchase of own shares 17.2.10

Quality 29.4.6
   buyers' rights A5.5
   correction of defects, easy A5.3.3
   cosmetic defects A5.3.3
   course of business A5.2.3
   damages A5.5.1
   description A5.3.2
   example A5.5.3
   exemption clauses A5.5.2
   drafting transfer of ownership contracts A5.1–A5.5
   fit for the purpose A5.1–A5.2, A5.3.3, A5.4
   goods supplied under the contract A5.2.2
   limitation of liability A5.5.2
   manufacturers A5.2.1
   price A5.3.2
   sale goods A5.3.2
   satisfactory quality 29.4.6, A5.1–A5.3
      definition A5.3.1
      duration of A5.3.4

Quality *cont*
    second hand goods   A5.3.2
    strict liability   A5.2.1
    unfair contract terms   A5.5.2
Quantity   A3.3.1
Quorum   12.4.7, 13.9.3–13.9.4

Race discrimination   2.2.1, 2.2.7
Receipts   3.2.1
Receivers
    administrative   24.9.3, 24.9.4, 24.10.1
    appointment of   18.5.4
    debentures   18.5.4–18.5.6, 18.8
    Official Receiver   23.3.3, 24.3.2
    power of sale   18.5.5
Records, failure to maintain   13.7.6
Recruitment   2.2.1
Redundancy   2.2.11
    age   2.2.11
    damages   2.2.12
    continuity of employment   2.2.11
    overlapping claims   2.2.12
    payments   2.2.11
    proof of   2.2.11
    time-limits   2.2.11
    unfair dismissal   2.2.10, 2.2.11
Registered office   10.2.3, 11.2.2
Reliefs
    agricultural property   22.4.3, 25.9.1
    assets, replacement of   22.4
    business property   22.4.3, 25.9.2
    capital gains tax   9.2.4, 21.2.4, 22.4, 25.7, 27.3.3
    carry across   3.4.2, 21.2.3, 25.3.2
    carry back   3.4.4, 21.2.3, 25.3.3
    carry forward   3.4.3, 3.4.4
    close companies   21.2.10
    conditions   22.4.1
    corporation tax   21.2.3–21.2.4
    deferral   22.4.1
    disposal of businesses   22.3
    Enterprise Investment Scheme   21.4.3, 22.4.1
    exemptions, interrelation between   22.4.1
    form of business organisations   25.9
    holdover   22.4.1, 25.7.2
    income tax   21.2.10, 21.4.2–21.4.3, 25.3
    incorporation of business   3.4.5, 22.4.1
    inheritance tax   22.4.3, 25.9
    instalment options   22.4.3, 25.9.3
    interest   25.6, 27.3.2, 27.3.2
    loans   21.2.10, 21.4.2, 27.3.2, 27.3.3
    loss   3.4, 21.2.3, 25.3
    national insurance contributions   25.5
    one year back relief   3.4.2
    partnerships   9.2.3–9.2.4, 22.4.3, 27.3.2, 27.3.3
    pensions   25.4
    reinvestment   22.4.1
    retirement   22.4.1, 25.7.2
    roll-over   22.4.1, 25.7.1, 27.3.3
    shareholders   21.4.2, 22.4.3
    sole traders   3.4, 22.4.3
    start up   3.4.1, 25.3.1
    taper   22.4.1, 25.7.1
    terminal   21.2.3, 25.3.3
    trading losses   3.4, 9.2.2
    Venture Capital Trust   21.4.3, 22.4.1
Remuneration
    auditors   15.3
    company secretaries   14.3
    corporation tax   25.6.1
    directors   13.6.1
        non-executive   13.5
    marketing agreement   33.3.3
    non-executive directors   13.5
    partnerships   5.5.1
Resale   A2.5.3
Resolutions
    accounts   12.5.6
    annual general meetings   12.4.4, 12.4.7–12.4.9, 12.4.14–12.4.16
    auditors   15.2, 15.4–15.5
        removal of   12.4.9
    board meetings   13.9.2, 13.9.6
    chairmen   12.4.11–12.4.12
    checklist   12.8.3, 12.8.5
    conversion   27.4.1
    directors   13.2
        removal of   12.4.9, 13.15.2
    elective   12.4.8, 12.5.6–12.5.7, 12.7.3–12.7.4, 15.2
    extraordinary   12.4.8, 12.8.5
    extraordinary general meetings   12.4.4, 12.4.7–12.4.9, 12.4.14–12.4.16
    liquidation   24.4.2
    minority shareholders   12.7.3, 12.7.9
    notice   12.4.8
    ordinary   12.4.8–12.4.9, 12.5.2, 13.2, 13.15.2, 17.2.2
    quorum   12.4.7
    shareholders   12.5.2, 12.5.6–12.5.7
        minority   12.7.3–12.7.4, 12.7.9
    shares   17.2.1–17.2.3
    special   12.4.8–12.4.9, 12.7.9, 12.8.5
        blocking   12.7.9
    types of   12.4.8–12.4.9
Restraint of trade   2.2.3, 5.17
Restrictive covenants   2.2.3
Retention of title   29.4.2
    all monies clauses   A1.5.3
    drafting transfer of ownership contracts   A1.5
    enforcement   A1.5.2
    identifying the contract goods   A1.5.2
    limitations   A1.5.4

Retention of title *cont*
   mixed goods   A1.5.3
   Romalpa case   A1.5.1
   tracing   A1.5.3
Retirement
   capital gains tax   22.4.1
   partnerships   5.14
   relief   22.4.1, 25.7.2
Risk
   accidental damage   A1.6.1
   bailment   A1.6.1
   breach of duty   A1.6.1
   drafting transfer of ownership contracts   A1.6
   examples   A1.6.4
   frustration   A1.6.3
   passing of
      ascertaining of   A1.6.2
      intention of   A1.6.2
   sale of goods   29.4.2
   significance   A1.6.1
Roll-over relief   9.3.4, 25.7.1–25.7.2
Romalpa clauses   29.4.2, A1.5
Rome Convention 1980   33.3.1

Salaries, *see* Remuneration, Wages
Sale goods   A5.3.2
Sale of businesses, *see also* Disposal of businesses
   capital gains tax   22.3.1, 22.3.4
   companies   27.3.1–27.3.2
   conversion   27.3.1–27.3.2
   corporation tax   22.3.1, 22.3.4
   going concerns   8.4.1
   individuals, by   22.3.1
   inheritance tax   22.3.1, 22.3.4
   partnership, dissolution of   8.4.1–8.4.2, 8.5
   undervalue, transactions at an   22.3.4
   unincorporated businesses   27.3.1–27.3.2
Sale of goods contracts, *see also* Drafting transfer of ownership contracts   29.1–29.4
   damages   29.4.5
   definition   29.2
   delivery   29.4.4
      late, effect of   29.4.4
      time and place   29.4.4
   description   29.4.5
   distribution agreements   31.3.2
   drafting   29.4
   implied terms   29.4.6
   intention   29.3.2
   instalments   29.4.2
   late payments   29.4.3
   non-payment   29.4.3
   payment   29.4.3
      date   29.4.3
   price   29.4.3
      calculation of   29.4.3
   quality   29.4.6
   retention of title   29.4.2
   right to sell   29.4.2
   risk   29.4.2
   satisfactory quality   29.4.6
   statutory framework   29.3
   transfer of ownership   29.4.2
   unascertained goods   29.4.2
Sales agency   31.2.1
Samples   A4.2.4
Satisfactory quality   29.4.6, A5.1–A5.3
Seals   10.6.7
Second hand goods   A5.3.2
Secret profits   13.10.1
Secretaries, *see* Company secretaries
Security, *see also* Charges
   creditors   23.3.5
   debentures   18.4, 18.5.3
   liquidation   24.6
   loans   18.4, 26.3.1
Selective distribution agreements   31.3.3
Service contracts   10.6.7, 13.6, 13.11.2, 13.12.3, 13.16.3
Services, *see* Supply of services
Services contracts   28.4.3, 30.2
Set off   3.4.2
Sex discrimination   2.2.1, 2.2.7
Shadow directors   13.2.6
Share schemes   21.3.3
Shareholders   12.1–12.3. *See also* Minority shareholders
   accounts   12.5.6–12.5.7
   agreements   10.8
   agricultural property relief   22.4.3, 25.9.1
   annual general meetings   12.4.1, 12.4.4, 12.5.2, 12.5.7–12.5.8, 12.5.12–12.5.13
   articles of association   10.8.1
      change of   12.6.2
   assets   22.2.3
   auditors   15.1
   best interests of the company   12.6.2
   business property relief   25.9.2
   capital gains tax   22.4.1, 25.7.2, 25.8.2
   capital taxes   21.4.4
   checklists   12.8.1
   Companies Act requirements   1.5.3
   corporation tax   21.4.6, 21.5.2
   debentures   18.10.1, 21.5
   debts   26.2.2
   decision making   1.4.2
   directors   1.4–1.4.2, 12.2.2, 12.3, 12.3.2, 12.5.1, 12.5.3, 12.5.7, 12.6.1
      fiduciary duties   13.10
      powers of   12.6.3
      removal of   13.15.1
      service contracts   13.6.2
   disposal of businesses   22.2.3, 22.4.3
   disposal of shares, capital taxation on   21.4.4

Shareholders *cont*
- dividends 12.3, 12.5.3, 17.4, 21.4.1, 21.4.6
- double taxation 25.8.2–25.8.2
- Enterprise Investment Scheme 21.4.3
- expenditure 21.5.1
- extraordinary general meetings 12.4.4, 12.5.2, 12.5.8–12.5.10, 12.5.13
- finance 19.2.1
- formation of companies 10.8
- fraudulent 26.2.2
- functions 12.3.2
- income tax 1.4.4, 21.4.1–21.4.2, 21.5.1
- inheritance tax 22.4.3
- interest 21.5.1
- joining the company 12.2, 12.5.5
- liability 26.2.2
- limited liability 12.3.1
- liquidation 24.6.5
- memorandum, subscribers to 12.2.1
- loans 21.4.1–21.4.3
- minority shareholders 12.6.2, 12.6.4
- minutes 12.5.8
- new 12.2, 12.5.5
- notice 12.5.2
- one-person companies 12.2.3
- partners, compared with 25.7.2
- private limited companies 1.4–1.4.2, 1.4.4
- profits on sale of shares 21.4.1
- register of 12.2.2, 12.2.3, 12.5.5
- resolutions 12.5.2, 12.5.6–12.5.7
- rights of 12.5–12.6
  - restrictions on 12.6
- sale of shares 21.4.1, 21.4.5
- Schedule D 21.5.1
- Schedule F 21.4.1
- share certificates 12.5.4
- sole members 12.2.3
- sole traders, compared with 25.7.2
- status of 12.2.2
- taxation 21.4
- *ultra vires* acts, restraining 12.5.11
- unfairly prejudiced, right not to be 12.5.14
- Venture Capital Trust 21.4.3
- voting 12.4.10, 12.5.1, 12.6.1
- winding up 12.5.15
- written statements, right to circulate 12.5.13

Shares 17.1–17.8 *see also* Shareholders
- allotment of 10.6.7, 10.7, 11.3.3, 12.3, 17.2.3, 17.8.1
- annual general meetings 17.2.1
- articles of association 11.3.3, 17.6
- bankruptcy 17.8.3
- board of meetings 10.6.7
- buy back 17.6
- capital 17.2.1
  - finance 19.1–19.2
  - maintenance of 17.2.9
- capital gains tax 21.4.4
- certificates 12.5.4
- checklists 17.8
- classes of 17.3
- creditors 17.2.9
- dealing 1.5.1
- death 17.7, 17.8.3
- debentures, comparison with 18.1
- directors 11.3.3, 13.2.2, 17.2, 17.2.1–17.2.6
- discount, issue at a 17.2.8
- disposal 21.4.4
- dividends 17.4
- employee share schemes 21.3.3
- extraordinary general meetings 17.2.1
- finance 19.1–19.2
- financial assistance for the purchase of own 17.2.10
- formation of companies 10.7
- income tax 21.4.1, 21.4.4
- issuing 17.2
- listing 1.5.1
- loans 17.2.10
- maintenance of share capital 17.2.9
- nominal capital 17.2.1
- offers 17.2.3
- ordinary 17.3
- partly paid 17.2.6
- payment 17.2.5
- personal representatives 17.7
- pre-emption rights 17.2.3–17.2.4
- preference 17.3
- premium, issue at 17.2.7
- procedure 17.2.4
- profits 21.4.1
- public limited companies 1.5.1
- qualification 13.2.2
- redeemable 17.3
- resolutions 17.2.1–17.2.3
- sale of 21.4.1
- schemes 21.3.3
- solvency 17.6
- stock transfer forms 17.5.1
- transfers 11.3.3, 17.5
  - procedure 17.5.1, 17.8.2
  - restrictions on 11.3.3, 17.5.2
- transmission of 17.7
- trustees in bankruptcy 17.7

Shelf companies 10.5, 11.2.3, 11.4
Small companies 10.7
Sole traders
- accounts
  - profit and loss 3.2
- agricultural property relief 22.4.3
- assets 22.2.1, 27.2.1
- bankruptcy 23.4.1
- capital
  - allowances 3.2.2
  - gains 3.4.2
  - losses 3.5

Sole traders *cont*
  capital *cont*
    profits   3.5
    capital gains tax   22.2.1, 22.4.1, 25.7.1–25.7.2, 27.2.3
    carry across relief   3.4.2
    carry back of terminal trading loss   3.4.4
    carry forward relief   3.4.3, 3.4.5
    companies, compared with   25.7.1
    converting the form of an expanding business   27.2
    debts   26.2.3
    definition of   1.2
    disposal of businesses   22.2.1, 22.4.3
    employees   27.2.4
    expenditure   3.2.1
      capital   3.2.2
      deductible   3.2.1
    formalities   27.2.1
    income profits   3.2
    income tax   3.2–3.2.1, 3.3, 3.4.2, 25.2.1–25.2.2
      closing tax year   3.3.4
      conversion   27.2.2
      date for payment   3.3.6
      first tax year   3.3.2
      illustration   3.3.5
      normal rule   3.3.1
      second tax year   3.3.3
    incorporation of business   3.4.5
    industrial buildings   3.2.2
    inheritance tax   22.3.4, 22.4.3
    liability   26.2.3
    names   27.2.1
    one year back for trading loss relief   3.4.2
    partners
      compared with   25.7.2
      conversion into   27.2
    plant and machinery   3.2.2
    profits
      assessment   3.3
      date for payment   3.3
      income   3.2
    receipts of the trade   3.2.1
      chargeable   3.2.1
    reliefs   3.4, 22.4.3
    set off   3.4.2
    sole traders, compared with   25.7.1–25.7.2
    start up loss relief   3.4.1
    taxation   3.1–3.5
    trading losses, relief for   3.4
Specific performance   A3.3.3
Stamp duties   27.3.4
Standard forms   28.2.3, A3.3.4, A3.4
Start up losses   3.4.1, 25.3.1
Starting up businesses
  accounts   2.3
  employees   2.2
  insurance   2.7
  intellectual property   2.8
  legal and practical considerations   2.1–2.8
  licences   2.6
  national insurance   2.4
  VAT   2.5
  Statement of terms   2.2.2
Stationery   10.6.3
Stock Exchange listing   1.5.1
Subsidiary companies   10.9, 34.8.2
Supply of services   30.1–30.3
  consideration   30.2.1
  exemptions   30.2
    clauses   30.2.2
  goods and services   30.3
  implied terms   30.2.1–30.2.2
  services contracts   30.2
  skill and care   30.2.1
  time for performance   20.2.1
  unfair contract terms   30.2.2
Surpluses   24.5

Table A   10.2.2, 11.3.2–11.3.3, 12.4.10
Taper relief   22.4.1, 25.7.1
Taxation   21.1–21.5 *see also* Corporation tax, Income tax, Reliefs, Taxation of partnerships, VAT
  accounting   2.3
  agency   33.4
  credits   21.4.1
  debentures   18.10.2
  directors   21.3
  distribution   33.4
  double   25.8
  employees   2.2.4, 21.3
  form of business organisations   25.1–25.10
  income profits   25.2
  marketing agreements   33.4
  national insurance contributions   25.5
  pensions   25.4
  private limited companies   1.4.4
  profits   3.1–3.5
  schedules, comparing   25.2.1–25.2.2
  shareholders   21.4
  sole traders   3.1–3.5
  tax rates   25.2.2
Taxation of partnerships   9.1–9.6
  assets, qualifying   9.3.4
  borrowings   9.2.4
  capital gains tax   9.3–9.4
    calculation of gain   9.3.3
  disposals,
    firm, by   9.3
    partners individually   9.4
  income tax   9.2
  inheritance tax   9.5

Taxation of partnerships *cont*
   losses   9.2.2
   membership, changes in   9.2.3
   payment of tax   9.3.5
   profits   9.2
   reliefs   9.2.2, 9.2.4, 9.3.4
   roll over relief   9.3.4
   tapering relief   9.3.4
   VAT   9.6
Time-limits
   accounts   16.2
   redundancy   2.2.11
   unfair dismissal   2.2.10
Time of the essence   A2.4.1
Tort and partnerships   7.2.4
Tracing   A1.5.3
Trade associations   34.5.4
Trade marks   2.8, 11.2.1
Trading
   corporation tax   21.2.2
   losses   3.4, 9.2.2, 21.2.3, 27.3.2
   partnerships   9.2.2
   profits   21.2.2
   reliefs   3.4
   sole traders   3.4
Transfers, *see also* Drafting transfer of ownership contracts
   articles of association   11.3.3
   ownership, of   29.4.2
   sale of goods   29.4.2
   shares   11.3.3, 17.5, 17.8.2
   undertakings, of   27.3.6
Travelling expenses   21.3.5
Trustees
   bankruptcy, in   17.7, 23.3.3–23.3.6, 23.4.1, 23.5
   directors   13.10.1
   shares   17.7

Ultra vires
   debentures   18.3.1–18.3.2
   directors   20.3.1
   liability   20.2.1, 20.3.1
   loans   18.3.1–18.3.2
   memorandum of association   20.2.1
   minority shareholders   12.7.8
   objects clause   20.2.1
   officers of the company   20.3
   shareholders   12.5.11
      minority   12.7.8
Undervalue, transactions at an   22.3.4, 23.5.4, 23.5.6, 24.8.5, 24.8.7
Unfair contract terms
   consumers   28.4.2, 28.5
   definitions   28.4.1
   delivery   A3.3.4, A3.4
   drafting commercial agreements   28.1, 28.4–28.6
   exemption clauses   28.1, 28.4–28.6, A3.3.4, A3.4
   flowchart   28.6.3
   guidelines   28.4.2
   implied terms   28.4.3
   limited liability clauses   28.1, 28.4–28.6, A3.3.4, A3.4
   quality   A5.5.2
   reasonableness test   28.4.2, 28.4.3, 30.2, A3.3.4, A3.4, A5.5.2
   regulations   28.5
   services contracts   28.4.3
   skill and care   28.4.3
   supply of services   30.2.2
Unfair dismissal   2.2.10
   age   2.2.10
   competence   2.2.10
   conduct   2.2.10
   continuity of employment   2.2.10
   damages   2.2.10, 2.2.12
   fixed-term contracts   2.2.10
   notice   2.2.10
   overlapping claims   2.2.12
   proof of   2.2.10
   reasons for   2.2.10
   redundancy   2.2.10, 2.2.11
   reengagement   2.2.10
   reinstatement   2.2.10
   time-limits   2.2.10
Unincorporated businesses
   capital allowances   27.3.2
   capital gains tax   25.7.1, 27.3.3
   companies, conversion into   27.3
   contracts   27.3.1
   conversion of form   27.3
   employees   27.3.6
   formalities   27.3.1
   income tax   27.3.2
   loans   27.3.2
   names   27.3.1
   incorporation of   25.7.1
   roll-over relief   25.7.1
   sale   27.3.1–27.3.2
   stamp duty   27.3.4
   trading losses   27.3.2
   VAT   27.3.5
United States   34.3.2
Utmost good faith   6.2

VAT
   conversion of form   27.3.5
   formation of companies   10.6.2
   partnerships   9.6
   registration   10.6.2, 27.3.5

VAT *cont*
   starting up businesses   2.5
   turnover   2.5
   Venture capital   19.2.4
Venture Capital Trust   21.4.3, 22.4.1
Voluntary arrangements   23.3.2, 23.6, 24.9.2
Voluntary liquidation   24.2, 24.4, 24.7.2, 24.8.2, 24.9.2, 24.10.3
Voting
   annual general meetings   12.4.10
   board meetings   13.9.2, 13.9.4
   casting votes   12.4.12
   chairman   12.4.12
   directors   12.6.1
   extraordinary general meetings   12.4.10
   prejudice   12.6.1
   proxies   12.4.7, 12.4.10, 12.4.13
   shareholders   12.4.10, 12.5.1, 12.6.1
   Table A   12.4.10

Wages, *see also* Remuneration   2.2.1
Winding up, *see also* Liquidation
   creditors   24.4.1, 24.4.2–24.4.3, 24.7.2, 24.10.3
   members' voluntary   24.4.1, 24.4.2–24.4.3, 24.7.2, 24.10.3
   minority shareholders   12.7.6
   partnerships, dissolution of   8.6
   shareholders   12.5.15
   minority   12.7.6
   voluntary   24.4.1, 24.4.2–24.4.3, 24.7.2, 24.10.3
Working time   2.2.5
Wrongful dismissal
   constructive   2.2.9
   contracts of employment   2.2.9
      repudiatory breach   2.2.9
   damages   2.2.9, 2.2.12
   fixed-term contracts   2.2.9
   liquidation   24.3.2
   notice   2.2.9
   overlapping claims   2.2.12
Wrongful trading   13.7.3, 20.4.3, 24.8.4, 26.2.1

Yellow Book, *see* Listing Rules